FIGURES IN A WILTSHIRE SCENE

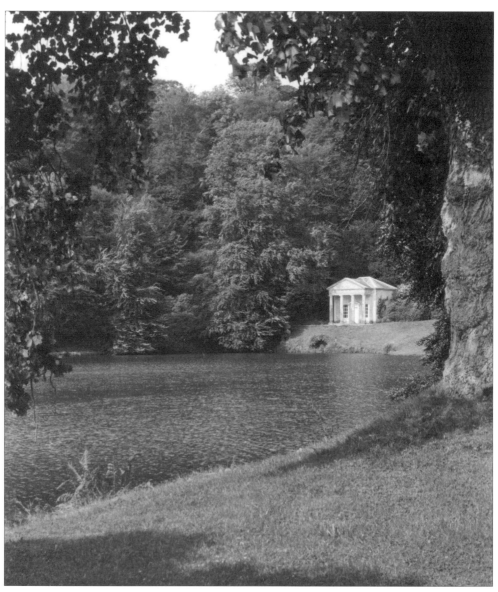

Stourhead: a Wiltshire Elysium created by Henry Hoare the Younger (Chapter 10)

Figures in a Wiltshire Scene

KEN WATTS

Historical studies of people connected by birth, residence or particular empathy with Wiltshire, relating them to the places with which they are associated

First published in the United Kingdom in 2002 by
The Hobnob Press, PO Box 1838, East Knoyle, Salisbury SP3 6FA

© Ken Watts 2002

British Library Cataloguing in Publication Data
A catalogue record for this book is available from the British Library.

ISBN 0-946418-11-X

Typeset in 9/11 pt Souvenir Light
Typesetting and origination by John Chandler
Printed in Great Britain by Salisbury Printing Company Ltd, Salisbury

About the Author

Ken Watts was born at Devizes in 1933 and has spent most of his life in Wiltshire. His interest in local history and topography is long-standing, and his early retirement in 1989 from his profession as an architect has enabled him to devote much time to these interests. Having spent much of his recreational time roaming over the countryside of Wiltshire and studying its history, he has developed a profound feeling for the county's history and its associations, about which he has written, in the words of a reviewer, 'with modesty and great learning'. His publications include *Snap, the History, Depopulation and Destruction of a Wiltshire Village* (1989), *Droving in Wiltshire; the Trade and its Routes* (1990), *The Marlborough Downs* (1993), *Exploring Historic Wiltshire; Volume 1, North* (1997) and *Volume 2, South* (1998), as well as magazine articles, walks booklets, and papers for archaeological journals. For several years he was a Countryside Commission warden on the Wiltshire section of the Ridgeway, and he has led many guided walks for a number of organisations in the Wiltshire countryside. His *Marlborough Downs* was compared to Crossing's classic *Guide to Dartmoor* and his two-volume *Exploring Historic Wiltshire* has been reviewed as being 'major books offering life-long reward . . . oozing historical detail and explanation, reliably and skilfully presented'.

Contents

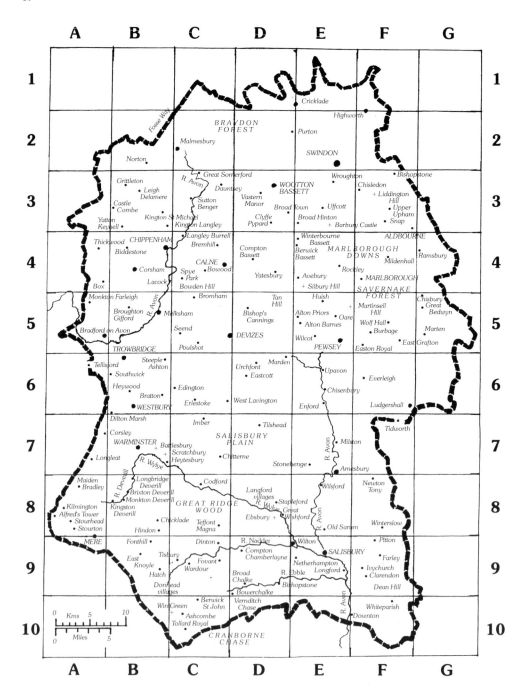

Map of Wiltshire showing the principal places mentioned

Introduction

Although my previous publications have generally concentrated on describing the attractions of landscape, this book differs in that it attempts to humanise the Wiltshire landscape by describing some of the persons associated with it. Since the landscape remains to be seen it concentrates on describing personalities, some of them being eminent persons while others are less well-known.

Practically everyone knows the fascination of visiting places associated with historical events or people. Although not readily apparent when walking or travelling around, these associations when known add a vital extra dimension to the enjoyment of such activities. This book consists of eighteen closely researched studies of people which attempt to evoke the spirit of place by describing and relating its persons to the places with which they are associated in Wiltshire.

A quotation from a poet and prose writer who was born in London to Welsh parents but grew to love Wiltshire aptly expresses the feelings which prompted the writing of this book:

> There are many places which nobody can look upon without being consciously influenced by a sense of their history. It is a battlefield, and the earth shows the scars of its old wounds; or a castle or cathedral of distinct renown rises among the oaks; or a manor house or cottage, or tomb or woodland walk that speaks of a dead poet or soldier. Then, according to the extent or care of our reading and the clearness of our imagination, we can pour into the groves or on the turf tumultuous or silent armies, or solitary man or woman.
> (from *The South Country* by Edward Thomas).

The chosen subjects are a purely personal selection, qualification for inclusion being by birth, residence, or a particular empathy with Wiltshire. Each chapter contains deeply-researched short biographies of its subjects and descriptions of their Wiltshire associations. A great deal of informative fact is interspersed with incidents, anecdotes and quotations in an attempt to humanise the book and closely relate the subjects to their places. The subjects are arranged chronologically and range from the future Roman Emperor Vespasian who conquered the west country, and the Saxon King Alfred of Chapter 1, to the German refugee professor of art and architecture Nikolaus Pevsner of the concluding chapter. People of national importance are included as are some who are less well-known but provide interesting subjects. Female subjects include Queen Jane Seymour, Mary Herbert Countess of Pembroke, and Miss Edith Olivier of Wilton.

Since the book is deliberately discursive its chapter-headings should not be assumed to indicate the sole content of the chapters. Opportunity has frequently been taken to introduce persons only loosely associated with the principal subjects or places described. Digressions are sometimes indulged because these allow the introduction of subjects who would not merit a chapter of their own. For this reason the comprehensive index of persons and places assumes considerable importance.

From Anglo-Saxon to Tudor times Wiltshire was an important county both politically and economically. It lay at the heart of the Anglo-Saxon kingdom of Wessex and it provided a royal power base in King John's disputes with his barons. Many of the itinerant Medieval, Tudor and Stuart kings were frequently in Wiltshire for the hunting that was provided by its many forests and deer parks. During the Middle Ages Wiltshire became of commercial importance as a centre of the woollen industry upon which the prosperity of England then depended, and Wiltshire continued to prosper throughout the centuries when wool represented the great wealth of England, but ultimately shared the decline in importance of the woollen industry.

The approximately chronological list of contents of this book demonstrates this change, although it must be emphasised that the introduction of persons who are sometimes loosely related to its principal subjects blurs the chronological arrangement. The early chapters are devoted to royalty and persons associated with the court, but as Wiltshire became politically less important and less prosperous the subjects change from being politically important to being either newly-rich landed magnates or artists and writers who were attracted to Wiltshire because it provided attractive rural environments which were conducive to their work.

Sources

Since the research for this book has been undertaken in such a wide variety of sources over many years it is practically impossible to list sources. As this book is intended for general reading I have not encumbered the text with innumerable references, although where sources have been heavily drawn upon they are acknowledged. Some general sources that should be acknowledged are:

> *The Victoria County History of Wiltshire*; the many volumes of the *Wiltshire Archaeological & Natural History Magazine*; *Wiltshire Notes and Queries*; *The Dictionary of National Biography*; Pevsner's *The Buildings of England: Wiltshire* (1963); many volumes of biography; magazine and newspaper articles; and obituary notices.

Most of my research was undertaken in the Wiltshire Reference and Local Studies Library at Trowbridge, where the staff, led by Michael Marshman, have provided me with unfailing help over many years. Grateful acknowledgement is made also to the Crafts Study Centre, Surrey Institute of Art & Design, University College, Farnham, for permission to reproduce work by Robin Tanner in Chapter 17.

Since this book has developed gradually over many years and has been reduced in size for publication I hope that readers will bear with any minor inconsistencies other than of fact. I will welcome any corrections of factual mistakes that readers may discover.

Ken Watts, Trowbridge, Wiltshire

Notes

The photographs are generally taken by the author who also drew the sketch maps.
To find the location of a place mentioned in the text readers should refer to the Index where most places are given a reference (e.g. **B4**) which will enable them to be easily found on the map of Wiltshire on page vi.

1   Wessex and King Alfred

including Vespasian and the Roman Conquest of Wiltshire

Wiltshire, which is situated at the very heart of the former Saxon kingdom of Wessex, is generally believed to derive its name from a West Saxon tribe called the *Wilsætas*, which settled at the south-eastern end of the Wylye Valley and gave their name first to Wilton and ultimately to Wiltshire. Although the precise details of the settlement of Wessex by the Saxons tend to be obscure, according to the *Anglo-Saxon Chronicle* Wessex, the kingdom of the West Saxons, was founded by Cerdic (died 534) and his son Cynric after they landed on the south coast in 495 AD and expanded their territories northwards. During the reign (560–92) of their successor Ceawlin the boundaries of Wessex were extended. The upper part of the Thames Valley was conquered in 571, Cirencester, Bath, and Gloucester were added in 577, and between 643 and 672 King Cenwalh annexed a large part of east Somerset. By the end of the 7th century the west of Somerset and about half of Devon had been added to the kingdom.

This area, consisting of Berkshire, Wiltshire, part of Gloucester, Somerset, Hampshire, Dorset, and part of Devon, is the area now generally regarded as Wessex, although during Egbert's reign (802–39) the addition of Sussex, Surrey, Kent, and Essex to the expanding kingdom explains the names of Sussex (South Saxons), Essex (East Saxons), and Middlesex (Middle Saxons). While Wessex remained a Saxon kingdom its capital was at Winchester, but after the Norman Conquest Winchester and Westminster became joint capitals and then during the Norman period London superseded Winchester as the capital and the name Wessex became disused.

Although the Romans had adopted Christianity as the official religion of their empire in 312 AD it practically died out in England after their departure and was only re-introduced in the Saxon period by missionaries working westwards from Kent. Christian Wessex was then from the late 8th century constantly attacked by heathen Vikings who appeared initially as raiders, but soon became a more positive threat to the kingdom. From his youth King Alfred's grandfather Egbert (died 839) fought the Vikings and as a result of his temporary annexation of Mercia in 828 became styled *bretwalda*, that is the overlord of Britain and the ruler of the *Heptarchy*, the seven English kingdoms of Northumbria, East Anglia, Essex, Mercia, Wessex, Sussex and Kent.

Under Alfred Wessex grew great although its boundaries remained unaltered until the peace settlement between Alfred and Guthrum the Dane in 878 added London, Middlesex, and part of Hertford to the kingdom, so that at Alfred's death all of England south of the Bristol Avon and the River Thames was within his kingdom of Wessex.

A little more than a century and a half later Harold II, the last Anglo-Saxon king of England, lost the throne of England to his rival Duke William of Normandy at the Battle of Hastings.

The revival of the name Wessex

After the Norman Conquest the name Wessex became obsolete and so it remained until it was revived by Thomas Hardy, when he described Dorset as 'South Wessex' in *Far From the Madding Crowd* (1874). When a Hardy chair of literature was in 1921 proposed for Southampton University its principal wrote to Hardy to thank 'the man who re-created Wessex and gave her back her soul'. Several letters and a leader in *The Times* in May 1925 proposed a University of

Wessex and although the idea was never realised the revived name caught the public imagination and it now has an emotive appeal to many people who have an awareness of history and live within the bounds of Wessex. When Queen Elizabeth's youngest son Edward took the title Earl of Wessex at his marriage in June 1999 he revived the old Saxon title last held by King Harold whose death at Hastings brought an end to Saxon England.

Vespasian and the Roman conquest of Wiltshire

A little more than eight hundred years before Alfred came to the throne of Wessex (a period equivalent to that from our time back to King John) the Romans conquered and then occupied Britain for almost four hundred years. At the time that the Emperor Claudius ordered the conquest of Iron Age Britain in 43 AD the area that later became Wiltshire was inhabited by two Celtic tribes. In the very south of the county were the Durotriges, while the rest of Wiltshire was held by the Belgae, a tribe which after strenuously opposing the Romans on the Continent had fled across the Channel and established themselves in north Wiltshire. Both of these tribes when emigrating to Britain had retained their tribal organisations and remained implacably opposed to Rome.

In overall command of the Roman invasion was Aulus Plautius, who after landing on the Kent coast struck north with his main force and occupied Colchester. After establishing himself in the south-east he decided on a three-pronged advance and the 2nd Augusta Legion was sent west to conquer the west country under the command of Vespasian (9–79 AD) who consequently became the first historical person to be associated with Wiltshire.

Vespasian, although he later became Emperor of Rome, at this time had yet to achieve any great success and we know little about his character. Gibbon recorded that: 'the birth of Vespasian was mean', and that: 'his merit was rather useful than shining, and his virtues were disgraced by a strict and even sordid parsimony'. From Suetonius we learn that Vespasian's father

Sabinus was first a tax collector and then a banker in Switzerland. Although his mother Vespasia Polla was from a good family Vespasian seems to have risen by his own military ability rather than by influence. After reaching senatorial rank he obtained more preferment by proposing special games to celebrate Emperor Caligula's victory in Germany and he married Flavia Dimitilla by whom he had three children before she died young.

Vespasian from a Roman coin

Under the Emperor Claudius Vespasian commanded a legion in Germany and then took part in the invasion and conquest of Britain. Later he governed a Roman province in Africa but fell upon hard times, resorted to mule-trading, and consequently acquired the nickname of 'mule-driver'. When touring with the court in Greece Vespasian displeased the Emperor Nero by falling asleep when he was singing and fled in fear for his life. Nero thereafter disliked Vespasian but could not afford to dispense with his military abilities and sent him to crush an uprising in Judaea. Following three attempted coups by other generals after Emperor Nero's enforced suicide, Vespasian was in 69 AD proclaimed Emperor by the army in Judaea. He returned to Rome and twenty-six years after conquering Wessex this veteran soldier became Emperor. His prudent financial management enabled him to undertake expensive building projects including initiating the construction of the Colosseum. He was deified and continued to be undisputed Emperor until his death in 79 AD.

In his advance westwards across southern England Vespasian was bitterly opposed by the Durotriges and the Belgae and 'fought thirty battles, subjugated two warlike tribes, and captured twenty *oppida* (hillforts) before the western tribes were reduced'. The hillfort known as

Roman 'lead road' from Mendip to the coast fording the Deverill near Kingston Deverill

Vespasian's Camp in a bend of the River Avon immediately west of Amesbury is generally assumed to be a fanciful name, although it could have been one of the hillforts stormed by Vespasian who, after conquering the west country, established a temporary Roman frontier running north-east from Dorset along the Severn with Wiltshire standing behind it in the frontier zone.

The line of Vespasian's advance cannot now be ascertained with any certainty. In advancing west from Winchester to Old Sarum he is likely to have approximately followed either the line of the later Roman road or the Dean Valley, and from Old Sarum he probably advanced west across Dorset remaining close to the coast from which he could be supported. He may however have sent part of his army north-west across Wiltshire up the valley of the River Wylye. This leads directly towards the lead mines of Mendip in Somerset which were one of the principal objectives of the invasion, and were being exploited by the Romans within a few years of the conquest.

If the Roman army advanced up the Wylye Valley it would have been confronted by the powerful hillforts of Scratchbury and Battlesbury, which may have been two of the twenty fortresses which Vespasian reduced. As they advanced the Romans would have looked for strong points to be occupied in order to safeguard their advance into hostile territory, and it is interesting that most of the Iron Age settlements and fortresses above the Wylye (Ebsbury, Grovely Earthworks, Grovely Castle, Hanging Langford

Camp, Stockton Earthworks, and Bilbury Rings) have revealed signs of Roman occupation. Items of Roman saddlery found at Bilbury Rings suggest that Roman cavalry were stationed in the hillfort, and a war cemetery has been found outside the north-west entrance to Battlesbury hillfort.

A mere six years after the conquest stamped ingots of lead reveal that by 49 AD Vespasian's 2nd Augusta Legion was working the lead mines of Mendip and exporting lead along the Roman 'Lead Road' which runs across south Wiltshire, crosses the River Deverill at the ford near Kingston Deverill, and continues along the ridge through Great Ridge and Grovely Woods towards Old Sarum, Winchester, and the south coast.

Roman 'lead road' following the ridge through Great Ridge Wood, looking east

After the conquest Celtic Britain became a peaceful province of the Roman Empire enjoying the *pax Romana* during which most of the native Britons continued to live much as they had previously done except that the more eminent members of society became Romanised-Britons. Then, early in the 5th century, the Roman army was withdrawn from Britain to go to the defence of Rome that was being threatened by foreign invaders.

The Saxon conquest

Most of the Romano-British settlements had been controlled by Romanised Britons and there is evidence that after the Roman army left a form of Roman civilisation survived for much of the 5th century, as the intermittent raids by the Saxons which had commenced in the Roman period developed into campaigns of conquest. These were resisted by the Britons using Roman military techniques under Romano-British commanders, but gradually the Saxons prevailed and gained control of the former Roman province. One Saxon advance was west along the Thames Valley into north Wiltshire, while in 495 an army under Cerdic and his son Cynric landed on the south coast and reinforced by the arrival of Port and his two sons in 501 gradually advanced north. The great post-Roman defensive dyke of Wansdyke which runs across Wiltshire may have been created as a barrier between these opposing Saxon armies.

In 519 Cerdic and Cynric won a battle at *Cerdicsford* (Charford) in the Avon Valley south of Salisbury. They then seem to have paused until 552 when they captured Old Sarum, Wilton was made the capital of their kingdom of Wessex, and in 556 the southern Saxons won a decisive battle over the Thames Valley Saxons at *Beranburh* (Barbury a few miles south of Swindon), and their conquest of Wiltshire was complete. By 575 Bath had fallen and the Anglo-Saxon kingdom of Wessex was firmly established as a pagan Saxon kingdom. This it remained until about 640 when it was evangelised by Bishop Birinus, the first Bishop of Winchester, and became the Christian kingdom to which Alfred succeeded in 871.

Alfred's birth and early life

The reputation of King Alfred as an undisputedly great historical figure has sometimes been overshadowed by the legends that have grown up around the so-called King Arthur, the semi-legendary Romano-British cavalry leader who in the 5th century AD organised British resistance to the Saxon invasions and heavily defeated them at Mount Badon (*Mons Badonicus*). Without mentioning Arthur the monk Gildas (*c.* 493–570) indicated that the Battle of Badon consisted of the siege of a hill, possibly a hillfort, and this is often presumed to be Liddington Castle in northeast Wiltshire, with Badbury nearby.

Particular difficulties arise over discussing the character and career of King Alfred because both primary sources upon which we have to rely are slightly suspect. Bishop Asser's *Life of King Alfred* was written by a man who was Alfred's friend,

owed his position at the court of Wessex to him, and may consequently have been over adulatory. The other primary source is the *Anglo-Saxon Chronicle*, which appears to have been re-written at Alfred's direction with the intention of glorifying Wessex and its kings. An added complication lies in the fact that the version of Asser's *Life* upon which we now rely was edited and adapted by Archbishop Parker when he printed the *Life* in 1574. The best-known stories about Alfred – the episodes of the cake-burning and of Alfred entering the enemy camp disguised as a harper – probably never happened, being legends invented by Medieval chroniclers.

Although King Alfred (849–c. 899) was born at Wantage, Wiltshire was at the heart of his kingdom of Wessex and his associations with the county are many and varied. Here he owned land (his Wiltshire estates which he bequeathed in his Will are described later, page 17), and he also campaigned throughout Wiltshire when opposing the Danes. In Wiltshire he fought many battles including the decisive Battle of Edington that was the most important event of his reign, and later he founded in Wiltshire defensive burhs at Cricklade, Malmesbury, Chisbury and Wilton (see later page 15). His name is associated with the commemorative Alfred's Tower on the southwest boundary of Wiltshire (it is actually a few yards across the Somerset border) and the Iron Age earthwork called Alfred's Castle just outside the county boundary at Ashdown Park.

This man who is now recognised to be one of the greatest of all Englishmen and a princial founder of the realm was born at Wantage in 849 as the fifth and youngest son of King Ethelwulf who ruled Wessex from 839 to 858. Since Alfred had four older brothers there can have been no expectation that he would succeed to the throne and in fact three of his brothers ruled Wessex before him. As the youngest son Alfred seems to have been destined for the priesthood, but as his brothers successively died he would have gradually recognised that the succession was approaching nearer to him, and ultimately it was thrust upon him.

The history of Wessex in the period leading up to Alfred's reign is confused because Alfred's father Ethelwulf for some unexplained reason divided his kingdom. He seems to have been an unenthusiastic ruler and may have regarded Wessex, which by his time covered most of southern England, as being too unmanageable to be governed by one man. Alternatively the *athelings* (princes) of the house of Wessex, being brought up to be aggressive and warlike in those troubled times, may have become ambitious and impatient to rule. Whatever the reason Ethelwulf allowed his eldest son Athelstan to rule East Wessex consisting of Essex, Kent, Sussex and Surrey, while he retained Wiltshire, Hampshire, Dorset and Devon for himself. Athelstan seems to have died shortly after his last mention in the *Anglo-Saxon Chronicle* in 851.

The precedent of sub-dividing Wessex was to have far-reaching consequences. In 833 Alfred was as a child sent to Rome and in 855 Ethelwulf, who was a religious man, took him to Rome for a second time. The *Anglo Saxon-Chronicle* for 855 records: 'And the same year he [Ethelwulf] proceeded to Rome in great state, and remained there twelve months, and then made his way towards home'. These visits to Rome suggest that Ethelwulf may have intended Alfred for the church. This second visit to Rome was to have unforeseen consequences. They stayed, as the *Chronicle* indicates, for about a year, and it was probably this prolonged exposure to Roman culture and civilisation that widened Alfred's horizons and explains how, after repelling the Vikings from his kingdom, he was able to transform Saxon Wessex into the most cultivated state seen in England since the departure of the Romans over four hundred years earlier. In recording that he 'made his way towards home' the *Chronicle* implies that Ethelwulf lingered on his way back, and when he and Alfred reached Wessex in 856 Ethelwulf's second and eldest surviving son Ethelbald opposed his father's resumption of the throne. Civil war was avoided by another division of the kingdom, with Ethelwulf retaining East Wessex and leaving the rest of Wessex to Ethelbald. Ethelwulf continued to reign East Wessex until he died in 858, and a gold inlaid ring with his name inscribed upon was found at Laverstock in the Bourne valley a short

distance east of Salisbury. At his father's death Ethelbald outraged convention by marrying his stepmother, his father's widow, and when Ethelbald died in 860 his short reign was described by Alfred's biographer Asser as 'lawless'.

Upon succeeding his brother Ethelwulf's third son Ethelbert managed to re-unite and rule Wessex from 860 to 865, five years described by Asser as a period of 'peace, love and honour'. When Ethelwulf's fourth son Ethelred became king in 865 he 'vigorously and honourably ruled the kingdom in good repute, amid many difficulties, for five years' (Asser). In this he was loyally assisted by his younger brother Alfred in opposing the Vikings who had now become much more persistant in their raids upon Wessex. In 871 the brothers fought five major battles which culminated in a triumphant Wessex victory at Ashdown at some unknown location in Berkshire, probably near the Uffington White Horse a little to the east of Wiltshire. Since he was born at nearby Wantage Alfred was probably familiar with this territory. Ashdown Park and a prehistoric earthwork known as Alfred's Castle three miles south-east of Bishopstone and just outside Wiltshire may have been the site of the Battle of Ashdown, at which Alfred's vigilance in his capacity as Ethelred's principal lieutenant ensured that the Saxon army of Wessex was not surprised and destroyed. Whilst King Ethelred remained at prayer Alfred with his levies intercepted the advancing Danes. The ensuing battle lasted all day and at its end the remains of the Viking host withdrew, leaving five of their earls dead beside a stunted thorn tree around which the battle had raged. Although this battle established that the Vikings were vulnerable it was not decisive because two weeks later the Vikings were victorious at Basing several miles south of Reading, and two weeks later a drawn battle was fought at Marten, probably Marten on the Roman road east of East Grafton in east Wiltshire.

As his older brothers successively reigned and died Alfred approached nearer to the throne, and when his last surviving brother King Ethelred died as a result of wounds sustained at Marten the precarious position of Wessex under constant threat from the Vikings demanded an adult fighting leader. The young Alfred had already proved his prowess in battle as second-in-command to his brother, and although Ethelred had two young sons Alfred was elected as the undisputed king. Possibly Ethelwulf had made provision for his sons to successively succeed him in order to avoid the dangers inherent in having his vulnerable kingdom left in the hands of a child king.

After succceeding in these improbable circumstances at a time when the kingdom was in grave danger Alfred rather surprisingly proved to be so successful in combating the Viking menace that he is the only English king ever to have had 'the Great' appended to his name,

The character of Alfred

It is remarkable that Alfred, who cannot have been brought up to rule, should have ruled Wessex so successfully in very desperate times and have become the saviour of his kingdom and ultimately of the whole of southern England. Since his was not an age of realistic portraiture we can have no idea about his appearance and it is perhaps inevitable that we are inclined to imagine him as he has been represented in Victorian paintings and statues. According to his friend and biographer Bishop Asser Alfred was 'more comely in appearance than his brothers, and more pleasing in manner, speech and

Alfred portrayed on one of his pennies

behaviour'. His stylised profile on his coins depicts him beardless and with rather coarse features, and we know that he suffered from a recurrent illness which was described by Asser as 'severe visitation of an unknown disease'. This malady, which may have been epilepsy, caused him acute anxiety which must have been aggravated by persistant worry caused by the constant onslaughts of the Vikings upon his kingdom.

Because of the disturbed times in which he lived Alfred's education was neglected and he only learnt to read and write late in life. It was perhaps fortunate that the younger sons of the royal house of Wessex were brought up as men of action, as hunters and as soldiers rather than as scholars, for such an upbringing enabled Alfred to fulfil his destiny as the military saviour of Wessex and England.

The Vikings

The Vikings (the original meaning of the word is uncertain) were Danish, Norwegian and Swedish sea warriors who raided much of north-western Europe between the 8th and the 11th centuries in search of plunder. Most of Scotland was attacked by the Norwegians known as Norsemen, England tended to suffer at the hands of the Danes, and the Swedes tended to go south and east from Sweden and played little part in the attacks upon England.

From the 6th to the 9th centuries England consisted of seven kingdoms known as the *Heptarchy*. The most powerful of the seven kings became known as the *bretwalda* and was acknowledged by the other six as their overlord. Wessex, the land of the West Saxons, lay south of the Thames and the Cotswolds and was adjoined by Mercia to its north and East Anglia (the land of the East Angles) to its north-east. Wessex extended to the south coast which made it so vulnerable to attacks by the Danes that the people prayed: 'From the fury of the Norsemen, good Lord deliver us'.

Christianity had been established in Wessex long before Alfred's time having been brought to England in 597. Within a century it had spread over most of the country but from the mid-9th century Christianity was endangered as the Christian Anglo-Saxon kingdoms which made up the then disunited England were assailed on all sides by the heathen Vikings who pillaged the monastic establishments. The Viking attacks had begun with a few isolated raids in search of plunder at about the end of the 8th century, but after about 835 they became a more persistent menace. Having originally come sporadically as marauders by 835 the Vikings became intent on conquest and in 851, when Alfred was only two, three hundred and fifty Viking ships anchored in the Thames, their crews burnt London and Canterbury, and then for the first time overwintered in England on the Isle of Thanet. Alfred's father Ethelwulf saved Wessex by his vigorous opposition to the Viking host at this time when the Christian continental kingdoms were falling to the heathens.

In 868 Ethelred and Alfred campaigned in Mercia to support their failing neighbouring Saxon kingdom from the Viking hosts. The *Anglo-Saxon Chronicle* records that:

> In this year [868] the same [Viking] host went into Mercia to Nottingham, and there took winter-quarters. And Burhred, king of Mercia, and his councillors begged Ethelred, king of Wessex, and his brother Alfred to help them fight against the host; and then they proceeded with the West Saxon levies into Mercia as far as Nottingham, and there came upon the host in the fortification, but there was no serious engagement, and the Mercians made peace with the host.

In 871 Ethelred and Alfred first defeated the Danes at Englefield in Berkshire and four days later 'led great levies' (*Anglo-Saxon Chronicle*) to Reading and there were defeated. Four days later the two armies fought at Ashdown and on this occasion the West Saxons were victorious, with Alfred playing a major part in the victory. Ethelred had now virtually succeeded in ousting the Vikings from Mercia to his north but in that year he was defeated and mortally injured at Marten.

Wiltshire places associated with Alfred

Anglo-Saxon kings were itinerant as were their Norman and Medieval successors. They progressed around their kingdoms staying on their own estates or those of their subjects, often for the deer and boar hunting that was offered in the extensive forests that existed in those times. Wiltshire was then particularly heavily forested and Alfred must often have been at his estates in the county, at for instance Chippenham and Wilton. Many other places in Wiltshire are also associated with Alfred who would have fought over most of the county when opposing Viking onslaughts on his kingdom. Within a month of

succeeding to the throne he was in 871 defeated by the the Danes at Wilton:

> And one month later king Alfred fought with a small force against the entire host at Wilton, and for a long time during the day drove them off, and the Danes had possession of the place of slaughter. (*Anglo-Saxon Chronicle*)

Some time later Alfred founded a nunnery at Wilton near his palace buildings which were probably sited at the present Kingsbury Square, and endowed it with his royal manor of Wilton.

In south-west Wiltshire Alfred was associated with Wardour, near Tisbury, which was mentioned in a late-9th century document. This informs us that King Alfred gave a judgement: 'while he stood washing his hands within the chamber at Wardour'. This suggests that he may have had an estate at Wardour, which was at the Norman Conquest held by the abbey he had founded at Wilton.

At Chippenham Alfred had a palace from which he hunted in the adjoining forests, and it was here that his older sister Ethelswith was married to King Burhred of Mercia to re-inforce the alliance of Mercia with Wessex against the Danes. Alfred was probably at Chippenham in 877 when the Danish host stormed unexpectedly into Wessex, and it was probably from there that he retreated into Somerset because the Danes immediately made Chippenham the base for their subsequent operations.

Swanborough Tump

King Alfred's statue at the centre of Pewsey emphasises his association with the Vale of Pewsey where he owned estates. Between Pewsey and Woodborough, beside the road a little south of Cocklebury Farm, is Swanborough Tump which was formerly a place of importance as the meeting place or 'moot' of the Swanborough Hundred. It was *Swanabeorh* in 987 – the name means 'barrow of the peasants' (or swains) – but it became known by the local people as Swanborough Ashes because ash trees grew on the mound. A document of 1764 which refers to a Court Leet to be held at 'Swanborough Ash' confirms that the Saxon moot remained the

Swanborough Tump, still a mound when this sketch was made in 1898

hundred meeting place well into the 18th century, but subsequently the location of Swanborough Tump was lost until the Rev. H. G. Tomkins identified it in 1890. It was not marked on the early editions of the Ordnance Survey nor was it, despite the 1764 reference quoted above, shown on Andrews and Dury's 1773 map of Wiltshire, but the name Swanborough Tump has now been reinstated on modern Ordnance Survey maps. In Swanborough Tump, now an insignificant shallow mound trodden almost flat by cattle and marked by a metal plaque on a post, we have a documented and little-regarded relic of Anglo-Saxon England. Here in the late-9th century when Wessex was being assailed by the Danes King Ethelred and his brother Alfred summoned their Council to decide how the Danes should be resisted. At this meeting Alfred's Will was drawn up on 26 October 899 to document the agreement reached between himself and Ethelred:

But it came to pass that we were all harassed with the heathen invasion; then we discussed our children's future – how they would need some maintenance, whatever might happen to us through these disasters. When we were assembled at Swanborough we agreed, with the cognizance of the West Saxon Council, that whichever survived the other was to give the other's children the lands which we ourselves acquired and the lands which King Ethelwulf gave us . . .

Elsewhere in the Vale of Pewsey Alfred by a land charter dated 892 granted an estate at North Newnton three miles south-west of Pewsey to Æthelhelm, his ealderman (earl) of Wiltshire. This charter precisely defines bounds which survive today as the boundaries of the present parish of North Newnton. The bounds are described as running from North Newnton church south-east 'along the Avon bank to stints ford' [at NGR 136567], then west along the present parish boundary through 'rush-slade' to 'Tioltas ford' [at Cuttenham Farm], north-west up the Avon [to NGR 101579] and north-east 'along the road' [a footpath following the Ridgeway crossing of Pewsey Vale] and through Gores to 'Bottle' [Bottlesford]. From there the bounds ran south-east following the stream 'along the wood' to near Butts Farm and looped 'across the wood' around North Newnton Wood to North Newnton church.

Alfred's retreat to Athelney

The Danes persistently continued their attacks upon Wessex and for the first six years of his reign Alfred fought, negotiated and treated with them, and when necessary paid them 'Danegeld' to gain some respite. In return for gold the Danes withdrew and left Wessex untroubled for several years, and then a few days after Christmas at midwinter in 876, at a time which was then normally a close season for warfare, the Viking hosts broke camp in East Anglia and swept in force and at great speed across Wessex to Wareham where they fortified a camp and were besieged by Alfred. Trapped and unable to plunder they sought a truce and agreed to leave Wessex but broke the treaty, siezed Exeter, and raided into

Devon. Alfred pursued them and forced them north into Mercia.

At midwinter 877-8 they came back, concentrated in force at the royal manor of Chippenham, and very soon they had overrun most of Wessex. The *Anglo-Saxon Chronicle* entry reads:

> 878. In this year the host went secretly in midwinter after Twelfth Night to Chippenham, and rode over Wessex and occupied it, and drove a great part of the inhabitants oversea, and of the rest the greater part they reduced to submission, except Alfred the king; and he with a small company moved under difficulties through woods [Selwood] and into inaccessible places in marshes.

During the winter of 877-8 Alfred remained with his 'small company of supporters' at Athelney in the Somerset Levels behind the barrier provided by the great Forest of Selwood, which straddles the Wiltshire–Somerset border and takes its name from the Old English *Sealwudu*, meaning 'sallow-wood'.

From the inundated Somerset Levels Alfred carried on a guerrilla war against the invaders, and it was at Athelney that the legend arose that while pondering the insecurity of his position he allowed some cakes to burn and was berated by a cowherd's wife. Only a few miles from Athelney was found the Alfred Jewel which was presumably lost at this time and is now in an Oxford museum. Around its rim is inscribed: *Ælfred mec heht gewyrcan*, meaning 'Alfred had me made'.

The advance out of Somerset into Wiltshire

The Anglo-Saxon Chronicle records how seven weeks after Easter 878 Alfred emerged from the marshes of Somerset:

> Then in the seventh week after Easter he rode to *Ecgbryhtesstan*, to the east of Selwood [Egbert – or Ecgbryht, Alfred's grandfather, had died in 839 ten years before Alfred was born], and came to meet him there all the men of Somerset and Wiltshire and that part of Hampshire which was on this side of the sea, and they received him warmly. And one day later he went from those camps to Iley Oak, and one day later to Edington; and there he fought against the entire

host, and put it to flight, and pursued it up to the fortification, and laid siege there a fortnight.

Alfred in his march eastwards into Wiltshire would almost certainly have marched along the old route known as the Hardway (part of the Harroway) and up Kingsettle Hill past the site of Alfred's Tower, then the principal way through the Forest of *Sealwudu* (Selwood). Somewhere east of Selwood he met his assembled troops at *Ecgbryhtesstan*, after which his advance would have been along or above the Deverill Valley.

The precise location of Egbert's Stone has for long been a matter of conjecture. From the nature of the name it was once thought to have been at Brixton Deverill, and the stones in a paddock beside the church at Kingston Deverill have also been suggested as the possible site, although it is now known that these stones were moved to their present position from nearby Court Hill comparatively recently. Danish traditions are strong in this area. A Danes' Bottom is found a little west of Kingston Deverill overlooked by Court Hill and Kings Hill, and until Victorian times fair haired children at Hill Deverill were referred to as 'Daners'.

A more likely candidate as Egbert's Stone is the large shire stone which exists at the point where Wiltshire, Somerset and Dorset meet near the head of large pond which was formed to drive the large water-wheel at the former Bourton foundry. This stone, which is not easily found as it is now toppled and is largely grassed over, seems to be a prime candidate as a place of assembly because, being a shire stone at the point where three counties meet, it would have been known to the people of those three counties.

Alfred's Tower

Anyone visiting the Stourhead district cannot fail to notice the massive triangular brick-built tower on the ridge overlooking Somerset on the county boundary, and just in Somerset on Kingsettle Hill. After completing in the second half of the 18th century the landscaping of the immediate surroundings of his Stourhead estate, Henry Hoare turned his attention to the outlying parts of his grounds and in 1762 decided to commemorate

King Alfred by constructing this immense tower, which he built beside the principal ancient crossing of Selwood from Somerset into Wiltshire. On 23 October he wrote to his daughter:

> I have one Scheme more which will Crown or Top all . . . I propose to erect a Tower on Kingsettle Hill where He [Alfred] set up His Standard after He came from His concealment in the Isle of Athelney . . .

Alfred's Tower was designed on a triangular plan to minimise the effects of wind in its exposed position by Henry Flitcroft, who about twenty-five years before had designed a very similar tower at Wentworth Woodhouse in Yorkshire, to commemorate the defeat of Prince Charles Edward Stuart at Culloden. Alfred's Tower was

Alfred's Tower on Kingsettle Hill

begun in late 1769 and finished in 1772, and above its door was placed a statue of King Alfred which was described by Henry Hoare in a letter in April 1770:

> A young lad of 18 Mr. Hoare sent from Bath has in 7 weeks finished a figure of Alfred the Great 10 feet high from a model given him to the Admiration of all the Spectators. He is a wonderful Genius & His countenance shows it. He lives with Mr. Hoare of

Statue of Alfred on the east side of Alfred's Tower

Bath. The Tower is now about 15 feet high and begins to Figure. I hope it will be finished in as Happy Times to this Isle as Alfred finished his Life of Glory in then shall I depart in peace.

The inscription on Alfred's Tower reads:

> Alfred the Great
> A.D. 879 on this summit
> Erected his standard against Danish Invaders
> To Him we owe
> The origin of Juries
> The Establishment of a Militia
> the Creation of a Naval Force
> Alfred the light of a benighted age
> was a Philosopher and a Christian
> The Father of his People
> The Founder of the English
> Monarchy and Liberty

The Battle of Edington

The most important event in the reign of Alfred and one of the most important events in English history now took place in west Wiltshire. Over a very long period a number of locations have been advanced as the site of the Battle of *Ethandune*, but authorities are now generally agreed that it was fought near Edington on the north escarpment of Salisbury Plain east of Westbury.

The countryside around Alfred's Tower and the head of the Deverill Valley cannot be very much changed since Saxon times, and Alfred would have seen a similar landscape to that which the poet Edward Thomas saw when he followed in Alfred's footsteps up Kingsettle in 1911 and saw ahead: 'those gentle monsters, the smooth Long and Little Knolls above Maiden Bradley, smooth, detached green dunes'. Thomas also saw ahead: 'White Sheet Downs, which are to be mounted', and the road making for: 'the scar of a huge quarry on the nearest slope of White Sheet, a little to the left of a lesser hill, a smooth rounded knoll or islet'.

We now cannot be certain what route Alfred followed. He would from Kingsettle Hill have probably made directly for White Sheet Hill visible three miles ahead and then unscarred by a quarry. In *The Lost Roads of Wessex* (1969) C Cochrane suggests that: 'A search through southwest England for an area that represented in its communication lines every phase of history might easily be met by the square mile around Alfred's Tower'. Alfred may have followed the line of the present Alfred's Tower Road and Long Lane Drove past Kilmington, although this seems to be a diversion of an older way which formerly ran through the present Stourhead estate until it was realigned by the enclosure of Stourhead in the 18th century. This old way ran from about a mile

east of Alfred's Tower first south-east along the shoulder of Six Wells Bottom, and after swinging east passed a short distance north of the obelisk and Stourhead House and continued through Drove Lodge on the B3092 and over Search Knoll to White Sheet. There the two routes converged and the decision would have been taken either to continue along the often waterlogged tumulus-lined way (formerly marked by the Ordnance Survey as a 'British Trackway')

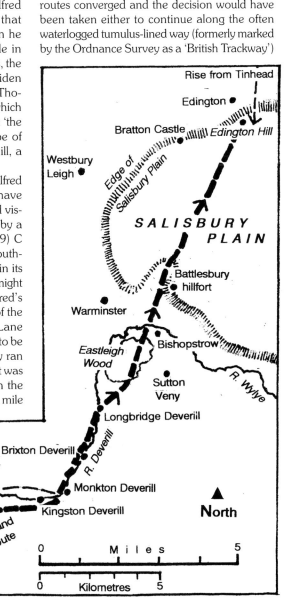

Conjectural route of Alfred to the Battle of Edington

Way over Search Knoll (left) viewed from White Sheet quarry

Alfred's alternative ways of approaching White Sheet from the west – left over Search Knoll; right Long Lane Drove

along the Deverill Valley under Long Knoll and Little Knoll past Dairy Farm to Kingston Deverill, or to follow the higher and drier ground over Rodmead Hill and Court Hill above Danes' Bottom to Kingston Deverill. From my own experience of walking extensively in this area I believe that Alfred is more likely to have followed the firmer high ground.

The day after assembling to the east of Selwood the Saxon army marched to 'Iley Oak', probably Eastleigh Woods above Bishopstrow south of Warminster. From Kingston Deverill the Deverill Valley could easily be followed through the Deverills to Longbridge Deverill, where

Eastleigh Woods would have been reached after a one-day march of about ten miles. Initial contact may have taken place at some point on the Plain between Warminster and Edington, as it seems unlikely that the Saxon army could have advanced unobserved by Viking scouts.

After camping overnight, probably in Eastleigh Woods, the next morning Alfred and his men would have continued past Bishopstrow and either up the present Sack Hill or between Battlesbury Camp and Scratchbury Camp on to the open expanses of the north-west corner of Salisbury Plain, where they would have marched across Boreham Down and Summer Down over

Head of the Deverill Valley from Long Knoll with Little Knoll on the left

an area used today by the School of Infantry for battle-training. Seven miles, or about three hours, after passing Battlesbury they would have reached the north escarpment of the Plain, probably at Edington Hill, for which the *Anglo-Saxon Chronicle* name was *Ethandune*. The name used in Domesday two hundred years later was the similar *Edendone*. This district may have been familiar to Alfred, as a moated site known as Palace Green (or Garden) at Westbury Leigh a little west of Westbury is believed to have been a palace of the Saxon kings, and here on Edington Hill the battle and the fate of Wessex was decided.

The route followed by the opposing Viking host when it marched from its base at Chippenham to meet the Saxon army at Edington would have been south from Chippenham past Lacock and Melksham, the total march being about twelve miles. The Vikings would probably have followed the high ground east of the River Avon over the heights of Bowden Hill and Sandridge Hill past the former Melksham Forest. The low ground past Keevil and Bulkington would then have to be crossed with the steep north escarpment of Salisbury Plain looming ahead.

The timing of the arrival of the respective armies would have decided the precise site of the battle. If the Saxons arrived first the site may have been at Edington Hill immediately south of Edington village, for the Saxons would surely have taken advantage of the high ground. If the Vikings were first on the scene they would have climbed the steep northern escarpment of the Plain and debouched at the top on level ground to meet the Saxon army on equal terms, in which case they are likely to have followed one or both of two surviving trackways on to the Plain. One of these climbs steeply from Bratton west of Edington Hill and over Patcombe Hill past White Cliff, and the other climbs from Tinhead at the east end of Edington and over Tinhead Hill to emerge on the wide expanses of Salisbury Plain. The Viking host can easily be imagined toiling up this latter track between steep grassy banks unaware that on these Wiltshire Downs at the north edge of Salisbury Plain they were about to suffer one of the most momentous defeats in European history at the hands of Alfred's army of Wessex

The siting of Westbury White Horse (not the present 18th-century horse but its predecessor which occupied its site and is traditionally believed to have been created two miles west of Edington Hill to commemorate the victory) is of little relevance to the precise battle site. To be visible from a distance the horse had to be sited on a steep slope and the horse in its present position is perfectly sited for such a monument, facing west to the setting sun and visible for many miles.

Edington Hill from Bratton hillfort

In November 2000 Lord Bath, a Wessex enthusiast, was present when a standing sarsen stone obtained from the Marlborough Downs was set up near the top of the road which runs from Bratton up to Bratton hillfort to commemorate Alfred's great victory.

The Battle of Edington was the most decisive event of Alfred's reign. Here, on the edge of Salisbury Plain near Westbury, the Danes were first decisively defeated and then besieged in their fortification. It is not clear whether this was their fortified base at Chippenham or the Iron Age hillfort of Bratton Castle. The historians Camden and Colt Hoare both believed that it was Bratton Castle rather than their base at Chippenham. In either case they held out for a fortnight until the Danish leader Guthrum sued for peace, gave hostages, and agreed to be baptised into the Christian faith and leave Wessex forever. He was baptised at Aller near Alfred's base camp at Athelney and Alfred was magnanimous in victory. After twelve days of feasting which symbolised Alfred's recognition of the need for the Danes and the Saxons to co-exist, Guthrum withdrew to Cirencester in the adjoining kingdom of Mercia and ultimately fulfilled his obligations under the treaty by returning to East Anglia.

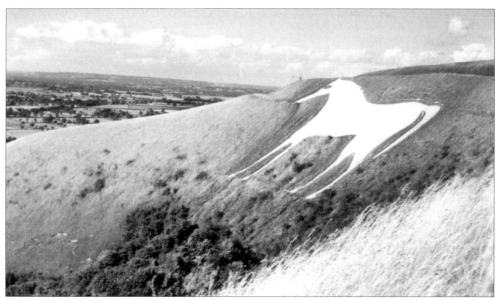

Westbury White Horse above Bratton

Early in the 20th century both G K Chesterton and Hilaire Belloc wrote essays entitled 'Ethandune'. Being uncertain about the precise location of the battle Chesterton described the battle as 'an elusive mirage' and as the place where the English were 'saved from being savages for ever'. Belloc wrote of the 'isolated hill' (Long Knoll above Maiden Bradley) from which 'a man perceives the two days march which Alfred made to overthrow the Danes at Ethandune', and described the battle as being 'of more moment to the history of Britain and Europe than any other'.

After Edington

After he had by his victory at Edington consolidated but not entirely secured his kingdom Alfred was able to turn his attention to other matters. The peace treaty drawn up after Edington left the Danes in control of England north and east of a line drawn approximately from Chester to London. Wessex was left intact and war against the Danes continued, but it was less desperate and sufficiently intermittent to allow Alfred to devote much of his life after 878 to military activities consolidating the defences of Wessex, and improving the organisation of his army, founding a

navy to intercept his marauding enemies at sea; but he also found time to improve his kingdom culturally, this being an activity in which he particularly revealed his greatness.

In 886 Alfred captured London and made a further treaty with Guthrum (who died in 890), finally partitioning England between them. The Danes retained the north and east, the area that became known as the Danelaw, and Alfred's authority was recognised over all of the rest of England including the entire south. Alfred's achievements prepared the way for his grandson Athelstan when he became king of Mercia in 925 to oust the Danes and the following year be recognised as the king of all England.

Alfred reforms the Army and founds a Navy

In the years following Edington Alfred first devoted himself to consolidating the defences of his kingdom. His army had traditionally consisted of the *fyrd*, a peasant militia which had to be called out in times of danger but tended to disperse to return home at key times such as harvest. The *Anglo-Saxon Chronicle* for 894 records how Alfred overcame this problem:

And the king had divided his levies into two sections, so that there was always half at home and half on active service, with the exception of those men whose duty it was to man the fortresses.

Alfred had also seen at first hand how effectively the Vikings fortified towns as military bases (for example Wareham when they raided into Wessex) and in the 880s arranged for a network of fortified towns to be established throughout his kingdom. We know a great deal about these fortresses as they were listed and described in the *Burghal Hidage*, written probably in the time of Alfred's son Edward the Elder. These *burhs* (Old English for boroughs) were used as refuges for the people in times of war and were sited so that most of the population lived within twenty miles of a *burh*. They also controlled the principal routes through Wessex but they were not entirely defensive. In addition to being sufficiently strong to withstand a siege they could also be used as bases from which troops could emerge to harry any marauding Vikings. The Wiltshire *burhs* were at Cricklade on the River Thames in the extreme north of the county, the strong hilltop town of Malmesbury in a loop of the River Avon in the north-west, Wilton situated in a defensible position between the Rivers Wylye and Nadder in south-east Wiltshire, and Chisbury Iron Age hillfort in the north-east. At Chisbury the exquisite ruined thatched early-gothic Chapel of St Martin may occupy the site of a Saxon church which served the *burh*, which presumably adapted the earthen ramparts of the Iron Age fortress as its defences.

Gothic ruined chapel at Alfred's Chisbury burh

Having also observed the mobility achieved by the Vikings by using their longships to sail inland up the rivers, Alfred now founded a navy equipped with similar ships which, according to the the *Anglo-Saxon Chronicle*, he designed himself. With these warships he was able to intercept invaders before they even set foot in his kingdom:

> Then the king ordered warships to be built to meet the Danish ships: they were almost twice as long as the others, some had sixty oars, some more; they were both swifter, steadier, and with more freeboard than the others; they were built neither to the Frisian design nor after the Danish, but as it seemed to himself that they could be most serviceable. (*Anglo-Saxon Chronicle*)

Alfred's scholarship

With regard to the cultural well-being of his kingdom, Alfred was aware that there were now no longer any good scholars in Wessex and being a man of action he took immediate steps to remedy this situation. The monasteries had been plundered and ruined by the Vikings and Alfred's education as a child had consequently been neglected. In the mid-880s the Welsh monk Asser (died 910) was brought to Alfred's court and became Alfred's friend. He was given the monastery at Amesbury and was made Bishop of Sherborne (892-910), and with his help Alfred, who had remained unable to read or write until he was past twelve, became literate in Latin as well as English.

A number of other intellectual men were attracted to Alfred's court and we know the names of six of them in addition to Asser. One was Plegmund, a Mercian priest who became Archbishop of Canterbury in 890. Another Mercian, Werferth, had by 873 been consecrated Bishop of Worcester. Two more Mercians were Werwulf, a member of Werferths episcopal household, and an Athelstan of whom we know nothing. The other two were learned monks, the Fleming Grimbald (c. 820-903) and the less important John, a continental Saxon. The details of the life of Grimbald, whom Alfred made abbot of his new minster at Winchester, are obscure, although Alfred mentions him as one of his teachers in his preface to his own translation in 896 of Gregory's

Cura Pastoralis, which he prefaced with a statement regarding the decay of learning in his kingdom and an indication of his intention to remedy this. In order to educate the clergy spiritually he sent a copy to each of his bishops, and he also ordered a selective translation to be made of Bede's *Ecclesiastical History*.

Alfred's court of Wessex now became recognised abroad as a centre of learning in which Alfred personally took an active part in translating several classic works from Latin into his native Old English. Although there is no evidence that Alfred ordered the writing of the *Anglo-Saxon Chronicle*, the history in annalistic form which has been described as 'the most important work written in English before the Norman Conquest', he probably ordered its revision as up to his time the chronicles merely listed isolated important occurrences. From about 890 the *Chronicle* became the systematic detailed compilation that has become a primary authority for the history of Anglo-Saxon England. Although Alfred's early literary work after 894 consisted of translations of existing books which were 'most necessary for all men to know', towards the end of his life he progressed to writing original works which offered ideas for his posterity by quoting from his own experiences to illustrate his ideas.

In addition to his literary activities Alfred turned his attention to the legal system of Wessex and issued a revised code of laws based upon those of his predecessors, the Kings Ine of Wessex and Offa of Mercia.

The Alfred legends

Alfred's astonishing reversal of fortune at Edington, from being an exile in hiding at Athelney to a victorious king accepting the full submission of the Vikings, has caught the imagination of Englishmen of many periods, but his story has been confused by legends that have been invented through the centuries. There is for example no contemporary evidence for the cake-burning episode at Athelney, nor for the story of Alfred entering the Danish camp as a spy disguised as a harper. These were inventions by 12th-century chroniclers which were further en-

hanced in the 13th century when the monk Matthew Paris (*c*.1200-1259) promoted Alfred in his writings as an example to contrast with Henry III who was then favouring his foreign favourites to the disgust of the English nobility. In the early Middle Ages the *Proverbs of Alfred*, probably written in the late-12th century, included an account of Alfred's life and quoted thirty-five proverbs alleged to be by him, all beginning: 'Thus quoth Alfred . . .', although they are attributed to him only on the basis of tradition.

During the 18th century Alfred was eulogised as a national hero and it was at this time that 'the Great' was first added to his name. Practically everyone knows the patriotic song *Rule Britannia*. It is the culminating theme of the musical medley which introduces the BBC Radio 4 programme early every morning, is played at the Service of Remembrance at the cenotaph in Whitehall, and is sung at the promenade concerts, but few know that it was inspired by King Alfred. At the time in the 18th century when Britain's sea-power was so powerful that she really did 'rule the waves', several popular stage productions took as their hero Alfred, and a masque called *Alfred* was in 1740 written by James Thomson and was set to music, probably by Thomas Arne. It included the song *Rule Britannia* in the context of Alfred having founded the navy to repel the Viking menace.

Even the essentially down-to-earth Dr Johnson (1709–84) became so interested in Alfred that he considered writing his life, and it was at this time that Henry Hoare of Stourhead erected Alfred's Tower on his Stourhead estate in south-west Wiltshire (see above, pages 9-10). This interest in Alfred continued in the 19th century when the historical painter Benjamin Haydon (1786–1846) committed suicide in his studio while working on a huge painting of Alfred and the first British jury, and the American poet Longfellow (1807–82) referred in his poem *Woodstock Park* to 'Alfred the Saxon King, Alfred the Great'.

On the presumed anniversary of Alfred's death in 1801 a monument to him was set up on the Isle of Athelney in the Somerset Levels, and in 1901 a statue of Alfred was erected at his former capital at Winchester. His statue at his birthplace in Wantage dates from 1877, and another at Pewsey in Wiltshire from 1911.

In spite of this recurring interest in King Alfred it is an interesting fact that although a number of the English kings named sons Arthur out of deference to the semi-legendary 'King' Arthur of the post-Roman period, no English monarch so far as I know named a son after Alfred until Queen Victoria named her second son Alfred, and by doing so for a time popularised Alfred as a christian name.

Summary of Alfred's achievement and his will

King Alfred grew up as the youngest of five sons of the royal house of Wessex and was never expected to reign and yet, when he unexpectedly become king of Wessex, he succeeded in retrieving an almost impossible military position, decisively defeating his enemies, expanding his frontiers, and reorganising the defences of his kingdom, and from his kingdom of Wessex became one of the principal founders of the realm of England. Although he was obliged to continue campaigning against his enemies for the rest of his life, Alfred in his later years greatly enhanced the cultural standing of his court by encouraging intellectuals and improving its literary standing. He also completely reorganised the legal system of his kingdom.

In spite of the fact that his education was neglected Alfred seems to have been endowed with a natural curiosity and his two visits to Rome before he was seven left him with an awareness of matters far beyond the boundaries of England. This was demonstrated when he married his daughter Elfhryth to Baldwin, Count of Flanders, and so founded an alliance with Flanders which lasted for many years.

Alfred died in about 899 at the age of fifty, a reasonable age for his time. He was buried in the Old Minster at Winchester and the *Anglo-Saxon Chronicle* carried this surprisingly low-key obituary:

In this year died Alfred, son of Ethelwulf, six nights before All Hallows Day. He was king over all England

except that part which was under Danish domination, and he ruled the kingdom twenty-eight and a half years. Then Edward, his son, succeeded to the kingdom.

Alfred's bones were subsequently moved and were ultimately lost. His wife Ealhswith outlived him by three years and died in 902. Five of his children survived to maturity, Edward his eldest son, Ethelward the youngest son, and three daughters, Ethelflæd the eldest, Ethelgifu, and Elfthryth the youngest

His Will made on 26 October 899 at Swanborough in the Vale of Pewsey (see earlier, page 8) reveals that Alfred held many estates in Wiltshire. An estate at Chiseldon near Swindon was left to Winchester, and his eldest son Edward was left Bedwyn, an estate possibly surviving from Roman times in the eastern part of Savernake Forest which included Chisbury Iron Age hillfort, one of the fortresses mentioned in the *Burghal Hidage*, and also an estate at Pewsey. Ethelweard, his youngest son, was left estates at Amesbury and at Dean in south-east Wiltshire. His youngest daughter Elfthryth was left Chippenham, which according to Asser was a royal estate, and also Ashton which was probably Ashton Keynes in the very north of Wiltshire rather than Steeple Ashton. His wife Ealhswith received an estate at Edington where Alfred had triumphed over the Danes.

Alfred left this modest assessment of his achievements:

This I can now most truly say, that I have desired to live worthily while I lived, and after my life to leave to the men that should be after me a remembrance in good works.

After Alfred

By the time of Alfred's death the Viking threat had lost much of its momentum. Recognising that he had been a caretaker king appointed by the nation out of expediency in its hour of need Alfred wisely left the appointment of his successor to the council of his kingdom. The choice lay between Alfred's son Edward and his nephew Ethelwold, the son of his elder brother Ethelred. Edward had distinguished himself as a soldier when taking an active role in support of his father, while Ethelwold had achieved nothing and the council understandably elected Edward king by general consent.

Alfred left his son Edward, who reigned 899–925 and became known as Edward the Elder, a kingdom in sound military and intellectual order. Edward built on these foundations and adopted a policy of aggression against the now-diminishing Viking threat. Instead of loyally supporting Edward and maintaining his own claim to the throne in the event of Edward being killed in action, the aggrieved Ethelwold siezed the royal palace of Wimborne and Christchurch in Dorset and was besieged by King Edward at Badbury Rings. He then fled during the night and turned traitor by joining the Vikings in Northumbria. By the end of Edward the Elder's reign in 925 all Viking territory south of the Humber had been absorbed into Wessex.

King Alfred's grandson Athelstan (c. 895–939) was heir to more than the throne of Wessex. Having been raised in Mercia he enjoyed the allegiance of the Mercians and in 924 was acknowledged their king the year before he succeeded his father Edward as king of Wessex. Athelstan was another great Saxon king with strong associations with Wiltshire where he greatly favoured Malmesbury. He rebuilt its great abbey, having in 930 granted to its burgesses as a reward for their assistance against the Danes five hundred acres as a common between Malmesbury and his estate at Norton, which is sometimes known as Malmesbury Common but alternatively as King's Heath. Rights to this common are still held today. During Athelstan's resistance to the Vikings in 937 two sons of Alfred's youngest son Ethelward were killed and were taken to Malmesbury for burial, and at Malmesbury Athelstan is commemorated by a recumbent effigy on a tomb chest near the altar in the abbey, although his body lies elsewhere in an unknown grave.

By converting Guthrum and his leaders to Christianity Alfred inadvertently prepared the way for a Viking to succeed to his kingdom. After Athelstan's death in 939 his successors became complacent, Alfred's measures for the defence of the realm lapsed, and only a hundred and seventeen years after Alfred's death the Christian Dane Cnut (or Canute) became in 1016 king of England and was succeeded by his son and grandson. For twenty-six years Danish kings held sway in England until in 1042 Saxon kings regained the throne and held it until 1066 when Duke William of Normany, a man of Viking descent, invaded England and assumed by conquest the throne of the former Saxon Kings of Wessex.

Only a hundred and sixty-seven years after his death Alfred's Anglo-Saxon kingdom had become subject to a foreign dynasty under a Norman king of Viking descent.

2 The Bassets and Marshals

in North and East Wiltshire

The surprising neglect of the Bassets and Marshals by Wiltshire historians and topographical writers is probably explained by the fact that both flourished during the confusing anarchy between Stephen and Matilda and the ensuing period during which most of the baronial class attempted to remain loyal to the throne but challenged the authority of John and his son Henry III as the current occupiers of that throne. These two important families held extensive estates in north and east Wiltshire at a time when, on the basis of its tax yield, Wiltshire was the fourth most important county in England. The Bassets of Wootton Bassett and the Marshals of Marlborough and Ludgershall, two families united by marriage and friendship, respectively held the important offices of justiciars and Earls Marshal of England, and they established in Wiltshire a royalist power base which was of great importance to King John and his son Henry III in their encounters with their barons.

The Bassets are now merely remembered because their name is appended to the names of several places around Wootton Bassett. They have tended to be dismissed with mere mentions that Wootton Bassett 'became the property of the Bassetts', 'belonged to the Bassetts' or that it 'got its name from the family of Bassett'. This neglect is probably explained by the fact that their male line died out early and the Basset heiress took their estates to the better-known but short-lived family of Despenser. Another factor which has contributed to the neglect of the Bassets is the disappearance from Wootton Bassett of practically everything connected with them. Their Vastern Manor House has been so much altered through the centuries that nothing survives from the time of the Bassets, and their great hunting park known as Vastern Great Park, which once enclosed much of the parish, is now divided agricultural land with farms bearing park-related names such as Highgate Farm, Park Ground Farm, Hookers Gate, and Old Park Farm. The park site has also been successively disrupted by the construction of the former Wilts and Berks Canal, the railway and the M4 motorway. The Hospital of St John which the Bassets founded in Wootton Bassett was dissolved at the dissolution of the monasteries, and there are no known Basset graves in the heavily remodelled church.

The former associations of the Marshals with Wiltshire are also virtually forgotten in spite of the fact that William Marshal was Marshal of England and a man of such scrupulous honour and loyalty to the crown that King John from his deathbed sought his forgiveness for the many ills he had done him.

The background to the Bassets and the Marshals

In the early Middle Ages the kings of England had no standing army. The barons then held their land of the king in return for military service and when summoned were expected to bring out their retainers in support of the monarchy, which was consequently entirely dependent upon the loyalty of the barons. At the death of King Stephen in 1154 Henry II (1133–89) of Anjou came to the throne as a result of an agreement between the two rival contenders for the throne, Stephen of Blois (c. 1097–1154) a grandson of the Conqueror, and Matilda of Anjou (1102–67), the only daughter of the Conqueror's son Henry I. By his marriage in 1152 to Eleanor of Aquitaine (1122–1204), previously the wife of Louis VII of France, Henry II acquired such vast possessions in France that his French territories after he came to the throne in 1154 exceeded those of the king of France. Henry and Eleanor had eight children, five of them sons – William (1153–56), Henry (1155–83), Richard (1157–99), Geoffrey (1158–86), and a late son John (1167–1216), who was his father's favourite.

After the premature death of Prince Henry, known as Young King Henry, Henry II was in 1183 challenged by his three surviving sons, and following the death of Geoffrey in 1186 Richard and John were encouraged by their mother Queen Eleanor, who was by this time estranged from Henry, to wage war against their father in his French possessions. At Henry II's death in 1189 his eldest surviving son succeeded as Richard I. He reigned for ten years, but was generally absent from England, and he impoverished the country to finance his crusading activities abroad which earned him the name of Richard the Lionheart. After Richard controversially nominated his younger brother John as his successor John reigned from 1199 to 1216. Against this background of anarchy the Bassets and Marshals became established in north Wiltshire.

Wootton Bassett and the Bassets

Wootton Bassett was in the early Middle Ages known as Wotton (meaning 'farm by the wood'), from being a small settlement located immediately south of the great Forest of Braydon. At Domesday Wotton was held by Milo Crispin and the Bassett suffixes were added when Wootton, Berwick and Winterbourne Bassett were acquired by Alan Basset by his marriage to Walter de Dunstanville's daughter and heiress Aliva in about 1212. The linear nature of Wootton Bassett is probably explained by the Bassets in the early-13th century extending Wootton away from the church. The resemblance between the straight wide High Streets of Wootton Bassett and Marlborough may not be coincidental. That at Wootton Bassett runs north-east away from the church and was probably developed after the Bassets were granted a market at Wootton Bassett. The similar High Street at Marlborough also runs north-east from the part-Norman church of St Peter and St Paul to the site of the old town around the Green. It seems to have been added in the time of the Marshals to link their castle site with the old town. The great width of Wootton Bassett and Marlborough High Streets suggests that both were created to accommodate markets.

Berwick Bassett, which reaches over Hackpen Hill almost to the former Templar preceptory at Temple, had been *Berewic*, meaning 'outlying grange' in 1185 in the records of the Knights Templar, and after the fall of the Bassets' successors the Despensers in 1326 the ownership of Berwick Bassett was disputed between the crown and Stanley Abbey and the parish was divided.

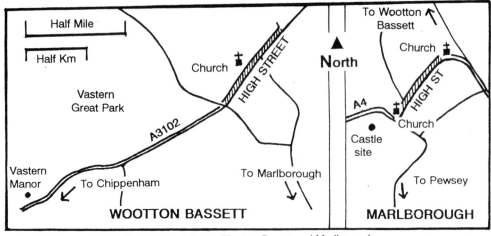

Comparison between Wootton Bassett and Marlborough

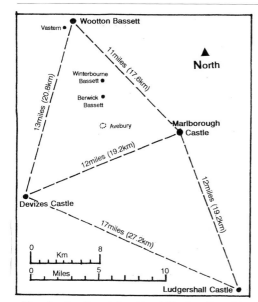

Plan showing the relationship of Wootton Bassett to the Marshal castles at Marlborough, Devizes and Ludgershall

Since in addition to Wootton Bassett they held Compton Bassett, Winterbourne Bassett, and Berwick Bassett, the Bassets exerted direct control over most of the area contained in a triangle between Wootton Bassett, Calne and Avebury, consisting of part of the upland plateau which lies between the principal western escarpment of the Marlborough Downs (Hackpen Hill), and the secondary escarpment which runs through Broad Town and Highway, together with the marshy ground which extends from the foot of this escarpment towards Hilmarton and Lyneham. Although the large church at Compton Bassett is largely Perpendicular, its 12th–13th century arcades led to speculation about a Basset involvement in its construction, particularly as the village was *Cumptone Basset* as early as 1228, and, according to John Aubrey, Gilbert Basset as a consequence of his opposition to Henry III in 1233 forfeited his 'house at Compton [Bassett]'.

The Basset name is derived from the Norman nickname Bass which was applied to persons of short stature. It is today used to denote low-pitched instruments and voices, and Basset is also used for the low-slung basset-hound. The Bas-

sets of Cornwall were an early Norman family. A Thurston Basset appears on the roll of Battle Abbey and Henry I's justiciar was Osmund Basset, as was Ralph Basset (died 1127) and his son Richard (died 1144). The office of justiciar arose from the Norman and Angevin kings having dual kingdoms in France and England necessitating a viceroy called the justiciar to rule England when the king was abroad. Administration of justice by the justiciar was often harsh and sometimes indiscriminate. The *Peterborough Chronicle* for 1124 records that:

> . . . before Christmas Ralph Basset and the king's thegns held a meeting of the Witan at *Hundehoge* in Leicestershire, and there hanged so many thieves as never were before, that was, in that little while, altogether four and forty men, and six men were deprived of their eyes. Many truthful men said there were many unjustly mutilated.

Ralph Basset was at his death in 1127 succeeded in the office of justiciar by his son Richard and the Bassets continued to be justiciars for several generations.

The appearance of the Bassets in Wiltshire is explained by Thomas Basset's marriage to a daughter of the Dunstanvilles, a name which recurs in Wiltshire history. The younger son of this

Compton Bassett church

marriage was Alan Basset (died 1232–3), who was a virtual contemporary of the celebrated William Marshal and was favoured by both Richard I and King John. Throughout the reign of the latter he was in constant attendance at court and he and his brother Thomas are listed in Magna Carta as king's counsellors.

Alan Basset left three sons, and the former great manor house of Vastern near Wootton Bassett was built by his eldest son Gilbert Basset who died in 1241, the younger sons being Fulk (died 1259) who became Bishop of London, and Philip who became justiciar and died in 1271. Early in his ecclesiastical career Fulk Basset was nominated by his father rector of Winterbourne Bassett church which he served from about 1214 to about 1239.

The loyalty of the Bassets to King John is a matter of interest at a time when the majority of the barons were in open rebellion. King John was probably well-known in Wiltshire where he often hunted. Pipe Rolls reveal that in addition to staying at the royal castles of Ludgershall and

King John from his effigy in Worcester Cathedral

Marlborough, he was often at unfortified places such as Clarendon, Bradenstoke and also at Melksham which then adjoined a royal forest. This frequent presence of the king may explain how north Wiltshire became a royalist base in the baronial wars between King John and his barons which followed the pope's anulment of Magna Carta. When that much maligned king died leaving the rebel barons holding half the shires of England, the royal party were in control of the west including Wiltshire and the Midlands, a situation that allowed John to be buried at Worcester and his young son to be brought from his safe haven at Devizes and crowned as Henry III at Gloucester. The animosity of the barons had been directed at John personally and not at the throne, and his death helped the untroubled succession of his son as Henry III, as did the fact that the Bassets remained loyal, although the major factor which ensured the boy Henry's succession was the loyalty demonstrated by the powerful William the Marshal.

The early Marshals

The Marshals emerged at the time when King Stephen and Matilda were contesting the throne. Stephen of Blois (c.1097–1154), a son of the Conqueror's daughter Adela, had been received at the court of Henry I and being an amiable fellow he became the king's favourite nephew and was given many English estates.

After Henry I lost his son and heir William drowned at sea in 1120 Matilda (1102–67) became the rightful heiress, but at Henry I's death in 1135 the barons refused to accept her and Stephen of Blois became the new king. Matilda had when very young in 1114 been married to the German Emperor Henry V and was therefore known as the Empress Maud. After the Emperor died in 1128 she married Geoffrey of Anjou and although the marriage was unhappy they agreed to make a joint bid for the lands and titles of Stephen, Geoffrey in France and Matilda in England. Matilda invaded in 1139 and a period of anarchy ensued from 1139 until 1152 during which the two rivals battled for the throne.

In about 1130 John Fitzgilbert, the son of Gilbert the Marshal who had succeeded his father as Marshal and married Sibyl the sister of Patrick of Salisbury, emerged as a great magnate in east Wiltshire, Berkshire and Hampshire, after inheriting the offices and estates of his father. He appears to have been a freebooter who plundered laymen and churchmen alike leading Wiliam of Malmesbury to describe him as 'the root of all evil, a very firebrand of hell'. During the wars between Stephen and Matilda he was as a supporter of Matilda described in the *Gesta Stephani* as:

> . . . a cunning man and very ready to set great designs on foot by treachery, in forcible possession of a very strong castle belonging to the king called Marlborough

and as:

> . . . that scion of hell and root of all evil, who was castellan of Marlborough, troubled the kingdom by increasing disorder; he built castles designed with wondrous skill, in the places that best suited him, from which he proceeded to terrorise the countryside.

John Fitzgilbert was a brilliant soldier who when Matilda was delaying the retreat of her army from the east towards his castle at Ludgershall in east Wiltshire by her insistence at riding side-saddle, persuaded her to ride astride and then with a small party fought a rearguard action near Wherwell in Hampshire which enabled her to escape. He then with some difficulty managed to follow her to Ludgershall.

The place of birth of John Fitzgilbert's son William Marshal (died 1219) is not known although it is probable that this greatest member of the family, who adopted Marshal as his surname, was born at his father's castle at Marlborough. John Fitzgilbert the Marshal died in 1165 having been granted large estates in Wiltshire, which included Marlborough together with North Tidworth and Clyffe Pypard, which the Marshals held into the 13th century.

The word 'marshal' was derived from the French *maráschal* meaning 'horse-servant', mare being derived from the same source. Marshal was used in Norman times for a man who looked after horses as a farrier or groom or was a dealer in

horses. At this time horses were of such immense importance to Medieval society that the name Marshal gradually grew in importance until it was used to designate the senior English earldom.

The Marshal castles in Wiltshire

Warfare in the 12th and 13th centuries involved holding and besieging castles, and in Wiltshire the Marshals were associated with the three important castles of Marlborough, Ludgershall, and to a lesser extent Devizes. Marlborough Castle originated when William the Conqueror built a timber castle which was rebuilt in stone by Bishop Roger of Salisbury in 1101. It was built on a high mound which has been generally assumed to be prehistoric although there is some doubt about this. During Henry I's reign (1100–35) the castle was probably entirely rebuilt to a standard fit to accommodate the king, and in the hands of Marshal John Fitzgilbert it played an active part in the conflict between Stephen and Matilda. The dependence of the king upon his barons was illustrated at Marlborough Castle when King John threatened to hang Robert FitzWalter's son-in-law. That fiery baron boldly told the king: 'You will not hang my son-in-law, by Gods body you will not!', and when the king referred the case for trial FitzWalter appeared at Marlborough accompanied by five hundred armed knights to ensure an acquittal.

King John was very much attached to Marlborough and there married in 1189 his first wife Isabella of Gloucester. When in 1200 he married his second wife, the twelve-year-old Isabelle of Angoulême, he immediately brought her to Wiltshire and left her for safety in Marlborough Castle while he went on a royal tour. Their five children Henry, Richard and three daughters were christened at Marlborough, possibly in the font now in Preshute church.

In about 1209 Marlborough Castle was strengthened and became an important strong point during the Barons Wars. It fell to Louis of France in 1216 but the year after John's death the royal party recaptured Marlborough in 1217 for the new king Henry III. When in 1220 William Marshal's son William Marshal II against royal instructions further strengthened

Remains of Ludgershall Castle

Marlborough, Henry III deprived him of the castle and developed it into a royal hunting extablishment associated with Savernake Forest. After Henry III's defeat by de Montfort at Lewes in 1264 the king's supporters seized Marlborough Castle, and when Henry III was restored after the Battle of Evesham in 1265 he held his last parliament at Marlborough Castle in 1267. After his death the castle was allowed to decline and by the early-15th century it was ruinous. Now practically nothing of it remains, although a conjectural reconstruction of it is included in the *Wiltshire Archaeological & Natural History Magazine*, volume 48 (facing page 140). Its site, south of the A4 Bath Road as it runs west out of Marlborough, is now occupied by Marlborough College.

Lacking a home other than Westminster the Angevin kings were constantly on the move, and Ludgershall was one of about six royal castles which they often visited. At Ludgershall we have one of the least-known but most interesting Medieval sites in Wiltshire, for here some standing castle remains survive at the north end of the village. Ludgershall Castle was initially built as a royal castle associated with Marlborough, the two castles being often held by a joint castellan. In the wars between Stephen and Matilda each party invested and captured strongholds and although these campaigns now defy logical description we know that Ludgershall Castle was held, as was Marlborough Castle, by John the Marshal for the Empress Matilda. After the strife ended he handed it to Matilda's son Henry of Anjou when he succeeded Stephen as Henry II. King Henry's son Richard I in 1189 granted Ludgershall to his brother John, who improved and repaired the castle and was frequently at Ludgershall for the hunting. By 1203 the North Park had been created adjoining the castle which became a stronghold in King John's wars with his barons. After the death of King John in 1216 Ludgershall lost most of its military significance and under Henry III became a royal residence and hunting establishment with two associated deer parks. From 1212 to 1222 the castle was held by William Marshal II who in 1222 surrendered it to Henry III. Between 1234 and 1250 it was transformed into a fortified hunting palace and by the late-13th century the extensive South

Park had been created. The Bassets' successors the Despensers held Ludgershall for a short time in the early-14th century.

The surviving remains of Ludgershall Castle are cared for by English Heritage and are freely accessible. They consist of earthen ramparts enclosing a large area around the remains of the castle keep and the palace. These ramparts appear to be prehistoric earthworks adapted as the castle bailey enclosure. The keep survives as a substantial ragged crag of flint walling standing to a height of about nine metres. The adjoining low walls of flint dressed with ashlar stone date from the 14th century when Henry III converted the castle into a hunting establishment, and it is now possible to stand on the spot at the east end of the Great Hall where Henry III held court.

At Devizes the warrior Bishop Roger of Salisbury (c.1065–1139) in 1109 began to construct a large castle to replace the timber castle built in 1080 by Bishop Osmund which had been destroyed by fire. Devizes Castle also featured in the civil wars in the reign of Stephen. When Matilda landed in England in 1139 to pursue her claim Stephen, aware of Bishop Roger's support for Matilda, forced him to surrender Devizes Castle, which later in the war became for six years from 1142 Matilda's headquarters. When Stephen was confirmed as king Devizes Castle became a crown property and a royal residence. King John was often at Devizes, as was his son Henry III who there maintained a sporting establishment and at Devizes imprisoned his chief minister Hubert de Burgh after his fall from power in 1232 (see page 29). Devizes Castle has been entirely destroyed and its site is now occupied by a Victorian house in pseudo-castle style.

All three of these royal castles of the Marshals had the normal hunting grounds associated with them which were such an attraction to the kings and barons at this time. Marlborough had Savernake Forest adjacent just as Ludgershall had Collingbourne Forest. Devizes Castle was less closely related to a forest, although Melksham Forest was within a few miles and adjoining Devizes Castle were two deer parks, Old or Great Park lying west of the castle site, and the New Park, which was also an early park, being at Roundway.

William the Marshal

John the Marshal's fourth son William was born in about 1146, probably in Wiltshire and possibly at Marlborough. The honourable character of William Marshal became evident early in his life when, during the wars between Matilda and Stephen, as a small boy of about four he was held

William Marshal from his effigy in the Temple Church, London

hostage by King Stephen, who took a liking to the child. When his father John the Marshal refused to surrender Newbury Castle the king resisted his supporters, who wished to catapult the child into the castle; he refused to harm the boy and on one occasion was seen playing an elementary form of conkers with him.

From thirteen to twenty-one William was sent to his father's cousin the Chamberlain of Normandy as a squire, preparatory to becoming a knight. In 1167 he was knighted and as a landless younger son became a brilliant warrior. For a time he led a team of tournament fighters and lived by selling horses and prisoners captured by his prowess. Tournament fighting was then a serious military training activity which sometimes took the form of pitched battles, and after one tournament William Marshal was seen with his head laid on an anvil having the dents hammered out of his helmet to allow it to be removed from his head! He was appointed tutor in chivalry to Henry II's oldest surviving son Prince Henry, but the period towards the end of the reign of Henry II was a particularly turbulent one. Henry II had married the strong-willed Eleanor, Duchess of Aquitaine (1122–1204), a remarkable woman who lived to be eighty-two when life expectancy was forty. She had been married to Louis of France (1137–52) but despised him as 'more monk than king'. When the marriage was annulled by the pope on grounds of consanguinity King Louis lost Aquitaine and Poitou, so that when Henry II in 1152 secretly married Eleanor in the year that she divorced King Louis the scene was set for three hundred years of warfare in France. Two years later Henry succeeded to the throne of England and by right of his wife to much of France.

Eleanor had by Henry II five sons but after 1168 they lived apart due to his open affair with Rosamund de Clifford, 'Fair Rosamund'. Having kept her last English Christmas at Marlborough Castle Queen Eleanor went home to govern Aquitaine from where, appalled by the murder of Thomas Becket in 1170, she in 1173 encouraged her sons to rebel against her husband. She was captured by Henry and remained confined for fifteen years, some of them at Old Sarum, until King Henry died and Richard I succeeded him in 1189. At Richard's death in 1199 Eleanor although aged seventy-seven acted decisively to secure the succession for her youngest son John and lived until 1204.

William Marshal inevitably became involved in these complicated royal politics as Henry II sought the help of his sons in controlling his immense possessions in France. In an attempt to avoid disputes over the succession he had his eldest surviving son crowned Young King Henry, but all of his sons were encouraged by their mother Eleanor of Aquitaine to go to war in France against their father. Young King Henry died in 1183 of dysentery when campaigning in France, and Geoffrey also died early leaving his brothers Richard (his mother's favourite) and John (his father's) to compete for the inheritance.

When in 1173 Young King Henry had under his mothers influence waged war against his father in France the young William Marshal stood by the young king and after his death in 1183 went on a pilgrimage (1183–87) to the Holy Land on his behalf. With his eldest son dead Henry II possibly encouraged Richard to rebel against him in France in order to enhance the prospects of his favourite son John. In June 1189 Richard rushed so hurriedly after his sick father and his army as they made for the safety of the fortress at Chinon that he omitted to wear his full armour, and when harrying King Henry's rearguard found himself at the mercy of the redoubtable William Marshal. He is alleged to have appealed to the Marshal by pointing out that he was unarmed, and William Marshal is said to have replied: 'No, I will not kill you, but I hope the Devil may!' When a temporary peace was arranged Henry II was devastated to find that high on the list of those to whom he was asked to grant amnesty was his favourite son Prince John who had unknown to him joined his opponents. Two days later Henry died forlorn and miserable at Chinon aged only fifty-six, estranged from his queen and heartbroken by the defections of his sons. It is said that he died cursing his 'devil's brood' and muttering 'Shame, shame on a conquered king'.

Although he has become an archetypal English hero the new king Richard I was like his brother John essentially French, being the son of parents from Anjou and Aquitaine. His only English blood came from his great-grandmother Maud, he spoke no English, and in his will directed that he should be buried in France. He was tenuously connected with Wiltshire in that his wet nurse Hodierna owned lands at West Knoyle in south-west Wiltshire, which was consequently known as *Knoyle Hodierne*. As a child Richard had been nominally given his mother's duchy of Aquitaine but, since his father insisted on retaining actual control, from the age of sixteen Richard waged war against his father in

Aquitaine. After succeeding to the throne in 1189 Richard regarded England as a subsidiary kingdom to be exploited to finance his crusading activities and he was an ineffective absentee king who spent only about six months of his reign in England.

Upon returning from his pilgrimage William Marshal was forgiven by King Richard who recognised his steadfast loyalty to his father. He was made a member of the royal household and was granted the hand of Isabella the heiress of Richard de Clare, 2nd Earl of Pembroke. By this marriage William Marshal became the 1st Earl of Pembroke of the Marshal line and acquired estates in four counties. He successively served four kings, Henry II, Richard I, John and Henry III, believing that his loyalty was to the throne rather than to its current occupant, and during Prince John's 1193 rebellion in England against his absent brother it was probably William Marshal who captured and held Marlborough for King Richard.

As a younger son William's prospects had been unpromising, but after John Marshal's sons Gilbert and Walter by his first marriage had died young without issue, and his own elder brother John died in 1194, William's fortunes unexpectedly improved. He succeeded his brother John as Marshal of England and inherited the family estates situated mainly in Wiltshire and Berkshire. He was also patronised by Eleanor of Aquitaine, Henry II's queen, and was made guardian and tutor to Prince Henry whom he coached in skill at arms. His land holdings were further enhanced by his marriage to Isabella of Pembroke and from being a younger son with few prospects William Marshal had by good fortune and a beneficial marriage become a great titled magnate with extensive land holdings, some of them in France and Ireland. When Richard I died abroad in 1199 William Marshal supported the claim of his brother John to the throne against the stronger claim of Arthur of Brittany. Perhaps, having been a younger son with few prospects, he sympathised with John as the fourth son of Henry II, who had unkindly dubbed him John 'Lackland'. In gratitude for his backing John retained William as his Marshal and he served him loyally.

By his marriage in 1200 to his second wife Isabel of Angoulême and acquiring her French possessions, King John made an enemy of her previous suitor John le Brun. This resulted in the war in France which ultimately cost John virtually all of his French possessions. In these years after 1200 William Marshal often fought for John in his French wars, although their relationship became strained when William was obliged to perform 'liege-homage on this side of the sea' to Philip of France in order to retain his estates in Normandy. For this King John unreasonably mistrusted and heaped indignities upon his Marshal who nevertheless remained loyal, counting his oath of allegiance to King John more important than many petty annoyances.

In 1206 King John's troops attacked William Marshal's Irish territories in Leinster while both he and Marshal were in England. Their relationship became more strained and from April 1208 to 1212 William Marshal withdrew to his Leinster estates where he was in both disfavour and exile. His relationship with the king gradually improved with their separation and then became fully reconciled when Marshal rallied the Irish lords to the king's support in 1212 and stood loyally by him in the Magna Carta crisis of 1215.

The Barons' Wars

The following year (1216) the majority of the barons of England took up arms against King John over his failure to abide by the provisions of Magna Carta, although the Bassets and the Marshals remained loyal to the throne. The rebel barons seized London and much of the campaigning took place in and around the Thames Valley, King John's pivotal stronghold being Windsor Castle, which was the principal royal garrison within easy reach of London. The Thames Valley has always been one of the major routes into the west towards Gloucester and Wales and its western end forty miles from Windsor was effectively commanded by the royalist Bassets and Marshals in north Wiltshire. It is also significant that the Marshals held estates in Berkshire, including Hampstead Marshal and a castle at Caversham on the Thames near Reading, to which William Marshal when terminally ill retired to die.

The rebel barons summoned assistance from abroad and offered the throne of England to Louis, the Dauphin of France, who landed in England on 21 May 1216. When he lost Winchester King John withdrew west and the campaign overflowed into Wiltshire where the former Lewisham Castle near Aldbourne is said to be named after Louis (alternatively Lewis) the Dauphin. After marching around Wiltshire and Dorset awaiting developments King John in September 1216 suddenly took the initiative by striking north to the Severn and then marching east to isolate his northern enemies from their allies around London. Having by this decisive action virtually won the war John suddenly died at Newark.

Towards the end of his life John recognised the staunch loyalty displayed by his Marshal and was recorded as saying : 'By the legs of God, I deem him the most loyal knight who ever was born in my lands', and is reputed to have said on his deathbed: 'Beg the Marshal to forgive me the wrongs I have done to him. He has always served me loyally, and he has never acted against me no matter what I did or said to him.'

The loyalty of the Bassets and Marshals to the throne is demonstrated by the fact that after King John died his young son Henry was brought from Devizes, where he had been lodged for safety, to Gloucester for his coronation. The Barons War came to an end when Louis the Dauphin rashly divided his forces and in May 1217 sent an army to reduce Lincoln Castle. There the formidable William Marshal caught up with them and, so excited that he forget to put on his battle helmet which he had to hurriedly retrieve before the battle, decisively defeated the French army. All the Frenchmen of importance were captured and only one English knight was killed. The plunder was so great that the battle became known as the Fair of Lincoln.

After securing the succession of Henry III, William Marshal after a lifetime of fighting and loyally supporting four successive monarchs sensed his impending end. In February 1219 he was taken ill at the Tower of London, surrendered his office, and asked to be taken up river to his estate at Caversham near Reading. Later that year Henry III recognising his immense debt to William Marshal moved his court to Reading to be near William who died a natural death aged over seventy at Caversham. His burial as a non-Templar in the Temple Church of the Knights Templar may be explained by one or several of the following circumstances. He had been on crusade on behalf of young King Henry after that prince had died young; his character was so honourable that the Templars may have requested the honour; and his father John Fitzgilbert the Marshal had, in 1155-6 after becoming a great land magnate in the Marlborough district, granted land at Rockley near Marlborough upon which the Templars founded their preceptory called Temple Rockley. It is also possible that William Marshal expressed the wish to be buried as a Templar knight. His body was carried to London and buried in the Temple Church of the Knights Templar where he is commemorated by a fine recumbent floor effigy. His exploits were related in the long French poem *Histoire de Guillaume le Maréchal*, written a few years later in about 1225.

The young Henry III

The new boy king's reign was initially hampered by the legacy of his father's unpopular reign. He inherited a turbulent kingdom with many of the barons in open revolt, although his Regents, first William Marshal and after 1219 Hubert de Burgh, ensured Henry III's succession and then stabilised the kingdom. Aware of inherent defects in the character of the new king William Marshall had addressed him from his death bed: 'Sire, I pray God that if ever I have done anything displeasing to Him he will give you the grace to be a gentleman. If it should happen that you follow the example of some evil ancestor [did he mean King John?], I pray Him not to grant you a long life.' William Marshal's fears for the character of the new king proved to be well-founded. In 1227 King Henry declared himself of age and in 1234 personally assumed full control of the country and began his long reign of misrule by emulating his father's mistake of alienating his barons. He proved to be an enthusiastic patron of the arts and architecture but a thoroughly bad ruler, and after marrying in 1236 Eleanor of Provence he invited waves of foreigners into England and gave them preference over the English barons who responded by threatening to evict both the king and his Poitevin adherents.

Hubert de Burgh at Devizes

One of the victims of the new regime was Hubert de Burgh (died 1243) who had been the gaoler of King John's murdered nephew and rival for the throne, Prince Arthur. He had married King John's divorced queen Avice of Gloucester and in 1227 was made Earl of Kent. Hubert was a bluff man of humble birth, characteristics which earned him many enemies who conspired against him so that he fell out of royal favour. In 1232 Henry III replaced him as justiciar with his father's old favourite Peter des Roches, the Poitevin who as Bishop of Winchester holding Downton in south-east Wiltshire had in about 1205 created the new town known as the Borough opposite Downton on the west bank of the River Avon.

The following story (which has a Basset connection) was recorded by Mathew Paris who heard it from the lips of Hubert de Burgh. After he was deposed de Burgh was confined in Devizes Castle under the supervision of four earls. His guardians were sympathetic to him as he was now a champion of the English barons against the foreigners, and when they heard that their prisoner was to be handed over to Peter des Roches they removed him to sanctuary at St John's church at Devizes. This sanctuary was violated by the king's agents who dragged de Burgh from the church and returned him to more severe restraint in Devizes Castle. Hearing of this violation of the right to sanctuary the enraged Bishop of Salisbury hurried to Devizes, excommunicated all the offenders, and then demanded of the king that de Burgh be returned to St John's church. This was done but the church was surrounded by royal soldiers intending to starve de Burgh out. Then on 30 October 1233 Gilbert Basset of Wootton Bassett rushed with a relieving force south from Vastern to Devizes, probably down the old 'Vize Way' across the Downs through Broad Hinton and Yatesbury (it was *la*

St John's church, Devizes

Visweia in the 13th century and is now Vize Lane) and freed de Burgh who eventually regained his estates and freedom and died a natural death in 1243, while Peter des Roches was at the insistence of the barons confined to purely spiritual duties as Bishop of Winchester.

Hubert de Burgh seems to have been an unscrupulous character. When William Longespée (died 1226), the Earl of Salisbury and the natural son of Henry II by Fair Rosamund, was shipwrecked and assumed drowned on his return from the French wars, de Burgh enlisted Henry III's support in a scheme to marry his nephew Raymond to Longespée's wife Ela. When the enraged Longespée landed in Cornwall he stormed off to demand redress from Henry III at Marlborough. He was subsequently taken ill at a banquet at Marlborough and eventually died at Old Sarum, some said poisoned by de Burgh.

The later Marshals and Bassets

After William Marshal died in 1219 he was succeeded in turn as Earl Marshal and Earl of Pembroke by five sons who were often provoked into rebellion by Henry III's policies. Three years after his father's death the eldest son William Marshal II demonstrated his loyalty by handing

Ludgershall Castle over to Henry III and was rewarded with the hand of the king's youngest sister Eleanor (1215–75). This marriage was probably intended to ensure the loyalty of William Marshal's sons, but when William Marshal II died without an heir in 1231 he was succceeded as 3rd Earl of Pembroke by his brother Richard Marshal, the second son of the first William Marshal. Richard had spent his early years on his estates in France and was like his father a liegeman of the French king. Henry III took exception to this, tried to prevent him from succeeding to the Earldom of Pembroke, and ultimately relented by allowing Richard to become the 3rd Earl. He did however continue to regard him with suspicion.

There is evidence of close friendship between the neighbouring families of Basset and Marshal, which was strengthened after Gilbert, the son of Alan Basset, married Isobel de Ferrers, a niece of the Marshal Earl of Pembroke. Henry III particularly disliked Gilbert Basset because of his refusal to meet his Poitevin favourites and his failure to respond to a summons to meet the king at Gloucester. In August 1233 he was attainted and his estates were forfeited. After the king's Poitevin ministers seized a Wiltshire manor (probably Compton Bassett) owned by Gilbert Basset the fierce Marcher Lords withdrew their allegiance to Henry III and Richard Marshal led the Marshal Rebellion of 1233–4 in Wales and Ireland against the control of the government by the Poitevins. In 1234 he was lured into a trap and killed on instructions given under the royal seal by Henry III's Poitevin ministers, but soon after this the king, faced with major rebellions, gave way and in 1234 dismissed his Poitevin advisers and re-instated Gilbert Basset, who in 1237 took part in a north versus south tournament which deteriorated into a pitched battle. Four years later Gilbert in 1241 died after a fall from his horse, and when his son Gilbert died immediately after his father the Basset estates devolved upon Fulk Basset, the Bishop of London, who died in 1259.

Richard Marshal was succeeded as 4th Earl of Pembroke by his brother Gilbert (died 1241), the third son of the first William Marshal. Although he had in 1233 joined the Marshal Rebellion in Ireland Gilbert was not a great warrior. He became a churchman and was forgiven by the king and allowed to succeed to the Earldom of Pembroke. He died as the result of a fall from his horse at a tournament and was succeeded in 1241 by William Marshal I's fourth son Walter as the 5th Earl. He too had been in open rebellion in Ireland in 1237 but was also pardoned, and like his brothers died without an heir. The fifth son Anselm Marshal (died 1245) became 6th Earl in 1245 but died that year without issue. The Earldom of Pembroke then passed through the female line to others and ultimately to William de Valence.

Vastern Manor House

Vastern, a short distance south-west of Wootton Bassett, was probably always a fortified site, as the name is a corruption of the Old English for fortress. That the Basset's Vastern Manor House was fortified is implied by the order for it to be demolished passed as a consequence of Gilbert Basset being attainted in 1233, but by 1234 he was re-instated and it is not clear whether the old house was demolished. If so it was soon rebuilt by the Bassets.

Vastern Manor House

The original Vastern House was walled and had a gatehouse, a chapel, and a prison probably used to incarcerate offenders in its extensive deer parks and the adjoining Braydon Forest. Account rolls suggest that it was associated with a large number of buildings which required frequent upkeep.

A legend that Richard III was born at Vastern Manor may have arisen from the fact that at the time when he was defeated and deposed at Bosworth in 1485 his mother Cicely Neville, Duchess of York (1415–95), was in possession of Vastern Manor and park. From a letter written to her by Richard III we know that her Wiltshire steward was William Collingbourne (executed 1483). This man, whose duties would often have brought him to Vastern, lived at Bradfield Manor which is now a farm with pointed windows and a 15th-century hall between Hullavington and Norton near Malmesbury. Two years before Bosworth he was executed as a traitor for writing:

> The Cat, the Rat, and Lovel our Dog,
> Rule all England under the Hog.

This couplet is explained by the fact that three of Richard III's strongest supporters were William Catesby ('The Cat'), Sir Richard Ratcliffe ('the Rat'), and Lord Lovel ('our Dog'), and that Richard III's emblem was a white boar ('the Hog').

Vastern House was progressively allowed to fall into decay and in the mid-19th century it was described as a crumbling farmhouse. Canon Jackson wrote an account of Vastern in volume 23 of the *Wiltshire Archaeological & Natural History Magazine*, but the house as it stands today, a mile south-west of Wootton Bassett on the north side of the A420, is almost entirely modern, although at its core may remain some fragments of the early-Medieval house. In 1866 the Meux family of brewers bought the estate and entirely renovated the house.

The later Bassets

Wootton Bassett in 1254 passed into the hands of Sir Philip Basset (died 1271) who became the most trusted servant of Henry III. He was the most important of the Bassets and was very highly connected by his second marriage to Ela, the widow of Thomas de Newburgh the 6th Earl of Warwick, and the daughter of William Longespée, Earl of Salisbury, a half brother to King Richard and King John. At the instigation of Walter of Wylye, Bishop of Salisbury, Philip Basset in 1266 founded the Hospital of St John at Wootton Bassett with Thomas de Gay as its rector. This hospital was situated in Wood Street and was intended to accommodate at least thirteen poor men of the parish and more if funds allowed, but it disappeared in 1406 when the then lord of the manor Edward Duke of York transferred its lands to Bradenstoke Priory.

Sir Philip Basset was a loyal baron but a moderate critic of Henry III's rule and in 1245 he was appointed by the barons one of the deputation which parliament sent to the Council of Lyons to protest against papal policy in England. Although he was still active on the part of the baronial party in 1258, when in November 1259 Henry III visited his kingdom in France, he was appointed joint justiciar to administer England during the king's absence. Although a member of the moderate opposition Philip Basset in 1259-1260 moved towards the king's party when the opposition to Henry III split. He broke with de Montfort and the extremist opposition, joined the king, and was rewarded with the castles of Oxford and Bristol. In the following year he became Sheriff of four counties and was entrusted with further castles at Corfe and Sheborne in Dorset, and when in April 1261 the king re-assumed power Philip Basset was made sole justiciar of England. He had no sons and his daughter and heiress Aliva Basset had married Hugh Despenser (died 1265), who by this marriage became his potential successor as justiciar. For a time Sir Philip Basset and Hugh Despenser served as joint justiciars but after the royalists assumed full power Basset acted alone and when the king again went to France in July 1262 he was left in sole charge of England. He presided at the October 1262 parliament and on Henry III's return met him at Dover to warn him that his opponents were gaining in power. In 1263 Hugh Despenser became justiciar while his father-in-law Sir Philip Basset actively supported the king in his attempt to regain control of his kingdom.

When Simon de Montfort went to war with the king Sir Philip Basset fought against the rebel barons under de Montfort in the royalist defeat at Lewes on 14 May 1264. He refused to surrender to his son-in-law Despenser until he was very badly wounded, but recovered from his wounds while imprisoned in Dover Castle. After Prince Edward escaped from captivity and defeated and killed de Montfort and Hugh Despenser at Evesham, Sir Philip Basset was released in August 1265 and despite pleading the cause of the barons was reappointed Sheriff of Somerset and Dorset and constable of Devizes Castle. In 1271 he died and the following year Henry III too died and was succeeded by Prince Edward as Edward I.

Sir Philip Basset provides an example of a man who became an important Medieval historical character but was soon forgotten. All that we really know of him is that as justiciar of England he was a man of national importance, that he remained staunchly loyal to the throne and was extremely brave in battle. His particular misfortunes were that he had no son, that his daughter Aliva married into the rising but doomed family of Despenser, and that her ambitious Despenser husband displaced him from his office as justiciar. Sir Philip Basset was at his death in October 1271, six years after the death in rebellion of his Despenser son-in-law, described as: 'noble, discreet and liberal . . . a man who greatly loved the English and the commonality of the land'. There can be few finer epitaphs.

Stanley Abbey

In addition to founding the Priory or Hospital of St John in Wood Street at Wootton Bassett, Sir Philip Basset gave land and property to the church at Marden in the Vale of Pewsey, and to Bradenstoke Abbey a few miles south-west of his manor of Wootton Bassett, for the souls of his wife and his brother Fulk, the former Bishop of London. Sir Philip was also associated with Stanley Abbey near Bremhill, the only Cistercian house in Wiltshire, and it was there that he was buried. His tomb disappeared when Stanley Abbey was demolished.

Stanley Abbey had been founded in 1151 at a site at Lockswell by Henry of Anjou (the future Henry II) at the suggestion of Empress Matilda's chamberlain Drogo. As Lockswell proved to be an unsuitable site the abbey was removed to the valley of the River Marden a mile south-west of Bremhill. Within fifty years of its original foundation Stanley Abbey was entirely rebuilt and the church in which Sir Philip Basset was buried was consecrated in 1266, only five years before his death.

Stanley Abbey in July 1201 withstood a siege when the Wiltshire outlaw Fulke Fitzwarin, who had quarrelled over a game of chess with King John when they were boys and been outlawed when John became king, held out with his men in Stanley Abbey for fourteen days although besieged 'by almost the whole county' including presumably Basset as justiciar. After surrendering Fitzwarin was in 1202 reconciled with the church.

Stanley Abbey flourished until the dissolution of the monasteries, when in 1538 it was granted to Sir Edward Bayntun of Bromham for £1200 paid in instalments. He demolished the abbey to provide building materials for his great mansion-house at Bromham which was itself destroyed during the Civil War. Although no public footpaths approach the site of Stanley Abbey it may be viewed from the redundant railway line which passes near the site, although practically nothing of the abbey survives except for some grass-grown earthworks, from which its plan was established by excavation in 1905.

The Basset deer parks

After acquiring Wootton Bassett before 1212 the Bassets in 1239 converted a great part of the manor into deer parks. Vastern Great Park occupied the area north of Vastern Manor House. It was contained roughly between the B4042 to its north, the A3102 to its south-east, and extending west to the minor road that runs through Hookers Gate Farm. The Little Park of the Bassets was a smaller park around Little Park Farm a mile and a half south-west of Wootton Bassett.

Alan Basset was in 1239 licenced by Henry III to empark Vastern Great Park by enclosing with

Former Vastern Great Park of the Bassets, now agricultural land, from Wootton Bassett

a hedge and ditch his wood at Vastern, and 3½ acres of his wood at Wootton Bassett within it. At the time of the death of his heiress Aliva, Lady Despenser, Vastern Old Park contained no less than 789 acres and a further series of enlargements ensued. The immensity of Vastern Great Park is best appreciated by standing on the B4042 at Highgate – which was the north gate of Vastern Great Park linking it with Braydon Forest – and looking south over the wide open countryside of the park.

Although they were wasted by Edward de Bohun and Mortimer during their 1321 campaign against the Despensers, the parks survived and after the executions of the Despensers in 1326 their history is particularly complicated.

Winterbourne Bassett church

Alan Basset's son Fulk Basset was rector of Winterbourne Bassett from 1214 to 1239 before he became Bishop of London. His brother was Sir Philip Basset whose daughter and heiress Aliva married Hugh Despenser and the Despensers, who succeeded the Bassets as lords of the manor, were probably responsible for the fine 14th-century work in the Decorated style at Winterbourne Bassett church. This 'unusually dainty detail'

(Pevsner) suggests that the north transept may once have been the Despenser chapel, and in a recess within its north wall there is a particularly fine carved stone tomb slab that from its 13th-century style is likely to have been part of a monument to a Basset or a Despenser. It consists of the figures of a married couple carved in high relief. John Aubrey recorded: 'In the north aisle under the window, which is of the fashion of Edw. III is an old nich, within which on a stone is the lineary figure of a man and his wife, of whose name there is no tradicion'. These figures became buried under masonry until 1842 when the burial register noted: 'In the north aisle . . . was discovered a stone coffin with two figures carved on the lid supposed to be the Founder & his wife'. The slab was then restored to its original position where it remains today.

The two figures lie on their backs, the man on the left with curly hair and beard and his right hand reaching across his wife and holding her by her right hand. This holding of right hands is believed to signify that the lady is an heiress. Taking into consideration the high quality of the carving and the late-13th century style of her dress it is fairly safe to assume that the lady is probably Aliva Basset who took the Bassett estates to Hugh

Despenser. The fact that their two Despenser sons were executed and are known to be buried elsewhere supports this suggestion. At her death in 1281 Aliva, who had remarried, held many estates including significantly the manors of Berwick Bassett and Winterbourne Bassett.

Conclusion

Having made their considerable mark on the national as well as the Wiltshire scene the Wiltshire Bassets died out when their male line expired with the death of Sir Philip Basset in 1271 and his daughter took the Basset estates to the Despensers. The Wiltshire estates of the executed Despensers were at first transferred to the queen, but in 1331 many of them were granted to Edward de Bohun, Earl of Hereford, who had been so active in bringing down the Despensers.

Despite the failure of their male heirs, more than six hundred years after the name Basset expired as a family name it survives as the second element of several place-names in north Wiltshire, although it is unlikely that one person in a thousand who uses a 'Bassett' place-name has any knowledge of the family from which it comes. Their friends the great family of Marshal have disappeared leaving even fewer traces of their former eminence, as have the successors of the Bassets, the ill-fated Despensers.

Winterbourne Bassett church

3 John of Gaunt at Upper Upham

including his son Henry IV and Geoffrey Chaucer

In an isolated and elevated situation at a height of almost 900 feet (274m) on the Marlborough Downs about six miles north of Marlborough stood the former Medieval village of Upper Upham, an unusual example of a settlement which was continuously occupied from early times and is associated with John of Gaunt, one of the greatest Englishmen of the 14th century. At Upper Upham a Romano-British building was succeeded by the Medieval village and then by an Elizabethan manor-house believed to have been built on or near the site of an early-Medieval hunting lodge associated with Aldbourne Chase. Being an outlying settlement on poor ground at the extremity of Aldbourne parish

Upper Upham and Aldbourne

Upper Upham was probably the site of the Earl of Lincoln's early-Medieval deer park, which was referred to in 1307 as existing in the parish of Aldbourne. The hamlet occupies a ridge overlooking Aldbourne Chase, a 'chase' being a hunting ground owned by a subject unlike a 'forest' which was owned by a monarch. Aldbourne Chase was formerly a royal forest because in 1066 William I appointed Waleran (or *Walderonde*) as his huntsman at Aldbourne and the

Walrond family who became hereditary rangers are believed to descend from him.

In 1229 Henry III gave Aldbourne to the Longespée Earls of Salisbury who conveyed Upper Upham to Lacock Abbey. In 1365 Edward III's son John of Gaunt, Shakespeare's 'time honoured Lancaster', received settlement of the Wiltshire parishes of Trowbridge and Aldbourne. William I and King John, and probably many of the intervening monarchs, had hunted Aldbourne Chase, and after he became the owner of Aldbourne John of Gaunt would probably have used it as a hunting manor. By tradition his hunting lodge was at Upper Upham where, as a great land magnate owning many widely-dispersed estates throught England, he would have stayed only intermittently.

Medieval taxation lists reveal that in John of Gaunt's time Aldbourne was the most populous parish in the Hundred of Selkley, returning in 1377 332 poll tax payers, 40 of them being at Upper Upham. Within Aldbourne parish were Aldbourne Warren and Lewisham Castle. The former, which had a national reputation for its rabbits, which were farmed for fur and for the table, was situated east of Upper Upham under

Aldbourne Chase, John of Gaunt's hunting chase from near Laines

West flank of Sugar Hill above Shipley Bottom, the site of Aldbourne Warren

Sugar Hill around Aldbourne Warren Farm. It existed in the time of John of Gaunt, and in 1410 his son Henry IV had rabbits sent to court from Aldbourne Warren. John Aubrey in the 17th century described the rabbits of Aldbourne Warren as: 'the best, sweetest, and fattest in England . . . a short, thick coney' (a 'coney' being a young rabbit). The warren survived until the Napoleonic Wars when it was ploughed to grow wheat.

Lewisham Castle stood a little over two miles south-east of Upper Upham, but we do not know its history subsequent to it being a minor castle during King John's war with his barons in 1216. This former castle was sited to command the important crossing of the old direct way from Aldbourne to Marlborough known as Stock Lane and the way which branches from the ridgeway track on Whitefield Hill, a short distance west of Upper Upham, and runs south-east to Ramsbury.

The present Upper Upham Manor house dates from a later time than John of Gaunt's, being an Elizabethan house built on or near the site of his former hunting-lodge, which had magnificent views south into Aldbourne Chase and north-west over Aldbourne Warren to the long bare mound of Sugar Hill.

John of Gaunt

John of Gaunt (1340–99) is with the exception of King Alfred the most eminent person to feature as a principal subject in this book. He was the son of a king (Edward III) and the father of a king (Henry IV), and his life spanned the latter part of the 14th century, the century which culminated in the usurpation and political murder of Richard II by his son.

We know little of his early life because as the fourth son of Edward III he was overshadowed by his powerful father and by the popular heir apparent the Black Prince. While the latter lived John was very much the younger brother whose military exploits were compared unfavourably with the triumphs of his idolised elder brother. After the deaths of the Black Prince in 1376 and King Edward III in the following year John of Gaunt became important as the old king's eldest surviving son, and found himself cast in the exalted position of Protector and effectively ruler of the realm for his nephew, the boy king Richard II, the son of the Black Prince. He now became one of the greatest noblemen in late-Medieval England.

Portraits of John of Gaunt appear to be scarce, although pictures of his father and his son who ruled as Edward III and Henry IV abound. At All Souls College at Oxford a stained glass representation of John of Gaunt exists – it is reproduced as the frontispiece to Sydney Armitage-Smith's *John of Gaunt* (1904) – but we may have a more realistic portrayal of him in the Wilton Diptych, now in the National Gallery, but deriving its name from having been for long in the collection of the Earl of Pembroke at Wilton House. The precise purpose and place of origin of this diptych is not known, but it seems to have been propogandist as it is full of symbolism which in fact provides a clue to its date. On its left-hand panel the kneeling Richard II is backed by three supporters, two of them crowned, while on the right-hand panel the virgin and child are depicted beneath the cross of St George and surrounded by angels. The three supporters standing behind the boy king are generally acepted to be from left to right his father, the deceased Black Prince as

The two panels of the Wilton Diptych

St Edmund the Martyr, his grandfather the late Edward III as Edward the Confessor, and an unknown person representing John the Baptist who may have been modelled on the young king's eldest surviving uncle John of Gaunt. The angels are uniformly dressed and wear Richard II's white hart emblem. The Wilton Diptych is often assumed to depict Richard II's coronation which took place when he was eleven, but the young king seems to be in his mid-teens in the painting and it may represent him a few years later, perhaps the occasion when he made his brave personal appeal at Smithfield to the peasants to disperse during the 1381 Peasants' Revolt. A clue

to the date of the painting lies in the fact that the angels wear collars of broom-cods ('cod' =small bag) which formed part of the insignia of Charles VI of France, whose second daughter Isabella was married at the age of seven to Richard II in November 1396.

In 1348 when John of Gaunt was eight the Black Death devastated England and killed from a third to a half of the populace. This high mortality disturbed the existing order and traumatized society. Men recognised that great changes were afoot and the loss of so many labourers significantly strengthened the bargaining power of those that survived. A smouldering discontent then simmered for most of John of Gaunt's life and contributed to the Peasants' Revolt which broke out in 1381 when he was forty-one.

By his first marriage John of Gaunt became Duke of Lancaster and owner of the Duchy of Lancaster manors in Wiltshire as well as the many Duchy estates in other English counties. He was an active man, a military leader of apparently limited capabilities, and a keen hunter. His name arose from the fact that after winning the naval Battle of Sluys on 22 June 1340 against the French and Spanish fleets, Edward III entered Ghent as conqueror on 10 July to be greeted by his queen Philippa of Hainault. She had recently given birth to their son who was thereafter known as John of Gaunt (Ghent).

At the early age of ten he was initiated into warfare when he joined his father and the Black Prince at the naval victory off Dungeness and he accompanied his father on a campaign in France and in an expedition against the Scots in 1355. In 1359–60 he again campaigned with his father in France and he continued to be active in his father's Continental wars, although he was overshadowed by his brilliant older brother Edward the Black Prince, the great warrior who, wearing the black armour from which he derived his name, gained an immense military reputation from successfully conducting the Hundred Years War with France on behalf of his father.

In 1370, with the Black Prince severely ill at Angoulême, King Edward sent John of Gaunt to replace his elder brother as his Lieutenant in Aquitaine. John was disconcerted when he found his brother so ill that he had to be carried about on a litter. The brothers for a time campaigned together but perhaps as a result of his severe illness the Black Prince, who was regarded as the epitome of chivalry, ordered an atrocity at Limoges. Chivalry was in the Middle Ages a strict code of honourable conduct which had arisen out of Arthurian romance and the crusades, but it applied only among the noble and gentle classes. Common people were excluded and at Limoges Froissart recorded:

> It was great pitie to see the men, women and chyldren [who] kneled downe on their knees before the prince for mercy, but he was so enflamed with yre [that] he toke no hede to theyme, so that none was herde, but all putte to dethe as they were mette withal, and suche as were nothing culpable.

John of Gaunt was said to have disapproved of his brother's cruel actions and may have been relieved when the Black Prince decided that in view of his chronic illness he must return to England leaving him in sole command. Although he appears to have been an adequate deputy commander under his father or the Black Prince, John of Gaunt proved to be less successful when given full command, and after six months of ineffectual campaigning he resigned his command and returned home to England.

John of Gaunt's marriages

In 1359 John of Gaunt married at Reading his first wife his cousin Blanche, the second daughter and joint heiress of the great warrior Henry, 1st Duke of Lancaster (c. 1299–1361). The wedding was celebrated in London by a tournament in which twenty-four knights vanquished all bearing the badge of the city of London, and then removed their helms to reveal that they were the king, his four sons, and nineteen of the leading barons of England.

In this marriage John of Gaunt was fortunate because the plague carried off both the Duke of Lancaster and his eldest daughter Maud, leaving Blanche as the sole heiress of Lancaster, her brother having been as a child drowned in the ford at Kempsford, a significant accident because had he lived John of Gaunt would not have be-

come Duke of Lancaster. Upon the death of his father-in-law in 1361 John of Gaunt succeeded to the Earldom of Lancaster and was then made Duke of Lancaster. His wife Blanche was described by Froissart, as the lady:

> . . . who died fair and young, at about the age of twenty-two years. Gay and glad she was, fresh and sportive, sweet, simple and humble semblance, the fair lady whom men called Blanche.

The home of the Lady Blanche had been at Kempsford where the River Thames forms the county boundary between Gloucestershire and Wiltshire. Henry Plantagenet, Earl of Lancaster, had acquired Kempsford by marriage, had there entertained Edward I, and to Kempsford he had also brought Edward II as a captive. Blanche of Lancaster took Kempsford and its castle to John of Gaunt, and after her death he in gratitude built the tower of Kempsford Church between 1381 and 1399 to her memory. Blanche died in 1369 of the plague while her husband was away campaigning in France, and was buried in the Old St Paul's Cathedral. Ever after John of Gaunt attended the annual memorial service at St Paul's whenever he was in England, and he left instructions that he should be buried beside her.

Edward III had from the 1330s attempted for political reasons to form alliances in Spain, especially with Castile. In 1342 he arranged to marry his young second daughter Joan to Pedro (1334–69), the heir to the throne of Castile, but she died of the Black Death in 1348 on her way to Castile. It was therefore no surprise when after the death of his first wife the Lady Blanche in 1369 John of Gaunt at the age of thirty-two married in 1372 as his second wife the seventeen-year-old Constance, the daughter and heiress of the late Pedro who, after becoming a vicious king known as Pedro the Cruel, had been deposed and murdered by his brother Enrique (Henry) of Trastamare (1333–79). From this time John of Gaunt pursued a claim by right of his new wife to the kingdom of Castile, but never succeeded in ousting Henry of Trastamare. As a result of his association with Castile – one of the kingdoms that was later amalgamated to form Spain – John of Gaunt is said to have at this time brought

Morris (or Moorish) dancing from Spain to England, and it is possible that Morris dancing was first performed in England at Upper Upham.

After the death of Constance of Castile in 1394 John of Gaunt in 1396 caused a scandal by marrying as his third wife his mistress Catherine Swynford. In 1397 their four children were legitimised as the Beauforts from whom Henry VIII and Queen Elizabeth were descended.

Campaigning in France

Soon after his second marriage John of Gaunt again demonstrated some shortcomings as a soldier. With the Black Prince terminally ill and Edward III aged sixty-one, he in August 1373 set out on his first fully independent command. Provided with a large army of eleven thousand men with substantial back-up resources he crossed the Channel hoping to recover control of Aquitaine. He also hoped also to cross the Pyrenees into Spain and press his claim to the throne of Castile but the campaign was an utter disaster. The French refused action and left John of Gaunt and his army marching ineffectually around the winter countryside lacking sufficient provisions. Disease set in and John of Gaunt ultimately returned to England with a very much depleted army and his military reputation in ruins, particularly as it was compared with the spectacular military successes which had been achieved by the Black Prince. In spite of this failure the death of the Black Prince in 1376 increased the standing of John of Gaunt as it left him as the eldest surviving son of Edward III.

It was probably for political rather than religious reasons that John of Gaunt opposed the clergy by supporting the theologian John Wycliffe (c. 1329–1424), who was later recognised to be 'the Morning Star of the Reformation' for initiating the Reformation of the English church, although this took place more than a hundred years after his death. Many of Wycliffe's theories were unacceptable to the contemporary church because he attacked the principle of papal authority; and they also asserted the superiority of secular over ecclesiastical power. It was probably this aspect of his beliefs that persuaded John of Gaunt to protect him, and when in February 1377

Wycliffe was tried at St Paul's for heresy John of Gaunt personally supported him. The trial descended into riot, and Wycliffe went free.

Among Wycliffe's followers who were executed as heretics was Richard de Cobham, Lord of Langley Burrell, who in 1413 was burnt for his beliefs on Steinbrook Hill south of Kington Langley.

John of Gaunt's nephew Richard II

Edward III was in 1377 succeeded by his nine-year-old grandson Richard of Bordeaux (1367–1400) whose life and reign as Richard II became inextricably mixed with that of his uncle John of Gaunt who acted as his Regent for twelve years from 1377 until 1389. Richard was the second son of the Black Prince, whose eldest son Edward after demonstrating great promise died aged six in January 1371 leaving Richard as second in succession after his father to the throne. His uncle John of Gaunt was for long Richard's loyal Regent and then his supporter, but towards the end of his reign became disillusioned when King Richard ignored his advice and became tyrannical.

Richard II, John of Gaunt's nephew

There was an element of doubt about Richard of Bordeaux's legitimacy, and John of Gaunt may as Edward IIIs eldest surviving son have resented the succession of his young nephew whose mother was the celebrated beauty Joan, Countess of Kent (1328-1385). Her taste in clothes was said to be extravagant and even indecent. She was known to later generations as 'the Fair Maid of Kent', and as the lady who by dropping her garter inspired the founding of the Order of the Garter in 1348.

Edington Priory, founded by William of Edington

In marrying Joan of Kent the Black Prince chose a lady with a complicated matrimonial past. At the age of twelve she had in 1340 married for love and by mutual consent Thomas Holland, Earl of Kent, but the following year she was forced into a marriage with William Montague, Earl of Salisbury, and during the 1340s her marital status remained in dispute. It was even rumoured that she had become Edward III's mistress, and in *The Raigne of the King* (published in 1596 and attributed to Shakespeare) Edward III dishonourably woos the married Countess of Salisbury and is only deterred by her threat to commit suicide. The dispute over her marriage was submitted to the pope who decided in favour of her first husband Thomas Holland. Within a few months of his death in 1361 in spite of the opposition of his father Edward III Joan was married to the Black Prince and in 1366 bore the son who in 1377 succeeded to the throne as Richard II.

Edington and William of Edington

One of the clergymen who had officiated at the marriage of the Black Prince to Joan of Kent was the Wiltshire-born William of Edington (*c.* 1300–66), the son of a prosperous Edington couple called Roger and Avise. After entering the church he became royal Treasurer in 1344 and Chancellor in 1346, and at Edward III's request first Bishop of Winchester and in 1366 Archbishop of Canterbury. He began the reconstruction of Winchester Cathedral and in 1362 he carried through parliament a statute that required all court pleadings at Westminster to be in English rather than in French. Despite his success in both ecclesiastical and secular fields William of Edington did not

forget his home village under the north escarpment of Salisbury Plain, and betwen 1352 and 1356 he built Edington Priory to house a dean and twelve priests. The Black Prince then persuaded him to make Edington Priory one of the two houses in England of the order of Bonshommes.

Almost a hundred years after Edington Priory was founded William Ayscough, the Bishop of Salisbury, was murdered at Edington. He was unpopular because of his constant absence from his diocese as Henry VI's confessor. He was also as the king's counsellor held responsible for many of the ills emanating from the court, and during the rebellion raised by Jack Cade in Kent he was attacked at the Bishop's Palace at Salisbury and fled to Edington Priory. On the way he was robbed of 10,000 marks and the following day, according to A. R. Maddison in his *Lincolnshire Pedigrees*:

> Many of his [Bishop Ayscough's] tenants intending to join Jack Cade, came to Edington, took him from mass, and drew him to the top of a hill, where they cleft his head as he kneeled and prayed – not far from Edington – and spoiled him to the skin, June 29, 1450.

In 1542 John Leland noted a chapel and hermitage which have now disappeared without trace on the hill above Edington Priory marking the place of Bishop Ayscough's murder. Of the priory only the magnificent monastic church of almost cathedral-like proportions (described by Pevsner as 'a wonderful and highly important church') survives, the rest of the buildings having been converted by the Paulett family into

Priory Farm shortly after they acquired them after the execution in 1549 of Lord Thomas Seymour of Sudeley, the original grantee at the dissolution.

Richard II's alleged illegitimacy

When the Black Prince died in 1376 a political crisis brewed in England. With the old king an aged dotard and his grandson Richard only nine, Peter de la Mare suspected that John of Gaunt had designs on the throne and boldly demanded that a council be appointed to ensure the succession of Richard.

On the other hand the complexity of the marital relationships of his mother Joan of Kent prompted some opposition to Richard's succession. Doubts were expressed about Richard's legitimacy and the Archbishop of Canterbury had warned that his legitimacy might be challenged. The Black Prince, aware of the rumours, had devoted the last few years of his life to ensuring the ultimate succession of his son, and on his death-bed persuaded his father and his brother John of Gaunt to promise to support Richard. Many years later during the 1399 demonstrations that led to Richard II's deposition the London crowd, probably at the instigation of the Lancastrians who were engineering his downfall, shouted 'bastard' at King Richard.

The Succession

Although by the 14th century the right of succession to the throne of England by primogeniture was well established it had not invariably been followed. The circumstances in which King Alfred succeeded his brother as king despite the fact that his elder brother left young sons have been described in Chapter 1; in 1100 Henry II succeeded his brother William II by opportunistically asserting that he was king when his brother Robert who was the rightful heir was absent in France; and when Richard I died in 1199 bequeathing his throne to his brother John, his nephew Arthur should by rights have succeeded.

Edward III's second son, Lionel of Antwerp, Duke of Clarence, had died in 1368, and until the death of the extremely popular Black Prince in 1376 John of Gaunt would not have dared to oppose Richard of Bordeaux's right to the throne, although many of the learned men of the time considered that as the eldest living son of the deceased king John of Gaunt should have succeeded. It was probably the old king's extreme affection for the Black Prince that ensured his son Richard's peaceful accession as Richard II.

Whilst his nephew nominally reigned John of Gaunt exercised the real power as Regent. A minority was in the Middle Ages a dangerous period and expectations of Richard as the apparent son of the idolised Black Prince were great. John of Gaunt has, as an ambitious man, tended to be regarded as the wicked uncle of the boy Richard II, in spite of the fact that he appears never to have demonstrated any interest in the English throne, preferring in the latter part of his life to pursue a claim to the throne of Castile by right of his second wife. He allowed his nephew to rule throughout his lifetime and in the interests of preserving peace he sometimes mediated between King Richard and his many powerful opponents.

Nevertheless rumours about his ambitions persisted and when at the parliament held at Salisbury in 1384 a Carmelite friar who accused John of Gaunt of plotting against the life of Richard II was found murdered the day before he was due to go on trial, his death was blamed on John of Gaunt. In that year (1384) John of Gaunt led a punitive expedition into Scotland as a reprisal for the Scots invading the north of England. Towards the end of 1385 King Richard, then nineteen, for some reason became suspicious of John of Gaunt and attempted to arrest him. He fled to his castle at Pontefract and in 1386 Richard, still distrustful of his uncle, encouraged him to make another attempt on the Castilian throne. John only succeeded in securing a promise that his daughter Catherine should marry the future king of Castile. Upon his return to England in 1389 John of Gaunt reconciled the quarrel that had arisen between his younger brother Thomas of Woodstock, Duke of Gloucester (1355–97), and his nephew the king which had almost broken into civil war. John of Gaunt was then made Duke of Aquitaine and was employed on several embassies to France.

At the age of twenty-three King Richard in 1389 declared himself of age and assumed control of his kingdom. For a time he ruled moderately but gradually became more autocratic. In 1397 John of Gaunt's brother Thomas of Woodstock, the leading figure in the Merciless Parliament which in 1388 had brutally condemned to death several of the king's supporters, was arrested by the king and probably murdered in captivity at Calais.

Despite the provocation of the murder of his younger brother and many other despotic actions by the king it was not John of Gaunt but his exiled son Henry Bolingbroke who under more provocation after his father's death usurped the throne.

Public hatred of John of Gaunt

As the effective ruler of the kingdom in troubled times John of Gaunt was with some justification blamed for many of the ills of the day. When John of Gaunt was eight in 1348 the Black Death which had been spreading eastwards across Europe reached England. Society was disordered by the high mortality and scarcity of labour resulted in an end of serfdom. Much unrest still existed when the deaths of the Black Prince and the king (in 1376 and 1377 respectively) left John of Gaunt effectively ruling the kingdom as Protector. The year 1377 was not an auspicious time to assume power as since the naval defeat off La Rochelle in 1372 the French war had gone from bad to worse and England was unable effectively to protect its south coast. The French raided up the Thames and also the Isle of Wight, Lewes, Hastings and Rye, and these indignities allied to high taxation, the aftermath of the Black Death, and the religious unrest fermented by John of Gaunt's protegé Wycliffe, caused a smouldering discontent with John of Gaunt's government and ultimately led to the Peasants' Revolt of 1381.

In the year (1377) of Edward III's death a new parliament was called in which John of Gaunt's steward Sir Thomas Hungerford (died 1398) was elected the first Speaker of the House of Commons, where he diligently promoted John of Gaunt's interests.

Aldbourne church

The Peasants' Revolt

This widespread rebellion of the common people in 1381 was provoked by the successive Poll Taxes of 1377, 1379 and 1381, which were levied upon both the rich and the poor and were a departure from previous taxation, which had been more fairly levied on property rather than persons. By allowing this unfair form of taxation John of Gaunt made a very serious mistake, as it brought him an unpopularity from which he never fully recovered.

The peasants took to the field in arms declaring that they would have 'no king called John', and on their march from Kent to London particularly targeted John of Gaunt's many estates. Upon reaching the capital they immediately made for his Palace of Savoy on the Strand, the most magnificent mansion in England. They hoped to murder the Duke, but as he was absent campaigning in the north the mob had to be content with plundering his palace and burning it to the ground, incidentally killing thirty of their number who were drunk in the cellars. John of Gaunt's good fortune in being absent is emphasised by the fact that three other principal objects of the mob's hatred, Archbishop Sudbury, Treasurer Hales, and John Legge who had dreamed up the Poll Tax, were dragged from the Tower of London and summarily beheaded. John of Gaunt's young son Henry Bolingbroke escaped by hiding in the Tower and lived to become King Henry IV. During negotiations at Smithfield the rebel leader Wat Tyler was struck down and killed. The leaderless rebels then dispersed, and the Peasants' Revolt was effectively ended.

John of Gaunt's Wiltshire estates

As the great Duke of Lancaster John of Gaunt owned many manors throughout the country. He was customarily followed by a retinue of three hundred, and owned more than thirty castles. His associations with Wiltshire arise from the fact that in 1365 he inherited through his first wife Blanche of Lancaster the Wiltshire manors of Trowbridge and Aldbourne. The manor of Aldbourne had as part of the Earldom of Salisbury been brought by Margaret, the grandaughter of William Longespée, by marriage to Henry de Lacy, 3rd Earl of Lincoln (1249?–1311). Henry was created Duke of Lancaster by Edward III in 1351. After his only son and heir died young his co-heiress Blanche, as we have seen, married John of Gaunt, and at the death of her father in 1361 conveyed the vast Lancastrian possessions to him. In celebration of his fiftieth birthday, Edward III in 1362 made John of Gaunt Duke of Lancaster.

At Aldbourne John of Gaunt according to tradition had a house on the site of the Court House adjoining the churchyard where, although the superstructure seems to be 15th-century, the cellars are older and may have been John of Gaunt's.

Upper Upham

On the hills above Aldbourne at the outlying hamlet of Upper Upham John of Gaunt is believed to have owned a hunting lodge which enabled him to enjoy the hunting in Aldbourne Chase. Although he owned many other manors throughout England John of Gaunt and his son the future Henry IV would as active military men have often visited Upper Upham with their respective entourages.

Upper Upham hunting lodge is now gone and an Elizabethen manor house has been built on or near its site. The house stands at an altitude of almost 900 feet (270m) on a ridge north of Aldbourne Chase. According to local tradition there was no water on the high ridge at Upper Upham and in order to bathe John of Gaunt and his retainers had to ride down to Aldbourne village. This may have been an infrequent occurrence for in Medieval times even the nobility bathed infrequently. King John had for example been regarded as exceptionally clean because he took eight baths in six months.

Geoffrey Chaucer

John of Gaunt from 1357 until his death patronised Geoffrey Chaucer (*c.* 1343–1400)

Upper Upham Manor on the presumed site of John of Gaunt's hunting lodge

Descent from Upper Upham towards Aldbourne

who was almost exactly his contemporary. Chaucer came from the bourgeoisie, being the son of a London vintner. As a youth or young man Chaucer became in 1357 a page to the king's second son Prince Lionel of Antwerp, later Duke of Clarence. He remained at court until 1359 and that year celebrated the wedding of John of Gaunt to Lady Blanche of Lancaster by writing *The Assembly of Foules*. He then accompanied the army which invaded France under Edward III in 1359 and was captured and ransomed by Edward III. His activities in the next six years are not known, but in about 1367 he married Philippa de Rouet, a lady-in-waiting to the queen and a sister of John of Gaunt's mistress Catherine Swynford.

Coinciding with his move to the entourage of John of Gaunt Chaucer emerged as a poet in 1369 with his *Boke of the Duchesse*, an allegory upon the death of John of Gaunt's first wife from the plague in 1369 four years after Aldbourne came into his possession. Chaucer relates how

John of Gaunt had wooed the beautiful Blanche, and wrote a song for her:

> Lord, hyt maketh myn herte lyght
> Whan I thenke on that swete wyght
> That is so semely on to see;
> And wisshe to God it myght so bee
> That she wolde holde me for hir knyght,
> My lady that is so fair and bright!

In the 1370s and 1380s Chaucer was frequently employed on diplomatic missions abroad and was granted several sinecure appointments. In 1374 John of Gaunt granted him a pension of £10 for life and he became Comptroller of Customs in the port of London. He continued to be employed on diplomatic missions abroad and in 1386 he became MP for Kent, but in that year he also lost most of his offices, possibly because his patron John of Gaunt was abroad. In 1387, the year in which his wife Phillipa died, Chaucer began to write his most famous literary work *The Canterbury Tales*. Upon John of Gaunt's return from abroad in 1389 Chaucer became royal Clerk of Works at the Palace of Westminster, in which appointment he supervised the reconstruction of Westminster Hall, building work at the Tower of London, and other royal works. He lost this appointment in 1391 for alleged failure to exercise adequate financial control and in 1394 Richard II granted him a pension of £20 for life. At the death of John of Gaunt and the accession of his son as Henry IV in 1399 Chaucer gained the favour of the new king but died the following year. His burial in Westminster Abbey led to the use of Poets' Corner as the burial place for poets, although his monument was not erected until 1555.

The fact that Chaucer's last official appointment was as deputy-forester in the royal Forest of North Petherton in Somerset suggests that he was probably interested in hunting and, having been for so long in the service of John of Gaunt, he would almost certainly have been at Upper Upham and hunted in Aldbourne Chase.

Richard II as King

Advised by John of Gaunt, Richard II ruled constitutionally until the mid-1390s, despite being opposed by a the very powerful baronial party known as the Lords Appellant. In 1388 three Lords Appellant, John of Gaunt's younger brother Thomas of Woodstock, Duke of Gloucester (1355–97), Robert FitzAlan, Earl of Arundel (1346–97), and Thomas de Beauchamp, Earl of Warwick (died 1401), accused five of King Richard's principal supporters of treason. The Appellants were later joined by Thomas Mowbray, Earl of Nottingham (1386–1405) and John of Gaunt's son Henry Bolingbroke, Earl of Derby, the future Henry IV. It is significant that John of Gaunt was not among the Appellants. The Merciless Parliament found the five guilty and sentenced them to death. King Richard was at this time insufficiently strong to protect his friends and they were executed, despite the pleas of Richard's first queen Anne of Bohemia for the king's former tutor Sir Simon Burley to be spared.

In 1394 Anne of Bohemia died childless from the plague and after an interval of two years King Richard in 1396 married a seven-year-old child bride Isabella of France (1389–1409). This marriage to a princess of the old enemy caused dismay in England, and Richard II's unpopularity after this marriage seems to have changed his character. He had lost his popular mother in 1385, his nearest advisers in the purge of 1388, and his beloved first queen in 1394. He now stood constitutionally alone, adopted French manners and ideas to impress his new child queen, and asserted his belief in absolute monarchy. In his isolation Richard seems to have brooded on his misfortunes and may even have become mentally unbalanced, because he resolved to revenge himself upon the powerful Lords Appellant. He particularly hated their leader, John of Gaunt's younger brother Thomas of Woodstock, Duke of Gloucester, who out of hatred for the French consistently acted against the king and his policies.

John of Gaunt now frequently found himself out of sympathy with his nephew the king, when for example he determined at all costs to hold Calais which had been captured by John's father Edward III in 1347 as a gateway for the English into France. John of Gaunt believed that the expense of maintaining Calais far outweighed its value but refused to take sides and tried to re-

main neutral in the constant disputes between his brother Thomas of Woodstock and the king.

Froissart relates in his *Chronicles* how Richard II personally lured Thomas of Woodstock from the security of his castle at Pleshey in Essex, led him into an ambush, and then had him taken across the Channel to Calais where he was strangled by four men. At the same time the Earl of Arundel was seized and publicly executed and the Earl of Warwick was exiled for life. Froissart (c.1337–c.1406), the French chronicler who came to England in 1360 and became secretary to Phillipa of Hainault, John of Gaunt's mother and the wife of Edward III, records how 'the Duke of Gloucester's death had greatly disturbed several of the great lords of England', particularly when the king seized all his lands which included Wiltshire manors at Gore near West Lavington and Tilshead.

Two powerful Lords Appellant who survived Richard II's 1397 purge were John of Gaunt's son Henry Bolingbroke, Earl of Derby, and Thomas Mowbray, Earl of Nottingham, who respectively became Dukes of Hereford and Norfolk. According to Froissart none now dared criticise the king who nevertheless feared to act directly against John of Gaunt's son. He therefore in 1398 contrived a quarrel between Hereford and Norfolk in the lists at Coventry and then decreed that they should settle their dispute by mortal combat in his presence, a strategem that would eliminate one of them. When his advisers warned the king that this would be unwise as public opinion considered that he had been responsible for the quarrel, he banished both men abroad, Bolingbroke for six years and Norfolk for life. Froissart then records how at Christmas 1398:

> John [of Gaunt], Duke of Lancaster, fell dangerously ill of a disorder, having been for a time very low-spirited on account of the banishment of his son and of the way in which his nephew Richard was governing the kingdom which, if pursued, he foresaw must be its ruin.

Henry Bolingbroke usurps the throne
By marrying Mary de Bohun, the heiress of the Earls of Hereford, Bolingbroke had in 1386 be-

come Earl of Hereford, and when his father died in 1399 he also inherited the Dukedom of Lancaster and became, in the words of Froissart: 'the most potent baron in England, and second to none but the king himself'. He was however not in England having been unjustly exiled and forbidden the kingdom. King Richard responded to this situation unwisely. Having already arbitrarily exiled Bolingbroke without any pretence of a trial he now took advantage of his enforced absence to extend his exile to life. He also siezed all of his immense properties and revenues and gave many of the Duchy of Lancaster estates to his favourites. He may have been merely attempting to remove the anomaly of the huge Duchy of Lancaster as a virtual state within a state, although he must also have feared his warrior cousin. Whatever the reason his actions were unjust and illegal, and they cost him his throne and his life.

In an attempt to regain some of his lost popularity the king now proclaimed a great tournament at Windsor, but so great was the feeling against him that Froissart tells us that: 'there was almost no one there,' most of the barons having boycotted the event. In spite of these ominous warning signs Richard unwisely absented himself from England on a campaign to placate Ireland, and while he was away the energetic Henry Bolingbroke, who but for his cousin's provocative behaviour would probably have remained loyal, invaded England. In July 1399 he landed at Ravenspur on the Humber in Yorkshire ostensibly merely to secure his estates. Most of the barons of England, who had viewed with concern Richard II's illegal annexation of first the Gloucester and then the Lancaster estates and feared for their own, flocked to his banner.

During his last years one of Richard II's principal advisers was Sir William Scrope, a member of a family with Wiltshire connections. Richard II had appointed him guardian of the realm during his absence in Ireland. The Scropes were a north-country family who were conspicuously loyal to the crown. A Sir Richard Scrope was chancellor in 1378 and 1381–2, and Sir William had been created Earl of Wiltshire in 1398 after having served in the French wars under John of Gaunt.

His youngest son Sir Stephen Scrope (died 1408) had become lord of Castle Combe in 1385, which was held by the Scropes for almost five hundred years. In 1394 Sir William was granted by Richard II the castle and town of Marlborough for life, and he became the king's principal adviser as well as his chamberlain and treasurer. As ambassador to France he had in 1395 gained more royal favour by negotiating Richard II's marriage with the French Princess Isabella. After Richard II's usurpation and death Richard Scrope, who was Archbishop of York, was beheaded in 1405 for conspiracy against Henry IV.

In King Richard's absence Sir William Scrope in his capacity as guardian of the realm confronted Henry Bolingbroke's army on his march towards London, but finding himself greatly outnumbered by Bolingbroke's constantly expanding army he fell back westwards to Bristol where he was captured and immediately beheaded without trial. Now aware of the extent of dissatisfaction with the king Bolingbroke changed his objective from simply regaining his birthright to that of deposing King Richard, and he occupied London with the assent of the Londoners. Richard, now generally referred to as Richard of Bordeaux rather than Richard the king, had hurriedly returned to England and was now in the west country. He was pursued by Bolingbroke into North Wales where he was lured out of Conway Castle and taken first to Flint Castle and then to the Tower of London. There the four men who had murdered Thomas of Woodstock at Calais were executed within sight of the terrified king, who in September abdicated the crown to Bolingbroke on the promise of his life.

On 30 September Henry Bolingbroke took advantage of the public discontent with Richard to claim the throne before parliament, and was crowned as Henry IV on 13 October. A few months later Richard conveniently died in suspicious circumstances as a prisoner at the Duchy of Lancaster castle at Pontefract, well away from the centre of affairs. His child queen Isabella (1389–1409), who had at her husband's insistence gone home to France, remained unconvinced of his death until 1406 when she remarried.

Having invaded merely to secure his rightful inheritance Henry Bolingbroke had now usurped the throne and become the first king of the House of Lancaster. These events set the stage for the prolonged dynastic struggles of the Wars of the Roses (1455–85) between the houses of York and Lancaster, which in 1485 at Bosworth established the Tudor dynasty on the throne of England. At his death in 1413 Henry IV was buried in the Trinity Chapel at Canterbury opposite the tomb of the Black Prince, the uncle whose son he had first usurped and had then probably murdered.

Henry IV at Upper Upham

Medieval kings and their nobles were itinerant and lived successively at all of their estates, particularly at those which offered good hunting. Henry IV when Henry Bolingbroke must often have hunted from Upper Upham with his father, who during the time that he was Protector would also probably have brought the young Richard II to Upper Upham for the hunting in Aldbourne Chase.

Henry Bolingbroke was born in 1367 two years after his father obtained Aldbourne and Upper Upham, and was thirty-two when in 1399 he inherited the Duchy of Lancaster estates which he was obliged to usurp Richard II to secure. After becoming king he would presumably have continued to visit Aldbourne to hunt from his father's former hunting lodge at Upper Upham.

The Duchy of Lancaster estates continued to be held as crown lands, and since the Plantagenet and Tudor kings were invariably enthusiastic hunters it is likely that most of the monarchs who succeeded Henry IV would also have hunted Aldbourne Chase from John of Gaunt's lodge at Upper Upham, until it was replaced by the present manor house in Elizabethan times.

John of Gaunt's character

When writing *Richard II* Shakespeare ignored John of Gaunt's unpopularity and invested his character with a great dignity. It was to John of Gaunt, his 'time-honoured Lancaster', that he gave the noble speech that, with its stirring references to 'This royal throne of kings, this sceptred isle', 'This happy breed of men', and 'This blessed plot, this earth, this realm, this England', is one of the most patriotic speeches in English literature.

In spite of the widespread suspicion about his aspirations to the throne with which John of Gaunt was regarded by his contemporaries, there is some evidence that his reputation is not justified. Events cast some doubt upon his characterisation as the most unpopular man in England and as the malignant uncle of Richard II. In his time the accession of minors to the throne was always a precarious event and powerful Regents were always likely to be regarded with extreme suspicion, especially if they had royal blood.

There is evidence that in spite of his exalted position John of Gaunt had a mild and generous disposition. He objected to his brother's massacre of civilians including helpless women and children at Limoges, and he is known to have ordered fuel and wine in the winter for the miserable prisoners in Newgate Prison. When he quarrelled with his fellow nobles he treated them generously, even when he was the target of assassination attempts in 1384 and 1394 by Robert de Vere, and in 1393 by the Duke of Norfolk. This was in marked contrast to the actions of his brother Gloucester, his nephew Richard II, and his son Henry IV, all of whom were particularly severe on their opponents. These attempted assassinations probably made John of Gaunt more popular with the common people.

John of Gaunt's unpopularity arose initially from the imposition of the unjust Poll Tax. It was then alleged that he had designs upon his nephew's throne, and yet although he exercised great power he kept the promise that he had made to his brother the Black Prince on his deathbed and supported Richard on the throne. In spite of the doubts expressed about Richard's legitimacy he recognised him as the rightful king and sought an outlet for his ambitions by claiming the throne of Castile by right of his second wife. He helped Richard II by mediating between the Lords Appellant and the king and in his last years in spite of his dissatisfaction with Richard II's rule and his anger at the unjust banishment of his son. He remained loyal and it was not until after the year after his death in 1399 that his son Henry Bolingbroke usurped the throne.

It is possible that John of Gaunt aspired to the throne but was unwilling to break his oath to his dying brother. King Richard always seems to have suspected him and in his extreme dissatisfaction at Richard II's last years of autocratic rule John of Gaunt may have suggested to his son

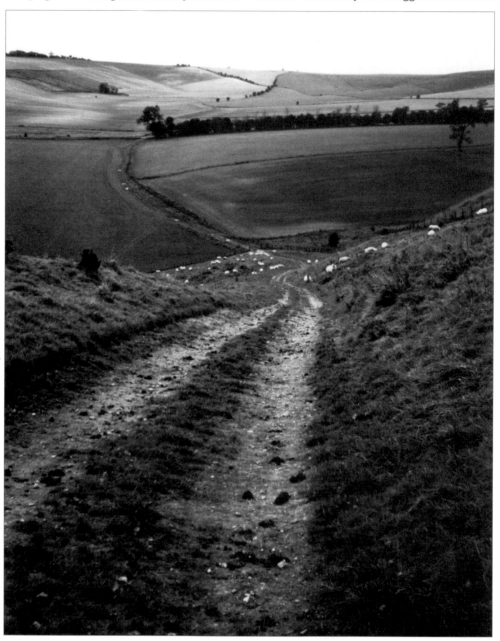

Shipley Bottom from Sugar Hill looking across Aldbourne Warren

Henry, who was not bound by his oath, that he should make a bid for the throne after his death. If King Richard suspected such a plot this could explain his apparently irrational and drastic actions in extending Bolingbroke's exile to life and seizing the Duchy of Lancaster estates immediately after John of Gaunt's death, which took place in 1399 at his favourite castle of Leicester.

The subsequent history of Upper Upham
Anyone who stands today on the ridge at Upper Upham and looks south past Snap in its coombe below to the wooded undulations of Aldbourne Chase in the broken downs to the south, or northwest to Sugar Hill, will see scenes very similar to those which John of Gaunt would have known over six hundred years ago when setting out with his entourage to hunt the deer in the Chase. I sometimes imagine that the deer that are frequently seen today in Shipley Bottom to the north of Upper Upham are descendants of the deer that John of Gaunt hunted here over six hundred years ago, and when walking down the ancient descent from Upper Upham past the Giant's Grave towards Aldbourne I often visualise John of Gaunt and his entourage of relatives and retainers, including his son who became Henry IV and Geoffrey Chaucer, riding down this way after hunting to bathe at Aldbourne. There John and his son would recognise the mainly 13th-century church of St Michael standing in its prominent position overlooking the green, although its noble tower dates from a period later than John of Gaunt's.

The Upper Upham house that we see today can bear no resemblance to John of Gaunt's hunting lodge, although its association with linear earthworks that could be the remains of a deer park pale suggest that it stands on or near the site of the original hunting lodge. At some time Lacock Abbey obtained Upper Upham, because at the dissolution it was in 1539 granted to John Goddard, a grazier described in contemporary documents as a 'woolman, who had since 1527 leased Upper Upham from Lacock Abbey'. By this acquisition John Goddard consolidated the fortunes of the Goddard family of North Wiltshire. His son Thomas in the late-16th cen-

tury rebuilt the manor house to an E-shaped plan in the Elizabethan style. The south-east front of the house includes a porch with the date 1599 and the initials of Thomas Goddard, his son Richard, and wife Elizabeth. The plainer north-west front has a fine Goddard coat-of-arms. Later the Goddards removed to Swindon and Upper Upham manor house fell into dereliction. In the mid-19th century it was ruinous and occupied by a farm labourer known to the writer Richard Jefferies. The poet Edward Thomas discovered the derelict manor and in 1909 described the house and its prominent situation towards the crest of the hill overlooking Aldbourne Chase. From the memoirs of his wife Helen Thomas we also know that Thomas seriously considered renting the manor house, which was in its derelict condition purchased in about 1910 by Miss Hanham (1872–1939), who had discovered it on a sketching tour, and when she married Sir James Currie in 1913 they sensitively rebuilt and extended the house while successfully preserving its Elizabethan style.

The front of the house was taken down and re-assembled as the centrepiece of a largely new house built of stone and flint with a stone-slated roof. Today (2002) the house is divided up and in shared occupancy, and some development has taken place at Upper Upham in the form of a redbrick crescent of houses around a green west of the house.

Aldbourne Warren
Immediately south-east of Upper Upham was Aldbourne Warren. Rabbit-warrens were areas of generally poor land devoted to the farming of rabbits to provide fur and all year round meat for the table. Rabbits were a significant food source in England from their introduction in the 12th century, and warrens are often mentioned in Medieval documents. Aldbourne Warren is of early foundation and must often have provided rabbits for the tables of John of Gaunt and his entourage, a suggestion that is supported by the fact that his son when Henry IV had rabbits sent from Aldbourne for the royal table. The southern edge of Aldbourne Warren appears to be defined by the remains of a rubble wall. This lies on the right to-

wards the bottom of the slope as you descend the old way which runs east from Upper Upham past high Clear Plantation and the Giants Grave round barrow towards Aldbourne village (illustrated earlier on page 44). The former rabbit warrens in this area are commemorated in the names of Liddington Warren Farm and Aldbourne Warren Farm, which stand beside the B4192.

The continuation of the line of John of Gaunt

After John of Gaunt's son usurped Richard II and became as Henry IV the first Lancastrian king, his son became Henry V, and John of Gaunt's great-grandson Henry VI became the last Lancastrian king. Gaunt's four children by Catherine Swynford, his daughter's governess who was first his mistress and then his third wife, were in 1397 legitimised by the pope and by Act of Parliament as the Beauforts, their name being taken from the castle of Beaufort in France where they were born. These children were John Beaufort (Earl of Somerset), Henry Beaufort (Cardinal), Thomas Beaufort (Duke of Exeter), and Joan Beaufort who married the Earl of Westmoreland. The Earl of Somerset's granddaughter by his son John Beaufort, Duke of Somerset, was Margaret Beaufort who married Edmund Tudor, Earl of Richmond, and by her John of Gaunt's blood was taken into the Tudor monarchy when her son Henry Tudor usurped the throne of Richard III and became Henry VII, the first Tudor king and the father of Henry VIII and grandfather of Queen Elizabeth I.

4   The Seymours of Wolf Hall

The great family of Seymour attained its eminence as a direct result of two particularly fortunate marriages. In about 1400 the Seymours became heriditary Wardens of Savernake by marrying into the Sturmy (or Esturmy) Wardens, and nearly a hundred and fifty years later they obtained great power and wealth when Jane Seymour married Henry VIII, at the time when he had recently appropriated the vast estates of the monasteries. Many of these estates were sold or granted by the king to his supporters, and the Seymours were the principal beneficiaries. The elevation of this comparatively unimportant Wiltshire family to national importance resulted from the desperate need of Henry VIII to obtain a legitimate son to secure the continuation of the Tudor royal dynasty which had been founded by his father Henry VII.

Anyone who would follow-up the Seymour presence in Wiltshire should visit Wolf Hall, their hereditary home east of Burbage, where in a single generation were born the three great Tu-

The way from Tottenham to Wolf Hall, looking south

dor Seymours, Queen Jane and her two older brothers Edward and Thomas. Although their house is gone, the ancient way by which the Seymours rode out from Wolf Hall with their retainers and royal visitors to enjoy their sport hunting boar and deer in Savernake may be followed north across the canal and railway past venerable oaks which may have looked down on the Tudor Seymours and upon Henry VIII who made them great.

The early Tudors and the Dissolution

After Henry Tudor usurped the throne of Richard III in 1485 and became king as Henry VII he was never secure on the throne. His son Henry VIII was similarly insecure and became obsessed with his need for a son and heir, which persuaded him to discard his first queen Catherine of Aragon after over twenty years of marriage because she had failed to provide him with a living male heir, and in 1533 to marry Anne Boleyn. As a result of difficulties with the pope over the divorce of Queen Catherine the king broke with Rome and destroyed papal authority in England, although in this the king was swimming with a tide of rapidly growing protestantism among all classes of his subjects. He in fact remained a catholic practising an unorthodox form of catholicism which denied the pope. In 1536 Anne Boleyn was executed after she too failed to produce a living son and was succeeded by Jane Seymour. Five years later the king after assuming the position of supreme head of the English church decided to dissolve the monasteries and appropriate their immense riches. Some of these he distributed to his favourites to secure their interest in the reformation of the church which would ensure that the old unreformed catholic religion would never return.

The early history of the Seymours

The Seymours were descended from a Norman family based at the town of Saumur-sur-Loire in Normandy, from which they derived their name. They came to England during the 13th century and in 1427 Sir William Sturmy (c. 1345–1427), the last of the hereditary Sturmy Wardens of Savernake, died leaving no male heir. One of his two daughters (Matilda) had in about 1400 married Roger Seymour of Hatch Beauchamp in Somerset who died in 1421, and at the death of Sir William Sturmy Roger Seymour's son John (1403–65) succeeded to the Wardenship of Savernake as the first Seymour Warden. He was followed by another John Seymour (1441–91) who was in turn succeeded by his son Sir John Seymour (1474–1536) of Wolf Hall, who married Margery Wentworth, and during the reigns of Henry VII and VIII achieved a distinguished reputation as a soldier. At the age of only twenty-three he led Henry VII's troops to victory against the Cornish rebels who were protesting over taxation in 1497. They were defeated at Blackheath by Sir John who was knighted on the field of battle. He then served as Sheriff of the three counties of Dorset, Somerset and Wiltshire, distinguished himself at the seige of Tournai, and in 1520 accompanied Henry VIII to the Field of the Cloth of Gold. He is however mainly remembered for being the father of his three illustrious children Jane, Edward, and Thomas. Had an older son called John, who died young and unmarried in 1520 lived, the history of the Seymours and of England would have been different. Sir John died in December 1536, seven months after his daughter Jane became Henry VIII's third queen.

On progress through the west of England in 1535 Henry VIII, accompanied by Anne Boleyn, had visited the Seymours at Wolf Hall. The following year he was disappointed when Anne gave birth to a still-born son and decided to be rid of her. She was tried and executed, and the king immediately married Jane Seymour who the following year produced the longed-for son. Many of the Wiltshire monastic estates which he had appropriated were then lavished by the king in his gratitude upon Janes Seymour's older

brothers – Sir Edward Seymour (c. 1506–52) who became Lord Protector and virtually king during the first part of the minority of his nephew Edward VI, and Thomas Seymour (c. 1508–49). Both of these Seymours were at the centre of affairs of state in England during the latter part of Henry VIII's reign and the initial part of the reign of his son Edward VI.

Queen Jane Seymour

Jane Seymour (1509–37) is a rather shadowy figure and not much is known of her early life before she became Henry VIII's third queen. A contemporary description of her is provided by the French ambassador Chapuys who wrote that she was: 'of middle height, and nobody thinks that she has much beauty. Her complexion is so whitish that she may be called rather pale. She is a little over twenty-five'. Jane had been 'long at court' as a lady-in-waiting to Henry's first two queens, Catherine of Aragon and Anne Boleyn, and the cynical Imperial ambassador wrote of her: 'You may imagine, whether being an Englishwoman, and having been so long at court, she would hold it a sin to be still a maid'.

Queen Jane Seymour

After at first resisting the advances of the king Jane was installed in accommodation at court accessible to the king with her brother Sir Edward as chaperone. Sir Edward may have in the Seymour interests encouraged her to yield to the king's advances, and if this was the case he was lucky after Jane became queen and soon provided the king with the longed-for son that he hoped would secure the succession.

We cannot now be sure precisely how the marriage between Henry VIII and Jane Seymour came about. Henry's roving eye may merely have alighted on Jane after he had lost patience with Ann Boleyn, but there are other possibilities. Jane may not have been as demure as she has been portrayed and may have schemed to supplant Anne as queen.

There are three possible reasons why Jane may have wished to secure the fall of Anne Boleyn. She may merely have simply aspired to being queen; as a catholic she would have been concerned at Anne's support for the reformation of the church; or she may have been encouraged by her ambitious brothers to attract the king's interest in order to further the family interests.

According to tradition Henry VIII first met Jane after hunting in the Forest of Savernake when he rode across the downs to be entertained at Wolf Hall as the guest of Sir John Seymour as the Warden of Savernake. At some time they were also at Littlecote House (seven miles northeast of Wolf Hall) where their initials are incorporated in one of the south windows, but the true story of their meeting is that Jane had been for some time at court and according to the historian John Lingard (1771–1851):

> . . . the Queen [Anne Boleyn] accidentally discovered Jane Seymour sitting on the King's knee. The sight awakened her jealousy; in a few days she felt the pains of premature labour, and was delivered of a dead male child.

Jane at first attracted Henry's interest by emulating Ann Boleyn and playing hard to get. She rejected a purse of gold, refused to become the king's mistress, and returned the king's letters unopened, but soon after Anne Boleyn was executed on 19 May 1536 Henry VIII secretly married her on 30 May in the Queen's Closet at York Place in London. Jane was twenty-seven and Henry was forty-five, and very much in decline.

After becoming Henry's third queen Jane dutifully took as her motto 'Bound to obey and serve'. Anne Boleyn had furthered reform of the church but Jane Seymour adhered to traditional catholicism and was consequently branded by Luther 'an enemy of the Gospel'. She persuaded the king to reinstate his catholic eldest daughter Mary as his heiress and criticised him for dissolving the monasteries, but had the good sense to draw back when the king sharply warned her to 'remember Anne Boleyn'. She died only twelve days after the birth of her son Edward, who secured both the immediate future of the house of Tudor and the short term prosperity of the Seymours, and was buried at Windsor. In a confused state of euphoria over the birth of a son and grief at the death of his queen King Henry founded an abbey in memory of her at Bisham in Berkshire, and a little later capriciously dissolved it! Ten years and two wives later he was buried beside Jane at Windsor.

Had she lived Jane might in the euphoria over the birth of their son have persuaded King Henry to halt the Reformation. It is therefore ironic that her son as Edward VI and her brother Edward Seymour as Protector Somerset ensured the continuation of the reformation of the catholic church.

Edward Seymour, Protector Somerset

The ambitious Sir Edward Seymour (c.1506–52) made the most of his opportunities as the brother-in-law of the king and the uncle of the heir apparent. He had served Wolsey and, although he was knighted in 1523, his career was unspectacular until his sister married the king. After Queen Jane's father died in 1536 Henry VIII in gratitude for the birth of his son lavished rewards upon Sir John Seymour's sons, the chief beneficiary being Sir Edward Seymour. His rise was meteoric. The month after his sister married the king he in June 1536 became Viscount Beaumont of Hache and was granted extensive monastic lands in Wiltshire to support his new title. In July 1536 he became Governor of Jersey and in August Chancellor of North Wales. He had also as

Edward Seymour, Protector Somerset

the eldest son inherited his father's estates and the hereditary Wardenship of Savernake, and was also granted more lands in Somerset, and in Wiltshire the former Duchy of Lancaster manor of Trowbridge with its by then ruinous castle. Membership of the King's Council followed in May 1537, and in October of that year he was created Earl of Hertford.

As the joint architect with Lord Chamberlain Cromwell in 1540 of the king's marriage to the protestant Anne of Cleves (1515–57) Hertford might have shared Cromwell's fall when the king found his new bride unattractive, but although Cromwell was executed Hertford was astute enough to avoid sharing his fall and to retain the king's confidence. He then strengthened his position by leading a successful punitive expedition into Scotland in 1544, and when the king led an abortive military expedition into France in July 1544 Hertford was left as Lieutenant of the Realm and was then summoned to France when the campaign faltered.

The Wiltshire monastic properties granted to Hertford were accepted on his behalf by his Wiltshire steward John Berwick (died 1574), who after Somerset's fall lived at Wilcot in the Vale of Pewsey, a property of Bradenstoke Abbey which he had purchased. Berwick held the advowson of Wilcot church where his monument dated 1574 and displaying his coat of arms, incorporating three bears as a play upon his name, may be seen in the north wall of the chancel. His elder daughter married into the Wroughtons of Broad Hinton and took Stowell Park at Wilcot to them.

King Henry had recognised that he was unlikely to live until his son reached his majority and decreed in his will that a sixteen-man Council of Regency should govern the nation during his son's minority, but during his terminal illness (December 1546–January 1547) the Seymours were active to secure their futures. On 23 January Sir Thomas was appointed to the Privy Council and the kings will, which had required the regency council to act in concert, was amended to allow authority to be vested in an individual. By this means the Seymours prepared the way for Hertford (Edward Seymour) to be nominated Protector, and at the king's death on 27 January 1547 the news was witheld for three days during which Hertford secured control of the boy king. The Council then at its first meeting nominated Hertford to be Protector and governor of the prince, and to support this position he was granted the title of Duke of Somerset which had been vacant since the 4th Duke had been executed after the Battle of Tewkesbury in 1471.

As Protector of the Realm Somerset was king in all but name. Already recognised as being a good soldier, he now proved himself to be a good administrator with sincere religious convictions, and it has been suggested with some justification that under him England experienced 'the first government to attempt social justice'. Somerset was a firm protestant and as the boy king had been brought up as a protestant Henry VIII's policy of 'catholicism without the pope' was under Protector Somerset translated from Reformation into a religious revolution in which protestantism replaced the old catholic religion.

The young King Edward would have been aware of the fate of the last boy king of England whose uncle had become Regent less than a hundred years before. In 1483 his namesake Edward V and his younger brother had been murdered in the Tower and his Protector uncle had usurped the throne as Richard III, only to lose it to the young King Edward's grandfather Henry VII. Awareness of this may have prejudiced the young king against his Seymour uncle, and in his diary he listed Somerset's faults as: 'ambition, vainglory, entering into rash wars in my youth . . . enriching himself from of my treasure, following his own opinion, and doing all by his own authority,' suggesting that had Edward VI lived to maturity he would have dispensed with his uncle Somerset.

After the death of his parents the boy king Edward VI (1537–53) was often in Wiltshire. John Aubrey who lived at nearby Broad Chalke a little over a hundred years later recorded how King Edward was lost by his courtiers when out hunting in Faulston Drove, immediately below the Ox Drove ridgeway south-east of Bishopstone in south Wiltshire. Protector Somerset would have been in his entourage on this occasion when the young king's party stayed at Wilton with Henry VIII's old friend the Earl of Pembroke, the man who a few years later was active in bringing about Protector Somerset's downfall – a service for which he was rewarded with many of Somerset's Wiltshire estates.

Somerset's particular failure as Protector was in foreign affairs. His scheme to unite the thrones by marrying the ten-year-old Edward VI with the five-year-old Mary Queen of Scots failed after 1547 when he led an army of 18,000 men into Scotland in an attempt to compel the Scots to agree to this marriage. Although the Scottish Regent the Earl of Arran was heavily defeated at Pinkie east of Edinburgh owing to lack of resources, the victory was not followed up and the English ultimately withdrew from Scotland. After failing in Scotland and provoking France into emnity the Protector left England with an impoverished exchequer.

Understandably by the standards of his time Somerset took advantage of his unexpected ex-

alted position to enrich himself. Henry VIII's widow Catherine Parr had a life interest in Savernake Forest of which Somerest was Warden and at her death in 1548 Savernake Forest was transferred into his ownership by letters patent of Edward VI. By this transfer of ownership to a subject Savernake technically became a chase (that is a hunting ground owned by a subject), but it continued to be described as a forest, implying continued royal ownership.

As an administrator Somerset governed the nation well and justly. He was generous to the poor and treated opposition gently by the standards of his time, but his humanity was both his strength and his weakness and it contributed to his downfall. During his 1544 punitive expedition into Scotland he had demonstrated his generosity towards his defeated opponents by deploring the fact that King Henry had instructed him to sack Leith and lay waste to Scotland, orders which led him to write that he 'could not sleep this night for thinking of the king's determination for Leith'.

As Protector of the Realm for his nephew Edward VI Somerset had in mid-1549 to deal with two rebellions, the Western Prayer Book Rebellion and Robert Kett's Norfolk Rebellion against enclosures. These occurred at the time when there were enclosure riots in Somerset, Wilts and Hants, and Scotland and France were threatening to invade. It is arguable that his sympathy for common men had encouraged them to rebel in the belief that they would escape lightly and their grievances would be redressed, and during the Kett Rebellion he sent a herald to Norwich offering the rebels pardon if they returned home. But the herald was insulted, and it was left to the rising John Dudley, Earl of Warwick, to put down with severity the rebellion in August 1549.

Somerset had kept his royal nephew under strict control and was so busy with his duties as Protector of the Realm that he had failed to cultivate the influence with the young king which his less involved brother Thomas achieved. The boy king had his mind prejudiced against Protector Somerset first by his envious brother Lord Thomas Seymour and after his execution by John Dudley, Earl of

Warwick, who as the Duke of Northumberland orchestrated Somerset's downfall.

Although his protestantism met with wide-spread approval Somerset's haughtiness offended many of his fellow courtiers. With all his virtues he was ambitious and avaricious. He pulled down an aisle of St Paul's Cathedral and proposed to demolish Westminster Abbey to provide materials for his palace Somerset House, and there is some evidence that he may have had aspirations to the throne. After he was elected Protector of the Realm Somerset seems to have become very arrogant. In documents relating to Amesbury Abbey he is described as 'The High and Myghtye Prince Edward, Duke of Somerset', and on the tomb of his father at Great Bedwyn he is 'Duke of Somerset, Earl of Hertford, Viscount Beauchamp, and Baron Seymour, Uncle to King Edward VI, Governor of his Royal Person, Protector of all his Dominions and Subjects, Lord Treasurer and Earl Marshal of England'. Letters at Longleat from Protector Somerset to his steward Sir John Thynne reveal that when referring to himself Somerset gradually dropped the singular 'I' and adopted the royal 'We', and he greeted King Francis I of France as 'brother'.

The execution for treason of his younger brother Lord Admiral Thomas Seymour (see later, pages 57-60) undermined Protector Somerset's position. He was censured for having signed his own brother's death warrant, and the very evident failings of Lord Thomas Seymour had demonstrated that even the Seymours were fallible. Opposition to Somerset grew and a power struggle developed between the Protector and the rising John Dudley (?1505–53), Earl of Warwick and from 1551 Duke of Northumberland. Warwick had gained status as a result of the ruthlessness with which he had put down the 1549 Norfolk Rebellion, and he criticised Somerset for having been lenient towards the rebels. It is possible that in early 1549 Protector Somerset had been distracted by the behaviour of his envious younger brother Thomas, which necessitated him ordering his execution in March 1549. By the end of September 1549 a majority of the Council wanted Somerset removed but his position was so strong that this could only be achieved by a

conspiracy. On a visit to the young King Edward at Hampton Court on 5 October 1549 Somerset received a warning that the Earl of Warwick and his supporters intended to pay him a 'friendly visit'. He summoned all loyal subjects to gather at Hampton Court but counter-proclamations were issued and he fled on horseback to Windsor Castle taking with him the boy king. This amounted to kidnapping the sovereign and now realising the gravity of his position Somerset summoned the Earl of Pembroke and the Duke of Bedford as commanders of the western army to come to his aid. They did not move, and Somerset's enemies followed him to Windsor, where on the 10 October he was arrested and conveyed to the Tower of London.

Few fallen politicians escaped after being sent to the Tower but Somerset for a time succeeded. He was released in February 1550 and temporarily resumed his duties but the determined campaign against him grew in momentum. He survived for a little over a year and a half until October 1551 when he was returned to the Tower, and in December was tried and convicted at a rigged trial for treason, the allegations being that he had displayed lack of enthusiasm in suppressing the 1549 rebellions and had been too lenient with the rebels. Evidence against him was gathered by torture, bribery, and by promises of free pardon to his alleged accomplices. He had been warned by his friend William, Lord Paget (1505–63), who had been Jane Seymour's secretary and then allied himself to Somerset, about being 'good to the poor', and when he was sent to the Tower crowds accompanied him all the way crying 'God save him'.

Somerset's generosity to the common people had alienated him from the powerful nobility who envied his supreme power, and he was beheaded on Tower Hill on 22 January 1552. The people regarded their 'Good Duke' as a martyr and preserved handkerciefs soaked by his blood as relics. Young Edward VI who had never liked his domineering uncle noted laconically in his diary: 'The Duke of Somerset had his head cut off upon Tower Hill between 8 and 9 in the morning'. Although some of Somerset's wife Anne Stanhope's relatives were executed for complicity that lady was, after a spell of imprisonment in the Tower, released, re-married, lived to the age of ninety, and died in 1587 having outlived her first husband by thirty-five years.

After the ailing Edward VI died in 1553 aged sixteen the throne went to the catholic Princess Mary, but only after John Dudley, Duke of Northumberland, had been executed in 1553 for attempting to place his protestant daughter-in-law Lady Jane Grey on the throne.

Sir Thomas Seymour, Lord High Admiral

The contrasting characters of the Seymour brothers were described about a hundred years after their deaths by Peter Heylyn in his *History of the Reformation* (1661):

> The Admiral [Thomas] was fierce in courage, courtly in fashion, in personage stately, in voice magnificent, but somewhat empty of matter. The Duke [Edward] was mild, affable, free and open, more easily to be worked on, but in no way malicious, and honoured by the common people, as the Admiral was more generally esteemed among the nobler. The Protector was more to be desired as a friend, and the other more to be feared as an enemy. The defects of each being taken away, the virtues united would have made an excellent man.

Thomas Seymour (*c.* 1508–49) was a handsome and athletic man, skilful in the tournament but extremely rash, and possessing little political acumen. Henry VIII's biographer Francis Hackett in 1929 aptly described him as having 'raw ambition on an empty mind'. He had courted the twice-widowed Catherine Parr (1512–48) but when in 1543 Henry VIII decided to marry her Thomas was despatched abroad as ambassador to Brussels. He was ambitious, and he became consumed with jealousy at the preferments that were showered upon his older brother. Aware of his weaknesses the Protector set him aside from mainstream politics by making him Lord High Admiral, but Thomas was prepared to go to almost any lengths to further his own prospects. He intrigued to put an end to the Protectorate and oust his brother, but being a man of action rather than a politician he lacked all discretion.

Thomas Seymour, Lord Admiral

Dissatisfied with his office as Lord Admiral Thomas Seymour resolved to improve his prospects by marriage, and immediately after King Henry's death wrote to the young Princess Elizabeth proposing marriage and eliciting the sharp reply that 'neither that my age nor my inclination allows me to think of marriage, I never could have believed that any would have spoken to me of nuptials at a time when I ought to think of nothing but sorrow for the death of my father'.

When Henry VIII died in 1547 Lord Thomas Seymour was about thirty-nine and the dowager queen Catherine Parr was thirty-five. Thomas Seymour lost no time in renewing his relationship with the dowager queen, who unhesitatingly secretly married him in June 1547. They lived sometimes at her houses at Chelsea and Hamworth, and at other times at his London house Seymour Place. When made aware of his brother's clandestine marriage Protector Somerset was furious, and the rift between the brothers was exacerbated by friction between their wives over the precedence given to Catherine Parr as the former queen over the Protector's wife Anne Stanhope. Catherine Parr had been a sympathetic stepmother to Henry VIII's children and may have expected to be made Regent during the minority of Edward VI, in which case she would have been disappointed by the appointment of her brother-in-law Edward Seymour as Protector.

Lord Thomas Seymour revealed himself to be an ambitious and dangerous intriguer in a number of ways. His ambition knew no bounds. After her father's death Princess Elizabeth, who as the daughter of the disgraced Anne Boleyn had experienced a precarious childhood, was befriended by her stepmother Catherine Parr and when Catherine married Thomas Seymour they were made the guardians of Elizabeth at their house at Chelsea. There Thomas Seymour committed indiscretions with the thirteen-year-old Elizabeth in a shameless bid for power. When Catherine Parr realised what was happening young Elizabeth was sent away and it was rumoured that she had become pregnant by Lord Seymour, and when Catherine Parr died in 1548 three days after giving birth to Lord Thomas Seymour's daughter Mary it was suggested that she had been murdered by her ambitious husband in order that he might marry the Princess Elizabeth. Despite being sternly warned not to persist in this idea by the Lord Privy Seal, Lord Russell, Lord Thomas Seymour continued to pursue his scheme to marry Elizabeth.

When Catherine Parr died in 1548 Lady Jane Grey (1537–54), a cousin of Edward VI, was also in her household and became a ward of Thomas Seymour who hoped to marry her to Edward VI. After Seymour was executed in 1549 Lady Jane returned to her parents. When Edward VI died in 1553 she was used as a pawn in an attempt to prevent the succession of the catholic Mary and was queen for nine days before being executed as a victim of her family's ambition.

Thomas Seymour had in his own interests been kind to the young King Edward and had gained favour with him behind Somerset's back by augmenting the meagre allowance that the Protector allowed him. When ingratiating him-

self with the young king the Lord Admiral seems to have entirely overlooked the possibility that the boy might have inherited the suspicious natures of his father Henry VIII and his grandfather Henry VII. The precocious young king had in fact viewed with suspicion his uncle Thomas's successive intrigues to marry the Princess Mary or Princess Elizabeth, who had been nominated by Henry VIII heirs to the throne in the event of Edward dying without issue. When rumblings about Lord Thomas Seymour's ambitions began to be heard it was a statement by King Edward ('We do perceive that there be great things which be objected and laid to my Lord Seymour, mine uncle, and they tend to treason') that decided his Council to bring a charge of treason against the Lord Admiral. According to Seymour family tradition Lord Thomas Seymour's ultimate offence was to be caught in the young king's quarters with a drawn sword in his hand with which he had killed the king's pet dog after it had raised the alarm. It was claimed that he was attempting to kidnap the king, and further investigation disclosed that he was preparing a rebellion in the west country against his brother's Protectorship.

Sharington of Lacock

The man who was instrumental in the conviction of Lord Thomas Seymour for treason was Sir William Sharington (c. 1495–1553) who in 1540 bought the dissolved Lacock Abbey for £783. In 1546 he became vice-treasurer of the Bristol mint and abused his position by making a fortune in three years by clipping the coinage. Sharington was also an amateur architect who

Sir William Sharington's conduit house on Bowden Hill above Lacock

advised Sir Thomas Seymour on his architectural ventures. The conduit house designed by Sharington for Lacock Abbey (which may be seen from the road near the top of Bowden Hill standing behind railings about fifteen yards north of the road) bears a marked resemblance to the conduit house at Thomas Seymour's principal house, Sudeley Castle in Gloucestershire. At Lacock Abbey Sharington demolished the abbey church, adapted the other buildings for his domestic use, and built the splendid octagonal Sharington's Tower at the south-east corner of the abbey.

Fearing that his misdemeanours at the mint might be discovered Sharington may have been blackmailed into joining Lord Thomas Seymour's plot and funding his proposed rebellion, in return for a promise of the Lord Admiral's protection. The government got to hear of his activities, Lacock Abbey was searched and on 19 January 1548–9 Sharington was arrested. Questioned at the Tower he admitted that he had financed many of Lord Admiral Seymour's works at Sudeley Castle and elsewhere, and claimed to have laid out a thousand pounds on Sudeley and fifteen hundred pounds on Bromham (see later, page 60). He was promised his life if he turned evidence and after preparing a long incriminating statement against the Lord Admiral he was released and allowed to buy back his estates. In 1552 he became Sheriff of Wiltshire. The following year he died and is commemorated by a pretentious monument in Lacock Church.

The arrest and execution of Lord Admiral Seymour

Lord Admiral Seymour had gambled for very high stakes and had lost. He was arrested on 17 January 1549 and was executed on a bill of attainder for treason on 20 March 1549 without being allowed to speak in his defence. His elder brother at first tried to save him but according to Sir Richard Colt Hoare, in his *Modern Wiltshire, Hundred of Mere* (1822), Protector Somerset's wife Ann Stanhope, who had resented the senior social position of Thomas Seymour's wife Catherine Parr as the former queen, encouraged her husband to sign his brother's death warrant.

Anne Stanhope, Protector Somerset's second wife

Ann Stanhope was described by Sir John Hayward in his life of Edward VI as a lady who was violent in accomplishing her ends, and Lloyd in his *State Worthies* also attributed the disaffection between the Seymour brothers to be largely due to animosity between their wives. Anne Stanhope was said to have warned her husband that he would never be safe while his brother lived, and he may have been secretly pleased to be rid of his troublesome younger brother.

On the night before his execution the Lord Admiral wrote letters to the Princesses Mary and Elizabeth warning them against his brother. The Princess Elizabeth, who as a young teenager may have been responsive to Lord Thomas's indecorous wooing, commented on his execution: 'This day died a man with much wit, and very little judgement'.

Although he too was born at Wolf Hall in Savernake Forest Thomas Seymour's connection with Wiltshire became rather more tenuous than that of his brother Edward, the Protector, who inherited the family Wiltshire estates and the Wardenship of Savernake, and also acquired many additional properties in Wiltshire. As a result of his marriage to Catherine Parr Thomas Seymour obtained the Vastern deer parks at Wootton Bassett (see Chapter 2) and a number of Wiltshire properties in addition to Sudeley Castle in Gloucestershire.

The Bayntuns of Bromham

Associated with the Seymours at the court of Henry VIII was Sir Edward Bayntun of the Wiltshire-based family which also prospered from the dissolution of the monasteries. In the 17th century the Bayntuns were one of the leading Wiltshire families, by this time based at Bromham near Devizes, although as the de Bentons they had earlier been at Faulston in south Wiltshire since the reign of Edward I. The Bayntuns acquired Bromham when, at the death in 1508 of Richard Beauchamp, Lord St Amand, Roches Manor at Bromham came to Nicholas Bayntun of Falstone who had married Joan, the junior heiress of the Roches. In 1516 John Bayntun was succeeded by his eldest son, later knighted as Sir Edward Bayntun, who rose to high estate under Henry VIII and died in 1578. He was vice-chamberlain to four of Henry's queens, a not inconsiderable achievement as they successively came into and went out of royal favour, and was entrusted with obtaining confessions from the men accused of having had treasonable relations with Queen Anne Boleyn. As governor of the household to Queen Catherine Howard he also gathered the evidence that led to her execution.

From his position at court Sir Edward was well-placed to prosper from the dissolution, and in 1538 he became lessee of the ecclesiastical manor of Bromham Battle by grant from the crown, and was thus enabled to unite the two Bromham manors under his ownership.

Bromham House (now Bromham House Farm) was built in the 16th century by Sir Edward Bayntun, who was also granted Malmesbury Abbey, which he immediately sold, and Stanley Abbey which he robbed of materials for Bromham House. This grand Bayntun house was built less than half a mile south-west

of the main road from London to Bath and Bristol, which then ran over Roundway Down and down Beacon Hill. The house was a particularly splendid one described by Leland as: 'nearly as large as Whitehall and fit to entertain a king', a function which it performed on a number of occasions. In 1535 Sir Edward Bayntun entertained Henry VIII and his court at Bromham House, and early in the 17th century there are records of visits by James I in 1613, 1618, and 1623, no doubt for the hunting in Bromham Park.

For a short time in the mid-16th century Bromham was in the hands of the Seymours. The *State Papers Domestic, vol. VI, Edward VI* reveal that at the death of Sir Edward Bayntun in 1544 his son Andrew agreed to exchange with Lord Admiral Thomas Seymour all their properties in Wiltshire. Bayntun fulfilled his side of the bargain but the unscrupulous Lord Thomas did not, although after he was executed Queen Mary restored Bromham to Andrew Bayntun.

Bromham House, which was on the site of the present farm, along with its deer park, were destroyed in the Civil War and the Bayntuns moved up the hill to Spye Park, where the former Bromham House gatehouse was rebuilt at the entrance to Spye Park on Bowden Hill above Lacock. The display of arms and initials on this gatehouse reveal that it had originally been built

Bromham church with its magnificent south chapel containing the Bayntun monuments

by Sir Edward Bayntun who died in 1544–45 serving the king in France.

The magnificent Beauchamp Chapel at Bromham church contains several Bayntun memorials. John Bayntun (died 1516) is depicted on a floor brass in full armour, and on the south wall is the canopied tomb of Sir Edward Bayntun (died 1578), the most important member of the family. It incorporates a brass depicting Sir Edward with his two wives and two children kneeling in line. In recesses under the east window are five niches in which are listed the names of the Bayntuns from 1679 to 1921. Also at Bromham, at the south end of the village, are the timber-framed and gabled College of the Poor almshouses which were built for the village by the Bayntuns in 1612.

The descendants of Protector Somerset

Jane Seymour's son by Henry VIII became king as Edward VI but died at the age of fifteen, leaving his throne to his sister Mary. Although Lord Admiral Seymour had a daughter Mary by Catherine Parr this child seems to have died in 1549. Protector Somerset left children from both of his marriages but, doubting the paternity of his two sons by his first wife Catherine Filliol, whom he had married in 1535 and divorced in 1537, he made arrangements to prevent them from inheriting his titles. The *Gentleman's Magazine* for 11 December 1757 recorded that the Filliol Seymours were: 'disinherited to gratify the pride and ambition of . . . Lady Anne Stanhope'.

Protector Somerset's eldest son and heir Edward by Anne Stanhope fell upon bad times after his father's execution in 1552. The family estates were forfeited, but Protector Somerset had been kind to the Princesses Mary and Elizabeth when they were out of favour, and both remembered their debts to him when they successively reached the throne. Queen Mary restored the Seymour estates to his son, who was at Queen Elizabeth's succession created Earl of Hertford, although he forfeited her favour when in 1560 he secretly married Lady Catherine Grey, the sister of Lady Jane Grey. Elizabeth had the marriage annulled and the couple imprisoned in the Tower, where Lady Catherine in 1561 gave birth to a healthy son. He was christened Edward in the chapel of St Peter-ad-Vincula, very near the headless remains of both his grandfathers. This son became Edward, Lord Beauchamp.

The Hertford imprisonment was benevolent, and another son christened Thomas Seymour was born. The queen was furious at the birth of another potential claimant to the throne and the couple were removed from the Tower and kept apart. Catherine died allegedly of a broken heart in 1568 and in 1570 Hertford was freed, although the queen never forgave him and he failed to get his sons legitimised until 1606, when James I was securely established on the throne of England.

At the end of the reign of Elizabeth the aspirations of the Seymours came very near to the throne. Hertford's son Edward Lord Beauchamp had as good a claim as James VI of Scotland and was proposed as a possible successor to the queen on her deathbed, but she declared that she would 'have no rogue's son in my seat' and nominated King James VI of Scotland as her successor.

The Filliol branch of the Seymours became a Devon branch of the family with holdings at Maiden Bradley in Wiltshire, which was conveyed to them by Protector Somerset as part of a settlement. They were however understandably aggrieved at their disinheritance. The last really great member of the family was Sir Edward Seymour (1633–1708), Speaker of the House of Commons, who has a magnificent monument in Maiden Bradley church. When asked by William III if he was 'of the Duke of Somerset's family' he haughtily replied: 'Pardom me sire, the Duke of Somerset is of my family'. At her accession Queen Anne made Sir Edward Comptroller of the Household and Ranger of Windsor Forest. He died in 1708, it is said as the result of being beaten up by an elderly village woman who had a grievance against him!

The principal Seymour properties in Wiltshire

In addition to their hereditary estates as the Wardens of Savernake the Seymours obtained an immense number of other estates as a result of their royal connections and their land-holdings are so numerous that space will allow only a small selection to be described here.

The greatest number of the Seymour properties in Wiltshire belonged to Protector Somerset as the elder brother, although Sir Thomas Seymour obtained some Wiltshire estates, including lands at Bratton, Tinhead, Edington, Imber, the former Abbess of Romsey estates based on Steeple and Rood Ashton, and the deer parks at Wootton Bassett. His principal land holdings were however elsewhere, in particular Sudeley Castle in Gloucestershire, from which he took his title of Lord Thomas Seymour of Sudeley. His estates were forfeited to the crown and granted to others after he was executed in 1649.

Seymour country around Wolf Hall

Before their rapid rise to national eminence under Henry VIII the Seymours resided at Wolf Hall, their home as hereditary Wardens of Savernake Forest in succession to the Sturmys. Wolf Hall stood in extensive grounds east of Burbage, surrounded by three deer parks called Suddene Park, Horse Park and Red Deer Park. The buildings were arranged around courtyards.

There was a 'Little Court', implying the existence of a larger court, and a chapel built by Sir William Sturmy. The gardens included the Great Paled Garden, My Old Lady's Garden, and My Young Lady's Garden.

After Edward Seymour attained national eminence during the reign of Henry VIII building materials from Wolf Hall were used to build their more grand Tottenham House in Savernake, which was more appropriate for their new position. Wolf Hall was then allowed to fall into dereliction and today practically nothing of the old house of the Savernake Wardens remains, although the Great Barn measuring 172 feet long by 26 feet wide, at which Henry VIII was fêted survived into recent times. Having been partly destroyed during the Civil War it still existed in an advanced state of dereliction when the Wiltshire Archaeological & Natural History Society visited Wolf Hall in 1923. Later it collapsed, although a sketch of it is reproduced in *Wiltshire Archaeological & Natural History Magazine* (volume 15, see below). Hooks high in its walls that were traditionally said to have supported wall-hangings for the celebrations of the royal wedding probably dated from other visits by the king in 1535, 1539 and 1543. Although the marriage of Jane Seymour to Henry VIII in 1536 is traditionally said to have taken place in the Great Barn at Wolf Hall, it in fact took place at Hampton Court. Ledger entries dated August 1539 account for a great feast 'at Wilfhaull against the king's coming thether' at the time when Edward Seymour (by then Earl of Hertford) was with

Barn at Wolf Hall (WANHM, vol. 15, facing p.144)

Thomas Cromwell (c. 1485–1540) arranging for the king to marry Anne of Cleves. The king and his entire court including Cromwell were entertained and there was feasting in the Great Barn at Wolf Hall for three days (9–12 August). Cromwell was executed the following year for his part in arranging the marriage with the unattractive Anne of Cleves, but Hertford escaped from sharing Cromwell's fate and the king made a final visit in 1543 when the Seymours owned many other estates in Wiltshire.

Wolf Hall from the east

The precise location of Wolf Hall has been a matter for some speculation. At present Wolf Hall Manor and Wolf Hall Farm stand respectively west and east of the point where the east to west road kinks for a short distance north to south, but old maps show Wolf Hall as a cluster of buildings standing north-west of the point where the road from the Bedwyns and Crofton then took a right-angled bend south. At some time this road from the Bedwyns was extended west to Burbage by creating the kink of the present road around Wolf Hall Manor, suggesting that the present manor house occupies the site of the old Wolf Hall, perhaps extending north across the road towards the existing building with tall chimneys known as the Laundry. This suggestion is supported by an account of a visit to Wolf Hall made by the architectural historian John Harris who became curator of drawings at the RIBA. In *No Voice from the Hall* (1988) he relates how as a student of architecture he stayed at Wolf Hall in November 1954 despite being warned that no one had stayed there since 1947. In his description of this visit he recorded seeing the 'Tudor wing at the back . . . opening on a kitchen', 'the interior, stuffed

with the left-overs from Tottenham Park?', and 'a library in chaos'. Harris also indicated that: 'Wulf Hall was made habitable for use while Flitcroft [the architect] and Lord Burlington were rebuilding Tottenham Park in the 1730s'.

The present Wolf Hall is screened by a dense tree screen. Pevsner described it as Victorian but mentions: 'in a dip a red-brick house with one Tudor wing with mullioned windows and a group of tall Tudor chimneyshafts (polygonal with projecting tops) and one wing refronted c.1740'. This house is the Laundry, which stands north of Wolf Hall Manor beside the lane along which the Seymours would have ridden north to Savernake Forest. This is probably the house described by John Harris. The old lane followed by the Seymours and their royal visitors to Savernake Forest still runs as a right-of-way north from Wolf Hall past the Laundry to Tottenham, the replacement house of the Seymours who remained at Wolf Hall until 1582. In that year they moved to Tottenham Lodge and stayed there until 1608, when Amesbury Abbey became their principal residence.

In the year of his sister's marriage to Henry VIII Edward Earl of Hertford was granted many properties, two of them (Monkton Farleigh and Easton Royal) being in Wiltshire.

Monkton Farleigh, a few miles east of Bath, had been founded in 1125 as a cell of the Cluniac Priory of Lewes in Sussex. A Georgian fronted manor house which now occupies the site is associated with some ancient buildings with lancet windows. A Monks Conduit House also survives standing over a spring. Here Bishop Jewel (1522–71), the first protestant to occupy the see of Salisbury, died after preaching his last sermon in Lacock church. Hertford sold Monkton Farleigh soon after acquiring it but in 1716 the Seymours recovered it by marriage.

Easton Royal was a Trinitarian Friary founded in 1245 which attained its 'Royal' suffix from being situated in the Royal Forest of Savernake. The Seymours had before owning Easton Royal patronised Easton Priory, which was their place of burial. Sir John Seymour was buried at Easton in 1536, as had been his first son of the same name who had died young in 1510. Edward Seymour, when Earl of Hertford, destroyed the friary buildings and erected on their site east of the road and opposite the church a mansion which was demolished in the 18th century. Today practically nothing remains of either the friary or the Seymour mansion except a series of banks. The Seymours continued to be buried at Easton Royal church until about 1590 when, it having become ruinous, the then Earl of Hertford rebuilt it but removed the memorials to his grandfather (Sir John Seymour) and father (Protector Somerset) to Great Bedwyn church. By then Tottenham House (a little west of Bedwyn) had become the new home of the Wardens of Savernake after Wolf Hall had been abandoned as being too humble for so eminent a family. Sir John's monument at Great Bedwyn consists of a tomb chest and effigy in gilded armour; Jane Seymour is commemorated by a window which incorporates heraldic stained glass from her home at Wolf Hall; and her brother Protector Somerset has a marble me-

Great Bedwyn church which contains the Seymour monuments

morial slab and a brass. There is also a wall brass with a depiction of a youth in a long gown, commemorating their elder brother John, whose early death in 1510 cleared the way for his ambitious brothers.

At the time of his execution in 1552 Protector Somerset was constructing an immense mansion, which would probably have been larger than his steward's house at Longleat, to replace Wolf Hall. This was in Bedwyn Brail a mile south of Great Bedwyn. Hundreds of workmen were employed on the construction of the house, a banked and ditched park-pale, and a huge water conduit fifteen feet deep and about 500 yards long (of which some signs remain). The house was to have been at the south end of Bedwyn Brail a little west of Hillbarn Farm and its extensive deer park was to have been surrounded by a bank and ditch enclosing an area south-east of the present canal, which included Castle Copse, Bedwyn Brail and most of Wilton Brail. The Kennet and Avon Canal appears to have adopted the line of the intended north-west pale of this park, which suggests that the bank and ditch may already have been excavated when at Somerset's execution all work was stopped and the building materials were used elsewhere.

In 1547 Maiden Bradley Priory, which had been founded as a hospital for lepers, came into Seymour's hands and in 1548, after Henry VIII's death, Savernake Forest – the Royal Forest of which he had been merely the Warden – and Marlborough Castle were conveyed by letters patent to Protector Somerset by Edward VI. Leland had in 1541 seen Marlborough Castle as the ruins of a once great castle, and soon after 1548 the Seymours converted the castle ruins into a fine dwelling house.

Amesbury Abbey was granted to Sir Edward Seymour in 1540 or 1541. The grant is dated 7 April 1541, but there is evidence that it was in his possession earlier.

Subsequent associations of several Seymour Houses

Long after Jane Seymour and her two powerful brothers were dead several Seymour houses in Wiltshire were, in the early-18th century, notable for their interesting associations. The disinherited first family of Protector Somerset by Catherine Filliol became owners of Maiden Bradley on the Somerset border, where a leper hospital at Priory Farm had been converted in 1189 to an Augustinian Priory. For most of his life Sir Edward Seymour (died 1707), Speaker of the House of Commons, lived at Berry Pomeroy in Devon, although after 1701 he lived at Maiden Bradley, which became the principal seat of the Dukes of Somerset, the Dukedom having been successfully claimed by this branch of the Seymours. Sir Edward's elaborate monument may be seen in Maiden Bradley church.

A letter dated 19 October 1786 from the Duke of Somerset's steward indicates that: 'Maiden Bradley House was built by Speaker Seymour for a hunting box'. It was then expanded into the large Palladian mansion illustrated in Colen Campbell's *Vitruvius Britannicus* but it is now much reduced in size. The Dukes continued to live at Maiden Bradley, but the 11th and 12th Dukes used the house only occasionally and it became virtually abandoned after the sons of the 12th Duke (born 1804) died young and the next in succession to the dukedom became his brother Archibald. The present Duke of Somerset, a Seymour descendant, lives at Bradley House.

Tottenham Lodge in Savernake, which was originally built as the Seymour's replacement for Wolf Hall, was in the 18th century entirely re-built as Tottenham House, an extremely important early Georgian Palladian house de-signed by Lord Burlington for his brother-in-law Lord Bruce, using as his architect his protegé Henry Flitcroft (see Chapter 10, page 150). Within a hundred years Tottenham was entirely remodelled in 1825.

During the early-18th century two Wiltshire ladies patronised important writers in former Seymour houses. At Marlborough Lady Francis Hertford, the grand-daughter of the First Lord Weymouth of Longleat, who had in 1713 be-come the wife of Lord Hertford, busied herself by elaborating the grounds of the house that her husband had recently built on the site of Marlborough Castle. One of the writers patronised by Lady Hertford was the Scottish born James Thomson (1700–48) who wrote the 'Spring' section of *The Seasons* at Marlborough in 1728, and dedicated it to the 'Countess of Hartford'. 'Spring' is said to have been written on the downs overlooking the River Kennet, and

the large sarsen stone which Thomson had used as a seat was brought down to the town and set up at the west end of Marlborough High Street outside the wall of St Peter's churchyard – but has has now disappeared.

Lady Hertford's benevolence to Thomson ended when he displayed a preference for eat-ing and drinking at Lord Hertford's table to pursuing his literary activities to please her. She also patronised a lesser figure in the local 'thresher' poet Stephen Duck (1705–56). An-other writer patronised by Lady Hertford was the hymn-writer Dr Isaac Watts (1674–1748). Lady Hertford lost her reason and lived to see her Marlborough home sold by her daughter. In the mid-18th century it was turned into the Castle Inn on the coach road from London to Bath, and in 1843 it became the nucleus of Marlborough College.

Contemporary with Lady Hertford's patron-age of writers at Marlborough, at the former Seymour property of Amesbury Abbey in the south of Wiltshire the Duchess of Queensberry patronised several writers. At the Dissolution the monastery was in 1541 granted to Protector Somerset, who dismantled its buildings and built a house on its site which was subsequently fre-quently remodelled. The Seymours retained Amesbury until 1720 when after passing through several hands it was in 1725 acquired by the Duke of Queensberry. In 1661 John Webb (1611–72), who had married a niece of Inigo Jones, built a Palladian house on the site of Amesbury Abbey for the Duke of Somerset. This house was in 1830 demolished and replaced by a Victorian Palladian mansion house of similar design.

Katherine, Duchess of Queensberry (1700–77) was the second child of Henry Hyde, 2nd Earl of Clarendon, and grand-daughter of Edward Hyde, the first Earl (Chapter 9). She married the Duke of Queensberry in 1720, but her eccentrici-ties were regarded by her contemporaries as amounting almost to insanity, and Walpole un-kindly referred to her as 'an out-pensioner of Bedlam'. At Amesbury she patronised John Gay (1685–1732) and Matthew Prior (1664–1721), who wrote her a poem beginning:

Thus Kitty, beautiful and young,
And wild as colt untamed.

At Amesbury John Gay is believed to have written *The Beggars Opera* (1728) which was forbidden at court. By patronising it the Duchess incurred the wrath of King George II who wrote a letter requesting her to abstain from appearing at court, to which the Duchess boldly replied that: 'she never came to court for diversion, but to bestow a great civility upon the King and Queen'.

The decline of the Seymours after Elizabeth

With the death of Queen Elizabeth in 1603 the direct relationship of the Seymours to the throne was ended although throughout the Stuart period they continued to be active in politics. In 1609 James I created Edward Seymour Baron Beauchamp, but he predeceased his father in 1612 and never became Earl of Hertford.

Sir William Seymour (born 1587) became Earl of Hertford in 1621 at the death of his grandfather. Before Lord Hertford's death this William Seymour married in 1610, clandestinely and without royal consent, Lady Arabella Stuart (1575–1615), a lady who was at least twelve years his senior and, having as strong a claim as James I to the throne, had been kept at court but forbidden to marry, because of the threat that any children would have posed to the succession. When the marriage was discovered Lady Arabella was imprisoned at Highgate and Seymour at the Tower. Both managed to escape and Seymour reached Flanders safely, but his wife was caught in the Calais Roads and was sent to the Tower where she died.

This William Seymour who succeeded to the Earldom of Hertford at his grandfather's death in 1621 become a rather dour protestant gentleman, understandably not particularly attached to the court of King James. He patronised the Wiltshire composer William Lawes (Chapter 8, pages 123-4) and at the accession of Charles I in 1625 he became one of the new king's devoted

friends, was created Marquis of Hertford in 1640, and became governor to Charles Prince of Wales in 1641. Throughout the Civil War Hertford was loyal to King Charles I as his General in the West and he was one of the king's supporters who offered their lives to save the king. When that failed he conveyed Charles I's body to Windsor for burial. At the Restoration in 1660 he was restored to the Dukedom of Somerset which had been forfeited by his great grandfather Protector Somerset, but the same year he died and was buried at Great Bedwyn.

During the 1630s, 1640s and 1650s the Seymour family suffered a succession of early deaths and ultimately Edward Seymour, of the older Devon (and Maiden Bradley) branch of the family which had been excluded from the Seymour titles for nearly two hundred years, claimed the Dukedom. His claim was validated and he became the 8th Duke of Somerset. From this Devon branch of the family came the autocratic Sir Edward Seymour (1633–1708) of Berry Pomeroy in Devon and of Maiden Bradley who in 1673 became the first elected Speaker of the House of Commons. Samuel Pepys found him: 'very high, proud and saucy', and Macaulay wrote of him: 'It was strange that the haughtiest of human beings should be the meanest'. When Queen Anne formed her first ministry in 1702 Sir Edward Seymour became Comptroller of the Household, Ranger of Windsor Great Park, and Master of Horse, but with the accession of George of Hanover in 1714 the Seymour influence declined.

In reflecting on the earlier Tudor Seymours it is interesting to speculate whether in their last hours Queen Jane Seymour, Lord Thomas Seymour, or Protector Somerset, all of whom died comparatively young, thought of their distant home at Wolf Hall, of their untroubled rural Wiltshire childhoods with their parents Sir John and Lady Margaret Seymour, and of how ambition had taken them from rural Wiltshire to the court at London, initially to great prosperity and then to their untimely deaths.

5   Wilton and Sir Philip Sidney

including his sister and her literary circle at Wilton

This curious seate of Wilton and the adjacent countrey is an Arcadian place and a paradise', wrote John Aubrey in the 17th century. He also recalled that Sir Philip Sidney had written his celebrated romance *Arcadia* in and around Wilton when staying with his sister Mary and her husband the Earl of Pembroke. Sidney was a romantic figure who contrived to attain the standing of a national hero, having apparently done little to earn such recognition, and it has been suggested that a perfectly adequate history of the Elizabethan period could be written without mentioning Sir Philip Sidney.

Wilton

Wilton in its easily defended position between the Rivers Nadder and Wylye has a long history. In the 6th or 7th century a Saxon tribe called the *Wilsætas* are believed to have given their name to Wilton and ultimately to Wiltshire. King Egbert founded here a Benedictine priory, a Saxon palace followed, and in the year of his accession (871) Alfred fought the Danes at Wilton and lost. He later made Wilton one of his four Wiltshire *burhs* for the defence of Wessex against the Vikings, and often spent Easter at the royal palace, which probably occupied the area around the present Kingsbury Square.

After Cnut's father Sweyn Forkbeard burnt Wilton to the ground in 1003 it was rebuilt, and in 1143 it was occupied by King Stephen. In the 13th and 14th centuries Wilton declined in importance when its neighbour New Sarum (Salisbury) in 1244 benefitted from the re-routing of the western road from Wilton to New Sarum.

At the dissolution of the monasteries Henry VIII's commissioners visited Wilton Abbey in 1533 and in 1544 the abbey was granted to Sir William Herbert (1501–70), one of Henry VIII's particular friends, who founded the Pembroke family fortunes. In 1577 his son Henry, the 2nd Earl of Pembroke, married as his third wife the beautiful Mary Sidney, and from that time until his death in 1586 her brother Sir Philip Sidney spent much time at Wilton because it was preferable to his own humbler and rather run-down home at Penshurst in Kent. Although Sidney was associated with Wiltshire for only nine years, those years were a period of intense literary activity. It should however be emphasised that the Wilton House that we see today is not the house that Sidney knew as it was extensively remodelled about sixty years after his death.

The Herberts

In his early years Henry VIII's father had as Henry Tudor from the age of five to fourteen been protected and raised by Lord Herbert of Raglan. The man who founded the fortunes of the Wiltshire Herberts and became the 1st Earl of Pembroke was William Herbert (*c.* 1501–70), whose father was an illegitimate son of a Yorkist Earl of Pembroke executed in 1469.

William Herbert was a roistering Welshman often known as 'Black Will Herbert' and described by Aubrey as 'a mad young fighting fellow'. It was alleged that he could neither read nor write, and after killing a man in Bristol he had fled to France and there served so effectively in the army of Francis I that the French monarch intervened on his behalf with Henry VIII. The king allowed him to return to England, where he soon established a reputation as a soldier and became a royal favourite. Soon after his return William Herbert's prospects were further improved when in 1543 his wife's sister Catherine Parr became Henry VIII's last queen. He was granted the monastic estate of Wilton, and was knighted for his part in suppressing the 1549 Cornish Rebellion.

William Herbert, who converted Wilton Abbey into a mansion house, remained close to King Henry, and became one of Edward VI's guardians. Protector Somerset often brought Edward VI to Wilton for his health, unaware that their host was to be instrumental in his fall from power. When Somerset suddenly became aware of the extent of the opposition to his rule and issued a proclamation calling on all loyal subjects to rally to the king and himself at Hampton Court, Herbert then published a counter-proclamation and backed Warwick in his power struggle with the Protector. By the boy king he was made first his Master of Horse and then, in 1551, the 1st Earl of Pembroke of the second creation. He took a prominent part in Somerset's trial and after Somerset's execution in 1552 was granted the Somerset estates in Wiltshire.

William, Earl of Pembroke, was a natural survivor who continued to prosper in troubled times. After in 1553 doing homage to Lady Jane Grey he abruptly changed course, supported the catholic Mary Tudor against Lady Jane Grey, and so became popular with Queen Mary and her consort King Philip of Spain. When Mary died he gained favour with Queen Elizabeth by being one of the nobles who greeted her at Hatfield at her accession. Being a member of the newly created aristocracy Pembroke was regarded as an upstart by the old-established Wiltshire gentry, particularly by his aristocratic neighbour Lord Stourton of Stourton.

Sir Philip Sidney's sister Mary became in 1577 the third wife of William Herbert's son Henry, the 2nd Earl (c. 1534–1601) – the courtier who had in 1553 married as his first wife Lady Catherine Grey, the sister of Lady Jane Grey. William, the 3rd Earl (1580–1630) and the son of Mary and Henry of Pembroke, became like his mother an enthusiastic patron of literature and the arts at Wilton. He was succeeded as 4th Earl by his brother Philip (1584–1650), a rougher character than his brother devoted to field sports. He was named after his uncle Sir Philip Sidney

and was a favourite of James I, although in 1641 he joined the parliamentary party and was in February 1642 made parliament's Lord Lieutenant in Wiltshire.

The standing of Sir Philip Sidney

Sir Philip Sidney (1554–86) is a rather problematical subject because his achievements as poet, courtier, diplomat and soldier failed to match the immense reputation which he was accorded for

Sir Philip Sidney

religious and political reasons after he was killed in his first campaign as a soldier. William Camden extravagantly described him as: 'the great glory of his family, the great hope of mankind. The most lively pattern of virtue, the glory of the world', although in both the political and literary spheres Sidney failed to realise these high hopes. John Aubrey described him as being 'extremely beautiful' and his portraits depict Sidney as a handsome clear-complexioned young man, although some contemporary accounts suggest otherwise. Ben Jonson said that 'Sir P. Sidney was no pleasant man in countenance, his face being spoiled with pimples', and his tutor and physician Thomas Moffatt recorded that his beauty was 'laid waste by small-pox', and that his face was disfigured with 'little-mines'.

Queen Elizabeth owed a considerable debt of gratitude to the Sidney family. Sir Henry Sidney had suffered substantial financial losses as a result of serving her loyally abroad and neglecting his own interests as her Lord Deputy of Ireland, and his wife had as a consequence of nursing her through small-pox in 1562 caught the disease and become so disfigured that she was unable to appear in public. Despite this Elizabeth appears to have always mistrusted their son Philip and obstructed his political progress, so that he was never in control of his future, while seeking preferment at the court of a queen who had inherited some of the fickle temperament of her father. Sidney died aged only thirty-two before his potential in either politics or literature had been fully realised, and yet he became the darling of both the court and the nation, and a symbol of the protestant cause at a time when the traumas of the religious upheavals of the reigns of Henry VIII, Edward VI, Mary and Elizabeth were remembered.

Sir Philip Sidney as a poet

Sidney was in his time extremely highly regarded as a poet, although today his poetry is entirely out of fashion and the work of several of his contemporaries, for example Shakespeare, Jonson, Donne, Spenser, Drayton and Marlowe, has much more appeal to the modern reader. He wrote of how he had 'slipt into the title of a poet' and seems to have had little regard for his poetry. Although none of his writings were published in his lifetime Sidney exerted extraordinary influence on the poetry of his own and succeeding generations, and his influence was enhanced by his reputation as a christian knight, as a protestant champion, and by his romantic death from wounds received in his first campaign as a soldier.

Philip Sidney was a friend of Spenser (c. 1552–59) who dedicated to him his *Shepheard's Calendar* and referred to Sidney as 'the president of noblesse and of chivalry'. His other particular friends were Fulke Greville (1554–1628) who also had several Wiltshire associations (see below), and Edward Dyer (died 1607). These friendships are confirmed in Sidneys poem:

> My two and I be met ;
> A happy blessed Trinitie ;
> As three most joyntly set,
> In firmest band of Unitie.

A later line of the poem included the initials E.D. [Dyer], F.G. [Greville] and P.S., [Sidney], confirming the identities of the 'blessed Trinitie'.

Sidney's friend Fulke Greville

Sidney's friend from childhood was Fulke Greville (1554–1628) who was associated with Wiltshire in a number of ways. He was descended from the great family of Greville woollen manufacturers of Gloucestershire who became the Lords Willoughby de Broke, acquired by marriage into the Willoughby family both Southwick Court and Brook House near Trowbridge, and took their title from Brook which was formerly Broke. The Grevilles also acquired for a time through the Willoughbys Wardour Old Castle in south Wiltshire, but sold it in 1544, the year before Fulke was born. Fulke Greville was an exact contemporary and a fellow school pupil of Philip Sidney and they remained close friends throughout their lives. After being knighted in 1597 Greville was Chancellor of the Exchequer from 1614 to 1621. He was at the age of sixty-six in 1620 created 1st Baron Brooke. James I granted him Warwick Castle and, after outliving Sidney by forty-two years, Greville was murdered in the Ghost Tower of Warwick Castle by an elderly manservant whom he had not included in his will.

Sidney's ancestry and early life

Philip Sidney was on his father's side a member of an ancient yeoman family of French extraction. In the reign (1272–1307) of Edward I a John de Sydenie owned a farm a few miles south of Guildford in Surrey. Sir William Sidney commanded the English right wing at Flodden in 1513, and his son Henry who was knighted in 1551 was brought up with the boy king Edward VI. Sir Henry Sidney (1529–86), who was three-times Lord-Deputy of Ireland, married Lady Mary

Dudley, a sister of the Earl of Leicester and daughter of the Duke of Northumberland. Sir Henry's psalter records that their eldest son Philip was born at a quarter to five on the morning of 30 November 1554.

In addition to being the heir of the Sidneys, Sir Philip was also the heir in the absence of their having legitimate children of the Earls of Warwick and Leicester. It was thought at one time that Leicester would marry the queen. These illustrious connections explain why Sidney was so well received when he went on his Continental travels, and they are also emphasised by the fact that his godfathers were Queen Mary's husband King Philip II of Spain, after whom he was named, and the Earl of Bedford, another man with Dudley connections and a long career of distinguished public service. It is rather ironic that Philip Sidney who became a protestant champion should have been a godson of Philip of Spain, the leading catholic monarch of his time, who when Sidney died fighting catholicism in the Netherlands noted succinctly: 'He was my godson'.

Sir Henry Sidney attempted to create an ancient noble ancestry for his family by paying the herald Robert Cooke six pounds to concoct a fictitious ancestry for him. The Sidneys were in fact descended from a late-13th century Surrey yeoman and during the 15th century had risen rapidly, their rise being accelerated by the marriage of Nicholas Sidney to Anne Brandon, the aunt of a later brother-in-law of Henry VIII. Their son William – Sir Philip Sidney's grandfather – was the founder of the Sidney family fortune, being knighted at Flodden in 1513. At the dissolution of the monasteries he was granted lands in Kent and Sussex, including the castle of Penshurst in Kent which became the Sidney family seat.

Mary Dormer, a niece of Philip Sidney's father, had been the favourite lady-in-waiting of Queen Mary, and two of his sisters (Mabel and Elizabeth) had died in the service of that queen. These catholic connections probably enabled the protestant Sidneys to weather the religious storms during the reign of Queen Mary, and resulted in Philip Sidney becoming Philip of Spain's godson. His relationships to so many of the great men of his time emphasises the insignificance of Sidney's political career.

In October 1565 Sir Henry Sidney was made Lord-Deputy of Ireland with a mandate to extend English control over the whole of Ireland, which had been partially conquered by Henry II and his successors, although during the 14th century the English hold on Ireland had been weakened by Scottish interventions, the Black Death, and Irish resistance. Sir Henry encouraged the 'plantation' of Ireland by English settlers but these were strongly resisted, and in 1578 he was dismissed and subjugation of Ireland was abandoned. On his meagre salary amounting to about five hundred pounds a year after expenses Sidney's father had been unable adequately to maintain the family seat at Penshurst. His son Philip described his home as 'not affecting so much any extraordinary kind of fineness' and as 'more lasting than beautiful' and it was probably the unpretentiousness of the rather run-down Penshurst that made Wilton House so attractive to him. In the words of John Aubrey: 'He lived much in these parts.'

Sir Philip's father died in May 1586 and was followed three months later by his wife Lady Mary, who had as a result of her disfigurement by smallpox led a reclusive life hiding her face from 'curious eyes'. Their son Sir Philip died in the autumn of the same year.

Sidney's education and travels
The young Philip Sidney grew up at Penshurst knowing that he was intended to be a courtier and a servant to his queen. It was his misfortune that he aspired to serve a great but vulnerable and capricious queen who always for some unknown reason obstructed his career. This behaviour may have been connected with the fact that Sidney gloried in the fact that he was a Dudley and the grandson of John Dudley, Duke of Northumberland (c.1505–53), who had attempted to place his daughter-in-law Lady Jane Grey on the throne in place of the catholic Mary.

Sidney was educated at Shrewsbury, where the puritanism of the masters was well-known and dramatic performances were an essential part of the curriculum. He shared his grandfather Northumberland's protestant religion and declared it more ardently than most of his contemporaries. At Shrewsbury school he met his lifelong friend Fulke Greville, and in 1568 he went to Christ Church at Oxford, which he left in 1571 to avoid the plague then raging at Oxford, and consequently did not take a degree. From 1572 to 1575 he is said to have spent two years on the Continent, although a lock of hair exists at Wilton House which was found with the following adulatory text dated 1573 attached:

> This locke of Queen Elizabeths own Hair was presented to Sir Philip Sidney by her Magestys own fair hands on which he made these verses and gave them to the Queen on his bended knee.
>
> ANNO DOMINI 1573
>
> Her inward worth all outward show transcend
> Envy her merit with regret commends
> Like sparkling gems her virtues draw the light
> And in her conduct she is alwaies bright
> When she imparts her thoughts her words have force
> And sense and wisdom flow in sweet discourse.

At the time when he left on his first Continental tour Philip Sidney was described by his uncle the Earl of Leicester as 'young and raw'. During this prolonged tour (1572–5) he was at the French court at the time of the massacre of St Bartolomew on 24 August 1572. He sheltered at the English embassy in Paris and then visited Germany, Poland, Hungary and Italy, where protestants were liable to be arrested as heretics. In Venice he was met by his cousin Richard Shelley, of the family from whom the poet sprang, but he was unimpressed by 'all the magnificent magnificences of all these magnificos'. When he decided to have his portrait painted as a record of his visit he discarded Titian as too old and, after hesitating between Tintoretto and Veronese, he decided on the latter, but the portrait is now lost. In 1575 Sidney returned to England, having been everywhere well received.

Astrophel and Stella

Upon his return to England in 1575 Sidney embarked on his life as a courtier. Eight years earlier, in August 1567, the Duke of Alva had descended with his Spanish army on the Netherlands to subdue the 'men of butter' who had revolted against Spanish occupation. England was at this time a comparatively minor nation and Queen Elizabeth's policy was to support the Dutch rebels financially but not intervene directly, in the hope that the Spaniards would be banished from the Netherlands without letting in the French who were now showing an interest in that country. Sidney now began to foster the idea of a protestant alliance between England and the Netherlands against the power of Spain. In that year (1575) Sidney became acquainted with Walter Devereux, the 1st Earl of Essex and Earl Marshal of Ireland (1541–76), and in 1576 he accompanied Essex to Ireland, of which he probably already had some knowledge from his father's appointments. The Earl's daughter was Penelope Devereux, and when they first met Philip Sidney was twenty-one and Penelope thirteen. An attempt was made by their families to arrange a marriage but Sidney demonstrated little interest in his prospective bride until she had become unattainable after marrying elsewhere.

Penelope Devereux is generally recognised to have been the Stella of Sidney's *Astrophel and Stella*, a sequence of 108 sonnets and eleven songs which he wrote between 1580 and 1584. He is believed to have obtusely arrived at the name Astrophel from the fact that a contraction of his name 'Phil. Sid.' was an abbreviation of *Philos sidus*. By substituting the Greek *astron* for the Latin *sidus* he arrived at *astron philos*, meaning 'star lover', the star being Penelope Devereux – whom he also referred to as Stella, meaning star. His passion for Penelope seems to have developed after she had been married against her wishes to Lord Rich in 1580. The Rich marriage was unhappy. Penelope became the mistress of Sir Charles Blount, and after divorcing Lord Rich she ultimately married Sir Charles in 1605, nineteen years after Sidney's death. Sidney refers to Penelope in his *Sonnet 37* as one that: 'Hath no misfortune, but that Rich she is'. His best-known sonnet is Number 31 which begins:

> With how sad steps, o Moone, thou climbst the skies,
> How silently, and with how wan a face

and has been described as being 'as fine as any of the lyrics produced in the Elizabethan age'.

The sonnets of *Astrophel and Stella* were widely circulated, and when they were posthumously published without the consent of Sidney's family in 1591 they prompted an outburst of imitative sonnet cycles. After Sidney's death Edmund Spenser in about 1589 wrote a pastoral which he called *Astrophel* in his friend's memory, and in 1591 he followed it with *The Ruins of Time*, a further elegy for Sir Philip Sidney, which he dedicated to Sidney's sister Mary. Sir Walter Raleigh also wrote *An Epitaph upon Sir Philip Sidney*.

Sidney's fall from Royal favour

In 1577 when he was twenty-six Philip Sidney was entrusted with a mission to the Elector Palatine and William the Silent. His future as a courtier then seemed assured, but he prejudiced his career when in 1580 he remonstrated with the queen against her proposal to marry one of her French catholic suitors, the Duke of Anjou and Alençon. In this he may have been merely the spokesman for the more powerful protestant objectors Walsingham and Leicester, but his letter to the queen was tactless in stressing the widespread opposition in the country to a catholic marriage. This protest appears to have blighted Sidney's career, for subsequently the queen seems to have mistrusted him, and he never attained any official appointment that accorded with his ambitions.

Now decidedly out of favour Sidney retired to Wilton for a year and then, although having apparently forfeited Elizabeth's favour, he was in 1583 made a Knight of the Garter as Sir Philip Sidney of Penshurst. That year he also sat in parliament as member for Kent but as he continued to be denied important office Sidney became progressively disillusioned and began to find attendance at court unappealing. The neglect encouraged his literary activities and he also began to seriously consider a military career fighting with the protestant forces on the Continent. He never fully regained the trust of the queen, who seems to have decided that he was a potentially troublesome man, and yet he longed to serve her by playing a part in the affairs of the nation.

In 1583 Sidney married Frances, the daughter of Sir Francis Walsingham, a lady who seems always to have meant less to him than Penelope Devereux and his sister Mary Herbert. Although he continued to spend much time away from home at Wilton during their three-year marriage Frances bore Sidney a daughter, while he continued to write sonnets to Penelope, the unhappy wife of Lord Rich.

In July 1584 Sidney obtained the appointment of joint Master of the Ordnance, and that same month Prince William of Orange was assassinated at Delft. The heraldry of the Sidneys of Penshurst included a pheon (that is a broad barbed arrow), and since Sir Philip was appointed joint Master of Ordnance the War Department has marked its property with a broad arrow. The death of William of Orange forced Elizabeth as the only protestant leader left in Europe to commit English troops to the Netherlands. An army was despatched under the Earl of Leicester, and in 1585 Sidney was appointed by the queen military governor of Flushing, a seaport on the south coast of Walcheren at the mouth of the River Scheldt, which had in the war against Spain been ceded by the Dutch to England to serve as an English garrison town. Sidney had now become directly involved in the religious war against Spain.

The queen's lack of consideration for Sidney is illustrated by an incident which occurred in the Netherlands in the last year of his life, when his father died from a chill caught travelling by barge from Bewdley to Worcester. Sidney applied for permission to visit England and settle his family affairs and comfort his sick mother – who it should be remembered had been disfigured by smallpox as a direct result of nursing Queen Elizabeth through that disease. She died later that year. Despite this fact, and Sir Henry's prolonged honourable and largely unrewarded service to the crown, the queen ordered Sidney to remain in the Netherlands.

A fact that is very relevant to Sir Philip Sidney's ultimate military career is recorded by Aubrey when he wrote that: 'Tilting was much used at Wilton in the time of Henry, Earl of Pembroke, and Sir Philip Sydney', for it is likely that Sidney's idea of adopting a military career as a substitute for his failed political career arose from his successes when taking part in the tournaments. These took place on the high ridge of downland known as Bemerton Heath, a mile north-east of Wilton and mid-way between Bemerton and Old Sarum, which had been one of the great Medieval tournament grounds after Richard I introduced into England the Continental practice of tournament jousting in 1194 at five sites in England. One of these was at Bemerton on 'the elevated airy down', in full view of the majestic fortress of Old Sarum on the one hand, and of Wilton and its venerable abbey on the other. Bemerton Heath is now covered by modern housing although a large open space survives at its centre and one of its roads is Tournament Road.

Sidney was, like his uncle Leicester, a fine horseman and patronised two Italian riding-masters who worked in England. A description survives of his equipage at a tournament which took place at Whitehall at Whitsun 1581:

> Then proceeded Mr Philip Sidney in a very sumptuous manner, with armour part blue and the rest gilt and engraven, with four spare horses having caparisons and furniture very rich and costly . . . He had four pages that rode on his four spare horses who had cassock coats and Venetian hose all of cloth of silver, laid with gold lace and hats of the same with gold bands and white feathers, and each one a pair of white buskins. Then had he thirty gentlemen and yeomen and four trumpeters who were all in cassock coats and Venetian hose of yellow velvet laid with silver lace, yellow velvet caps with silver bands and white feathers, and every one a pair of white buskins.

Arcadia

Sidney's finest literary works were his pastoral romance *Arcadia* and his *Apology for Poetry* which was renamed *Defence of Poesie. Arcadia* was written in 1580, the year that he spent out of royal favour at Wilton, and became regarded as the greatest of Elizabethan prose romances. Arcadia was a district of the Peloponnesus in Greece and was according to Virgil the home of pastoral simplicity. *Arcadia* exists in two versions, the original completed in 1581 known as the *Old*

Arcadia, and the second version made by Sidney 1583–4 but never completed and known as the *New Arcadia*. The latter was printed in 1590 and then reprinted in 1593 as a composite of both versions, and it was this that was the only version available to readers until the *Old Arcadia* was discovered in 1906. The published version was for long known as *The Countess of Pembroke's Arcadia* because she had suggested the subject to her brother, who dedicated the work to his 'dear lady and sister', who saw it page by page as it was written, and after her brother's death in collaboration with Fulke Greville revised and expanded *Arcadia*. Sidney's dedication reads:

> You desired me to do it, and your desire to my heart is an absolute commandment. Now it is done only for you, only to you: if you keep it to yourself, or commend it to such friends who will weigh errors in the balance of goodwill, I hope, for the father's sake, it will be pardoned, perchance made much of, though in itself it have deformities. For indeed, for severer eyes it is not, being but a trifle, and that triflingly handled. Your dear self can best witness the manner, being done in loose sheets of paper, most of it in your presence ; the rest by sheets sent unto you, as fast as they were done . . .

Longford Castle

Much of *Arcadia* was written by Sidney when riding out on the vast Pembroke estates in south Wiltshire, principally in Vernditch Chase on the Dorset border, but also at the ruins of the Norman priory of Ivychurch and the adjoining Clarendon Park in south-east Wiltshire. His 'Castle of Amphialeus' was based on Longford Castle, south-east of Salisbury in the Avon Valley. Aubrey tells us:

He [Sidney] was often at Wilton with his sister, and at Ivy-church (which adjoyns the parke pale of Clarindon Parke) situated on a hill that over-lookes all the country westwards, and North over Sarum and the plaines, and into the delicious parke (which was accounted the best of England),

and that: 'Mary, Countess of Pembroke, much delighted in this place' [Ivychurch], which was then leased by the Pembrokes from the Dean and Chapter of Salisbury.

Vernditch Chase was in Sidney's time far more extensive than the comparatively small wood that survives today. Ivychurch Priory was demolished in 1888, although two Norman columns from an arcade and the springing of their arches still stand, some carved remnants are built into the wall of Ivychurch Farm, and some small paired Norman

Remains at Ivychurch Priory where Sidney wrote part of Arcadia

columns from Ivychurch were in 1897 incorporated in the village drinking fountain at Alderbury. John Aubrey recorded how Sidney :

> . . . was wont, when hunting on our pleasant plaines, to take his Table booke out of his pocket, and write downe his notions as they came into his head, when he was writing Arcadia (which was never finished by him) . . . These Romancy Plaines, and Boscages did no doubt conduce to the heightening of Sir Philip Sidney's Phansie.

Although Sidney considered *Arcadia* 'but a trifle' it became the most popular work of fiction for a hundred and fifty years after its composition. Such popularity is now difficult to comprehend, a fact debated by that fine poetry critic Edward Thomas when he wrote in 1914:

Vernditch

. . . we should like to know, why and how *Arcadia* and similar books appealed to the men and women of England from 1590 to 1630, during which ten editions were called for. What kind of truth and beauty they saw in it; what part of humanity was moved by it; whether they detected the influence of Wilton and Salisbury Plain.

Arcadia has never been universally admired. Milton thought it 'vain and amatorious', Hazlitt considered it to be 'one of the greatest monuments to the abuse of intellectual power upon record'. In more recent times T. S. Eliot described it as: 'a monument of dullness'.

Sidney's New World episode

Recognising that his career as a courtier and diplomat was being stifled by the queen, and having little regard for his poetry, Sidney turned his thoughts to becoming a soldier, with the intention of becoming a protestant champion in opposition to catholic Spain's occupation of the Low Countries. When England was in 1585 granted by treaty control of Flushing, Brill and Fort Rammekens as security for English aid to the Netherlands against the catholic league, the Dutch wanted Sidney, for whom they had a high regard, to be Governor of Flushing. Queen Elizabeth however demurred and Sidney, fearing that someone else would be appointed, dreamt up an alternative scheme to embark upon an expedition to the New World. Sir Francis Drake (*c.* 1540–96) was approached, and a land and sea expedition was arranged to be jointly led by Drake and Sidney, with Drake being the nominal leader until they left England.

Drake assembled his ships at Plymouth and in August 1585 summoned Sidney, who secretly left court accompanied by Fulke Greville and went down to Plymouth. They found that the fleet was not ready to sail and there was friction between Sidney and Drake. Fulke Greville began to smell a rat and his suspicions were justified when Drake wrote to the queen disclosing Sidney's intentions and Elizabeth immediately ordered Sidney to return to London. The entire episode was probably a stratagem to force Elizabeth's hand and, whether or not the queen believed that Sidney had really intended to accompany Drake to the New World, she reluctantly appointed him Governor of Flushing. She would not have been pleased at having been outwitted.

Sidney's death and funeral

Having secured his appointment Sidney sailed to the Netherlands and was enthusiastically received at Flushing, while Fulke Greville remained behind at court in some disfavour for his part in the matter. Soon after his arrival at Flushing on 23 September 1586 Sidney decided to join an attack by Sir John Norris on a Spanish column of troops near Zutphen which was making for Arnhem. It appears to have been an ill-conceived escapade, for Norris had only 300 foot and 200 horse, the latter including 60 young gentlemen of birth whom he had been particularly ordered to take care of, while the enemy column numbered about 3,000 foot and 1,500 horse. Despite these odds Norris in a fit of bravado attacked the column and succeeded in inflicting heavy losses, although he failed to prevent the column from getting into Zutphen. While waiting for the enemy to appear Sidney, according to Fulke Greville, discovered that his friend Sir William Pelham had failed to put on his cuisses (leg-armour). Unwilling to fight better protected than his friend, Sidney discarded his own leg armour, had one horse shot under him, mounted another, and was then hit by a musket ball a little above his unprotected knee. He succeeded in riding back to camp where his wound was treated.

It was at this point that the legend arose about Sidney's gallant conduct for which Fulke Greville (who was not present) is the only authority. In his *Life of Sir Philip Sidney* Greville wrote:

In which sad progress, passing along by the rest of the army, where his uncle [Leicester] the General was, and being thirsty with excess of bleeding, he [Sidney] called for a drink. But as he was putting the bottle to his mouth, he saw a poor soldier carried along, who had eaten his last at that same feast, ghastly casting up his eyes at the bottle. Which Sir Philip perceiving, took it from his head before he drank and delivered it to the poor man with these words, 'Thy necessity is yet greater than mine.' And when he had pledged this poor soldier, he was presently carried to Arnhem.

Although this story may be authentic it could equally be part of the propaganda which was mounted after Sidney's death, which occurred after he was removed to Arnhem. Here he died on 17 October after enduring twenty-six days of intense suffering. On his deathbed he wrote a will leaving his estates including Penshurst to his brother Robert, his junior by nine years. Dr John James, who was present at Sidney's bedside at his death, wrote: 'Few ages have brought forth his equal, and the very hope of our age seemed to be utterly extinguished in him'. Leicester wrote to Walsingham notifying him of Sidney's death and suggesting, rather pointedly in view of Elizabeth's treatment of Sidney, that: 'none of all hath a greater loss than the Queen's Majesty herself'.

Queen Elizabeth had never favoured Sidney. There may have been something in his personality that displeased her, or she may never have forgiven him for opposing her proposed French marriage when she was forty. She openly lamented the failure of this proposal, and later referred to Sidney as 'that inconsiderate fellow'. Possibly she held his ancestry against him, remembering that he was a grandson of the Duke of Northumberland who had attempted to subvert the succession by placing his daughter-in-law Lady Jane Grey on the throne instead of her sister Mary in 1553. Two years after Sidney's death the queen, perhaps in a fit of remorse, appointed Sidney's brother Sir Robert Sidney Governor of Flushing, a post which he held for twenty-eight years before becoming Earl of Leicester.

The Elizabethans left the world with an ostentation which matched their exuberant life-styles. Sidney's body was conveyed by boat from Arnhem to Flushing, where it lay in state for eight days. On 1 November it was brought with great ceremony to England in *The Black Pinnace* and was landed at Tower Hill.

Sir Philip Sidney's romantic death in an ill-advised skirmish against the armies of catholic oppression in the Netherlands caught the imagination of the nation, and his funeral on 16 February 1587 rivalled in grandeur that of a peer of the realm. His father-in-law Sir Francis Walsingham 'spared not any cost to have this funeral well-performed', and the populace of London thronged the streets to see his cortège pass. Sidney's charger was ridden by one of his pages bearing a symbolic broken lance, this page being Henry Danvers (1573–1643), the second son of Sir John Danvers of Dauntsey in Wiltshire, who according to Aubrey 'accounted himselfe happy that his son was so bestowed'. Henry Danvers was to figure prominently in national history as the Earl of Danby. He was a favourite of James I's son Prince Henry, and was knighted in 1633.

Sir Philip Sidney's monument in Old St Paul's was less imposing than his funeral. His tomb and that of Sir Francis Walsingham were crowded by the ostentatious adjoining tomb of Queen Elizabeth's favourite Sir Christopher Hatton (1540–91), who had gained her favour by his dancing, causing the following doggerel couplet to be circulated:

> Sir Philip, Sir Francis have no tomb,
> For great Sir Christopher takes all the room.

Sidney's capacity for friendship is illustrated by the inscription which associates his name with two monarchs on the tomb of his friend Fulke Greville at Warwick. It reads:

> Here lies the body of Fulke Grevile, Knight, Servant to Queen Elizabeth, Counsellor to King James, and Friend to Sir Philip Sidney.

Mary Herbert, Countess of Pembroke

That Sir Philip Sidney was frequently at Wilton over the nine years from 1577 to his death in 1586 was entirely due to the fact that his sister

Mary (1561–1621) in 1577 became Countess of Pembroke by marrying at sixteen into the Pembrokes, who had then owned Wilton for merely twenty-six years.

Mary, Countess of Pembroke

Mary Sidney was both learned and beautiful. She spent most of her childhood at Ludlow Castle where her father resided as President of Wales. She was well educated and her brother Philip, who was seven years her senior, was her constant childhood companion. When her sister Ambrosia died in 1575 Queen Elizabeth wrote a letter of condolence to her parents suggesting that their other daughter Mary should come to court. Her parents complied and in 1575 at the age of only fourteen Mary became a member of the royal household and accompanied the queen on her royal progresses. Two years later she became the wife of the widowed Earl of Pembroke and went to live at the family seat at Wilton. Her husband was celebrated for his prowess at tilting and was appointed Lord Lieutenant of Wiltshire, and in 1586 Lord President of Wales, the office that had been held by his wife's father Sir Henry Sidney.

In addition to several salacious stories about her Aubrey provides us with a short description of Mary Countess of Pembroke:

> She was a beautiful Ladie and had an excellent witt, and had the best breeding that that age could afford. Shee had a pritty sharp-ovall face. Her haire was of a reddish yellowe.

Aubrey also tells us that Mary Sidney was: 'the greatest patronesse of witt and learning of any Lady in her time'.

Nine years after her marriage, Mary Herbert suffered in a single year (1586) the triple deaths of her father, her mother, and her brother Sir Philip Sidney. In her grief she dedicated herself to completing the literary works that her brother had contemplated or left incomplete. Sir John Harington believed that her poetry would 'outlast Wilton's walls'. When at his death in 1601 her husband left her ill provided for, James I gave Mary an estate at Ampthill in Bedfordshire where she built Houghton House, which became the 'palace beautiful' of Bunyan's *The Pilgrim's Progress*. This house is of interest in that in style it resembled Longford Castle with classical loggias, but with corner towers in the style of the old Wilton House prior to the addition of its Palladian front in the mid-17th century. Mary died in 1621 having outlived her brother by thirty-five years, during which she had patronised at Wilton many men of letters. She lies beneath a small brass before the altar in the choir of Salisbury cathedral and her beautiful epitaph – for long believed to have been written by Ben Jonson but now attributed to William Browne – reads:

> Underneath this marble hearse,
> Lies the subject of all verse;
> Sidney's sister, Pembrokes mother
> Death! ere thou hast slain another
> Wise and fair and good as she,
> Time shall throw a dart at thee.

Writers at Wilton in the late-17th century

The pastoral poet William Browne (1591–1643) was one of the galaxy of brilliant writers who were attracted to Wilton by Mary, Countess of Pembroke, when she established what is best described as an academy of literature at Wilton House during the time (1570–1601) of her husband the 2nd Earl of Pembroke, and of her son William, the 3rd Earl (1601–1630). After her death in 1621 the 'academy' continued for a time under Philip, named after Philip Sidney, who was the 4th Earl from 1630 to 1649. Aubrey, who made Mary Herbert the subject of one of his *Brief Lives*, tells us that 'In her time Wilton was like a college, there were so many learned and ingenious persons'.

In addition to Sir Philip Sidney and William Browne, who according to Anthony Wood was taken into the Herbert household and there 'got wealth and purchased an estate', other writers who were frequently at Wilton House included Spenser (c. 1552–99), Shakespeare (1564–1616), Ben Jonson (c. 1573–1637), who addressed his *Epigram to the Honoured Countess* to Mary, and Isaak Walton (1593–1640). These were virtual contemporaries except for Isaak Walton who was of a later generation.

Spenser addressed his long poem *The Faerie Queene* to Mary, Countess of Pembroke, and sang her praises as:

> The gentlest shepherdess that lives this day
> And most resembling both in shape and spright
> Her brother deare.

Another Elizabethan poet and dramatist who joined the Wilton literary circle was Samuel Daniel (1562–1619), who became tutor to the 3rd Earl of Pembroke and then to Lady Anne Clifford. Later he went into the household of James I's queen Anne of Denmark, and in 1604 became Licencer for the Children of the Queen's Revels. This post he resigned in 1605 when it was alleged that his tragedy *Philotas* was sympathetic to the 1600 rebellion of the Earl of Essex. He recovered his position at court but retired to Beckington in Somerset on the borders of west Wiltshire, between Frome and Trowbridge, where he died and is commemorated by a fine wall monument in the church erected by Lady Anne Clifford. His most famous lyric begins:

Care-charmer sleep, son of the sable night,
Brother to death, in silent darkness born.

During the Romantic period Daniel's poetry was greatly admired by Lamb and Wordsworth, and also by Coleridge who found his language as 'pure and manly' as that of Wordsworth.

At Wilton Shakespeare is believed to have produced some of his plays, and credible tradition suggests that he acted here in 1603 before James I in *As You Like It*. His friendship with the Pembrokes has prompted the suggestion that the 'W H' who was the 'onlie begetter' of Shakespeare's sonnets was a Herbert, possibly the 3rd Earl William Herbert, particularly as the first folio of Shakespeare's works was dedicated in 1623 to the 3rd Earl of Pembroke and his brother Philip the 4th Earl.

The playwright Philip Massinger (1583–1640) was the son of Arthur Massinger (d. 1603), who was the Earl of Pembroke's solicitor and became MP for Weymouth and Shaftesbury. In Massinger's play *A New Way to Pay Old Debts* (1633) Sir Giles Overreach is based upon a Wiltshireman, Sir Giles Mompesson (1584–c.1681) who became notorious for corruption, was found guilty by the House of Lords and banished, but contrived to live nearly thirty years in retirement in Wiltshire before dying in about 1681. As his wife was a St John he was buried in Lydiard Tregoze church near Swindon with a monument near the chancel.

Although archaeology was not then recognised and Stonehenge was in the 17th century generally regarded as a mere mysterious pile of stones, in the 16th century visits to 'the stones' first became fashionable. The Wilton poets sometimes visited Stonehenge, and several were inspired to write about the ancient monument. Sidney wrote:

Near Wilton sweet, huge heaps of stone are found
But so confused that neither any eye
Can count them just, nor reason reason try
What force brought them to so unlikely ground

and Spenser refers to Stonehenge in *The Faerie Queene* (Book ii: 10). Samuel Daniel speculated:

And whereto serves that wondrous trophy now

That on the goodly plain near Wilton stands?
That huge dumb heap that cannot tell us how
Nor what, nor whence it is nor with whose hands
Nor for whose glory it was set to show
How much our pride mocks that of other lands.

George Herbert

Most of the poets associated with Wilton were merely visitors, but a short-term resident of this area was was the saintly parson-poet George Herbert (1593–1633). He was a distant relative of the Earl of Pembroke, and was already associated with Wiltshire in several ways when towards the end of his short life he became from 1630 to 1633 vicar of Bemerton beside the River Nadder between Salisbury and Wilton. George Herbert's appointment was due to Mary Pembroke's son William, the 3rd Earl of Pembroke (1580–1630), who in the last year of his life persuaded Charles I to appoint him vicar of Bemerton and Fugglestone.

George Herbert's father died when he was three and in 1608 his mother Magdelen Herbert married Sir John Danvers of Wiltshire who was twenty years her junior. At Westminster School Herbert was a classical scholar and an accomplished musician, music being his 'chiefest pleasure'. In 1612 he published a volume of Latin poems mourning the early death of Prince Henry. He studied at Trinity College, Cambridge, where he became public orator 1620–7 with a view to a career at Court. In 1624 and 1625 he was MP for Montgomery and was hesitating between the attractions of a court or a religious life when the almost simultaneous deaths of his two principal patrons, the Duke of Richmond and the Marquess of Hamilton, and of James I in 1625 blighted his prospects at court.

Herbert now took holy orders and was ordained in 1630. At Lord Danby's house at Dauntsey in north Wiltshire he had met Jane Danvers, the daughter of Charles Danvers of Bayntun. It is said that Jane's father was so impressed by George Herbert when he met him on a visit to Dauntsey that he did all he could to further the match. They were married at Edington church east of Westbury and for a year lived at

Dauntsey House, but when in 1630 the rector of Bemerton was made Bishop of Bath and Wells George Herbert obtained his living. Although Herbert was of the Laudian party which opposed the puritans and advocated that churches should be embellished, in his pious life as a clergyman he practised the christian humility that pervades his writings, and at Bemerton he spent the few years left to him caring for his parishioners with humility and charity and writing the spiritual poetry for which he is now remembered.

Bemerton church

Most of Herbert's poetry is included in *The Temple* (1633), a collection of 160 religious poems which provided the Anglican church with its finest expression in verse, and was read by Charles I in prison. In prose he wrote *A Priest to the Temple*, which his first biographer Isaak Walton considered to be 'plain, prudent, useful rules for the country parson', although it was not printed until 1652. The reputation as a poet that Herbert obtained in the 17th century waned in the 18th century, but Coleridge did much to restore it with an appreciative notice in *Biographia Literaria* (1817), and today George Herbert's poetry is held in high regard, much higher than Sidney's.

Bemerton church and rectory were restored by George Herbert, who after leading a blameless life died at his rectory in 1633. He was buried near the altar and commemorated by a modest wall tablet inscribed 'G H 1633'. His church was the little 14th-century church of St Andrew with its timber belfry, which still contains the bells

which Herbert tolled for his congregation. The new church of St John was built much later in 1860. Opposite the old church stands George Herbert's flint-built rectory with its garden running down to the Nadder, the house which Isaak Walton described as 'the good and more pleasant than healthful parsonage', suggesting that the house may then have been insanitary and could have contributed to George Herbert's early death at the age of only forty, just three years after he moved into it.

Herbert was the subject of one of Aubrey's *Brief Lives*, and his friend Isaak Walton wrote his biography which was published in 1670. He was a keen musician, and Walton describes how Herbert walked twice a week from Bemerton to Salisbury to hear the music in the cathedral, an experience that he regarded as 'heaven on earth'.

Bemerton parsonage house

Palladianism at Wilton

The Wilton House that we see today differs greatly from the Wilton House known by Sir Philip Sidney and his sister Mary. The house with which they were familiar would have been the rambling buildings of the Medieval abbey as adapted by the 1st Earl of Pembroke into a mansion. The principal accommodation, including the great hall, was then in the north wing and was

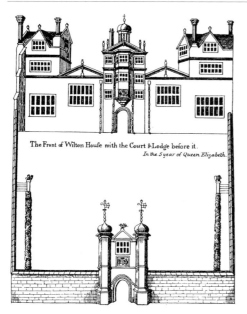

The Front of Wilton House with the Court & Lodge before it.
In the 5 year of Queen Elizabeth.

Wilton House as Sidney would have known it (from WANHM vol. 15)

approached through an archway in the east wing. Coaches drove through this arch into an inner quadrangle, the house being entered through a porch which is known as the Holbein porch, from allegedly having been designed by Hans Holbein the Younger (1497–1543), the German painter who was often in England and painted many eminent Englishmen. Pevsner wrote of Wilton: 'Of this house, which was built round a courtyard, the general shape remains, and certainly the so-called HOLBEIN PORCH, now a garden ornament to the W of the S front, but originally the porch from the courtyard to the Great Hall, which lay in the N range'. If Pevsner's dating of this porch as about 1560–70 is correct Sidney and his sister would have known it.

Wilton is a place of immense significance in the development of Palladianism in Britain, because here may be seen in Wilton House one of the greatest 17th-century Palladian buildings in Britain, which provided a model for many later buildings in that style, the covered bridge which is a fine example of the early-18th century second-phase of Palladianism and was copied at Stowe and Prior Park, and several small build-

ings designed by Sir William Chambers (1723–96), sometimes known as 'the last of the Palladians'.

The south front of Wilton, which was added to the house in about 1650, became the prototype for a particular type of Palladian building with raised corner towers which, although this form seems to have arisen at Wilton by accident because the existing building had corner towers, was subsequently frequently emulated by the 18th-century Palladian architects, a fine example being Lydiard Park near Swindon in north Wiltshire.

The scheme for re-fronting Wilton House had been suggested to the 4th Earl of Pembroke by Charles I who was frequently at Wilton. One of King Charles's virtues was his supreme taste in art and architecture, and the 4th Earl took his cue from his king and encouraged at Wilton the pursuits of art and literature. Aubrey, an almost contemporary observer who should have known the truth, recorded that the king encouraged Pembroke to rebuild Wilton in the Palladian style practised by his royal surveyor Inigo Jones:

> His Majesty intended to have it [Wilton House] designed by his own architect, Mr Inigo Jones, who being at that time engaged in His Majestie's buildings at Greenwich could not attend to it; but he recommended it to an ingenious architect Monsieur Solomon de Caus, a Gascoigne, who performed it very well; but not without the advice and approbation of Mr Jones; for which his Lordship settled a pension on him [de Caus] of, I think, a hundred pounds per annum for life, and lodging in the house. He died in about 1656.

Aubrey has evidently confused two members of the de Caus family because Solomon (1576–1626) left England in about 1613 and died in France, having been engineer and possibly also drawing master to Prince Henry, who died in 1612. His son or nephew Isaac de Caus was a designer of gardens and grottoes employed at Wilton by Philip, 4th Earl of Pembroke.

The architect of the south front of Wilton House has been a matter of some discussion. Its design was for long attributed to Inigo Jones, who seems to have been involved, although in 1650

Wilton House: the Palladian south front

he was seventy-seven and he died in 1652. Consequently the design is now usually attributed to John Webb, who had married Inigo Jones's niece and often worked with him. The Wilton south front is a very restrained exterior, in marked contrast to the exuberance of the magnificent state rooms which lie behind it, and in this respect it fulfils the maxim expressed by Jones that a building should reflect the temperament of a wise man, in that: 'outwardly every wise man carries a gravity, yet inwardly has his imagination set on fire and sometimes licentiously flies out'.

The south front of Wilton House has an unusual appearance for a Palladian building because its centrepiece is not the usual columnar and pedimented feature, but a Venetian window embellished with figures reclining above the arched centre light. This is explained by the fact that the frontage as built is less than half the length of the original design, which was intended to have a pedimented central feature and a similar range to its west repeating what now exists. Drawings prepared by de Caus showing this full-width frontage related to the formal garden which he was designing and the scheme for the reduced frontage have survived. The reduction seems to

have been a consequence of the uncertainties raised by the Civil War, during which the Earl of Pembroke transferred his allegiance from his friend the king to parliament just in time to save his estates.

The exquisite covered Palladian bridge at Wilton was built in 1737 to the design of Roger Morris (1695–1749) although the architect Henry, 9th Earl of Pembroke (1693–1751), is often credited with its design.

Lady Anne Clifford,Countess of Pembroke

Mary, Countess of Pembroke, lived until 1621 and in 1630 Lady Anne Clifford (1590–1676) married as her second husband Mary's son Philip, the 4th Earl of Pembroke (1584–1650), and became Countess of Pembroke. This interesting lady was the sole surviving child of George, 3rd Duke of Cumberland, a former Elizabethan privateer. At the age of nineteen she had married the twenty-year-old Richard Sackville (1588–1623) who that year (1609) became 3rd Earl of Dorset. To finance his extravagant life-style at Knole in Kent he sold the more easily disposed elements of his inheritance and mortgaged the house. Lady Anne's father left his estates to his brother, apparently unaware of an entail that made his daughter his rightful heir, and Lady Anne was obliged to enter into lawsuits to secure her Cumberland inheritance. After securing it despite general opposition Lady Anne's marriage became tempestuous, as she fought to keep her vast estates out of the hands of her spendthrift husband, whom she nevertheless regarded with affection and described as 'the best and most worthy man that ever lived'.

When Richard Sackville died in 1623 leaving huge debts, Lady Anne vowed never to marry again, but in 1630 she was persuaded to marry Philip, the 4th Earl of Pembroke, and become mistress of Wilton House. The architectural historian Sir Roy Strong has pointed out how much influence Lady Anne, an enthusiastic builder, then had on the reconstruction of Wilton House and gardens which was begun in 1632, two years after her marriage to the 4th Earl.

After the death of her husband in 1650 Lady Anne returned to her estates in the north of England, where she spent a pleasurable old age, living to be eighty-six, busying herself by restoring her houses, entertaining her many grandchildren, and acting as hereditary High Sheriff.

Sidney's posthumous reputation

A fully authorised edition of Sidney's work was published in 1590 by his sister Mary Herbert, and it was with this posthumous publication of his work that the idea of Sidney as the perfect image of militant protestant Christianity emerged. Although Charles Lamb wrote: 'Sydney's sonnets – I speak of the best of them – are among the very best of their sort', his poetic legacy is now regarded as being of no great significance. On his deathbed at Arnhem Sidney confessed that 'he had walked in a vague course', and his life was perhaps best summed up by Fulke Greville when he suggested that his friend never found 'a fit stage for his eminence to act upon'.

During his life and after his death there seems to have been an orchestrated campaign to enhance Sidneys reputation as poet, politician and soldier. Despite his recognition as a great poet in his time Sidney's poetry has not maintained its popularity and is seldom read today. His career as a courtier and diplomat was blighted by Elizabeth's distrust, and even as a soldier Sidney never achieved any real reputation, as he was mortally wounded in his first campaign, although as a result of his romantic death he became a national protestant icon.

Wilton: the Palladian Bridge

6 John Aubrey
of Easton Piercy and Broad Chalke

At the east end of Seend the road executes a short loop around a large house which is perched in an imposing position on the edge of the Seend Ridge, with extensive views south to the north escarpment of Salisbury Plain. When passing this house, which is now known as Seend Park, I am invariably reminded of the Wiltshire writer and antiquary John Aubrey (1626–97) because Joan Sumner, the lady who brought the breach of promise action against him which led to his ultimate financial ruin, lived for a time at an earlier house on this site. Aubrey was a native of Wiltshire who circulated in the very highest society, associated with royalty, and always retained an immense pride in his Wiltshire birth, which he revealed when he wrote of his fellow Wiltshireman Thomas Hobbes: 'Though he left his native countrey at 14, and lived so long, yet sometimes one might find a little touch of our pronounciation'.

The two parts of Wiltshire with which Aubrey is particulary associated are in the north of the county the sparsely populated area of scattered farms west of the A429 around Kington St Michael, and in the south the village of Broad Chalke situated on the little River Ebble between the Ebble-Nadder Ridge and Cranborne Chase. He was born in the former, was particularly fond of Broad Chalke and nearby Cranborne Chase, and he inherited from his father properties in both areas, but he was also familiar with most of Wiltshire.

Aubrey is one of the most attractive of all Wiltshire personalities. There is something very appealing about the way in which he muddled through life and managed somehow to extricate himself from his many difficulties by making virtues out of necessities. His agreeable character is attested by the fact that despite all his troubles he kept most of his friends. On the other hand his reputation has suffered because he so much relished life and was so easily distracted from any enterprise which he took up that he was incapable of finishing any work that he started. His reputation was also adversely affected by the vindictiveness of his associate Anthony Wood (1632–95), the Oxford historian and antiquarian with whom he had a stormy relationship, although it should be recognised that Wood, who described Aubrey as 'magotie-headed and sometimes little better than crased', was derogatory about many of his associates. In fact Aubrey had a number of very good friends who were much more significant than Anthony Wood. These included the philosophers Hobbes and Locke, the diarist John Evelyn, and the mathematician and architect Sir Christopher Wren, in addition to the scientists Boyle and Newton, writers Isaak Walton and Samuel Butler, and the poets Marvell and Dryden. Aubrey was also a founder member of the Royal Society.

Although an obsessive collector of facts and myths John Aubrey regularly failed to present them in an orderly form that would make them useful to his contemporaries or his successors, a fact that he recognised when he admitted: 'I now set things down tumultuarily, as if tumbled out of a Sack'. He died believing that he was a failure who had frittered away his inheritance and made no mark in the world, but posterity has judged otherwise and John Aubrey would not have believed the esteem in which he is held today as a brilliant observer and recorder of the 17th-century scene, a pioneer field archaeologist, as a biographer of his contemporaries, and as a peerless relater of amusing and sometimes scurrilous incidents. He was a master at recording the memorable mo-

John Aubrey (from WANHM *vol. 4)*

ment, as when he recalled the Bishop of Oxford when confronted by a man with a large beard addressing him as 'You behind the beard'.

It is arguable that the writing of biography began with Aubrey's manuscript notes for his *Brief Lives*, which although they were written in the 1660s did not appear in print until 1898. After being for long dismissed as mere credulous gossip these are now evaluated at their real worth, and Aubrey's writings provide one of the great delights of studying Wiltshire history. His gossipy sometimes inaccurate and often gullible and ill-informed tales and short biographies reveal a zest for life and a consuming curiosity that are an invariable joy and provide for us invaluable insights into the life of late-17th century England.

Aubrey's birth and early life

John Aubrey was born in a delightful and still unfrequented part of rural Wiltshire, the hamlet of Easton Piercy in the parish of Kington St Michael. He was the oldest son to survive of a prosperous Herefordshire family, and his birth occurred at a time when the country was enjoying the long period of calm that was soon to erupt into the Civil War. Easton Piercy (the name means 'East town of Fitz Piers') now consists of three ancient farms – from west to east Upper Easton Piercy Farm, Easton Piercy Farm, and

Lower Easton Piercy Farm – strung along Cromhall Lane, the minor road which runs west from Kington St Michael to Yatton Keynell.

The Wiltshire Aubreys claimed descent from the Aubreys of Herefordshire, John Aubrey's grandfather on his father's side being William Aubrey, a Doctor at Law at the court of Elizabeth who called him 'her little doctor'. He was a master in Chancery and in the Court of Requests whose great love was to return home and make merry with his friends, and it may have been from William Aubrey that his grandson inherited his sociability and his capacity for making lifelong friends. William's son, John Aubrey's father, was Richard Aubrey, whose mother was from the well-known Wiltshire family of Danvers. Richard Aubrey inherited substantial estates but got them so encumbered that after his death his children never succeeded in disentangling them. Richard Aubrey died in 1652 and was buried in the southeast corner of Kington St Michael church, but his son John, as with so many of his good intentions, never got around to erecting a monument to him.

Kington St Michael church

John Aubrey's mother Deborah was only fifteen when she married Richard Aubrey and sixteen when John was born. She was the daughter and heiress of Isaac Lyte of Easton Piercy (died 1672), a prosperous London alderman who in 1675 built at Kington St Michael the Lyte

The Lyte Almshouses, Kington St Michael

Almshouses, six gabled cottages with mullioned windows and an inscription, which may still be seen in the main street of the village.

In the early years of his reign Charles I revived an ancient unrepealed statute of Edward II which required all men of property to accept a knighthood or be fined. The limit was set at property worth in excess of forty pounds a year, and it was stipulated that those who declined the knighthood must compound – that is pay a fine – for their refusal. Among those who paid at Easton Piercy in 1630–1 were John Aubrey's father 'Richard Awberry' and his maternal grandfather 'Isaac Lyte of Easton Pearcy, Gent'.

John Aubrey was born 'very weak and like to dye' and was consequently hurriedly 'christened that morning before morning prayer'. We know from his own account that during his childhood he suffered a severe illness at a time when plague often raged, child mortality was rife, doctors were generally amateur quacks, and medical treatment was primitive. But he survived and grew up: 'in a kind of Parke far from Neighbours and no Child to converse withall', confirming that Aubrey was born in a house at Lower Easton Piercy in the park created by Nicholas Snell after he had bought St Mary's Priory at the Dissolution and created a park over the open area north of Lower Easton Piercy Farm and west of Priory Farm.

Aubrey's birthplace has now been destroyed and its precise position at Lower Easton Piercy is uncertain, although we know that when

Aubrey's grandfather Isaac Lyte sold Lower Easton Piercy in 1575 he retained some land on the brow of the hill above the brook and facing south-east. On that land he built the house which Aubrey later painted and marked the window of the room in which he was born with a cross. His painting shows the house surrounded by trees.

Aubrey's birthplace, now destroyed, at Easton Piercy (fom WANHM vol. 4)

After the house was rebuilt it was again drawn by Aubrey in its more fashionable form. John Britton (see later, pages 94-6) remembered seeing Aubrey's birthplace in the 1780s 'in a state of ruin, with doors and windows removed, and walls nearly covered with ivy, the floors either fallen in or much decayed'.

Aubrey's birthplace at Easton Piercy, drawn by him in 1669 after rebuilding

Aubrey tells us in his writings that as a result of his lonely childhood isolated from other children he turned to the local country people for companionship. These early associations with adults probably explain his love of society and his credulity in his later life, for he tells how: 'When I was a child (and so before the Civill

Warres), the fashion was for old women and mayds to tell fabulous stories nightimes, of Sprights and walking of Ghosts, &c'. He became receptive to such tales, for example when he recorded the story of a shepherd being lured by a fairy fiddler to a place under Hackpen Hill (near Avebury) which resounded with music. It is however interesting to note that the Ordnance Survey gives the name Fiddler's Hill to an area west of Hackpen Hill opposite Broad Hinton. From hearing such tales in his childhood Aubrey became superstitious and at times credulous, but that is

Hackpen Hill where Aubrey heard the fairy fiddler

to judge him unfairly by the standards of our own times. Aubrey would have known Hackpen Hill from visiting his 'old cosen Ambrose Brown' who lived at Winterbourne Bassett not much more than a mile west of Hackpen Hill.

As a child Aubrey 'cared not for play' but had a 'strong and early impulse to Antiquities', probably against parental opposition, because he records that his father 'was not educated to learning, but to hawking'. His lonely life probably prompted Aubrey to amuse himself by studying and he tells us how even before he went to school he was: 'inclin'd by my Genius, from my Childhood to the Love of Antiquities, and my Fate dropt me in a Country most suitable for such Enquiries'. He also delighted in conversing with old people, regarding them as 'living histories'.

Aubrey's love of history was partly fuelled by his nostalgia for the world of his childhood and youth prior to the Civil War, and for the earlier monastic world that was swept away by the Dissolution. Among his papers is a description of the old nunnery at Priory Farm at Kington St Michael, in which he tells of the nuns learning needlework,

confectionery, surgery, physics, writing and drawing. He records how: 'Old Jacques could see from his House the Nuns of the Priory of St Mary (juxta Kington) come into the Nymph-Hay with their Rocks [cleft sticks used in hand-spinning] and Wheels to spin, and with their Sowing Work'. This he considered to be: 'a fine way of breeding-up young women'.

Loving a scandal Aubrey relates with relish how Nicholas Snell, the Abbot of Glastonbury's bailiff at Kington, took advantage of the Dissolution of the monasteries to buy the manor of Kington St Michael for about £804, using money said to belong to the Abbot. This manor included the Priory of St Mary's, a Benedictine priory for nuns established before 1155 on the site of the present Priory Farm at Easton Piercy. The priory park contained carp ponds and allotments to which the villagers had rights, but having acquired the manor Nicholas Snell enlarged the park by imparking West Field, and 'shutt the people out of the park and took away their allotments'. Since he had been born in the parish in 1626, only about ninety years after the event, Aubrey's information was probably correct. Snell prospered, became a Member of Parliament, and was knighted.

Aubrey's early education

When he was eight John Aubrey began his education in 1633 at a Latin school held in the church at Yatton Keynell. The following year he moved to a school run by the rector of Leigh Delamere in the adjoining parish. To go to Yatton Keynell he would have travelled one and a half miles west along Cromhall Lane. His way to school at Leigh Delamere would have been the direct route north past Easton Piercy Farm along the lane which now declines into a public field path across the fields to Leigh Delamere church. He described this journey as 'a mile's fine walk', and then characteristically admitted that he 'had a fine little horse and commonly rode'. Although only nine he formed at Leigh Delamere a close friendship with his teacher the Rev Robert Latimer.

Oxford University and the Civil War

In 1638 Aubrey was sent to Blandford School in Dorset which he described as 'the most eminent

Schoole for the education of Gentlemen in the West of England'. At Blandford he was a fellow pupil of Sir Walter Raleigh's great nephews Walter and Tom Raleigh, and recorded that they were 'proud and quarrelsome'. Then at the age of sixteen he in 1642 entered Trinity College at Oxford and loved university life, but this was soon disrupted by the outbreak of the Civil War. With London held by parliament the king's court made Oxford its headquarters and in August 1643, although his family were royalists, a combination of small-pox and Civil War drove Aubrey home from Oxford and he 'for three years led a sad life in the country', principally at his father's farm at Broad Chalke which was then known as Chalke Farm but is now Manor Farm, a little east of the church at the bottom of Church Bottom. Aubrey's farmhouse is now gone and its site is occupied by a later building. Although Aubrey is known to

The present Manor Farm on the site of Aubrey's farm at Broad Chalke

have farmed at Broad Chalke, the fact that he recorded that there were 'no better trouts in the kingdom of England' than in his pond at 'Naule' suggests that he may also have had Knowle Farm. This, although it adjoins Bower Chalke, is within Broad Chalke parish with Knowle ('Naule') Pond beside it.

Despite the presence of the king at Oxford the war at first hardly affected south Wiltshire, although a Major John Morgan of the king's army was sheltered in a garret in the Aubrey farm at Broad Chalke when he 'fell sick of a malignant fever' when marching into the west. From Aubrey's point of view the worst aspect of the Civil War was the action of the puritans after obtaining power in destroying the ancient imagery

and enrichments of the churches. This prompted Aubrey's first positive venture into antiquarianism when, at the age of only eighteen, he commissioned drawings of the remains which had survived the Dissolution of the ancient island abbey at Osney next to Oxford. Aubrey recorded that: 'Now the very foundation is digged up' and these drawings provided the only record after the abbey was finally razed to the ground. They were used in Dugdale's *Monasticon* with a protracted acknowledgement recording that:

> The Noble Ruines of this Fabrick were drawn from a love to Antiquity, while yet a Youth at Oxford, and (which was not a little lucky) but a short time before they were entirely destroyed in the Civil War, secured now as it were revived, are dedicated to Posterity, by John Aubrey of Easton Piers in the County of Wilts, Esq.

The Aubrey family suffered financially in the Civil War, his father being fined for his royalist sympathies. A parliamentary committee met at Faulston House three miles east of Broad Chalke and the *Falstone Day-Book* for 8 January 1646 recorded that: 'Richard Aubrey of Broadchalke, gent, has already paid £7 in North Wiltshire towards his five and twentieth part there. Now he pays to us at Falstone £33 in sixty fat sheep and £60 in money, accepted for his fine here and in Herefordshire'.

At home Aubrey did not get on well with his father who had little interest in learning. Towards the end of the Civil War he in February 1643 'with much adoe . . . gott my father to lett me to my beloved Oxon againe' and resumed his studies at Oxford where, together with his further education at the Middle Temple in London which he entered in April 1646, he 'enjoy'd the greatest felicity of his life'. Then, at Christmas 1648, he had to return home to his dying father and reluctantly assume responsibility for the management of the family estates.

Aubrey's discovery of Avebury

In January 1649 Aubrey at the age of twenty-three first saw the Marlborough Downs when staying at Marlborough Castle and hunting around Avebury with a party of royalist companions. He writes:

Salisbury-plaines, and Stonehenge I had known from eight years old, but I never saw the Countrey about Marleborough, till Christmas 1648: being then invited to the Lord Francis Seymour's, by the Honourable Mr Charles Seymour (then of Allington near Chippenham, since Lord Seymour) . . . The morrow after Twelf day, Mr Charles Seymour and Sir William Button of Tokenham (a most parkely ground, and a Romancy-place) Baronet, mett with their packs of Hounds at the Greyweathers. These Downes looke as if they were Sown with great Stones, very thicke; and in the dusky evening they looke like a flock of Sheep: from whence it takes its name.

Their hunting was probably over Fyfield Down east of Avebury which today remains littered with sarsen stones, despite the depradations of sarsen cutters who have exploited them for building stone. Aubrey's description of these stones as being 'like a flock of Sheep' has been echoed by the Ordnance Survey who mark the area as 'Grey Wethers', a 'wether' being a castrated sheep.

Scattered sarsen stones on Fyfield Down where Aubrey hunted with a royalist party and discovered Avebury and Silbury Hill

The meeting at Marlborough Castle may have been a royalist assembly for political intrigue under the cover of hunting, and at the end of that month Aubrey was horrified by the execution of Charles I.

During this first visit to the Marlborough Downs Aubrey saw Avebury monument and Silbury Hill which were the discoveries of his life, because the archaeological significance of

Avebury and its associated monuments was not then recognised. They aroused in Aubrey his lifelong enthusiasm for investigating the antiquities of his native Wiltshire, to which he devoted so much time, leaving his business affairs to look after themselves.

Aubrey inherits at the death of his father
At home at Broad Chalke Aubrey inneffectually managed the family estates, and when his father died in 1652 he merely recorded that he had left debts amounting to £1,800. He ignored the substantial estates that were left to him in Wiltshire, Surrey, Brecknock, Hereford, Monmouth, and Kent, although some of these properties were admittedly encumbered with lawsuits. At this time Aubrey was generally living at Broad Chalke rather than Easton Piercy, although at Broad Chalke he disliked being isolated in the country remote from society. Now, with money in his pocket and no accountability to his father, Aubrey embarked on a spendthrift course of dilettantism and undertook to write *The Natural Historie of Wiltshire*, which he opened with an endearing modesty:

> I was from my childhood affected with a view of things rare, which is the beginning of philosophy; and though I have not had leisure to make any considerable proficiency in it, yet I was carried on with a strong impulse to undertake this taske: I knew not why, except for my own pleasure.

His 'strong impulse' proved to be insufficiently strong because, as has been already noted, Aubrey consistently demonstrated his inability to complete his 'taskes'. Although the book was never published it has fortunately survived in manuscript. Its original observations that the ground rose with age and that ancient remains underground became visible when viewed from a height establish a claim for Aubrey as being the first serious English archaeologist.

Misfortunes
Although Aubrey never married he now found himself in great difficulties with a succession of ladies. He was 'hair breadths from matrimony' on a number of occasions, and he recorded how: 'My mother fell from her horse and brake her

arme the last day of April (1649 or 50) when I was suitor to Mris. Jane Codrington'. He never mentions this lady again but in 1651 he writes: 'about 16 or 18 April, I saw that incomparable good conditioned Gentlewoman, Mris. M. Wiseman, with whom at first sight I was in love'. His interest in Mrs Wiseman seems to have lasted for some time because he recorded: '1656. This yeare, and the last, was a strange year to me, and full of Contradictions: silicet Love (M.W.) and Lawe suits'. From this date Aubrey became involved in a succession of disputes in connection with his properties. He was obviously a disinterested manager of his estates who was easily distracted by his time-consuming interests in everything but his financial affairs. These soon became desperate and he ultimately lost everything but his friends, who loyally stood by him in his later years when he was virtually penniless.

Contemplation of marriage then brought Aubrey to Salisbury. He appears to have abandoned thoughts of Mary Wiseman and in 1657 was paying court to Katherine Ryves when she suddenly died. Characteristically Aubrey deplored the loss of her fortune rather than the lady herself:

> 1657 : Novemb. 27, obiit Domina Katherina Ryves, with whom I was to marry; to my great Losse (2000 pounds or more, besides counting care of her brother, 1000 pounds per annum).

During this courtship Aubrey must often have visited Katherine Ryves's home at Sherborne Place (No. 65 The Close), which stands directly opposite the cathedral cloisters in The Close at Salisbury. This house, which obtained its name from having been the prebendal house of Sherborne Abbey, had been rebuilt in the 15th century. It became known as The King's House after James I stayed there on visits to Salisbury in 1610 and 1613 as the guest of Thomas Sadler (c. 1561–1634), a son of William Sadler of Wootton Bassett who had acquired the house by marriage. Thomas Sadler, who was a JP and the Registrar to six Bishops of Salisbury, was knighted in 1623 for his hospitality at Salisbury to the king and his court. After several rebuildings The King's House was later used for educational purposes,

The King's House (now Salisbury Museum) in Salisbury Close

first in the 18th century as Mrs Voysey's school, then from 1851 until 1978 as the diocesan training college for schoolmistresses, in which capacity it was attended by Thomas Hardy's sisters. From 1978 to the present it has been the Salisbury and South Wiltshire Museum.

In 1659 Aubrey initiated a project for a county history of England for which he undertook to provide the section on Wiltshire with the assistance of others. He had learned to survive under the Commonwealth but in 1660 was delighted when King Charles was restored to the throne.

Although none of his work had been published it had been widely circulated in manuscript and by this time he had a great many eminent friends. In 1662 he was nominated as one of the ninety-eight original Fellows of the Royal Society, an honour of which he was justly proud. Charles II, who had visited Stonehenge and attempted unsuccessfully to count the stones when he was hiding at Heale House in the valley of the Salisbury Avon after his defeat at Worcester, heard of Aubrey's interest in Avebury and his pronouncement that Avebury: 'did as much excell Stoneheng as a Cathedral does a Parish Church'. The outcome was that Aubrey showed the king around Avebury and conducted him and his brother the Duke of York (later James II) to the top of Silbury Hill. At the royal command he in 1663 surveyed Avebury with a plain table, and he also made a similar survey of Stonehenge during which he discovered the depressions known as the Aubrey Holes which still bear his name.

In June 1664 Aubrey set off on a long anticipated visit to the Continent, but as might have been expected this enterprise went wrong. In August he recorded: '. . . had a terrible fit of the Spleen, and Piles, at Orleans. I returned in

October. Then Joan Sumner.' This ominous last phrase heralded the most disastrous of his matrimonial problems, which was alluded to at the beginning of this chapter.

Joan Sumner and Seend

As a result of his financial troubles Aubrey had in 1662 finally sold his Herefordshire properties, and it was at about this time that he became associated with the village of Seend. A marriage licence dated 1660 exists at the Salisbury Diocesan Registry for 'Awbry, John, of Easton Pierse, and Mris. Joan Sumner of Sutton Benger, sp.' to marry. Aubrey had met Joan Sumner at the house of her brother John Sumner, now Seend Park, at the east end of Seend to which she had moved from Sutton Benger after her father died when she was in her teens. The house that we see today does not appear to date from Aubrey's time, having been given a later frontage, although it may incorporate parts of the old house as windows at its rear formerly had transomes and the mouldings appear to be early. The 18th-century front facing the road has above its door the Sumner arms, which the family assumed apparently without the sanction of the College of Heralds.

Aubrey records how he lived for fourteen months with Joan Sumner at her 'howse' (presumably at Seend) which may explain the familiarity with Seend which he demonstrated in the following description of the village:

> When King Henry VII lived in Flanders with his aunt the Dutchess of Burgundie, he considered that all or most of the wooll that was manufactured there into cloath was brought out of England; and observing what great profit did arise by it, when he came to the crown he sent into Flanders for clothing manufacturers, whom he placed in the west, and particularly at Send in Wiltshire, where they built severall good houses yet remaining; I know not any village so remote from London that can shew the like. The cloathing trade did flourish here till about 1580, when they removed to Troubridge, by reason of (I thinke) a plague; but I conjecture the main reason was that the water here was not proper for the fulling and washing of their cloath, for this water, being impregnated with iron, did give the white cloath a yellowish tincture.

In 1666 Aubrey described an iron ore field that he saw at Seend as the best he had ever seen, considered that it might be exploited for medicinal purposes, and in 1684 mentioned a well over the chalybeate springs at Seend.

More misfortunes

The year 1666 proved, as already indicated, to be a particularly disastrous one for Aubrey, who recorded eloquently that 'this yeare all my business and affaires ran kim kam'. (The meaning of *kim* is not now clear, although *kam* is a Celtic word meaning 'crooked' or 'gone awry'). His business matters had for long been chaotic, but a new element now complicated his affairs when Joan Sumner sued him for breach of promise. In December 1667 he was arrested in Chancery Lane, the case was heard at Salisbury and Winchester, and substantial damages were awarded to Joan. This proved to be the last straw in the ruination of John Aubrey, who wrote sadly: 'Sold Easton-Pierse, and the farme at Broad Chalke', and then characteristically: 'Never quiett, nor anything of happiness till divested of all, 1670, 1671, when Providence raysed me (unexpectedly) good Friends'. He then indicated that he had hopes of 'enjoying a happy delitescency'.

While hiding from his creditors at Broad Chalke in 1671 Aubrey amused himself by writing, or rather starting to write, a rustic comedy, set at Christian Malford Green east of Draycot Cerne. This play included a clergyman who was hunted to the alehouse by his friend James Long with his pack of hounds, but as so often with Aubrey's projects this too came to nothing.

After he had been obliged to dispose of his homes at Easton Piercy and Broad Chalke Aubrey led an itinerant life staying at the homes of his various friends. He was often in London, but in Wiltshire he stayed at Sir James Long's at Draycot, and later with a relative, James Bertie, the First Earl of Abingdon, at West Lavington.

Aubrey's association with Anthony Wood

In about 1671 Aubrey met Anthony Wood (1632–95), the antiquarian and historian, a meeting that was to influence the remainder of Aubrey's life. Anthony Wood was a tempestuous man who got on with nobody. He was an ineffective writer because his unpopularity was so immense that no one would co-operate with him and he was consequently obstructed in his researches. By contrast Aubrey was affable and popular and had a wide circle of eminent friends, attributes which made him an admirable foil for Wood. In spite of Wood's difficult character Aubrey collaborated with him for twenty-five years, although the irascible and probably envious Wood was frequently derogatory in his references to Aubrey.

In addition to the research that he undertook on behalf of Anthony Wood, Aubrey continued to work on projects of his own. Now penniless he contemplated entering the church, and in 1677 he was in such dire straits that he was selling his prized books, but still he remained optimistic. By 1679 he was engaged on his *Brief Lives*, a series of short biographies of his friends and contemporaries, which in 1692 he submitted in a bound-up form to Anthony Wood for his opinion. Wood then proceeded to break open the binding and mutilate the work by cutting out and losing large tracts of the manuscript, and according to Aubrey he also 'imbezilled the Index of it'. This prompted Aubrey to deposit his mutilated work in the Ashmolean with strict instructions that Anthony Wood was under no circumstances to be made aware of its whereabouts. By this action he ensured that his *Brief Lives* survived to be published long after his death and provide both an amusing read and an invaluable source of information for historians.

Wood was expelled from Oxford in 1693 as a consequence of publishing his *Athenae Oxonienses* (1691–2), a biographical dictionary of Oxford bishops and writers which contained some very severe judgements on his contemporaries. Some of Aubrey's notes used by Wood reflected on Lord Clarendon, and Wood was prosecuted. These difficulties finally soured the relationship between Aubrey and Wood who died aged sixty-three in 1695. Aubrey survived him by four years.

John Aubrey was also a friend of his fellow historian and biographer Thomas Fuller (1608–61), the author of *The History of the Worthies of England* which was posthumously published in 1662. He may have provided Fuller with some of his Wiltshire material, although Fuller was also connected with Wiltshire, having married Eleanor (sometimes Ellen), the daughter of Mr Hugh Grove the MP for Salisbury, who lived at Chisenbury, a hamlet in the parish of Enford in the valley of the upper Salisbury Avon. Eleanor Fuller died in 1641 and the marriage is not widely known because during the interregnum it was suppressed. This was because Eleanor's half-brother was Captain Hugh Grove, the royalist who joined Colonel John Penruddocke in his 1655 Wiltshire rising against Cromwell, for which they were both executed at Exeter.

As a moderate royalist and chaplain to Lord Hopton (1598–1652), the commander of the royalist forces in the south-west 1642–6, Fuller was probably with Hopton at the Battles of Lansdown near Bath and Roundway Down near Devizes in the summer of 1643.

In 1686 Aubrey was offered two chances to go to the New World. First he was offered by a Captain Poyntz, to whom he had rendered some undefined favour, a thousand acres of land in Tobago. The same year he was also offered by William Penn six hundred acres in Pennsylvania. He was advised how to exploit their potential but as usual he let these offers slip, perhaps because he was sixty in 1686 and may have considered himself too old, or he may have been unwilling to abandon his interest in history and his many loyal friends whom he valued so highly.

Aubrey's Wiltshire friends

Like many Wiltshiremen Aubrey delighted in the exhilaration that is to be found in high places, and recorded his delight in the extensive views that could be enjoyed from hills such as Chalke Down above his farm at Bower Chalke, with its trees 'shorn by the south and south-west winds'. It was was probably as a result of staying with Francis Potter at Kilmington that he knew Long Knoll above Maiden Bradley, a vantage point from which he recorded seeing forty miles to the Fosse Way near Cirencester, the Isle of Wight, Salisbury spire, and the Severn.

Long Knoll (from which Aubrey enjoyed the panoramic views) from White Sheet Downs

Francis Potter (1594–1678) was a painter, mathematician and 'mechanick'. He was a member of the Royal Society and was born at Mere rectory, took degrees in art and divinity, and in 1637 succeeded his father as rector of Kilmington where he remained for fifty years. Aubrey tells us that he resembled a monk, that 'his house was as undeckt as a Monkes cell', and deplored the fact that 'such a delicate inventive Witt should be staked to a private preferment in an obscure corner'. He also noted that Francis Potter was in about 1640 the first person to suggest the 'Transfusion of Blood out of one man into another'. Potter died completely blind and was buried at Kilmington.

Aubrey's 'most familiar learned acquaintance' was Lancelot Moorehouse (sometimes Morehouse) whom he described as: 'a very learned man, and a solid and profound Mathematician'. Moorehouse, who had been curate at Broad Chalke where Aubrey presumably first met him, became parson of Pertwood three miles east of Kingston Deverill, from where he went to Little Langford in the Wylye Valley where he died.

Another good Wiltshire friend was Edward Davenant, a mathematician who was for a time the parson of Poulshot, near Seend. He generously loaned Aubrey £500 for a year and would take no interest.

While still a boy at school at Leigh Delamere Aubrey in 1634 met and became friendly with a much older fellow Wiltshireman, the philosopher Thomas Hobbes (1588–1679), who has been described as: 'the greatest political philisopher to have wriiten in the English language' (*The Oxford Companion to British History*). Hobbes's father was the minister of the church which stood at Westport outside the west gate of Malmesbury, but had to flee after striking a colleague at his church door. Aubrey tells us that Hobbes was born prematurely when: 'his mother fell in labour with him upon the fright of the Invasion of the Spaniards in 1588', and he was very particular in giving the precise location of the place of Hobbes's birth which was:

> at his father's house in Westport, being that extreme howse that pointes into, or faces, the Horsefayre ; the farthest howse on the left hand as you goe to Tedbury, leaving the church on your right.

Aubrey first met Hobbes when the philosopher visited Leigh Delamere to renew his acquaintance with Robert Latimer, who had taught him at Westport before he went to Oxford. Hobbes served the Cavendish family of Hardwick in Derbyshire and stayed with that family for most of his life apart from a period during the interregnum. In 1640 he fled to France for fear that he would be accused of advocating royal absolutism, and from 1647 he was tutor to Charles, Prince of Wales, while he was in exile. For his treatise on 'the matter, Forme and Power of a Commonwealth Ecclesiastical and Civil' Hobbes adopted the name *Leviathan* (1651), which is Hebrew for a monster of the waters. In Hobbes's book this represented the sovereign power. In *Leviathan*, which was in 1955 described as the 'greatest, perhaps the sole, masterpiece of political philosophy in the English language', Hobbes claimed that: 'The condition of man . . . is a condition of war of everyone against everyone', and that man was essentially a selfish creature and his life was: 'solitary, poore, nasty, brutish and short'. He also suggested that liberty should be restricted and that the power of monarchs should be limited. These theories for a time brought Hobbes the disfavour of Prince Charles and the enmity of the Church, which suspected him of being atheist, although Aubrey recorded that Charles II 'thought Mr Hobbes never meant him hurt'. When Hobbes returned to England in 1652 and made his submission to Cromwell he was forbidden to publish anything on controversial subjects.

Early in 1660 Aubrey wrote to Hobbes informing him of the imminent return of the king, and at the Restoration he regained royal favour and was granted a pension of £100 a year, which the king incidentally conveniently forgot to pay. Parliament seriously considered whether the Great Fire and the Great Plague were God's punishment for the theories advanced in *Leviathan* but Hobbes escaped censure.

Hobbes did much of his thinking when walking, and had an ink-horn fitted into his staff in order that he could immediately record any thoughts that came to him. At eighty-six Hobbes, claiming that he had nothing better to do, translated the *Iliad* and the *Odyssey*, and both were published in 1682. It is typical of John Aubrey that he recorded the insignificant but amusing fact that Hobbes in his old age was: 'very bald . . . and sayd that he never tooke cold in his head, but that the greatest trouble was to keepe-off the Flies from pitching on the baldness'. With his last words Hobbes coined the expression: 'I am about to take my last voyage, a great leap in the dark'.

The Danvers family of Dauntsey and West Lavington

John Aubrey's mother came from the Danvers family who had acquired Dauntsey in the 15th century by marriage. Henry Danvers became a page to Sir Philip Sidney (see Chapter 5, page 76), a fact of which he was inordinately proud. Despite spending a very active life as a soldier Henry Danvers lived to a be an old man. He was knighted in his teens for gallantry during the siege of Rouen in 1591, but in 1594 he was alleged to have with his brother Charles been responsible for the murder at Great Somerford for some unknown reason of Henry Long, a case which caused an uproar throughout the country. Henry and Charles Danvers then fled to France, where they served in the French army with such distinction that Queen Elizabeth pardoned them, and in 1598 they returned to England. Charles then accompanied Essex to Ireland and was in 1600 executed on Tower Hill for complicity in the Essex plot against Elizabeth, but Henry served with distinction in Ireland, was made Lord Danvers by James I and Earl of Danby by Charles I, and died in 1654 during the Commonwealth. He has a splendid ornate tomb in West Lavington church.

The third brother was Sir John Danvers (1588–1655) who married first Lady Herbert, the widowed mother of George Herbert. Aubrey, who referred to Sir John as: 'my Relation and Faithfull friend', tells us that: 'she [Lady Herbert] was old enough to have been his Mother' and that Sir John 'married her for love of her Witt'. It was when at Dauntsey for the 'choice air' that the poet George Herbert met his wife Jane Danvers, the daughter of Charles Danvers of Bayntun (died 1626), and married her at Edington (see Chapter 5, page 78).

In 1628 Sir John Danvers obtained the West Lavington estate by his marriage to his second wife, Elizabeth Dauntsey (1604–36), the daughter and co-heiress of Ambrose Dauntsey of West Lavington. Aubrey was a great friend of 'my cosen, John Danvers', of whom he wrote: 'He had a very fine fancy, which lay for Gardens and Architecture'. Sir John laid out the gardens at West Lavington in a style that was transitional between the formal style of the 17th century and the 'irregularities' of the 18th. Sir John Danvers was the regicide most abhorred by the royalists because, although in July 1644 he had been entrusted with the safe keeping of two of the children of Charles I (the Princess Elizabeth who was born in 1635 and died young and Prince Henry, Duke of Gloucester), he then signed the death warrant of Charles I. This, according to Aubrey , was to spite his sister and ingratiate himself with Cromwell, and to negate his brother Danby's influence. He escaped the retribution of the royalists by dying in 1655 before the Restoration.

Aubrey recorded of Sir John that: 'The Mannor of Dauntsey in Wilts was forfeited to the Crowne by Sir John Danvers his foolery'. After his estates had been forfeited as a consequence of his having signed the king's death warrant – Sir John was posthumously attainted on 12 July 1661 – the West Lavington estate was granted by the Crown to Clarendon's father Henry Hyde, Lord Cornbury and others as trustees to carry out the wishes of Sir John's son Henry Danvers, who had died young and unmarried at the age of twenty in 1654. By the marriage of his sister Anne Danvers West Lavington went to her husband, Sir Henry Lee of Ditchley in Oxfordshire. They had joint heiresses Eleanor and Anne, and Eleanor became sole heiress and the first wife of another of Aubrey's friends James Bertie, 1st Earl of Abingdon, who through her acquired West Lavington. He died in 1699 and was succeeded by Montagu, 2nd Earl of Abingdon. Aubrey recorded that in 1682 James, Earl of Abingdon, who also was related to Aubrey, made a hare warren at West Lavington (was this the area now known as The Warren?), and in about 1686: 'built a noble portico, full of water workes, which is on the north side of the garden, and faceth south'.

At West Lavington Aubrey: 'enjoyed the contentment of solitude' in the Earl of Abingdon's gardens while he arranged his *Miscellanies*. He therefore knew these gardens, which are now virtually gone, and wrote:

> The garden at Lavington is full of irregularities, both naturall and artificiall, *sc.* elevations and depressions. Through the length of it there runneth a fine cleare trowt stream; walled with brick on each side, to

hinder the earthe from mouldring down. In this stream are placed severall statues. At the west end is an admirable place for a grotto, where the great arch is, over which now is the market roade . . . It is almost impossible to describe this garden, it is so full of variety and unevenesse.

The stream now runs beside the road through the village and only a possible remnant of the garden described by Aubrey survives in The Warren with its lake to the west of the A360 south of West Lavington, which is accessible by public footpath and is well worth visiting.

John Britton

When in the 19th century a stained glass window in Kington St Michael church was dedicated to John Aubrey and John Britton, the Rev Jackson mentioned that the two men were: 'born as to time within 146 years; as to distance within a mile of each other'.

John Britton

It is appropriate that the writer and topographer John Britton (1771–1857) should figure in this chapter devoted to John Aubrey, for in addition to being born in the same village as Aubrey he wrote Aubrey's life and made the first positive attempt to arrange Aubrey's disordered papers into some sort of order.

Britton was the first son and the fourth child of a baker, maltster, shopkeeper and farmer at Kington St Michael. His birthplace has, like Aubrey's, been destroyed. At the time of Britton's

John Britton's birthplace at Kington St Michael, now destroyed

birth Kington St Michael was a self-sufficient rural community situated about a mile from the turnpike road. Britton there grew up following the usual pursuits of a country lad, and was educated in a rather rudimentary way as a residential pupil at schools at Foscote, Yatton Keynell, Draycot Cerne and Chippenham. Later Britton's letters to William Cunnington, Colt Hoare's collaborator in his archaeological investigations, reveal his sensitivity over the fact that he lacked a proper education and was largely self-educated. His letters also suggest that he had a sense of inferiority which sometimes led him to be vain about his undoubted successes. At this time in his early teens Britton enjoyed visiting his grandfather at Maidford immediately east of Norton at the south-west end of Malmesbury Common. At thirteen he was brought home to help with the baking, bread delivery and farm work, but his purchase at a manor house sale of a bundle of books for a shilling changed his life.

His autobiography (published in two volumes in 1850) suggests that there was antipathy between Britton and his father, which may have caused him to leave home in 1787 when he was sixteen. He went with his maternal Uncle Hillier

by coach 'at a speed of about five miles an hour' to London and subsequently looked back at the sixteen years he had spent at home at Kington St Michael as wasted years.

In London his uncle tied him by a six-year apprenticeship (1787–93) to a wine merchant, and after progressing from being a cellarman to clerk he composed a song, which was pirated by a publisher who sold more than 70,000 copies. For a short time he performed in the theatre and from his meagre earnings he bought books from bookstalls. After recovering from a prolonged illness Britton became an attorney's clerk and a sociable young man. Of this period he recorded that his 'bookish amusements were very desultory and miscellaneous' until he met a publisher called Wheble who had started his career in Salisbury. Wheble suggested to Britton that he should collaborate with Edward Brayley (1773–1854) on writing *The Beauties of Wiltshire*, to exploit the current fashion for topographical writings and ancient buildings. In search of material Britton in 1798 studied the Aubrey manuscripts at Oxford and was well-received at Bowood by Lord Lansdowne, who encouraged him by putting him up for four days and giving him the run of his considerable library. Britton regarded this meeting as the launching of his writing career. At about this time he also met Colt Hoare and William Cunnington (see Chapter 11), but he later believed that he was slighted by Colt Hoare and regarded him as his rival.

The first two volumes of *The Beauties of Wiltshire* appeared in 1801 with most of its illustrations drawn by Britton. The third volume was not published until 1825. It is not known where Britton learned to draw.

Britton has tended to be regarded in Wiltshire as just another topographer, and his reputation has been overshadowed by that of John Aubrey, although his illustrations were for their time unusually accurate, and their influence on architectural style in the 19th century was recognised by Kenneth Clark in his authoritative *The Gothic Revival* (1928):

> The man who popularised engravings of Gothic by publishing them cheaply and in great numbers was

John Britton . . . Britton deserved his success. His text was painstaking and his illustrations . . . achieved an accuracy and detail never before attempted. Though Britton's volumes were a commercial venture, they did not merely feed a craze ; they gave the average cultivated man a far truer idea of Gothic forms than he had hitherto had, so that after their publication the old fantastic parodies of Gothic were no longer possible. Britton killed Ruins and Rococo.

The Beauties of Wiltshire was so successful that Britton was commissioned to write The Beauties of England and Wales (1803–1814) in twenty-five volumes. For this massive undertaking many artists were employed to prepare the plates. The Cathedral Antiquities of Great Britain came out intermittently until 1835 when he was sixty-four, and during the rest of his long life Britton wrote many more books on archaeology and architecture. His Life of Aubrey appeared in 1845 and he also edited Aubrey's Natural History. When engaged in writing about Fonthill he was befriended by the normally unapproachable William Beckford.

In his last years after 1853 Britton was a leading light on the committee which founded the Wiltshire Archaeological and Natural History Society based at Devizes, and his collection of papers, books and drawings formed the nucleus of the society's original library. He died on New Year's Day 1857 and was buried in Norwood Cemetery in London, his grave being marked with an eleven foot high monolith, which was deliberately left unwrought to resemble one of the stones of Stonehenge in his native Wiltshire. As recently as 1937 a street in Clerkenwell was named Britton Street in recognition of his work on London topography.

In Wiltshire Britton has been less recognised. The site of his birthplace in Kington St Michael is now occupied by the village hall, which has built into its wall an almost indecipherable stone commemorating his birth, this stone having been presumably salvaged from his home when it was demolished. In 1857 the stained glass window jointly commemorating John Aubrey and John Britton was installed at the east end of the south aisle of Kington St Michael church, and the Royal

Institute of British Architects funded an inscription on brass to his memory in Salisbury Cathedral.

Aubrey on education

In about 1680 Aubrey developed in writing an idea on which he had worked since 1669, when he wrote An Idea of Educating Young Gentlemen, which he considered to be his most valuable work. In this he perhaps ill-advisedly attacked the methods of the celebrated Dr Busby, the head of Westminster School, who had educated many illustrious men including Sir Christopher Wren, John Dryden, and John Locke. Aubrey's theory was to desist from forcing children to learn by intimidation and persuade them to take such delight in their studies that they underook them willingly. Exercise was also to be encouraged, and Aubrey thought that about six schools run on these lines would be enough to serve the entire country. His ideas sound surprisingly modern and were far in advance of his time, but after he had pursued them for several years and failed to obtain a sponsor for them Aubrey finally abandoned the idea.

Aubrey's Wiltshire

As a result of his apparent incessant travelling about Wiltshire and his insatiable curiosity John Aubrey became familiar with the geography, history, and folklore of most parts of the county. He admired both north and south Wiltshire, having lived in both, and everything and everyone interested him. In addition to his native countryside around Easton Piercy, he was particularly fond of his farm at Broad Chalke, the Ebble Valley, and the countrysides of Cranborne Chase and Vernditch Chase, of which he wrote:

About Wilton and Chalke, the downes are intermixt with boscages, nothing can be more pleasant, and in the Summer time doe excell Arcadia in verdant and riche turfe and moderate aire . . . The innocent lives here of the shepherds do give us a resemblance of the Golden Age . . . In this tract is ye Earle of Pembroke's noble seate at Wilton ; but the Arcadia and Daphne is about Vernditch and Wilton ; and those fine romancy plaines and boscages did no

Church Bottom descending from the Ox Drove to Aubrey's Manor Farm at Broad Chalke

doubt conduce to the hightening of Sir Philip Sydney's phansie.

Vernditch Chase, although now greatly reduced, retains much of its arcadian quality which Aubrey so enthusiastically admired. It might have been lost had it not been acquired before the Second World War by the composer Balfour Gardiner (1877–1950), who with his nephew the pioneer environmentalist Rolf Gardiner (1902–71), planted millions of trees on Cranborne Chase in an attempt to recreate the historic landscape. Rolf Gardiner recorded in *The Countryman* how:

> During a period of more than forty years, first Balfour, at my instigation, and then I alone planted some three million trees on the chalk downs and among the hazel coppices of this impoverished district of north-west Cranborne Chase . . . I was determined to restore in some measure the hill-and-vale economy devised by the Saxon 'minsters' which created the manors and parishes of Wessex.

Today Vernditch Chase (the name means 'fern ditch' and Grims Ditch runs through it) is one of the most beautiful places in Wiltshire, par-

ticularly in springtime when the beech woods break into leaf, are carpeted with bluebells, and nightingales still sing from its thickets. Anyone who visits Vernditch will appreciate Aubrey's enthusiasm for this part of Wiltshire.

Aubrey's travels took him to all parts of his native county, for example to Bowden Park above Lacock. This was in 1681 the seat of his friend George Johnson, Solicitor to the Treasury, and MP for Devizes, who had in 1667 been granted the reversion of the Mastership of the Rolls. Unfortunately the then Master, Sir Harbottle Grimston, lived until 1685 and George Johnson predeceased him in 1683, having waited sixteen years to succeed to an appointment which he never attained. According to Anthony Powell in *John Aubrey and His Friends* (1948) this George Johnson 'trebled his estate (upon which were the remains of a Roman iron forge) by finding marl under the soil', marl being a rich clay used as manure.

Aubrey's death and burial

After he had squandered away his inheritance Aubrey lived for part of his time at Draycot Park at the expense of the royalist Colonel Sir James

Long. He was particularly grateful for this hospitality and in the second manuscript of his *Brief Lives* nominated 'Sir James Long, baronet of Draycot' as one of his particular *amici*.

Having been a churchwarden at Bower Chalke Aubrey longed to be buried beside Gawen's Barrow, a mile and a half south of Broad Chalke, and now almost flattened, of which he wrote:

> I never was so sacralegious as to disturbe, or rob his urne . . . Let his ashes rest in peace : but I have oftentimes wisht that my Corps might be interred by it : but the Lawes Ecclesiastick denie it.

Anyone who goes to the site of Gawen's Barrow, situated immediately west of the road which runs south from Broad Chalke towards Vernditch Chase (at NGR SU036234), and enjoys the views from it west over Bower Chalke will understand why Aubrey wished to be buried here with views across the landscape that he loved.

Having lived just long enough to publish his *Miscellanies* and dedicate them to the Earl of Abingdon, Aubrey died in 1697 'surprized by age' at the age of seventy-one, probably at Oxford and, according to Rawlinson in his introduction to Aubrey's *Surrey*, on his way to Draycot in Wiltshire to visit the widow of Sir James Long, who often entertained him in his later days. An entry in the register of St Marys Church at Oxford reads: '1697,

JOHN AUBERY A Stranger was Buryed June 7th'. It seems a pity that Aubrey being such an ardent Wiltshireman should have been buried at Oxford as a 'Stranger', rather than as he had wished beside Gawen's Barrow above the Ebble Valley near his beloved farm in south Wiltshire.

Aubrey's Reputation Today

John Aubrey is now sufficiently recognised to have been the subject of a memorable one-man television play, and his writings are well known to Wiltshire historians, although the only work that he published in his lifetime was his *Miscellanies* (1696). Towards the end of his life he expressed the hope that some 'public-spirited young Wiltshire man' would polish and complete his writings and this wish was belatedly granted. His Wiltshire writings are contained in two publications. *The Natural History of Wiltshire* was produced in an edited limited edition by John Britton in 1847, and his other papers were in 1862 edited by Canon J E Jackson as *Wiltshire ; the Topographical Collections of John Aubrey*. His *Brief Lives* containing invaluable short biographies of his friends and contemporaries has been more widely disseminated in a number of editions. It first appeared in an edited edition in 1813, in 1898 it first appeared in a two-volume unabridged form, and there have been more editions.

7   A Wiltshire Republican

Edmund Ludlow of Hill Deverill

The upper part of the Wylye, known as the Deverill, is one of the most beautiful and peaceful areas of Wiltshire. Despite its tranquillity in the 17th century the Deverill Valley produced one of the most militant men of the Civil War, a republican MP who, after parliament had won the Civil War and had converted England into a republic by executing the king for having ruled despotically, quarrelled with Oliver Cromwell when he made himself king in all but name, and then went into a prolonged exile when the monarchy was restored in 1660.

The early-17th-century unrest in Wiltshire

When the Stuarts became kings of England in 1603 they had ruled the kingdom of Scotland for three centuries, during which they had often been humiliated by the aggressive Scottish aristocracy. They had no experience of parliament on the more democratic English model, and James I as the first English Stuart monarch made far-reaching demands of his parliaments, but had the good sense lacking in his son Charles not to press his demands too hard. Having experienced problems with his parliaments over royal prerogative, after his eldest son Prince Henry died young James I is said to have prophetically warned his second son: 'You will live to have your bellyfull of parliaments', but Charles I ignored his father's advice and demonstrated a complete lack of understanding of the English people. This may have been due to the fact that he had very little English blood, being on his father's side a Franco-Scot and on his mother's a Germano-Dane.

The origins of the Civil War arose during the first fifteen years (1625–40) of Charles I's reign, during which he behaved as an absolute mon-

arch by attempting to rule without calling parliaments. Unrest appeared early and continued until about 1640, provoked by the king's imposition of forced loans, arbitrary royal enclosure, and illegal taxation without the sanction of parliament. This unrest was manifested at many places in Wiltshire. New enclosure fences were torn down in Braydon Forest, and at Great Wishford at the lower end of the Wylye Valley protesters were organised into an officered army. When in 1627 the king decided to enclose the royal Forest of Selwood, at Cley Hill Farm near Warminster Sir John Thynne's tenant Mr Thomas Carr in 1631 resisted the enclosure. The trained bands were called out but were sympathetic to Mr Carr and refused to act, as did some gunners when artillery was called up from Bristol.

Cley Hill, near Warminster

Some of the objectors to the king's arbitrary rule were landowners such as Sir Giles Eyre (died 1655), a member of the family from Brickworth Park in south-east Wiltshire who in 1606 built the brick gazebo known as Eyre's Folly on Pepperbox Hill overlooking his estate. Sir Giles was one of many upper class protesters who opposed Charles I's oppressive measures prior to the Civil War. In 1640 he was imprisoned for refusing to

Eyre's Folly (known as the Pepperbox) at the west end of Dean Hill above Brickworth

pay a forced loan illegally demanded by the king, and his monument at the west end of Whiteparish church bears an inscription describing his opposition.

Such events demonstrate the widespread resistance to royal power that existed prior to the Civil War, and was often supported by people of rank.

The emergence of the Ludlows

During this period of unrest a republican family emerged in the valley of the Deverill. Sir Henry Ludlow (1592–1643) of Maiden Bradley, one of the most outspoken republican members of the Long Parliament, was on 7 May 1642 sternly reprimanded by the Speaker for boldly stating that Charles I was not worthy to be king, prompting a royalist wit to pen the lines:

'Who speaks of peace', quoth Ludlow,
'Hath neither sense nor reason,
For I neer spoke in the House but once,
And then I spoke high treason'.

When in November 1642 King Charles attempted to defuse parliamentary support in Wiltshire by offering a pardon for the inhabitants of the county, the specific exceptions were four high-ranking Wiltshiremen, Sir Henry Ludlow, Sir

Edward Hungerford, Walter Long, and Sir John Evelyn of West Dean, all men from families well-known to Wiltshire historians, with the possible exception of Sir John Evelyn.

The Evelyns and Pierreponts of West Dean

Early in the 16th century John Evelyn (1554–1627), of a Surrey family who in the second half of the 16th century were granted a lucrative monopoly in the manufacture of gunpowder, bought the manor of West Dean in the extreme south-east of Wiltshire.

The Evelyn house at West Dean is now entirely gone. It stood at the west edge of the village immediately north of the railway line, and was a grand house illustrated by Colt Hoare, and shown by Andrews and Dury on their 1773 map of Wiltshire with very extensive formal landscaped grounds, of which few signs remain. John Evelyn died in 1627 and was succeeded by Sir John Evelyn (1601–85) who, although knighted by King Charles in 1641, joined the parliamentary party, became very active in the Civil War, and was declared a traitor by the king. Sir John was a distant relative of his famous namesake the diarist and author John Evelyn (1620–1706), with whom he has often been confused. Although the diarist as a royalist would presumably have disapproved of Sir John, he occasionally mentions him, for example:

1698-9. January. My cousin Pierrepont died. She was daughter to Sir John Evelyn, of Wilts, my father's nephew. She was widow to William Pierrepont, brother to the Marquis of Dorchester, and mother to Evelyn Pierrepont, Earl of Kingston; a most excellent and prudent lady.

At his death in 1685 Sir John Evelyn left West Dean to his grandson, subject to a life interest in favour of his daughter Elizabeth, the mother of Evelyn Pierrepont (*c.* 1665–1726), 5th Earl and later Duke of Kingston, and a grandson of Sir John Evelyn. Upon the death of his mother in 1699 he inherited the West Dean property. His son the 2nd Duke of Kingston married the notorious Wiltshire-born lady Elizabeth Chudleigh (1720–88), the grand-daughter of the Bradford on Avon clothier John Hall, who once appeared in a masque as Iphigenia in a dress that was so diaphanous that Lady Mary Wortley Montagu (see below) commented that: 'She was so naked that the high priest might easily inspect her entrails'.

Elizabeth Chudleigh first aroused the interest of the Earl of Bath, almost married the Duke of Hamilton, and attracted the attention of George II. Despite being already married she married bigamously in 1768 Evelyn Pierrepont, Duke of Kingston, and so became Duchess of Kingston. She then travelled widely on the Continent and when the duke died in 1773 Elizabeth inherited his substantial fortune. The outraged family challenged her on the grounds that the marriage was bigamous, she was tried before the House of Lords in Westminster Hall and was found guilty. By some means she contrived to retain the Kingston estate, which included Kingston House at Bradford where she sometimes resided. She again travelled abroad, met Catherine the Great of Russia (1729–96), and died in Paris aged sixty-eight.

The 1st Duke of Kingston was the father of the writer and intellectual Lady Mary Wortley Montagu (1689–1762) who, after her mother died in 1694, although still a child, acted as hostess at her father's table and had a carving tutor to teach her how to carve meat. She grew up to be an intellectual and was often with her grandmother at West Dean, and it was from there that in about 1712 she eloped with her commoner husband Edward Wortley Montagu, who had been rejected as an unacceptable suitor by her father, who sold West Dean in 1725. From 1716 to 1718 Lady Mary Wortley Montagu was abroad with her husband, who was ambassador to Turkey, where she became interested in vaccination for smallpox, and upon her return in 1718 she introduced vaccination into England. For the succeeding two decades she was a member of society and a great friend of Alexander Pope (1688–1744), but they quarrelled in 1727, for some reason that has never been conclusively explained. In 1739 she left her husband and lived abroad in France and Italy, where Walpole met her in 1740 and described her as an 'old, foul, tawdry, painted, plastered personage'.

Edmund Ludlow's ancestry and early life

As their name suggests the early Ludlows had been prominent in Shropshire, where a John of Ludlow was licenced in 1291 to crenellate his manor house at Stokesay Castle, and created the earliest surviving example of a fortified manor house. They then retained Stokesay for ten generations from 1291 to 1497, and it was their activities as wool merchants that brought them to Wiltshire by way of Chipping Campden and Shipton Moyne, the latter not far from Malmesbury but just over the boundary in Gloucestershire. They first appeared in Wiltshire in the 15th century when William Ludlow (died 1478) and his wife Margaret acquired an interest in Tidworth Manor and William became parker of Ludgershall Park. He also held Ludgershall Manor and was MP for Ludgershall from 1432 to 1437. Although this William Ludlow does not feature prominently in history he held the significant office of butler to three monarchs – Henry IV, V, and VI – the 'Royal Butler' being then Comptroller of the Royal Household.

At the accession of Edward IV in 1461 William Ludlow as a Lancastrian lost all his offices, including the parkership of Ludgershall. The Tidworth estate then passed through a succession of Ludlows including John Ludlow who died in 1487, George Ludlow the High Sheriff of Wiltshire who died in 1580, Sir Edmund Ludlow who died in 1624 having been MP for Hindon, Sir Henry Ludlow and his son Edmund Ludlow, the subject of this chapter, who sold the Tidworth estate.

The first Ludlow to appear at Hill Deverill was the William Ludlow mentioned above, who acquired the manor in 1440. The fine Ludlow tomb chest which is now in the Bath Chapel of Longbridge Deverill church was removed from Hill Deverill church to Longbridge Deverill when then former was made redundant in 1984. It displays shields with the arms of three families who married into the Ludlows – Margaret Rymer who married William Ludlow, Philippa Bulstrode who married Jack Ludlow (died 1519), and Jane Moore who married William Ludlow (died 1533).

The Ludlow arms (*Argent, a chevron between three martins heads, erased sable*) also appear on the monument to Edward Baynard (died 1575) in Lacock church, Robert Baynard (died 1501) having married Elizabeth the daughter of John Ludlow, by whom he had thirteen sons and five daughters! More Ludlow heraldry appears at the exquisite 15th-century manor house at Great Chalfield, near Bradford on Avon, as a result of the marriage of Thomas Tropenell (c. 1405–88), the builder of Great Chalfield, to Margaret the daughter of the William Ludlow of Ludgershall mentioned above. Their tomb in Corsham church also displays the Ludlow arms.

In 1576 'Edmund Lewdelowe, gentleman' paid tax as lord of the manor of Hill Deverill. His later namesake, the subject of this chapter, was the eldest son of Sir Henry Ludlow by his wife Elizabeth, a daughter of Richard Phelipps of Montacute in Somerset, some of whose family were royalists, as after the Battle of Worcester in September 1651 Colonel Robin Phelipps, a younger son of the Montacute family, came to King Charles in hiding at Trent near Sherborne and helped in guiding him across Wiltshire to the Sussex coast, where he embarked for France.

Edmund Ludlow (c. 1617–92) is believed to have been born at his father's farm of Newmead, situated in the Deverill Valley under Brimsdown Hill and a mile and a half south-east of Maiden Bradley, which was according to Aubrey ruined during the Civil War. He became lord of the manor of Hill Deverill, about four miles north-east of Newmead.

By the 17th century the Ludlows were numerous in Wiltshire. Two Ludlows from the Dinton branch of the family emigrated to America, and Edmund's grandfather Sir Edmund Ludlow, the head of the family during the reigns of Elizabeth and James I, had a younger brother Thomas Ludlow of Dinton, who at his death in 1607 left four sons. Roger Ludlow emigrated in 1630 and in 1639 became deputy-governor of Connecticut. The youngest son George Ludlow (1596–1656), who was baptised at Dinton in 1596, also emigrated and became an active member of the Massachusetts council and a sixteenth-part owner of the Pilgrim Fathers' ship the *Mayflower*. Although Edmund Ludlow was only three when George Ludlow emigrated, he knew

Edmund Ludlow from the first edition of his Memoirs

of his cousin George (who lived until 1656) and mentioned him in his *Memoirs*. Had George lived four years longer, Edmund might when obliged to flee from England in 1660 have joined his relatives in America rather than gone to Switzerland.

Edmund Ludlow had five brothers and four sisters. He was educated at Blandford School and at Trinity College Oxford, where he matriculated in September 1634. In November 1636 he took his BA and in 1638 was admitted to the Inner Temple. At Oxford he was described as being of a 'gruff, positive humour, resolutely bent upon whatever his own will suggested', and the events of his subsequent career suggest that this description was accurate. His *Memoirs* suggest that the only humour that he possessed was unconscious, and his attitude to marriage was pecuniary, as when seeking a wife he offered his friends ten per cent commission if they could find him a wife worth four thousand pounds a year. When he married a Welsh heiress Elizabeth, a daughter of William Thomas of Wenvoe in Glamorgan, his first mention of her in his *Memoirs* was a description of how he had invested her dowry! His wife's Welsh family long resented the acquisition of her property by an Englishman, and it is said that when Edmund Ludlow died and she became a widow aged seventy-three, a member of the Thomas family, then in his thirties, married her in 1694 solely in order to recover the Welsh estates for the family. She died in February 1701–2.

Outbreak of the Civil War

The Ludlows of Newmead and Hill Deverill were neighbours of the Thynnes of Longbridge Deverill and of Longleat but, unlike the Thynnes, did not remain aloof from the Civil War. A number of members of their family were extremely active in support of parliament and Edmund Ludlow is remembered almost entirely for his activities during the Civil War and the subsequent Commonwealth. He was twenty-six when war broke out in 1643 and forty-three at the Restoration of the monarchy in 1660. The rest of his life he spent in obscurity in exile.

For most of the Civil War the north and west of Wiltshire and the areas around Swindon, Marlborough and Salisbury, were sympathetic to parliament, while the east and the extreme south of the county were either neutral or inclined to be royalist. When war broke out Ludlow was convinced that no one would fight for the king, but he nevertheless met at the Inns of Court Mr Richard Fiennes and Charles Fleetwood, both men with Wiltshire connections, to be instructed in arms in case they should ever be required to fight. These three men then attached themselves to the Earl of Essex after he was appointed parliamentary commander.

Ludlow's activities during the Civil War

His upbringing by his republican father and the undemocratic actions of Charles I had made Edmund Ludlow a convinced republican parliamentarian, and during the war he was very active on behalf of parliament, particularly in his native Wiltshire. Having joined the Earl of Essex as one of the hundred gentlemen who formed his bodyguard, Ludlow saw action early in the Civil War. He was at Powick Bridge near Worcester when Essex on 23 September 1642 engaged Prince Rupert, and he fought at Edgehill a month later on 23 October. In January 1643 Ludlow was ordered by Sir Edward Hungerford, the parliamentary commander in Wiltshire, to raise a troop of horse. This he did from men on his father's estate, and was then made a captain of horse in Sir Edward's regiment. There is a local tradition that at some time during the Civil War Ludlow used the mill at Hill Deverill as a headquarters.

Parliamentery strategy in the Civil War was to deprive the royalists of their houses, and Ludlow's most celebrated exploit as a soldier occurred at Wardour Castle near Tisbury. The staunchly catholic Arundells of Wardour had in the early-17th century encouraged a pocket of recusancy, and the parishes around Wardour contained fifty to sixty per cent of the catholics in Wiltshire, and are said to have contained the greatest concentration of catholics outside London. Wardour was therefore an early prime target for the puritans, and in April 1643 Sir Edward Hungerford brought seven hundred men to Wardour with Ludlow as one of his officers. He then augmented his force to about thirteen hundred and besieged the castle of the Arundells.

Old Wardour Castle

The sieges of Wardour Castle

Wardour Castle had been acquired by the Arundells, who in 1570 updated the accommodation using Robert Smythson as their architect. Nevertheless at the time of the Civil War the castle remained substantially that built by Lord Lovel,

Old Wardour Castle

consisting of a tall hexagonal tower keep built around a hexagonal inner court with a bailey surrounded by a defensive wall with corbelled turrets. It was probably at this time that the now deserted and forlorn little 16th-century gateway was built nearly half a mile south-west of the castle on what was formerly the main drive to the castle from the present A30 under White Sheet Hill.

Gateway in Wardour Park

Being strongly catholic the Arundells sided with Charles I in the Civil War, but when Hungerford and Ludlow appeared before Wardour the Arundell fighting men were away and the castle was held by the doughty Blanche, Lady Arundell (1583–1649), then aged sixty, a grand-daughter of Margaret, Countess of Salisbury, and the second wife of the 1st Baron Arundell, who in her husband's absence heroically defended Wardour Castle. With only about twenty-five fighting men she courageously held out for five days but after the castle was undermined and partially blown up she was forced to surrender. According to a contemporary account the Articles of Surrender required:

> First, that the ladies and others in the Castle should have quarter. Secondly, that the ladies and servants should carry away all their Wearing Apparel, and that six of the serving Men, whom the Ladies should nominate, should attend upon their persons, wheresoever the Rebels should dispose of them. Thirdly, that all the Furniture and goods in the house should be safe from Plunder and to this purpose one of the six, nominated to attend the Ladies, was to stay in the Castle, and take an Inventory of all in the House, of which the Commanders were to have one copy and the Ladies another.

Only the first condition was observed. The ladies were given safe conduct and were sent to Shaftesbury, but were deprived of all their possessions and left with only the clothes that they were wearing. The castle was also looted and five cartloads of plunder were sent off to Shaftesbury, and it was wryly suggested by the royalists that: 'The one use of the inventory was to let the world know what my Lord Arundell lost and what these rebels gained'. This was probably no fault of Ludlow, who was at Wardour under the command of Sir Thomas Hungerford.

After Hungerford departed leaving Ludlow as the parliamentary governor of Wardour young Henry 2nd Lord Arundell, whose father had died at the royalist headquarters at Oxford, arrived before Wardour with some cavalry and demanded its surrender, although his unsupported cavalry posed no threat to the castle. In December 1643 Captain Christopher Bowyer appeared at Wardour with infantry and the castle was closely invested, but Ludlow stubbornly resisted. After Captain Bowyer was killed he was succeeded by Colonel Barnes, who erected a siege work on the hill and continued to invest the castle without assaulting it. As Ludlow's garrison began to run short of provisions the royalist commander summoned reinforcements under Sir Francis Dodington. He brought up some Irish troops who took an active part in the final stages of the siege. Dodington invited Ludlow to surrender but he stoutly held out until 16 March, when he agreed to negotiate. On 18 March he met Dodington and Arundell in the grounds and grudgingly surrendered the castle, after having resisted for three months. According to his *Memoirs* he surrendered against his will and only because his men had become discouraged. Ludlow's sick and wounded were held at Wardour for a time before being sent to Bristol. During the time that he was besieged at Wardour Ludlow's father Sir Henry died and he inherited his estates.

The ruins of old Wardour Castle from its former drive

Wardour Old Castle was rendered uninhabitable during its sieges and by subsequent slighting, and today it remains in the ruinous condition that makes it one of the most picturesque places in Wiltshire. The battered hexagonal castle keep stands within its surrounding bailey wall beside a picturesque lake that was created in the 18th century, as was a gothick dining pavilion with ogee-headed windows, and a terrace with yew trees and a grotto of tufa stone built in 1792 by the grotto specialist Josiah Lane of Tisbury.

Adjoining Old Wardour Castle is the house built by the Arundells after the destruction of their castle, which is now in the care of English Heritage and is well worth visiting.

At the time when it was under siege in the Civil War Wardour Old Castle was adjoined by several deer parks, which must have provided good eating for its besiegers. These deer parks extended for about a mile west of the castle, with the Fallow Deer Park nearest the castle and the Red Deer Park to its west, extending as far as Parkgate Farm. After the siege the surviving deer were released, and although the deer parks were re-established they have been obliterated by 18th-century landscaping.

Although catholics continued to be repressed after the Civil War the Arundells eventually recovered their fortunes by a number of advantageous marriages, and in the late-18th century the 10th Lord Arundell (died 1834) built New Wardour Castle three-quarters of a mile north-west of the old castle. This vast house, the largest Georgian house in Wiltshire, was designed by James Paine in his rather bleak late-Palladian style and built between 1769 and 1776, incorporating a magnificent catholic chapel which was allowed on condition that it was not obviously a church. The chapel was therefore embedded in the west wing of the house, and it was later extended and enriched by the architect Sir John Soane. Here at Wardour Paine created one of the great architectural experiences of Wiltshire. From the deliberately sombre low-ceilinged entrance hall the visitor emerges into a high, brilliantly top-lighted rotunda staircase hall, with a cantilevered staircase. This rotunda was described by Pevsner as 'the most glorious Georgian interior in Wiltshire'. After having been for many years Cranborne Chase Girls School, New Wardour Castle was in the mid–1990s converted into luxury flats.

Ludlow's later career in the Civil War

After Ludlow surrendered Old Wardour Castle he was in violation of the terms of the surrender sent to the royalist headquarters at Oxford by way of Broad Chalke, Salisbury and Winchester. At

New Wardour Castle

Oxford he was imprisoned, but early in 1644 he was exchanged for three high-ranking royalist officers and was commissioned as major in the regiment of horse commanded by Sir Arthur Haslerig (died 1661) in the army of Sir William Waller. Haslerig was one of the five MPs whom Charles I had attempted to arrest in parliament and by this act had finally provoked the Civil War. Because his cavalry regiment wore old-fashioned armour they were known as 'Haslerig's lobsters'.

For a time Ludlow commanded the parliamentary garrison at Faulston House near Bishopstone in south Wiltshire. There he 'with his troop somewhat restrained the excursions of the King's garrisons thereabouts' (Ludlow's *Memoirs*). Faulston House was erected on the site of a castle built by William de Braose, one of King

Faulston Manor near Bishopstone where the Parliamentary Commission met. The round dovecot is the remains of a Medieval castle tower

John's barons. One round tower of this former castle survives today converted into a dovecot, and it was from Faulston House that the Parliamentary Committee for Wiltshire during the Civil War levied fines on 'malignants', that is persons who supported the royalist cause.

The sometimes over-enthusiastic activities of the Ludlow family on behalf of parliament are confirmed by several entries in the *Falstone Day Book* which on 23 March 1647 recorded that Captain William Ludlow's troopers were accused of 'disorders' and 'taking free quarter', and Captain Ludlow was ordered to punish the offenders. Two of Edmund's uncles (Benjamin Ludlow and Robert Ludlow) died serving parliament, as did his cousin Gabriel, who was killed at Edmund's side at the Battle of Newbury, and his younger brother Robert (1621–43), who died as a royalist prisoner.

In July 1644 Sir William Waller promoted Edmund Ludlow to colonel and sent him to raise another regiment of horse in Wiltshire. There in August 1644 he attacked royalist strongholds at Stourton and at Witham Park, the latter just over the county boundary in Somerset, and the home of the royalist general Lord Hopton. On visiting Maiden Bradley he found that his father's house at Newmead had been plundered and ruined by the royalists.

On 28 May 1644 parliament made Ludlow its Sheriff of Wiltshire, and for the rest of the Civil

War he generally campaigned in his home county, although he was at the Second Battle of Newbury in October 1644, the siege of Basing House in November 1644, and he also accompanied the attempt to relieve Taunton in December 1644. It was at Newbury that his cousin Cornet Gabriel Ludlow was killed.

Action at Salisbury

Salisbury Close with its defensive surrounding walls and gates was successively held by both sides in the Civil War. In December 1644 Ludlow evicted a royalist garrison and attempted to fortify the formidable bell tower with his new Wiltshire Regiment. Although it was demolished in 1790 and its stones were sold and used to build Alderbury House, descriptions and prints of the campanile which Ludlow fortified at Salisbury reveal that it was a formidable structure. One night in January 1645 Ludlow's small force in The Close was surprised by a superior force under Sir Marmaduke Langdale. Ludlow counter-attacked past the Poultry Cross into the Market Place, and pursued the enemy down Endless Street. Ludlow's regiment then fought a gallant defensive action in the streets and for a time held out in The Close, but finally withdrew and fought a fierce rearguard action at Harnham Bridge before drawing off through Odstock to Fordingbridge.

That Ludlow was prepared to profit from the Civil War is suggested by an interesting note in the papers of Bishop Seth Ward of Salisbury, which reads: 'Bishops Hall sold by state to Col. Ludlow who sold it on and it was partly pulled down and the rest converted into an inn'.

During the ensuing period when the New Model Army was being formed little is heard of Ludlow. He was recommended by the committee which selected officers for the command of a regiment, but the Wiltshire Committe objected on the grounds that he was indispensable in Wiltshire. In May 1646 the esteem with which Ludlow was regarded in Wiltshire led to his election as an MP for Wiltshire, with Mr James Herbert, the second son of the Earl of Pembroke, the two former Wiltshire MPs having been Ludlow's deceased father and Sir James Thynne,

the latter being 'disabled from sitting as a suspected royalist'. In 1650 Ludlow bought the manor of East Knoyle which had been ecclesiastical property, but in 1661 it was restored to the church trustees.

Ludlow's continued opposition to Cromwell

An old adage suggests that power corrupts, and during the Commonwealth Cromwell effectively assumed the prerogatives of royalty when he used the rising by Penruddocke in Wiltshire (see below) as the excuse for appointing major-generals over specific areas to suppress any further opposition. In his *Memoirs* Ludlow frequently expressed his dislike of Cromwell's Protectorate, particularly when he assumed supreme power, and he also objected to the 'folly and profusion' of the body of Cromwell lying in state at Somerset House. He could not bring himself to describe the funeral, merely writing:

> I purposely omit the rest of the Pageantry, the great number of persons that attended on the body, the procession to Westminster, the vast expense in Mourning, the state and magnificence of the Monument erected for him, with many other things that I care not to remember.

Cromwell had when in power treated his outspoken and inveterate enemy generously, and it has been suggested that 'Cromwell could comprehend and bear with Ludlow, but Ludlow was not big enough to comprehend Cromwell'.

The Penruddocke Rising

After the Civil War had been won by parliament and Cromwell was in power during the Interregnum, a revolt occurred in south Wiltshire. The particularly beautiful grouping of church, manor house, park and lake at Compton Chamberlayne, above the River Nadder west of Salisbury, was for over three hundred years until they sold it in 1930 the home of the Penruddockes, a Cumberland family who came to Compton in the 16th century. Sir John Penruddocke was appointed Charles I's Sheriff of Wiltshire on 29 September 1643, and was in January 1644 ordered to raise as many troops as he could muster in Wiltshire. In September 1644 he was succeeded as royal Sheriff by Sir Walter Long, who soon gave way to Sir James Long.

Early in 1655, a little over ten years after his father was appointed as Sheriff, his son Colonel John Penruddocke (1619–55) planned a rising against Cromwell. The Penruddockes had lost relatives serving the king in the Civil War and had also suffered heavy fines for 'malignancy'. Although the Penruddocke Rising has often been assumed to be an isolated local rebellion, in fact parallel risings took place in Shropshire, Nottingham, and the North of England. All of them failed, but the widespread nature of the revolt explains the severity with which it was treated. The historian Lord Clarendon suggested that Cromwell encouraged the widespread risings in 1655 to provide the pretext for imposing a more severe military control of the nation by the major-generals.

A few years earlier John Penruddocke had with John Aubrey been guests of Lord Francis Seymour at the royalist gathering at Marlborough, at which Aubrey discovered Avebury and Silbury. Early in 1655 preliminary royalist 'meetings of foxhunters' were arranged in Wiltshire (at Everleigh, Ludgershall, Salisbury, West Knoyle, Compton Chamberlayne, and other places) to plan the rising. Penruddocke's principal supporter was Hugh Grove, from the family that had come to Wiltshire from Buckinghamshire in the mid–15th century and had become established at Chisenbury in the upper Avon Valley in about 1650.

On Sunday 11 March 1655 about sixty horsemen assembled by arrangement in Clarendon Park east of Salisbury under Sir Joseph Wagstaff, and were joined by about forty more. Penruddocke and Grove were present and led them to Blandford where more mounted troops joined them. Now numbering about two hundred they returned to Salisbury on 12 March and there arrested Chief Justice Rolle and Baron Nicholas who were then presiding at the Salisbury Assizes. They also attacked the Sheriff's house, which was resolutely defended by Major Henry Wansey from Warminster, and then proclaimed Charles II king.

After failing to gather much support in Salisbury Colonel Penruddocke and Hugh Grove led their party south to Downton, then on to Blandford, Sherborne and Yeovil, before retreating west into Devon. Reduced to about a hundred by desertions they were dispersed at South Molton by troops under a Captain Crook. Sir Joseph Wagstaff escaped and fled abroad, but Colonel Penruddocke, Hugh Grove, and about sixty more were captured. Penruddocke and Grove were taken to Exeter. The list of prisoners sent to parliament by Captain Crook indicates that they were not all from Wiltshire. Colonel Penruddocke was taken to London and interviewed by Cromwell at Whitehall, where the two men seem to have formed a good opinion of the other. On 9 April he was returned as a prisoner to Exeter passing through Salisbury on the 11th. At Salisbury some of the rebels were later tried and several were hanged.

Back at Exeter Penruddocke and Grove were tried and sentenced to death as traitors. Penruddocke and Grove wrote to their judges asking them to petition the Lord Protector for mercy on their behalf, and it was said that Cromwell was inclined to be merciful, but it was ultimately decided that examples had to be made and they were beheaded on 16 May. Mrs Arundell Penruddocke spared no effort but failed to obtain a reprieve for her husband. To his credit Cromwell expressly forbade the usual horrific deaths for traitors of hanging, drawing and quartering. Both men died bravely, Grove declaring that he died a loyal subject of Charles II, and Penruddocke stating: 'The cause for which I am now to die is Loyalty, in this age called High Treason'. Seven of their colleagues were hanged at the same time, and others suffered transportation. Penruddocke's farewell letters to his wife, which have survived, are so moving that many years later Steele and Addison published them in *The Lover*.

Grove was buried at Exeter, as was Penruddocke initially, although surviving accounts suggest that his body was later returned to Compton Chamberlayne and buried in a small vault beneath the family pew, where a headless skeleton was subsequently discovered.

Penruddocke's Rising provided the excuse for Cromwell to divide the entire country into military districts subject to martial law under major-generals. Ludlow expressed strong opposition to this 'cantonisation' of England, and it was Cromwell's assumption of almost regal power that finally alienated Ludlow from him, especially after he had declared a preference for monarchy. His relations with Cromwell had always been strained and in his *Memoirs* Ludlow recorded how their discussions about the Constitution in January 1648 had descended into farce, when Cromwell hurled a cushion at his head and Ludlow responded by chasing Cromwell out of the room, this being probably the only occasion when a high-level political discussion deteriorated into a pillow-fight!

Parliament originally had no intention of executing the king. It had hoped to come to an arrangement which would allow the king to reign provided that he undertook to do so democratically, with legislation and taxation sanctioned by parliament. Charles I was executed because he refused to accept this, and so persistently broke undertakings that Cromwell realised that he was so untrustworthy that no settlement was possible. It was then decided that he must die, and Ludlow was appointed one of the king's judges at his trial in January 1649. The fortieth signature on the death warrant of the king, who was executed on 30 January 1649, was 'Edm. Ludlowe'.

Ludlow as Deputy Lieutenant of Ireland

In spite of their differences Cromwell in 1650 appointed Ludlow deputy in Ireland to his son-in-law Henry Ireton (1611–51), possibly to get him out of the way. When Ireton suddenly died in November 1651 parliament first instructed the army to obey Ludlow and then nominated Charles Fleetwood (c. 1618–92) as commander in Ireland over his head. Fleetwood, one of the principal Cromwellian soldiers, is connected with Wiltshire by being elected MP for Marlborough in 1649. He remained commander-in-chief in Ireland 1652–5, having in 1652 married Cromwell's daughter Bridget, the widow of Henry Ireton who had died the previous year. Later, having become one of Cromwell's 'lords',

Fleetwood took a leading part in the overthrow of his son Richard Cromwell in 1659. He was made commander-in-chief by the Rump Parliament and together with Lambert moved to oppose General Monck's march south to restore the monarchy.

By the time that Fleetwood reached Ireland in October 1652 Ludlow had effectively conquered the country. He later claimed that during his four years of service in Ireland he had spent £4,500 of his own money in the parliamentary cause.

With the execution of the king and the abolition of the House of Lords England was now for the first time a republic. All of Ludlow's aspirations had now been realised, but he became even more disillusioned with Cromwell when he assumed almost regal powers as Lord Protector, and refused to recognise him in that office. When in January 1655 Ludlow was found to have been circulating leaflets hostile to his government Cromwell reluctantly ordered Ludlow to remain in Ireland. In 1655 he disobeyed orders by crossing the Irish Sea and landing at Beaumaris in Anglesey where he was immediately arrested and imprisoned in Beaumaris Castle. After six weeks he was granted an interview with Cromwell, at which he claimed that, since the government was controlled by the army, it was unlawful and refused to give an undertaking not to act against it.

Ludlow again elected to Parliament

Parliament now found itself in the difficult position of having one of its most popular generals threatening to oppose its will. Ludlow was allowed to retire with his relations to Essex, at some distance from his home and power base in Wiltshire. After Cromwell's death in 1658 he attempted to re-unite the republican party and opposed the election of 'Tumbledown Dick' Cromwell as Protector. In 1659 he was candidate for the Hindon constituency and held election meetings at Yarnfield and at East Knoyle, was elected, and resumed his seat in parliament. In the Long Parliament of that year he was appointed a member of the Committee for Public Safety. On 9 June he was made Lieutenant-Colonel, was given command of a regiment, and again made commander in chief of the army of Ireland, which he proceeded to reorganise by appointing republicans as its senior officers.

After Richard Cromwell fell and General Monck marched south from Scotland to restore the monarchy, Ludlow was on the point of joining General Lambert (1619–83) to oppose Monck when Lambert's army melted away.

Ludlows escape to the Continent and exile

At the Restoration of the monarchy in 1660 Ludlow was impeached, his accusers including General Monck who had effectively brought about the Restoration. Ludlow was plotting a rebellion by the republican regiments when on 14 May 1660 parliament decreed that all who had sat in judgement on Charles I should be secured, and from his hiding place in London he saw the crowds returning from welcoming Charles II home.

Although he surrendered to parliament Ludlow soon recognised that his life was in danger and he finally fled to the Continent. For a while the country was unaware of his escape and £300 was offered as a reward for his arrest. Rumours circulated that Ludlow would soon be the greatest man in England, but he was quietly travelling across France to Geneva. When the king's judges began to be apprehended and returned to England for execution he moved on to Vevey on the north bank of Lake Geneva, where he was welcomed and granted asylum and protection. He was hunted by Charles II's agents, several attempts were made on his life, and although they were foiled Ludlow fortified his house and went incognito by adopting his mother's maiden name and signing his letters 'Edmund Phillips'.

In 1663 Ludlow's wife joined him in exile, but since his *Memoirs* end at 1672 the later part of his life is rather obscure. His letters reveal that he continued to observe closely events in England, and in 1685 he was invited by the Duke of Monmouth to assist him in his attempt to usurp the throne of James II but refused, possibly on the grounds that he was then sixty-eight, or more probably because he was so opposed to royalty that he had no wish to exchange one king for another.

Ludlow's long period of exile was interrupted after nearly thirty years by the revolution of 1688, which put the protestants William of Orange and his wife Mary on the throne. Misjudjing the situation Ludlow came to London in June 1689 hoping for a reprieve. In London his house became a meeting place for republicans, attention was drawn to his presence in London, and parliament was asked to proclaim him traitor. On 7 November an address was proposed on the subject of Ludlow to the king by the Speaker, Sir Edward Seymour of Maiden Bradley. King William offered a reward for Ludlow's arrest but he again escaped, this time to Holland, some said with the connivance of the authorities.

Ludlow's death and burial at Vevey

Disappointed at his inability to obtain permission to return to England Ludlow placed an inscription over his door in Vevey which read: *Omne solum forti Patria, quia Patris, 1686* (translated by Macaulay as: 'To whom God is a father, every land is a fatherland'). Edmund Ludlow died in 1692 and was buried in St Martin's Church at Vevey leaving no issue. During his long exile he had written his *Memoirs of the Civil War* which were originally written in the 1660s as *A Voyce from the Watch Tower* and published in 1698–9 in three volumes, possibly by Ludlow's friend Slingsby Bethel (died 1697), the former Sheriff of London with whom Ludlow and his wife were on friendly terms. There were subsequent editions, including a brilliant one by Sir Charles Firth who added an account of *The Civil War in Wiltshire*. Ludlow's *Memoirs* were for long regarded as a minor classic, providing one of the most reliable original sources of information on the Civil War and particularly on the republican opposition to Oliver Cromwell, but when part of the original manuscript was discovered in 1970 comparison revealed that the published text had been revised to make Ludlow's opinions far more extreme than those expressed in the original.

Hill Deverill Manor House and Church

During his long enforced exile of more than thirty years in Switzerland Ludlow must often have thought nostalgically of his home beside the river

Edmund Ludlow's home, the Manor House at Hill Deverill

at Hill Deverill. The Manor Farmhouse that we see today is not the house that he would have known. It was remodelled in the time of Queen Anne by his successors the Cokers long after he had left it. The present house has arched and mullioned windows and is attached to a very long fifteen-bay barn with three porches associated with a 15th–16th century farm building that Ludlow would have known. These buildings stand near the now redundant Hill Deverill church in a remote situation beside the River Deverill. The former extensive grounds with ponds and many outbuildings are now gone. Local tradition suggests that the manor house once had a moat and a drawbridge. The Ludlow arms survive above a gateway, may also be seen on a house in Monkton Deverill, and they are reproduced in Colt Hoare's *Hundred of Mere* (page 176).

The beautiful chest tomb to Edmund's ancestor John Ludlow, the grandson of William Ludlow, with traceried sides and heraldic shields bearing the arms of Ludlow impaling others and supported by angels, was removed when Hill Deverill church was deconsecrated in 1984 to Longbridge Deverill church, where it now serves as an altar tomb in the Bath Chapel.

The Ludlows lost Hill Deverill when their male line died out and a Ludlow heiress Elizabeth (died 1765) married Sir Henry Coker, who then became lord of the manor.

The subsequent Ludlow connection with Heywood

Long after Edmund Ludlow's death the Ludlow family became established at Heywood near Westbury, which from the 13th century to the Reformation was owned by Stanley Abbey and leased to tenants. At the dissolution of the monasteries Heywood was acquired by Sir Edward Bayntun, whose son Andrew conveyed it to Henry Long. The Longs sold Heywood to Sir James Ley, who in 1620 became Chief Justice of the Kings Bench. In 1626 he was created Earl of Marlborough by Charles I. At Heywood he built a new house in the Jacobean style which passed at his death to his son Henry, Earl of Marlborough, who died in 1638 leaving Heywood to his son James, Earl of Marlborough (died 1665). He in turn sold Heywood to Henry, Earl of Danby, who died in 1644.

Around 1700 Heywood was acquired by the Phipps family. William Phipps, the Governor of Bombay, was born at Heywood and died in 1748. In 1789 Thomas Peckham Phipps sold Heywood to the clothier Gaisford Gibbs (died 1791). His widow Elizabeth married Abraham Ludlow, and Susan the heiress of Gaisford Gibbs, married the son of Abraham Ludlow, another Abraham who died 1822. By this marriage Heywood became the property of the Ludlows. Heywood House then passed to the

Lopes family. Henry Charles Lopes (1827–99) was an MP and a JP for Wiltshire and Somerset. In 1897 he was created Baron and out of deference to the Ludlows took the title of Baron Ludlow of Heywood. The house was soon after 1869 rebuilt in its original Jacobean style.

This descent of Heywood House to the Ludlow descendants of Edmund Ludlow explains how the inscription which Edmund had placed over his door during his exile at Vevey was for long kept at Heywood House, which is now used as offices by the National Trust.

Ludlow compared with Clarendon

Edmund Ludlow's long exile for his political beliefs and his writing his memoirs of the Civil War during that exile is a sad story that invites comparison with that of the royalist Lord Clarendon, the subject of Chapter 8, who endured similar misfortunes. These two men who loyally served England according to their beliefs and gave so much for the causes which they served were obliged to live out most of their later lives in exile from their native Wiltshire which they both loved.

Had he not escaped into exile it is interesting to speculate whether at the age of forty-three Ludlow would have died the death of a traitor, as did the other surviving regicides. He might have escaped death because he had regularly quarrelled with Cromwell, although his reputation as an inveterate republican would have counted very much against him.

As it was he lived to the age of seventy-five and died naturally in his bed at Vevey.

8 Dinton and Lord Clarendon

with the Lawes brothers

Everyone interested in the history of Wiltshire will sooner or later find their way to Dinton. The claim of this village to fame lies in the fact that during the 17th century the families of Hyde and Lawes, which had come to Dinton in the previous century, produced three men who achieved fame at the court of Charles I, and suffered considerable hardships as a result of their support for that ill-fated monarch. It seems disproportionate that such a small village should have produced three men of national eminence at one time. The greatest of these three men was Edward Hyde, who changed the course of British history by being the principal agent in the Restoration of the monarchy after it had been abolished after the Civil War. As Charles II's first minister he was then created Earl of Clarendon, became one of the greatest of English historians, and was also the grandfather of two queens of England. The other two Dinton men were the Lawes brothers who attained celebrity as musicians and composers at court.

Dinton is an attractive village that nestles under a steep wooded ridge of down about eight

Grovely Woods, the former royal forest, seen from above Dinton

miles west of Salisbury. Two miles to its north Grovely Woods occupies a parallel ridge to that above Dinton, and a mile south of the village the River Nadder flows between Dinton and Fovant on its way to join the Avon near Salisbury. Until the early 19th century the principal road at Dinton was the Teffont to Salisbury road, that ran along the sandy ridge north of the village, from which a cross road plunges south down a dramatic winding declivity to Dinton, and to the north descends more gently and runs past Marshwood Farm to Dinton Beeches at the west end of Grovely Woods.

At the Dissolution of the monasteries the principal landowner at Dinton was the Abbess of Shaftesbury.

Edward Hyde's ancestry and birth

Edward Hyde (1608–74), who became the Earl of Clarendon, was the third son of Henry Hyde (c. 1562–1632), a country gentleman with Cheshire associations who owned an estate at Purton in north Wiltshire and leased another at Dinton. The Hyde family had been settled at Norbury in Cheshire from the time of Henry III and their connection with Wiltshire began when Robert Hyde, the great-great-grandfather of Edward, married Margaret Hollard of Dinton. Some of the Hydes had been lawyers who had prospered in the aftermath of the dissolution of the monasteries, and Henry's father Laurence Hyde of West Hatch had looked after the business affairs of Sir John Thynne of Longleat. After the Dissolution he was granted properties on the sites of both the present College of Matrons and the Hungerford Chantry off Choristers' Green in The Close at Salisbury. He died eighteen years before his grandson Edward was born and is commemorated by a large brass in the floor of the sanctuary of Tisbury church inscribed: 'Here lyeth Laurence Hyde of West Hatch Esqr., who had issue by Anne his wife, six sons and four daughters and died in the Incarnation of Our Lord God 1590'.

After his father's death in 1590 Henry Hyde was by a family arrangement granted the lease of Dinton rectory for life, but early in the 17th century he moved from Dinton to Purton because he preferred as he said: 'to live upon his own land, the which he had purchased many years before, and to rent Dinton, which was but a lease for lives, to a tenant'. He had served in the later Parliaments of Queen Elizabeth, but after the queen's death in 1603 never again went to London, although he lived for another thirty years. His son Edward recorded: 'From that time, he lived a private life at Dinton aforesaid, with great cheerfulness and content, and with great general reputation throughout the whole country'. On 3 April 1597 Henry Hyde married at Trowbridge parish church Mary Langford (1570–1661), a lady from a family of prosperous Trowbridge woollen manufacturers. Edward recalled that his father's wife Mary Langford: 'was married to him [Henry Hyde] above forty years, never was in London in her life', and that his father: 'lived till he was seventy years of age'. In 1631 he paid a £17. 10s. 0d (£17.50) fine as a composition for refusing to accept a knighthood.

Towards the end of his life Henry Hyde decided to spend the rest of his time in Salisbury, where he had a house prepared for him in The Close. He moved to Salisbury in late 1632 and died within a few days of moving. Edward Hyde related the circumstances of his father's death with a typical 17th-century earthiness, how he suffered from an indisposition that obliged him to frequently make water, one day toured the Salisbury churches to choose a place to be buried, and after deciding on the cathedral rushed home to relieve himself and died.

The long-held belief that Edward Hyde was born at his mother's home town of Trowbridge is disproved by a 1608 entry in the Dinton parish registers which reads: 'In this year, the two-and-twentye day of February, Henry Hide

Dinton Church

of Dinton, gent., had a son christened named Edward'. Edward Hyde also states in his *Life* that he was: 'born at Dinton in the county of Wilts . . . and was always bred in his fathers house under the care of a schoolmaster'. His birthplace was probably the house which stands a short distance west of Dinton church which was formerly the Rectory House, but is now known as Hyde's House. At the Dissolution it was acquired by the Arundells and then passed through several families to Laurence Hyde, who obtained it in the reign of Elizabeth by marrying the widow of its former owner.

Hyde's House in its parkland setting

As a boy young Edward was sent to Purton in north Wiltshire to recover from a serious illness at his father's other home, which still stands in the centre of the village. Being a third son he was originally destined for the church, but after his two older brothers died young (Laurence as a child and Henry aged twenty-six) Edward unexpectedly became father's heir and after attending Magdalen Hall at Oxford took up law as his career.

In the following account of his life Clarendon is generally referred to as Edward Hyde up to 1661, and thereafter as Clarendon.

The Langfords of Trowbridge

The marriage in 1597 of Edward's father Henry Hyde to Mary Langford (1570–1661) of Trowbridge is a matter of interest, since it has sometimes been implied that he married beneath himself. In fact Mary's mother was Mary Hyde, a daughter of Laurence Hyde of West Hatch, and the Langfords are believed to have been a family with a distinguished past which emanated from the Langford villages in the Wylye Valley.

Clarendon House at Purton

Most of the prosperous families in the Wylye Valley made their money from a combination of sheep farming and woollen manufacture, and it is likely that the Langfords were involved in these activities, because in 1490 William Langford and his son Alexander, Mary Langford's great-great-grandfather, moved to Trowbridge at a time when the woollen industry was being removed from the cottages into weaving establishments. In 1544 Alexander Langford senior and junior purchased Castle Mills at Trowbridge, together with other properties at Bradford on Avon and Freshford, to add to their expanding west Wiltshire estates.

Some of the Langfords moved away but Edward, the great-grandson of William Langford, stayed at Trowbridge and there he married Mary Hyde. The registers of St James's Church at Trowbridge reveal that on 10 December 1570 their daughter, another Mary, was baptised, that Edward Langford was buried on 9 December 1594, and that in April 1597: 'Mr Henry Hide and mistris Marie Langeforde was married the 3 daie'. From his marriage to Mary, who was the co-heiress of her recently deceased father, Henry Hyde acquired several properties in Trowbridge, and in his will he mentions a 'great house at

Trowbridge', and lands and tenements at Studley, Hilperton, and elsewhere, which he had obtained through his Langford wife. Edward Hyde had no reservations about the standing of the Langfords and quartered their arms in his own.

Mary Langford was probably born at the top of The Parade in Trowbridge where part of Edward Langford's timber-framed house is said to survive behind the later facades of the former Usher's offices and the Crowing Cock Café. By Henry Hyde Mary became the mother of the Earl of Clarendon, the grandmother of Clarendon's daughter Anne Hyde, Duchess of York, and the great-grandmother of two queens of England – Mary II and Queen Anne. Edward Hyde inherited from his mother properties at Trowbridge where he is commemorated by Clarendon Avenue and Clarendon School.

Probable birthplace of Mary Langford at The Parade, Trowbridge

Edward Hyde's early life and character

Edward Hyde was described by his friend the diarist John Evelyn as being of a: 'jolly temper, after the old English fashion'. He is recorded as being fat and pompous in manner, characteristics which are borne out by his portrait by Lely. After being schooled privately at Dinton the future Earl of Clarendon in 1622 went to Magdalen Hall at Oxford. It is an indication of the standing of the Hydes as a county family in Wiltshire that Edward Hyde was recommended to Dr Langton, the president of Magdalen, in a letter written by James I, which was because of its late arrival apparently ignored until a Secretary of State pursued the matter. From Magdalen Hyde graduated with a BA and in 1625 went to study law at the Middle Temple, where his uncle chief justice

Edward Hyde, Earl of Clarendon

Sir Nicholas Hyde was treasurer. In 1633 he was called to the bar.

Edward Hyde's character was summarised by Sir Philip Warwick, who knew him personally, in his *Memoires* (1682):

> Sir Edward Hyde was of a cheerful and equable conversation, of an extreme industry and activity, and of a great confidence which made him soon at home at a court. His natural parts were very forward and sound, his learning was very good and competent and he had a facility both of tongue and pen which made him willingly hearkened unto and much approved : and having spent much of his study in the law, this made his speech and writings the more significant, and his language and style very suitable to business, if not a little redundant.

Gilbert Burnet (1643–1715), Bishop of Salisbury from 1689, was rather more critical of Hyde, alleging that: 'he took too much upon himself and meddled in everything, which was his greatest error', but then relented and admitted that: 'upon the whole matter he was a true Englishman and a sincere Protestant'. In his frank assessment of his own character Edward Hyde admitted to being very ambitious and over-indulging his palate, but claimed that he never spoke a profane or loose word, that he was inclined to be over proud and liked to wrangle and dispute, and that he was

generous and had a contempt for money. He also asserted that his integrity was unblemished and that he was above temptation.

In addition to being a lifelong royalist Clarendon was a religious man and a firm believer in the Anglican church. His writings contain frequent references to the goodness of God and he rather pompously recorded how, when he was summoned to receive promotion from Charles I, the king: 'took notice of his affection for the church', for which: 'he thanked him more than for all the rest', and how he replied that: 'if he had commanded him to have withdraw his affection and reverence for the church, he would not have obeyed him'.

Edward Hyde's marriages and children

Edward Hyde married first in 1629 when he was twenty. Anne Ayliffe was a Wiltshire lady from Grittenham whom he described as: 'a young lady very fair and beautiful, the daughter of Sir George Ayliffe, a gentleman of a good name and fortune in the county of Wilts . . . and by her mother (a St John) nearly allied to many families'. By this marriage Edward Hyde rose a little up the social scale, but within a few months of her marriage Anne died suddenly at Reading of small-pox, aged only twenty. As his second wife Edward Hyde 'after a widowhood of near three years' in 1632 married Frances Aylesbury (1617–70) the daughter of Sir Thomas Aylesbury, who held offices as Master of Requests to the King and Master of the Mint. His second wife, in a marriage which lasted 'five or six and thirty years', bore Edward Hyde 'many children of both sexes'. These included a daughter Anne, who was to marry secretly James, Duke of York, to the consternation of both Charles II and her father, and die before her husband became king, unaware that two of their daughters were to become queens of England.

Charles I and his Parliaments

The manner in which Charles I in the early-17th century provoked unrest among his ordinary people has been described in Chapter 7 (pages 99-100). He was equally high-handed with his parliaments, choosing to rule by divine right and levy taxation without recourse to parliament. In the first three years of his reign from his accession in 1625 until 1629 he called three parliaments and then dismissed them, because they all opposed his unconstitutional methods and the favours that he showered upon his favourite the Duke of Buckingham. The period from 1629 to 1640, in which Charles I governed without calling parliaments, became known as the 'eleven years tyranny', but in desperate need of funds he was in 1640 obliged to call the Short Parliament, which was so-named because it lasted only from 13 April until 5 May when it was dissolved.

Charles I's troubles arose from the fact that he consistently demonstrated dual standards. In his private life he was a cultured gentleman but in his public dealings he was far from honourable. His word could never be trusted and he was ultimately executed because it had been proved impossible to negotiate with him. His reign was a case of a monarch governing harshly in order to conceal his weakness, and using the court of Star Chamber to maintain royal authority.

After his training at Middle Temple was completed Edward Hyde's work for some London merchants brought him into contact with Archbishop Laud (1573–1645), the king's adviser and chaplain, who thought well of him. In his *Life* Edward Hyde admits that he 'well knew how to cultivate such contacts'. His friends at this time included Ben Jonson, John Selden, Charles Cotton, Sir Kenelm Digby, and Thomas Carew.

Edward Hyde was by his own account in his early career particularly industrious. He writes of how he:

> grew so much in love with business and practice, that he gave up his whole heart to it; resolving by a course of severe study, to recover the time he had lost upon less profitable learning; and to intend nothing else, but to reap all those benefits to which the profession could carry him.

As soon as he began to accumulate money Hyde started to enlarge his paternal estate by purchase. During Charles I's troubled reign many lawyers were entering parliament, and in 1640 he was elected as the member for Wootton Bassett to the Short Parliament called by Charles

I merely to vote him funds. When the new parliament insisted on addressing the nation's grievances the king unwisely dissolved it.

In the subsequent Long Parliament, to which he was elected as member for Saltash in 1641, Hyde became the principal advocate against the prerogative courts which had been abused by the Stuarts, and he headed the committee against ship money, but when John Pym demanded that the king's advisers should be chosen by parliament he objected. He now realised just how far the opposition was prepared to go and from this time was a moderate royalist acting in opposition to Pym. He soon attracted the king's notice and became one of his principal advisers, the others being Queen Henrietta Maria, whose advice the king generally followed, and John Digby, Earl of Bristol (1580–1653). Digby, after having been an adviser to James I, had in the 1620s been accused by Prince Charles of trying to convert him to catholicism, but had returned to power after the assassination of the royal favourite Buckingham at Portsmouth in 1628. While the queen and Digby often offered bad advice Edward Hyde attempted to reconcile the king and parliament by urging him to rule more democratically. Had this advice been followed the Civil War would have been avoided and the king would have kept his head.

Parliament now presented the Grand Remonstrance drawn up by John Pym which listed grievances and demanded the king's action in remedying them. The king's response was drafted by Hyde, but King Charles now resolved to ignore his sound advice that:

> Your Majesty well knows that your greatest strength is in hearts and affections of those persons who have been the severest asserters of the public liberties, and so, beside their duty and loyalty to your person, are in love with your inclination to peace and justice.

The intractability of King Charles is demonstrated by the fact that John Pym (c. 1584–1643), a moderate man who had been the MP for Calne in Wiltshire, was provoked by the king's behaviour to become the leader of the parliamentary revolution. His dominance of the opposition in parliament became so great that he was known as 'King Pym'.

On 4 January the king, after conferring with the queen, decided upon the extreme measure of arresting five of the most reactionary members of parliament. He entered the house with a file of troopers, demanded use of the Speaker's chair, and then found that 'the birds had flown'. This act caused a furore, the city rose in arms and, no longer feeling safe in his own capital, the king left London only to return several years later as a prisoner for his trial and execution.

Shortly before the outbreak of the Civil War Edward Hyde rode in the fields between Westminster and Chelsea with Nathaniel Fiennes (1608–69), who lived in Wiltshire at Newton Tony east of Amesbury. He was the favourite son of William Fiennes, Lord Viscount Saye and Sele (1582–1662), and became in 1662 the father of the redoubtable lady traveller Celia Fiennes. He was an ardent parliamentarian who became a roundhead colonel and was Governor of Bristol when it was attacked by the royalists in July 1643. When its defenders ran out of ammunition the citizens indicated that they did not wish their city to be stormed and plundered. Fiennes consequently surrendered and was allowed to march out with his troops. Being the second port in the kingdom Bristol was a great prize for the royalists, and when accused of cowardice over its surrender Colonel Fiennes demanded a trial, at which he was found guilty and sentenced to death, although the sentence was remitted after he had suffered banishment for some years. On this ride between Westminster and Chelsea Edward Hyde, according to his own account, was asked by Nathaniel Fiennes: 'What it was that inclined him to adhere so passionately to the church which could not possibly be supported?', to which Hyde answered that 'He could have no other obligation than that of his conscience'. He also emphasised that 'He had no relation or dependence upon any churchmen', but that he 'could not conceive how religion could be preserved without bishops'.

Colonel Fiennes's daughter Celia Fiennes (1662–1741) spent her girlhood at the family manor house at Newton Tony where she was probably born. Her mother was Francis, the daughter of another roundhead colonel, Richard Whitehead, from the same part of Wiltshire. Three uncles of her own and five of her uncles by marriage fought for parliament in the Civil War. In the late-17th century Celia Fiennes travelled over England from Lands End to the Scottish border on horseback and recorded her experiences in *Through England on a Side Saddle in the Time of William and Mary*.

The Fiennes manor house stood west of the road through Newton Tony. When The Croft was built about 1948 its foundations were exposed, and a cob wall north of the site is associated with the former manor house, which became a mere farmhouse after Wilbury House was built early in the 18th century.

Hyde was as a member of parliament appalled by the king's unconstitutional act in attempting to arrest the five members, and very nearly deserted the royalist party, but ultimately slipped away from London and joined the king when he raised his standard at Nottingham.

Sir John Glanville of Broad Hinton

The Speaker of the House of Commons when Edward Hyde entered the Short Parliament in 1640 was John Glanville (1586–1661) who lived at Broad Hinton near Wootton Bassett. He was a Devon man, a lawyer and a judge, who had been MP for Plymouth since 1614. Sir John was descended from Henry II's Lord Chief Justice Sir Ranulf Glanvil, and Bishop Burnett described him as being: 'a man of generous and just disposition'. He took part in the impeachment of the king's great favourite Buckingham in 1626 and spoke so strongly against ship-money taxation that the parliamentary opposition to the king had high hopes of him but, having shown some sympathy for parliament's cause, Glanville like Edward Hyde finally committed himself to the king. His home was the manor house at Broad Hinton which he bought in 1640 from the Wroughtons, who had long been established there. After it was burned down during the war he lived in the gatehouse, as described by John Evelyn in his diary entry for 16 July 1654:

> We went to another uncle and relative of my wife's, Sir John Glanville, a famous lawyer, formerly speaker

of the House of Commons; his seat is at Broad Hinton, where he now lived but in the Gatehouse, his very fair dwelling-house having been burnt by his own hands, to prevent the rebels making a garrison of it.

According to other accounts Broad Hinton house was burnt by parliamentary troops, suggesting that Sir John may have made the most of it and cultivated royal favour by claiming that he had destroyed his own house in the royalist cause. That the house was indeed burnt is apparently confirmed by the fact that some farm buildings at Manor Farm to the north of Broad Hinton appear to be built from stones which have been subjected to fire. The gatehouse was probably on the present drive which runs south-south-east from Manor Farm, this being the approach shown on old maps.

In 1644 Sir John Glanville fell into the hands of parliament and was disabled from being an MP. In 1645 he was sent to the Tower and also fined as a 'malignant', but he compounded for his freedom and was released. He lived to see the Restoration and is commemorated in Broad Hinton church by an inscribed tablet in Latin with a scrolled open pediment and side garlands on the north wall of the chancel. His second son Lieut-Colonel Francis Glanville (1617–45) died fighting for the king at the siege of Bridgwater, having already served for six years in the king's army. He has a grander monument consisting of a life-size alabaster figure standing in full armour in a niche with his real armour above. His place of burial is not known.

Edward Hyde's Civil War

Hyde remained head of the royalist party in the Commons until May 1642, and after joining the king remained staunchly loyal to the crown throughout the war and became the king's principal adviser. He drafted for the king the moderate pronouncements providing for a balanced government which helped to strengthen the royal party, although many who knew the king were aware that he would not regard himself as being bound by these undertakings and consequently threw in their lot with parliament. Edward Hyde was present as a non-combatant

at the first battle of the Civil War fought at Edgehill on 23 October 1643. After this battle the king felt sufficiently strong to reject peace overtures offered by parliament.

Edward Hyde had earler become involved in fund raising for the royalist cause, and parliament expelled him from the House of Commons in August 1642. While the royalist headquarters was at Oxford he lived at All Souls College. In February 1643 he was knighted, but was profoundly distressed by the death of his great friend the statesman and writer Lucius Cary, Viscount Falkland (1610–43) at the Battle of Newbury in September 1643.

Early in 1645 the king decided to send the fifteen-year-old Prince Charles into the west country to drum up royalist support, and a council of advisers including Sir Edward Hyde was formed to accompany him, and left Oxford for Bristol on 4 March. One of the major royalist problems throughout the Civil War was squabbling among the generals. The royalist Lords Goring and Greville in the west had promised much during the winter, but had alienated the people by their harsh measures and were now utterly at odds with each other. There was no co-ordinated command structure, the generals acted independently and spent much of their time blaming each other for their failures. At Bristol while the prince's council argued interminably Sir Edward Hyde kept the young prince severely in his place, and the whole western enterprise had already proved to be utterly ineffective when, on 14 June 1645, the royalists were decisively defeated by the New Model Army at Naseby.

Edward Hyde's first exile

After Naseby Sir Edward Hyde accompanied Prince Charles into exile, first to Scilly and then, it having been decided that Scilly was not defensible against parliament's navy, for two years in Jersey. In this first exile he began to write his *History of the Rebellion and Civil Wars in England*. After Charles I's execution in January 1649 Hyde became principal adviser to Prince Charles and much of his time was spent at Antwerp and Breda, where he was often in severe financial distress. From Brussels he wrote: 'We are all without a dollar, and have been long, and they who have neither money nor credit are likely to keep a cold Christmas'.

From November 1649 until March 1651 Sir Edward Hyde accompanied Lord Cottington on a futile embassy to Spain, and for the ensuing nine years he served Charles II at his impecunious and factious court in exile. In 1658 he was made Lord Chancellor, and after Oliver Cromwell's death that same year he advised Prince Charles to accept restoration to the throne subject to a future parliament.

The Restoration and Clarendon's title
On 2 January 1660 General Monck marched south from Scotland with a Scottish army, on 3 February he was in London, and on 21 February his troops allowed the excluded members of the Long Parliament to resume their seats. Parliament then dissolved itself and the new parliament pronounced Prince Charles king as Charles II. He landed at Dover on 23 May accompanied by James, Duke of York.

On the eve of the Restoration there was an attempt by catholics and presbyterians to exclude Sir Edward Hyde from power, but he was naturally in great favour with the new king, who wrote to his wife: 'I must make Ned Hyde Secretary of State for the truth is I can trust nobody else'. The king made Hyde Baron Hyde of Hindon and chief minister, and at the coronation in April 1661 he was created Earl of Clarendon, taking his title from the ancient Clarendon estate in south-east Wiltshire east of Salisbury. In his usual desperate need of money Charles I had mortgaged Clarendon Park for £20,000 to Sir Edward Hyde, who was not above feathering his nest, as was usual for holders of high office at that time. He recorded how 'without any noise or scandal' he had procured many land grants from his master Charles I and one of these was Clarendon Park. Samuel Pepys in his diary records the circumstances in which Sir Edward Hyde obtained Clarendon Park.

Since the royal exchequer was almost invariably impoverished Hyde assumed that the debt would never be repaid and that Clarendon would remain his own. Although during the Common-

wealth Hyde had as a royalist in exile forfeited Clarendon and it was sold by the Commonwealth parliament, after the Restoration the sale was invalidated, Sir Edward Hyde was reinstated to the ownership, and when made a peer by Charles II he took his title from Clarendon which was his principal Wiltshire property.

The remains of Clarendon Palace on the estate from which Edward Hyde took his title

A few years later Clarendon unexpectedly lost the estate from which he had taken his title. In his diary entry for 22 February 1664 Pepys recorded how: 'the King [Charles II] hath this day sent his order to the Privy Seale for the payment of this £20,000 to my Lord Chancellor [Clarendon] to clear the mortgage'. It was said that the money was raised from the sale of Dunkirk to France. After regaining royal ownership the new king gave Clarendon to General Monck (1608–70), who had been instrumental in ensuring his Restoration to the throne, and was rewarded with the title of 1st Duke of Albemarle.

To support his new title Clarendon was given three manors in Oxfordshire which had been confiscated from the deceased Wiltshire regicide Sir John Danvers of Dauntsey, who according to Aubrey: 'To revenge himselfe of his sister, the Lady Gargrave, and to ingratiate himselfe more with the Protector to null his brother, earl of

Danby's, Will, he contrary to his own naturall inclination, did sitt in the High Court of Justice at the King's Triall'. According to Anthony Wood Cornbury Park was 'Procured of the King by Clarendon at the Restoration and from it he took his second title of Lord Cornbury'.

Anne Hyde marries James, Duke of York

After the Restoration things for a time went well with Hyde who as Earl of Clarendon was at the peak of his career, although his position was about to be undermined. His troubles began when the heir apparent James, Duke of York, announced that he had contracted to marry Clarendon's daughter Anne Hyde (1638–71). During their exiles Anne, as a lady-in-waiting to the Princess of Orange, had entered into an arrangement to marry the Duke of York and was now in an advanced state of pregnancy. Clarendon out of his great respect for the monarchy, and possibly fearing trouble, was outraged and even suggested that his daughter should be

Clarendon's daughter, Ann Hyde, who became queen of James II

sent to the Tower. The king was at first disconcerted but then decided to make the best of the situation and decreed that the marriage should proceed. It took place at Clarendon's London residence Worcester House on 3 September 1660. Charles I's queen Henrietta Maria, who had always hated Clarendon, rushed over from France in an attempt to prevent the wedding. As soon as he had the king's permission the Duke of York had second thoughts and tried to extricate himself from marrying Anne. Despite the fact that he was twenty-six he pleaded that: 'the contract had been made in the warmth of youth', and he was backed by his friends who in a notable excess of loyalty asserted that they had all enjoyed her favours! The king alone came out of it well and having insisted that the marriage should proceed visited Anne in her confinement but the child died.

Anne Hyde was described by Pepys as downright plain, but in due course she proved to be a very good manager, as was to be be expected of a daughter of Clarendon. She ably organised her husband's life until she died, a fact which James grew to recognise and appreciate. They had eight children, four sons and four daughters, but of these children only Mary and Anne survived infancy. Anne died an avowed catholic in 1671 unaware that both of her surviving daughters would become queens of England in their own rights when James failed to produce by her a male heir who lived. By his second wife, Mary of Modena, he had only the Old Pretender who never succeeded in obtaining the throne abandoned by his father.

Clarendon's fall from favour

For seven years after the Restoration Clarendon remained in power, but his politics were old-fashioned, his strict morals were entirely at odds with the profligate court of Charles II, and he made enemies by not concealing his disapproval of the lax behaviour of the king and his courtiers. The marriage of his daughter Anne to the prospective king also generated widespread suspicion about his motives and prompted a wit to pen the lines:

Then the Fat Scrivener doth begin to think
Twas time to mix the Royal blood with ink.

In his high office as Chancellor Clarendon was as we have seen not above looking after his interests. He admitted that under Charles I he had exploited his position to obtain royal properties when they were obtainable cheaply, and Aubrey related the story told him by the Welsh judge David Jenkins (1586–1663) that he could have been made one of the judges of Westminster Hall 'if he would have given money to the Chancellor Hyde'. Aubrey's collaborator Anthony Wood found himself in trouble after indiscreetly publishing an allegation of corruption made by Aubrey against Clarendon, which prompted his son the 2nd Earl of Clarendon to issue a writ against Wood for libel, although his father had been dead for twenty years.

Clarendon also became unpopular at court because of his inability to satisfy the expectations of those cavaliers who contrasted his good fortune with their own lost fortunes, and the building by Clarendon in 1664–1667 of his magnificent town house called Clarendon House in Piccadilly was a particular irritant to the impoverished cavaliers. This house, which was designed by the royalist gentleman architect Sir Roger Pratt (1620–85), was demolished in 1683, although prints of it survive. Another source of trouble was the generation gap between Clarendon and the king and his courtiers because, according to Macaulay, Clarendon had: 'an inordinate contempt for youth which alienated him from the younger men and made him disliked by the majority of the House of Commons'.

Dissatisfaction with Clarendon was building up in all quarters, and it was exacerbated when during the Second Dutch War in 1667 the enemy fleet broke the defensive chain across the Medway, fired the laid-up British fleet, and towed away the flagship the Royal Charles. Although by his meticulous control of finances Clarendon may have underfunded the navy, the troubles were probably more attributable to the fact that society had been severely unsettled by the Great Plague and the Great Fire which had descended upon London in 1665-6, and were regarded as dreadful judgements on the immorality of the court. London was in a panic and Pepys thought there would be a revolution. A scapegoat was required to deflect criticism away from the king

and his court, and the choice perversely fell upon Clarendon, the man who more than any other had objected to the morals of Charles II and his courtiers. A peace was signed with Holland the following year on terms that were advantageous considering the circumstances, but the British public expected revenge for the indignity that Britain had suffered and blamed Clarendon for what they considered to be a dishonourable peace.

There can be no doubt that the easy-going and indolent Charles II had grown to resent being constantly lectured as if he were still a schoolboy by Clarendon about the duties of kingship, and in Clarendon's hour of need when he was mourning the recent death of his wife the king was unwilling to jeopardise the throne for which he had waited so long. He abandoned his loyal servant, just as his father had for expediency broken his solemn promise and sacrificed his principal adviser the Earl of Strafford.

The mob came out, broke the windows of Clarendon's new house in Piccadilly and dug up his trees, and Clarendon was threatened with impeachment for high treason. To his credit Clarendon's son-in-law James, Duke of York, tried to defend his father-in-law in the House of Lords, where the former Wiltshire MP Denzil Holles (1599–1680) was one of the four peers who protested against his banishment.

To be fair to the king he had offered Clarendon an honourable retirement as a country gentleman such as his father Henry Hyde had so much enjoyed, but Clarendon was not prepared to relinquish power and retire. That the king may have felt some pangs of conscience about abandononig his old servant is suggested by his letter some weeks later to his Lieutenant in Ireland James Butler, 12th Earl of Ormonde (1610–1688):

> The truth is his [Clarendon's] behaviour and humour was grown so insupportable to myself and to all the world else, that I could not longer endure it; and it was impossible for me to live with it and do those things with the Parliament that must be done or the Government will be lost.

the significant phrase being 'or the Government will be lost'.

Clarendon was by no means without fault for he had by his behaviour alienated the court and had made few friends. In 1666 he was fifty-seven, a good age for his time, and he was severely incapacitated by gout. He should have been prepared to retire. It is likely that he had become impossibly difficult as a result of pain from his gout, which had grown more acute as he grew older. The king had in the past always been considerate of this disability in his old minister, and had often visited him to discuss official business rather than require him to come to court. It was therefore significant that when he demanded Clarendon's seals of office King Charles required him to deliver them to him personally at ten o'clock in the morning, although he was aware that his gout often kept Clarendon in bed on some mornings.

By his failure to support Clarendon the king disgraced and forced into exile the man who had devoted his life to serving both his father and himself, who had done his best to persuade Charles I against his ill-advised declaration of war against his parliament, and had stood by his king during the Civil War. He had also guided the future Charles II in his exile and taught him the responsibilities of kingship, negotiated his restoration to the throne, and then loyally served him as his first minister.

The Lawes brothers

In the early-17th century music flourished in England, so that Aubrey could write of Bishop;s Cannings: 'This parish in these dayes would have challenged all England for musique, foot-ball, and ringing'. Dinton was at this time the home of Henry and William Lawes, contemporaries of Clarendon who achieved fame as musicians and composers at Charles I's court. They were the sons of Thomas Lawes (died 1640) of Dinton, a vicar choral of Salisbury Cathedral.

Henry Lawes (1596–1662), who was baptised at Dinton, became a student of John Cooper, who after studying music in Italy had assumed the Italianised name Giovanni Coprario. After Henry VIII's suppression of the monasteries the Chapel Royal had assumed great importance as the centre of music in England.

Portrait of Henry Lawes, c. 1642

Henry Lawes in 1622 joined the Chapel Royal and became a member of the king's band. He is believed to have sung as a counter-tenor and revealed great ability in composition. In 1634 he set John Milton's *Comus* so brilliantly that Milton wrote in his Sonnet 13 of:

> Harry, whose tuneful and well measured song
> First taught our English music how to span
> Words with just note and accent – not to scan
> With Midas ears, committing short and long.

Henry Lawes's best-known work is his setting of *The Angler's Song* ('Man's life is but vain') from Isaak Walton's *The Compleat Angler*. He wrote three *Books of Ayres and Dialogues* in 1653, 1655, and 1658, and more of his songs were published by Playford between 1652 and 1659. In all he wrote over 430 songs, and was regarded by his contemporaries as second only to John Dowland as a songwriter.

Henry's younger brother William Lawes (1602–45) was born at Salisbury in 1602, the year that Thomas Lawes became a lay vicar at Salisbury. He like his brother studied under Coprario, was also a counter-tenor, and achieved similar fame as a composer. Fuller says that he was patronised by Edward Seymour, Earl of Hertford, at Amesbury Abbey (which was frequently visited by Charles I when Prince Charles) and he was music tutor to James I's children. In 1625 he became 'publick and private musician' to Charles I. William demonstrated more versatility than his brother Henry by writing in addition to music for masques a great deal of instrumental music.

Undated portrait of William Lawes

In 1642 William Lawes joined the king's Life Guard in a 'safe' capacity as commissary officer but in September 1645 was killed at the siege of Chester 'by his own adventuresssness', shot by a stray musket ball. Charles I mourned his early death and described him as 'the Father of Musick'. His brother Henry survived the Civil War but referred in his *Second Book of Ayres* (1655) to having: 'lost his fortunes with his master [Charles I] of blessed memory', and although he regained his court appointments at the Restoration he died two years later at the age of sixty-seven, leaving ten pounds for the poor of Dinton.

The Lawes brothers are now generally not highly regarded and their music is seldom performed, although they are recognised to be part of the new movement in English music which arose at the time when secular music at the Stuart court of Charles I was superseding the religious music that had tended to prevail until the dissolution of the monasteries. Although Henry Lawes was extravagantly praised by John Milton for his setting of *Comus*, by Robert Herrick for his settings of his verse, and was very highly regarded

in his own time, the declamatory style of his songs in which the almost spoken word dominated the instrumental accompaniment has not endeared his music to later composers, and in the early-20th century Sir Hubert Parry – who married into the Pembrokes of Wilton – expressed some reservations about his music. Henry Lawes's younger brother William is now regarded as the greater of the two brother composers and his music has survived better, perhaps because it was usually instrumental. John Aubrey's collaborator and rival Anthony Wood of Oxford considered that William Lawes's music broke the conventional 17th-century rules of mathematical composition, an innovative characteristic that has caused it to be recently described as 'varied and individual'. To mark the fourth centenary of William's baptism on 1 May 1602, the Lawes brothers were the joint subjects of a series of five programmes in the series 'Composers of the Week' on BBC Radio 3.

The Hyde and Lawes houses at Dinton

Edward Hyde was probably born at Hyde's House, which stands a little north-west of the church in a fine situation looking south over Dinton Park, now a National Trust open area from which it may be viewed. Behind its early-Georgian south front hides an ancient house and dovecot dating from the time when the Abbess of Shaftesbury owned the manor of Dinton. In Hyde's time it was known as the rectory house and only became known as Hyde's House after it was given to the National Trust. The Hyde name is also commemorated in Hyde's Copse which stands on the hill a third of a mile northeast of Dinton church.

Hyde's House, the 18th-century south front

After Clarendon's time Hyde's House was in about 1725 given a fine though rather bland Georgian south facade. This stone-built front is of five bays with a hipped tiled roof with dormers, thee central three bays being brought very slightly forward and accented by a dentilled pediment, the dentils being extended along the eaves of the end bays. Each window is dressed with moulded surrounds and triple rusticated keystones, and the central door has a pedimented doorcase with engaged Ionic columns. The whole ensemble is a high quality frontage in the early-18th century Wren style, with more than a little hint of Palladianism.

About a quarter of a mile east of Dinton church, at the point near the village shop where the minor road from the church joins the B3089, stands the stone farmhouse known as Little Clarendon. It was formerly known as Hayters, and its present name may be misleading as there is no record Hyde ownership. Little Clarendon is a large house dating probably from the late-15th century, although one buttress suggests an earlier date. Its grounds beside the B3089 contain a small catholic chapel created in 1921 from an outbuilding by Mrs Engleheart, the wife of a former owner.

Adjoining Little Clarendon to its west is Lawes Cottage, a quite large cottage-style 17th-century house with a symmetrical many-windowed front and a roof which was until recently thatched. Despite its name there is no documentary proof that Lawes Cottage was the home of the Lawes family.

Clarendon's writings

One of Clarendon's claims to fame is as a historian. When first exiled during the Commonwealth in Scilly and Jersey he wrote between 1646 and 1648, with the approbation of Charles I, his great three-volume *History of the Rebellion and Civil Wars in England*. The first page is dated 18 March 1646, indicating that he started his *History* at the time that he was writing state papers and advising the king with whom Cromwell was at this time still negotiating. Clarendon's *History* was written: 'with all fidelity and freedom of all I know of persons and things'. It was intended to record the events and circumstances of the Civil War in the

hope that Charles I might yet come to an agreement with parliament and be restored to the throne.

Little Clarendon at Dinton

When finally banished from the court of Charles II, Clarendon in his second exile between 1668 and 1670 wrote in France his three-volume *Life of Edward, Earl of Clarendon*, with the intention of placing on record the story of his life and vindicating his actions, principally for the benefit of his children. Although it achieves more literary eminence than his *History* attained, since he had few references to hand when it was written the *Life* contains more inaccuracies. Clarendon then attempted to write a fuller history of his times and for this he added to his *History* the parts of his *Life* which had not been used in the former book, and produced the *History of the Rebellion and Civil Wars in England* that was first published by his second son Laurence Hyde, Earl of Rochester, in 1702–4. The style and readability of Clarendon's writings more than compensate for their occasional inaccuracy.

As chancellor of Oxford University after 1660 Clarendon sought to improve the lax discipline at his old university and proposed an academy to teach fencing, dancing and riding. He retained his love of Oxford and in 1672 the proceeds from the publication of his *History* were devoted to founding the Clarendon Press, the predecessor of the Oxford University Press, which had its first premises in the upper part of Wren's Sheldonian Theatre at Oxford.

Clarendon's second exile and death

King Charles perhaps finally persuaded Clarendon to go into exile with an undertaking that if he did so his estates would be saved for his sons, although after surrendering his seals of office to the king Clarendon still remained reluctant to go. After visiting him on 27 August 1667 his old friend the diarist John Evelyn wrote:

> Visited the Lord Chancellor, to whom his Majesty had sent for the seals a few days before; I found him in his bed-chamber, very sad. The Parliament had accused him, and he had enemies at Court . . . He was my particular kind friend, on all occasions.

A month later Evelyn recorded on 26 October: 'My late Lord Chancellor was accused by Mr Seymour in the House of Commons'.

While the Commons discussed impeachment Evelyn found his old friend sitting disconsolately in the garden of his new house in Piccadilly, watching the gates being set up which opened on to the fields to its north. The following day he heard that Clarendon had finally fled the country. He set out for France on 29 November 1667, and as he left he looked up to where his opponents were gloating over his departure and admonished them saying: 'Pray remember that, if you live, you will grow old'. After landing at Calais Clarendon stayed for a while in that area, perhaps hoping to be recalled. His letter resigning the Chancellorship of Oxford University was sent from Calais and dated 7 December. After being seriously ill at Calais he went to Avignon where he stayed until June 1668, and in July he proceeded to Montpellier in the south of France, where he remained for three years until June 1671. He then moved to Moulins, 150 miles south of Paris where he spent three tranquil years. In May 1674 he moved to Rouen and it was from there only four months before his death that he appealed to Charles II to allow him 'to die in his own country'. His letter was not answered, and at Rouen on 9 December 1674 he died, his final hopes of a return to England and perhaps to his home at Dinton unfulfilled. His grandson Lord

Cornbury was present at his death and he was then belatedly honoured by being brought home for burial in Westminster Abbey, where his daughter Anne, Duchess of York, had been buried three years earlier.

Many years later Horace Walpole summed up the contradictions in Clarendon's character: 'In his double capacity of Statesman and Historian, he acted for liberty but wrote for prerogative', and Fosse's verdict in his *Judges* was that Clarendon would:

> ever be regarded with admiration and reverence for his devoted adherence to Charles I during his misfortunes, and to Charles II for nearly 20 years after – the almost universal verdict, after two centuries of investigation – an unreserved acknowledgement of his loyalty, his wisdom, and his integrity.

Clarendon's grand-daughters as Queens
By Anne Hyde (Clarendon's daughter) James, Duke of York, had eight children, of whom only two daughters survived infancy. Two of their sons James and Edgar Stuart were successively in 1664 and 1667 created Barons of Dauntsey, the estate in north Wiltshire in which Henry Hyde acquired an interest as trustee after the regicide Sir John Danvers had forfeited it, but both sons died young. Had either lived he would have become heir to the throne, but their deaths in infancy left the way open for Clarendon's two protestant grand-daughters to reign as queens of England. Queen Mary (1662–94) occupied the throne as joint monarch with her husband William of Orange (1650–1702) from 1689 until her death in 1694, and when William died childless in 1702 he was succeeded by Clarendon's other grand-daughter, 'Good Queen Anne' (1665–1714). She was the last monarch of the House of Stuart, to which her grandfather Edward Hyde, Earl of Clarendon, had been so conspicuously devoted.

9 East Knoyle and Sir Christopher Wren

including William Talman, and the Wyndhams of Clouds

Eight years before the Earl Clarendon, the subject of the previous chapter, was elected as Edward Hyde to the Short Parliament, a Wiltshire-born man who also left his native village and became a celebrated national figure was born at East Knoyle, about eight miles west of Clarendon's birthplace at Dinton in the extreme south-west of Wiltshire five miles north of Shaftesbury. East Knoyle has recently regained some of its former tranquillity since the A350 road was re-routed to by-pass the village. The particular claim of East Knoyle to fame is for being the birthplace of the most eminent of English architects, Sir Christopher Wren.

The history of East Knoyle

As late as 1570 East Knoyle was known as *Estknoyle alias Bisshopes Knoyle* from having been in the Middle Ages a manor of the Bishops of Winchester. At the Dissolution of the monasteries in the mid-16th century the Still family became its owners and it ultimately came into the possession of the Wiltshire family of Seymour, which explains the name of the village inn being the *Seymour Arms*. Among the Seymour lands was the Clouds estate which the Seymours sold in 1877 to the Hon Percy Scawen Wyndham in order to finance the reconstruction of Knoyle House, which was destroyed in the 1950s for road widening. In the late-19th century Clouds House (see later, page 141) was built on the hill to the north-west of the village and became a centre of political, literary and artistic activities.

Wren's parentage and birth

As virtually all of his adult life was spent away from Wiltshire it may be argued that Sir Christopher Wren is a rather tenuous Wiltshireman. He was

however born and spent his boyhood at East Knoyle and he maintained a link with Wiltshire by retaining a small copyhold at East Knoyle until 1662.

Sir Christopher Wren

Wren was born in 1632, the fifth child of Dean Christopher Wren (1591–1658), whose principal living was East Knoyle. An older brother, another Christopher Wren, was born the previous year but died as a baby. Dean Wren was brought up in the high church tradition and was very well-connected. He was a former fellow of St John's College at Oxford and became Dean of Windsor in succession to his elder brother Matthew Wren

(1585–1667), who became successively Bishop of Hereford, Bishop of Norwich, and died as Bishop of Ely. They were sons of a London mercer, Francis Wren (1553–1624). The bishop's son, another Matthew Wren, became secretary to James II when he was Duke of York. Dean Christopher Wren was at one time chaplain to Lancelot Andrewes (1555–1626), the divine who had been active in the production of King James's Bible, and became under James I successively Bishop of Chichester, Ely and Winchester.

Dean Wren married Mary, the twenty-one year old daughter of Robert Cox, the squire of Fonthill Bishop where he was rector from 1620. Their children were Catherine (born 1626), Susan (1627), Elizabeth (born 1631 but died as an infant), Christopher (born 1630 and also died as an infant), Christopher the architect, born 1631, Elizabeth (1633) and Anne (1634). Christopher Wren was born in lodgings at a house which later became a shop called Haslam's, which stood opposite the post office as the road swings left when entering the village from the north, the Wrens being at the time absent from their rectory because it had been damaged by fire. Wren's birthplace was demolished in 1878, and Dean Wren's rectory was refronted in 1799 and is now called Knoyle Place. When Christopher was young his mother died and his eldest sister Catherine assumed her role in the family.

Knoyle Place, East Knoyle

As a child Christopher was delicate and he grew up to be to be almost diminutive, although he lived to the age of ninety-one in a plague-ridden age when life expectation was not high. When he was six his father in 1638 petitioned the king against the actions of a Mr Thornhill in un-

dermining his pigeon-house at the rectory causing it to collapse. Dean Wren's ownership of a pigeon-house, which was the prerogative of the rich, is an indication of the relative prosperity of the Wrens at East Knoyle. When Thornhill was found to be manufacturing and exporting saltpetre to the enemies of the king he fled the country.

A great deal of information about the Wren family in general and Sir Christopher in particular is contained in the *Parentalia*, compiled by his son Christopher and published in 1750 by the architect's grandson, another Christopher Wren.

Plasterwork at East Knoyle Church

Dean Wren was an amateur architect with sufficient reputation to have been asked in 1634 to design a building for Queen Henrietta Maria. At East Knoyle immediately before the Civil War he in 1639 commissioned a plasterer called Robert Brockway from *Quinten* (Frome St Quintin) in Dorset to embellish the chancel of his church with decorative plasterwork, to illustrate the Bible to his parishioners. It has been suggested that the kneeling figure incorporated in this plasterwork on the north wall of the chancel of the church illustrating Psalm 55 is a portrait of Dean Wren. This plasterwork was described by Sir Nikolaus Pevsner as 'a surprise and a delight' and by the rather mystified Wiltshire antiquarian Sir Richard Colt Hoare as 'a strange and quaint performance'. It was executed when Christopher Wren was seven, and one wonders whether Dean Wren discussed the designs with his son who was a precocious child.

While the plasterwork was being installed the church was visited by a troop of roundheads who took exception to it as idolatrous, until it was pointed out that it represented Christ's ascension. Nevertheless they damaged the work and Dean Wren was accused of 'heretical practices' by the parliamentary Faulston Commission. Despite being supported in writing by several eminent Wiltshire parliamentarians (George Danvers, James Herbert the son of the parliamentary Earl of Pembroke, William Stephens, and Sir John Evelyn of West Dean), who pointed out that Dean Wren: 'had been a painful labourer in the work of the Ministry these Thirty years', he was fined

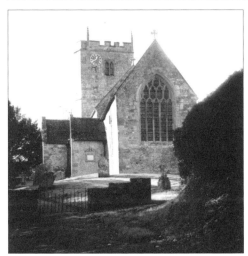

Wren's father was rector of East Knoyle Church

and replaced as rector of East Knoyle, although it is said that he stayed on in the parish as a schoolmaster. His plasterwork somehow survived the interregnum and may be seen today. Dean Wren also designed a new roof for East Knoyle church. These building works suggest that Wren may have inherited some of his architectural abilities from his father.

The Wrens in the Civil War

At the outbreak of the Civil War Christopher Wren was only eleven, but he was a member of an essentially royalist family. The Wren family suffered for their support of the king and Wren's father ultimately had to flee to his son-in-law William Holder at Bletchingdon in Oxfordshire. According to John Aubrey, who knew Christopher Wren, Mr Holder was: 'very helpful in the education of his brother-in-law [the young Christopher Wren] . . . of whom he was as tender as if he had been his own child, whom he instructed first in geometrie and then in arithmetique'. Christopher's Uncle Matthew, the Bishop of Ely, suffered more severely by being imprisoned for eighteen years in the Tower of London.

Wren's father may have supported the king's party more actively than has been generally recognised. At the start of the war he at first retired to Windsor, but when in August 1644 the parliamentary general Edmund Ludlow (see

Chapter 7) was besieged at Wardour Castle by Colonel Barnes it is said that Dr Wren brought to Wardour from Windsor Lord Hopton's warrant. This commanded Colonel Barnes to send a troop of horse to his aid to enable him to collect his East Knoyle rents which had been appropriated by parliament's general Sir Edward Hungerford in a fund-raising sweep through south Wiltshire.

On another occasion, after Cromwell had dispersed Colonel Long's regiment of horse near Trowbridge in March 1645, a Mr George Style of East Knoyle deposed that a large company of royalist horse arrived at East Knoyle accompanied by Dr Wren. In the autumn of 1645 a Mr Marshman also swore an oath alleging that Dean Wren had encouraged his parishioners to support the clubmen in their rising against the depradations of both armies in the war, and on 29 August 1645 he was fined £40 by the Parliamentary Committee at Faulston in south Wiltshire. The young Christopher Wren would presumably have been aware of his father's royalist activities as he did not leave Westminster School for Oxford until 1646, and would probably have spent his holidays at home at East Knoyle, which was bought by Edmund Ludlow in 1650, although he forfeited it in 1661 after the Restoration.

Wadham College and the Royal Society

Young Christopher Wren was first educated by the Rev William Shepherd, a local clergyman at East Knoyle. In about 1640 he went away to Westminster School where he remained until 1646 under the celebrated Dr Busby, and then in 1649 he went to Wadham College at Oxford as a Gentleman Commoner. There, having had a good grounding from his brother-in-law William Holder, he indulged in many actitivities and began his brilliant career by studying anatomy, astronomy and mathematics.

At Oxford Wren is said to have written a poem commemorating the achievement of Sir William Petty (1623–87), the political economist ancestor of the Lansdowne family of Bowood. Petty had achieved celebrity by reviving Anne Green after she had been hanged at Oxford for the murder of her illegitimate child. He became professor of music at Gresham College in London and, during the Interregnum, a land surveyor and landowner in Ireland. He also designed a double-hulled 'unsinkable' boat which unfortunately sank! When challenged to a duel by an expert swordsman Sir William, having as the challenged party the choice of weapons and venue, deliberately disconcerted his challenger into withdrawing by choosing carpenter's axes in a darkened cellar.

Many years after his death in the mid-19th century it was decided that Sir William Petty should be commemorated by one of the most prominent landmarks in the county. The Lansdowne Monument was set up by his descendant Lord Lansdowne on Oldbury Hill above Cherhill in a situation from which it is visible for many miles around. It seems however that after the monument was completed Lord Lansdowne decided that it should bear his name rather than be known as the Petty Monument, and Petty, who was a native of Romsey, is now commemorated by a Victorian recumbent effigy in Romsey Abbey. The 1845 contract reveals that the Lansdowne Monument cost £1,359, and that it was built by Daniel and Jones of Bradford on Avon, builders for whom my grandfather worked towards the end of the 19th century.

Lansdowne Monument on Cherhill Down, initially built to commemorate Wren's friend Sir William Petty

Soon after it was founded in 1612 Wadham College became an important centre of scientific activity. In the great room over the gateway met from 1652 until 1659 the Oxford Philosophical Society, a group of intellectuals including Wren that in 1662 moved to London and under the patronage of Charles II, and became the Royal Society.

Wiltshire was well represented among early members of the Royal Society. Its first president was Lord Viscount William Brouncker (1620?–84), a mathematician and courtier who in 1665 became a Commissioner to the Admiralty. He was one of the Brounckers of Melksham and Erlestoke, where their name is commemorated in several place-names. Another founder member of the Royal Society was Thomas Willis (1621–75), the eminent physician and doctor to James II who was born at Great Bedwyn. Willis undertook important pioneering researches in medicine and initiated the modern treatment of asthma. Part of the brain is today known as Willis's circle. John Aubrey, another founder member of the Royal Society, described Willis succinctly and rather unkindly as being of 'middle stature: dark and brindle haire (like a red pig), stammered much'.

Aubrey described Wren as his 'deare friend' and often reported his conversations, although Wren was not a subject of his *Lives*. He recorded that in 1661 Wren investigated a haunting at Tidworth in east Wiltshire. A local militia officer Mr Mompesson had objected to the persistent drumming at Ludgershall of an itinerant drummer called William Drury from Uffcott near Broad Hinton in north Wiltshire. He released the man but confiscated his drum and took it home to Zouch House at Tidworth. From that time his house was plagued for several years by poltergeist activities and persistent drumming, which became so notorious that the Wiltshire writer Addison based a play called *The Haunted House* on the incident.

In 1657 Wren became Professor of Astronomy at Gresham College in London. He was also twice elected MP, first for Windsor in William and Mary's first parliament (1689),although the return was declared void, and then in 1701 for Weymouth. He seems however to have been inactive in politics and appears later in life to have concentrated on his architectural career and deliberately remained clear of the political scene, perhaps remembering the experiences of his father during the Civil War and the eighteen-year imprisonment of his Uncle Matthew in the Tower. Not being allied to any political party may have proved to be advantageous to Wren in his long career as it enabled him to survive in office during the political upheavals of the late-17th and early-18th centuries.

Wren becomes an architect

With the Restoration of Charles II to the throne the fortunes of the royalist Wrens took a predictable turn for the better. In 1661 Christopher Wren, then recognised as a mathematician and astronomer, was asked by the king to supervise the fortification of Tangier, and was also offered the reversionship of Sir John Denham's office as Surveyor-General of the Royal Office of Works. When offered this appointment Wren was a bachelor of twenty-nine and despite having become Savillian Professor of Astronomy at Oxford he may have been concerned about his long-term financial future, as in the 17th century few scientists were able to exist by science alone.

Before Wren's time the profession of architect was unknown. Buildings were then generally designed by associations of craftsmen or by amateur architects who drafted rough designs for buildings and supervised their construction in a very casual manner, major decisions of detail being left to the craftsmen.

Some time before Wren went to Oxford building work had been undertaken between 1610 and 1613 at Wadham College by Thomas Holt, who had already executed architectural work at Oxford. Holt worked in a mixed gothic and classical style and his work may have influenced Wren when he unexpectedly took up the practice of architecture, for Wren did not design exclusively in the classical baroque style. He added Tom Tower in the gothic style to the Tudor gatehouse of Christ Church at Oxford, and some of his London city churches were given gothic spires and towers. In 1682 Wren designed St Mary's church at Aldermary in a form of Tudor gothic, and his originally non-traditional plan for St Paul's Cathedral was amended by his clients into an essentially gothic plan with a long nave to satisfy liturgical requirements.

Wren had been practising architecture in a limited way before he was offered the Royal Surveyorship. As early as 1663 he had been a member of the Commission for repairing Old St Paul's Cathedral, and his first original building was the chapel of Pembroke College at Cambridge (1663), for which he was commissioned by his aged uncle, now restored to his former bishopric at Ely. Gilbert Sheldon then appointed Wren to design the Sheldonian Theatre at Oxford which was built 1664–9 to accommodate university functions. Immediately after the fire of London in 1666 Wren was appointed one of six commissioners appointed to decide how London should be rebuilt.

He produced a plan for the rebuilding of London which included many often radiating straight streets and vistas that was not universally admired. In the following century Sir Joshua Reynolds (1723–92), the first President of the Royal Academy, in his *Thirteenth Discourse* on art pointed out that one of the attractions of our old towns was that their streets had not been regularly planned and had grown piecemeal, and that if London 'had been built on the regular plan of Sir Christopher Wren, the effect might have been, as we know in some parts of the town, rather unpleasing; the uniformity might have produced weariness'.

Although his plan for London was never adopted Wren already recognised that his future lay in architecture. In 1665 he had been sent by the king to Paris, where he stayed for nine months and escaped from the plague then raging in London. In Paris he furthered his architectural knowledge by studying the design and construction of the most eminent French buildings, and wrote in a letter: 'I shall bring you almost all France on paper'. In Paris he met the great Italian architect Bernini, admired his unexecuted design for the Louvre, and wrote: 'The Design I would have given my skin for; but the old reserved Italian gave me but a few minutes view'. Wren then busied himself in: 'surveying the most esteemed Fabricks of Paris and the country round'.

Although he had at first declined the Surveyorship on the grounds of ill-health Wren finally accepted it in 1668, significantly the year before he married Faith, a daughter of Sir John Coghill of Bletchington in Oxfordshire. Her father probably demanded that his prospective son-in-law should have reasonable prospects in order to support his daughter. Faith Coghill died seven years later in September 1675, and in 1677 Wren married as his second wife Jane, a daughter of Lord Fitzwilliam of Lifford.

Christopher Wren's architectural style

For reasons that will become apparent it must be emphasised that Wren's mild baroque architectural style bore little resemblance to the flamboyant baroque style of southern Europe. Andrea Palladio (1518–80) had during the previous century invented in Italy a more severe classical style based on Roman architecture and a system of mathematical proportions. Although this Palladian style had in the early-17th century been brought to England by Inigo Jones (1573–1652), after his death the strict Palladian style had practically died out until Wren revived it and anglicised it into his mild English baroque style of the latter part of the 17th and the early-18th centuries. His style is much more restrained than that of the Italian baroque architects, being closer to that of Palladio but less severe and correct. The restraint of the Wren style is generally attributed to the more sombre nature of the northern European temperament, although other factors are that protestantism rather than catholicism was the official religion of England, and that Wren never visited Italy. He seems to have received some of his classical style by way of Dutch architectural manuals which his friend and fellow member of the Royal Society John Evelyn is known to have brought to England. Although Wren never visited the Netherlands John Evelyn had visited Holland in 1641 and brought back several Dutch manuals of architecture, including a Dutch translation of Serlio's *Books of Architecture*. Consequently Wren often designed restrained harmonious non-baroque buildings employing homely red bricks – rather than the more noble stone – in a rather Dutch style, an example being Chelsea Hospital for old soldiers which was described by Carlyle as 'obviously the work of a gentleman'.

Wren's work at the Office of Works

Wren held the Surveyor-Generalship of the King's Works for fifty years. At the head of the Office of Works was the Surveyor-General, with below him the Deputy Surveyor and then the Comptroller of Works, all three being much-coveted appointments. As the Royal Surveyor Wren rebuilt or extended several royal palaces, including Hampton Court, Kensington, St James's, Westminster, Whitehall, and Winchester, as well as Windsor Castle. In addition to designing Chelsea Hospital for soldiers he also designed part of Greenwich Hospital for seamen. Some of his principal achievements were the designs for the fifty-three splendid London city churches which he designed on severely cramped sites between 1670 and 1711 as replacements for the churches destroyed in the Great Fire of 1666. The ingenuity exhibited by Wren in overcoming the severe limitations imposed by the restricted sites of these churches revealed his true genius, and the city churches are often regarded as his greatest work. Although he occasionally designed in a revived gothic style, most of these churches are masterpieces in restrained baroque, as was his *tour-de-force*, the replacement St Paul's Cathedral in London, which he designed and supervised between 1675 and 1710.

There is no Medieval precedent in Britain for the steeples with which Wren crowned his city churches. They rose in distinct diminishing stages with convex and concave ornament similar to the steeples of the Amsterdam city churches and the flèches of the town halls of Leyden and Haarlem. The Italian Renaissance style of architecture generally reached England indirectly through Holland, the publications of the Italian master architects being generally first translated into Dutch and then from Dutch into English, and ties between England and Holland were at this time strong for two reasons. Firstly, Holland shared with England the protestant religion, and secondly Charles II and many of his courtiers had spent the greater part of their exiles during the Commonwealth in Holland, where they had become familiar with Dutch architecture. That Wren developed his classicism as a result of consulting Evelyn's library seems likely, and his characteristic use of large areas of high quality brickwork dressed with stone quoins and cornices in his domestic buildings and palaces seems to have been derived from Dutch practice.

St Paul's Cathedral

Wren was however no mere copyist and he revealed his true architectural and structural genius when he was appointed to build a new cathedral to replace Old St Paul's Cathedral, which was already ruinous before it was finally destroyed in the Great Fire of London in 1666. This was Wren's great opportunity, particularly as both he and the king were determined on a modern building which broke with gothic tradition. He was immensely disappointed when his first design, in the form of a Greek cross plan with one arm extended as a vestibule, was rejected by the clergy, who wanted a more traditional design with a long nave and choir to accommodate their liturgy. He then produced the 'warrant' design (of which there is a large model in the cathedral), which was authorised. This in fact bears little resemblance to the building as constructed because Wren drastically and secretly amended the design, apparently with the approval of the king. Although St Paul's was to be the first cathedral to be built in England to serve the Anglican faith Wren turned for inspiration to Italy, and decided to crown his design with that essentially Renaissance feature – a dome. This decision was particularly controversial because at that time no dome existed in England, and domes were generally regarded as symbols of Roman catholicism.

More than two hundred years earlier, between 1420 and 1437, Brunelleschi had added a double-shelled dome to the gothic structure of Florence cathedral. Wren is known to have studied drawings of this dome, although even today the means by which Brunelleschi constructed his dome without the use of supporting timber centreing (temporary supporting framework) is not entirely understood. In the intervening two centuries the Italians had continued to construct domes, but Wren's dome at St Paul's is remarkable for being the first dome to be built in England. It is in fact a pseudo-dome, because Wren's English workmen were incapable of constructing a true dome. He therefore ingeniously supported the heavy masonry lantern of St Paul's on a massive brick cone over which he applied a lead covered false outer dome constructed of timber. Inside the cone he also provided a brick

under dome, creating the impression of a dome both externally and internally although the external and internal 'domes' were of entirely different profiles. In designing St Paul's with its very high dome and two tall towers it has been suggested that Wren may have had in mind the possibility of astronomical observations being taken from the former, and scientific experiments being conducted in the latter. During the construction of his cathedral Wren went every week to St Paul's and was hoisted up inside his great dome to a great height in a basket to inspect the work.

Upon first seeing St Paul's Cathedral the great painter and aesthete William Hogarth (1697–1764) considered it to be 'the epitome of beauty' and nominated Wren 'the prince of architects'.

Wren's associate and rival William Talman

Most people who recognise Sir Christopher Wren to be the greatest English architect of all time know nothing of William Talman (1650–1719), another Wiltshire-born architect who attained a national reputation and was, like Wren, employed at the Office of Works. During their tenures of offices there, Wren for fifty years as Surveyor-General 1668–1718 and Talman as Comptroller of Works over the shorter period 1689–1702, these two Wiltshire-born architects exerted immense influence on the development of English architecture over one of its most prolific phases.

If Wren was influential in the appointment of Talman as Comptroller of Works he may soon have regretted it, because Talman was a difficult man who regularly fell out with his private clients, and he very soon became Wren's rival. When part of the new buildings at Hampton Court collapsed killing two workmen in the year of his appointment, Talman went out of his way to lay the blame on Wren. He also accused Wren of nepotism over the appointment of a clerk of works, and in 1699 he attempted to obtain for himself Wren's appointment as Comptroller of Works at Windsor under the pretence of a reorganisation.

Because of his rather unusual name it has been assumed that Talman was a Dutchman, at a time when Dutch architecture was exerting considerable influence on English architecture. He was in fact the second son of William Talman, a gentleman with a small estate at Eastcott near Devizes. The name is in fact not as un-English as it might first seem. It appears in 16th-century Wiltshire records and a 'William Taleman' is listed in the 1332 Wiltshire tax lists at Great Hinton, only seven miles west of Eastcott where the architect William Talman was born. The name perhaps originated as a descriptive one applied to a tall member of the family, or alternatively to someone who was employed as a tallyman, the 1332 version having been Taleman.

The *Wren Society Papers* reveal that a William Shergall sold the Eastcott estate to Talman's father in 1660. That he was previously a tenant is suggested by the fact that young William was baptised at nearby West Lavington in 1650. The Talman home was probably Eastcott Manor House, where the gateposts with their late-17th century pineapple finials may have been designed by William Talman.

Talman senior died in 1663 when William was only thirteen and his eldest son Christopher inherited the estate which he sold in 1683. William's inheritance was three houses in Westminster. Since he was only thirteen when his father died William may have continued for a time to live at Eastcott with his brother. By 1693 he is known to have been living in London, as is to be expected of the holder of the office of Comptroller of Works. In the 1693 articles for the work which he did at Chatsworth he is described as: 'W. Talman of the parish of St James within the liberties of Westminster, in the County of Middlesex, Gentleman'.

Talman presents an intriguing subject because practically nothing is known of his architectural career prior to his appointment in 1689 at the age of thirty-nine to the important office of Comptroller of the Kings Works. To obtain such an appointment he must have gained great experience and a considerable reputation as an architect. There is evidence that early in his career (1678) Talman was patronised by Lord Clarendon's son Henry, 2nd Earl of Clarendon, and in 1685 a judgement awarded him £800

owed by the earl. Although he receives no mention in Pevsner's *Wiltshire* volume of *The Buildings of England* (1963) he may early in his career have practised in his native area around Devizes, and could therefore have designed some of the fine unattributed local houses of the period, houses such as Urchfont Manor (before 1688 and very near his birthplace), and now the Wiltshire residential college of further education, Courthill House west of Potterne, and Dial House at West Lavington (c. 1685), none of which has a known architect associated with its design.

Urchfont Manor east front, possibly by William Talman

The identity of the designer of Ramsbury Manor, a very important moderately sized brick-built mansion in east Wiltshire, has never been conclusively established and has always been a subject for some speculation. This house was built in about 1680 nine years before Talman became Comptroller of the Kings Works, and Hill and Cornforth in *English Country Houses: Caroline* (1966) describe Ramsbury as 'one of the most beautiful houses in England' and suggest that its designer was 'probably a London man in the Wren *atelier*'. This raises the possibility that Talman may have been the designer, as by 1680 he could have started to practise in London and become known to his fellow-Wiltshireman Wren. Ramsbury Manor House has some quirky features, notably the strange two-bay (not the usual uneven bays) pedimented centrepieces on its north and south elevations, which would be consistent with William Talman being its designer. Howard Colvin in later editions of the *Dictionary of British Architects 1600-1840* ascribes Ramsbury to Wren's friend Robert Hooke (1635–1703) on the grounds that he was a friend and 'architectural adviser' to its owner the lawyer Sir

William Jones, and the fact that after Sir William died during construction Hooke on 9 August 1682 visited the uncompleted building with his executor. This in my estimation is not conclusive, because Talman could have designed Ramsbury and then, as was his habit, quarreled with his client leaving someone else, who could have been Hooke, to take over the construction.

That William Talman was as a young man not exclusively employed as a west country architect is proved by his known involvement in the design of the now destroyed Thoresby House in Nottinghamshire, sometimes attributed to about 1671, but more probably dating from the mid–1680s. This house, which is both Talman's only known early commission and the first large scale English country house to be designed in the style of an Italianate palace, may have established the reputation that led to Talman's appointment to the Office of Works in 1689. Talman is also known to have been the architect of many other important country houses, including Chatsworth House in Derbyshire (1687–96) for the Duke of Devonshire, Swallowfield in Berkshire (1689–91) for Henry, Earl of Clarendon, and Dyrham Park (1698–1700) north of Bath for William Blathwayt, the Secretary of State to William III. While working at Chatsworth he obtained his official appointment at the Office of Works, and most of his other major private commissions came after that date. The designs for these houses reveal Talman's knowledge of Italian architecture, which influenced most of his buildings, in contrast to Wren who was (as already noted) more influenced by Dutch and French architecture.

Talman's quarrelsome nature which led him to dispute with most of his private clients and to intrigue against Wren, who had been Surveyor-General for twenty-one years when Talman was appointed Comptroller of Works in 1689, was emphasised by his rival Sir John Vanbrugh. He succeeded him at the Office of Works and wrote of the 'vexation and disappointment' of those who employed Talman. Talman was in fact approached to design Castle Howard, but the Earl of Carlisle found him so arrogant that he replaced him with Vanbrugh who provided his client with a magnificent baroque masterpiece. Other reper-

cussions may have accrued from this incident, because it was the influential Earl who in June 1702 obtained for Vanbrugh Talman's post as Comptroller of Works.

Talman was undoubtedly an architect of great ability. The eminent architectural historian Sir John Summerson suggested that he, rather than Wren, was largely responsible for the bold square outline of Hampton Court Palace, because this type of rectangular building is nearer to Talman's style than Wren's. Talman is known to have been very much involved in the modernising of the old Tudor palace at Hampton Court, and the *Dictionary of National Biography* states that Talman 'was responsible for the carrying out of the extensive additions and alterations to Hampton Court Palace, begun in 1690 from the designs of Sir Christopher Wren'.

Talman in his later life seems to have severed all connection with Wiltshire and died and is buried at Felmingham in Norfolk.

Sir Stephen Fox and the buildings at Farley

One of the places in Wiltshire possibly connected with Wren as architect is the tiny village of Farley, six miles east of Salisbury in the south-east of the county, and the birthplace of the great financier and administrator Sir Stephen Fox (1627–1716). According to the *Dictionary of National Biography* Stephen Fox 'took an active part in the escape of Charles to Normandy after he was defeated at Worcester on 3 September 1651'. The writer may have confused Stephen with his brother John Fox (1611–91), who is known to have assisted Prince Charles, although it is possible that both were involved. After leaving Heale House near Salisbury in the early hours of Sunday 12 October the king rode east, crossed the Bourne valley probably near Winterbourne Earls, and rode through through Clarendon Park Corner. According to local tradition the royal party was surprised by a detachment of parliamentary cavalry near Farley and hid in 'Dean Hedge between Farley and The Livery'. They then passed south of the Winterslow villages, entered Hampshire at Tytherley, and the prince ultimately embarked from the Sussex coast.

Most of the landowners in south-east Wiltshire were at this time parliamentarians and it is likely that it was here, in their home district, that the royalists John and Stephen Fox assisted the king in his escape. Stephen Fox attained sufficient favour with Charles II to share his exile, and in Holland he organised Charles's meagre finances so effectively that the prince was able to live in the comfort that was so important to him. Stephen Fox is believed to have undertaken dangerous missions to England on behalf of the king. He was knighted in 1655 and after the Restoration continued in high favour, was given the manor of East Meon in Hampshire, and was made Paymaster General to the Forces. In 1680 he was appointed one of the Lord Commissioners of the Treasury, and that year, on 6 September, John Evelyn wrote in his diary of Sir Stephen:

> This gentleman came first a poor boy from the choir of Salisbury . . . his Majesty being in exile, and Mr Fox waiting, both the King and Lords about him frequently employed him about their affairs, and trusted him both with receiving and paying the little money they had.

Sir Stephen used his high offices, as was usual with holders of high appointments at this time, to enrich himself, although John Evelyn found no fault with this and described how upon his return to England at the Restoration Sir Stephen demonstrated such dexterity in handling money that he obtained preferment, and was 'believed to be worth at least £200,000, honestly got and unenvied, which is next to a miracle'.

Sir Stephen Fox pursued a long career in politics under James II, William of Orange, and Queen Anne. In 1670 he began to buy up estates in his native Farley area and in 1678 purchased the lease of the Manor of Pitton and Farley from the cathedral authorities. From the fortune that he had amassed he decided to bestow almshouses and a church on his native village.

Sir Stephen first financed the almshouses opposite Farley church which were founded in 1682 for three old men and three old women, and a few years later he built Farley church. This replaced an old church of flint and thatch that reputedly dated

from about 1190, and was situated about three hundred yards west of the present church in Chapel Close, where no signs of it now survive.

Fox Almshouses at Farley by Wren's associate Alexander Fort

The man principally associated with the building of Farley almshouses was Alexander Fort (died 1706), who was described in 1682 in the *Wren Papers* as the 'Master Joyner in the Office of His Majesties Works [under Wren] and Surveyor of the building of the Hospitall and house at Farley'. He was paid £50 for 'severall Modells and Journeys about that Work'. In 1678 Alexander Fort had obtained the reversionship of the post of Master Joiner, and he succeeded to the post under Wren around 1685, about the time that the Farley almshouses were completed. The almshouses consist of a long low range of building in brick with tiled hipped roof, their centre being of four bays. The wings that flank the centre each consists of lower two-storeyed ranges, and the latticed windows are of the traditional mullion and transom cross type.

Alexander Fort was a local man, the son of Thomas Fort of Salisbury. He was a member of Wren's group and was often associated with him. He executed work on Salisbury Cathedral, first alterations to the choir and then making and carving the Bishop's throne in 1671–2, both projects for which Wren provided the designs, witnessed the contracts for the work, and acted as techical adviser. Bishop Seth Ward, Sir Christopher Wren and Alexander Fort were on friendly terms, and when Fort died in 1706 he had become a prosperous man. His wife Elizabeth was granted probate of his will and his son Thomas Fort tried to obtain his father's official appointment but was refused because he lacked sufficient capital to undertake crown works.

Sir Stephen Fox knew Wren, with whom he had frequent dealings at the Office of Works, for example in 1682 when he originated the idea and served on the Commission for the building by Wren of Chelsea Hospital for old soldiers from 1682–91. At this time when travel was slow and arduous it was usual for busy architects to employ local men to supervise their work in distant places, and Wren was certainly a very busy official architect. It is possible that he was involved in the design of the almshouses at Farley and employed the local man Fort as his site architect to supervise the work, although it must be admitted that the building is very traditional and shows little sign of Wren influence. If Alexander Fort was indeed the site architect for Wren he must have departed widely from the original design.

Wren may have been involved in the design of Farley Church

In the case of the classical church which was also built at Sir Stephen's expense opposite the almshouses a few years later, the involvement of Wren is on stylistic grounds more likely. Farley church was built during the 1680s and was completed by 1689. It is in the style of Wren, and Alexander Fort was again involved. The church is of brick with stone dressings, and in plan it consists of a nave with transepts and chancel with a west tower. The round-headed windows have continuous running mouldings, the roofs are tiled and hipped, and the tower has a parapet with urns. The north transept is the Fox family chapel.

Wren's other possible work in Wiltshire

There was always understandable concern about the stability of the ancient and exceptionally tall and slender spire of Salisbury, and following a number of fierce thunderstorms in 1668 the Dean and Chapter called in Wren to report on its stability. Wren's fellow astronomer and friend Seth Ward (1617–89) was then Bishop of Salisbury, having been appointed in 1667. After making his survey Wren expressed concern about inadequate foundations and buttressing and suggested long-term measures, although little seems to have been done apart from 'the bracing ye Spire towards ye Top with Iron'. The slender spire still stands, perhaps because its builders left the original scaffolding inside as permanent support.

It is possible that Wren's contribution to Salisbury Close – of which Bill Bryson wrote in *Notes from a Small Island*: 'There is no doubt in my mind that Salisbury Cathedral is the single most beautiful structure in England and The Close around it the most beautiful space' – was greater than has been acknowledged. Wren's name has like that of Inigo Jones become associated with innumerable buildings that were not designed by him. Nevertheless, in view of Wren's known connection with Salisbury and the fact that he was Wiltshire-born, it is interesting to speculate whether he could have been involved in any of the buildings in Salisbury Close. Pevsner suggests that he probably had some involvement in the design of the College of Matrons (1682) which was founded by Seth Ward for the widows of

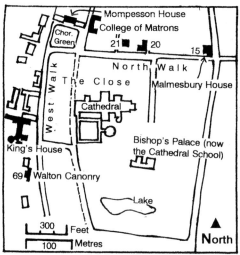

Salisbury Close

clergymen, but may have been designed (with Wren's help?) by its sponsor Thomas Glover of Harnham. The building is long, low, and symmetrical, of brick with stone dressings with a pediment accenting its long centre and an octago-

College of Matrons, Salisbury

nal lantern. It is also possible that Wren was consulted about the design of Malmesbury House (No. 15 The Close) where the seven-bay two-storeyed facade and the late-17th century summerhouse date from his time. This house is situated at the east end of North Walk beside St Ann's Gate which leads into the north-east corner of The Close. It originated as three canonries built in 1228 and known variously as Cole Ab-

bey and Copt Hall. Malmesbury House, which remains partly Medieval, was in 1651 leased by John Coventrye, a royalist who was involved in Charles II's escape past Salisbury to the coast after his defeat at Worcester. When in 1665 Charles II brought his court to Salisbury to escape the Great Plague then raging in London he stayed at this house. From 1660 to 1685 Malmesbury House was leased by the Harris family, there being a succession of James Harrises. Between 1704 and 1719 the house was extended for James Harris, the philosopher's father, in the Wren style by Wren's associate Alexander Fort.

James ('Hermes') Harris III (1709–80) was born at Salisbury and moved in the most distinguished literary and musical circles. He studied like Wren at Wadham College and obtained his nickname from writing *Hermes, or A Philosophical Inquiry Concerning Universal Grammar* (1751). He inherited Malmesbury House in 1733, became an MP, and held posts at the Admiralty and the Treasury before becoming Comptroller of the Queen's Household. His house became known as Malmesbury House after 1788, when the diplomat James Harris IV, a friend of the Prince Regent, was created Earl of Malmesbury.

Malmesbury House is of two storeys and seven bays with one attic dormer in its hipped roof and a pedimented doorway. The interiors are richly stuccoed and the house contains busts of Shakespeare, Jonson and Milton, which reflect the literary interests of 'Hermes' Harris. It has several eminent associations and was visited by Dr Johnson, who was described by Mrs Harris as: 'more beastly in his dress and habits than anything I ever beheld. He feeds noisily and ferociously'. Another distinguished visitor was the

Mompesson House in Salisbury Close

composer Handel who was twice saved from bankruptcy by 'Hermes' Harris, and is said to have composed in a first-floor room built into The Close wall adjoining the St Ann Chapel. In this chapel he conducted some of his works, including the pastoral *Daphnis and Amaryllis* to a libretto by Harris, who was devoted to music and particularly to the work of Handel, who left him some of his opera manuscripts.

Several other houses in Salisbury Close, including No. 53, Mompesson House (dated 1701) and the Walton Canonry (1719) are of a quality,

Wren Hall (left) in Salisbury Close

Elsewhere in Wiltshire the Longleat Papers reveal that the fine doorcase of Lord Weymouth's Grammar School at Warminster was 'Made by the directions of Sir Chr. Wrenn'. This rather attenuated flat corniced doorcase with engaged Corinthian columns was designed for Longleat but was for some reason moved to its present position in Warminster. The Hungerford Almshouses at Heytesbury are also rather tenuously linked with Sir Christopher Wren, as they

Walton Canonry in Salisbury Close

style and date that make it possible that Wren was involved, directly or indirectly (see later, page 142), in their design.

Hemingsby (No. 56 at the west side of Choristers' Green) was re-built in 1717 as the residence of the warden of the Choristers' School and is named after the first warden, Alexander of Hemingsby. It seems to have been rebuilt at the expense of Sir Stephen Fox with whom Wren was associated. The adjoining Wren Hall (No. 56c, dated 1714), the present name of the former Cathedral School, although its name is recent may have originated it from a tradition of Wren having worked in The Close.

Wren's doorcase at Lord Weymouth's Grammar School, Warminster

are said to have been rebuilt to a design based on Morden College at Blackheath (1694) which is linked with Wren.

Wren's fall from office

Having seen the tribulations suffered by his father and his uncle for their political affiliations during the Civil War, Wren later in life appears to have avoided politics, and yet his final downfall came about for political reasons. Towards the end of his long life in 1714 George of Hanover succeeded Queen Anne and it was deemed that the change of royal house should be marked by a change in the style of official buildings. This had been anticipated by Lord Shaftesbury when he suggested, in his *Letter concerning Design* (1712), that: 'a new national taste' was necessary to replace that of 'a single court architect [Wren] with too much of the Gothick'. It was decided that the homely Dutch-influenced William and Mary and Queen Anne styles which were strongly associated with the House of Stuart should be superseded by the bleaker Georgian style of architecture based on ideas adapted from Italian classicism, as promulgated by Palladio in his *Quattro Libri*, which were now translated into English as *The Four Books of Architecture*. A number of other Palladian manuals, several of them dedicated to George I, were from 1714 published in England to promote the Palladian style which was to be used for future official Hanoverian buildings, and in 1718 the octogenarian Wren was dismissed from the Office of Works, which he had graced for so long, to make way for an amateur practitioner of the new Palladian style.

Sir William Benson of Wilbury

Wren's successor was Sir William Benson (1682–1754) who had been High Sheriff of Wiltshire in 1710. He was a poet, pamphleteer, and politician, and the eldest son of William Benson who had been Sheriff of London 1706–7. Like most gentlemen of his time the younger William Benson had acquired a superficial knowledge of architecture. He lived at Wilbury House near Newton Tony in south-east Wiltshire east of Amesbury, having bought the Wilbury estate in 1709 when he was twenty-seven, and built Wilbury House based on an unpublished design by Inigo Jones. This made it of importance as the first 18th-century building to be built in the Palladian style in England. It has now been greatly altered.

Pevsner (in his *Wiltshire* volume of *The Buildings of England*) illustrates Wilbury House as originally built and stresses that its importance lies: 'less in its appearance now than in its appearance as it was first built and illustrated in *Vitruvius Britannicus*'. The building was originally a single-storeyed villa of seven bays with hipped roof and balustraded cupola and a tetrastyle (four-columned) pedimented Corinthian portico. Benson was the elder Henry Hoare's cousin and Wilbury greatly influenced the design of Stourhead House when it was built by Henry Hoare the Elder. In 1734 Henry Hoare the Younger bought Wilbury house for £14,000 from Benson and much later Percy Wyndham lived at Wilbury House while Clouds was being built for him at East Knoyle (see later, page 141). The influence of Sir William Benson on the house and garden at Stourhead is decribed in Chapter 10, page 146.

After George I's dissolution of parliament in January 1715 Benson became MP for Shaftesbury. He had spent some time at the Court of Hanover where, by his work on the fountains of Herrenhausen, he had ingratiated himself with the future George I and prepared the way for his appointment to replace Wren as Royal Surveyor. Wren's clerk and friend the architect Nicholas Hawksmoor (1661–1736) was greatly incensed at Wren's dismissal and described how: 'in extream need of employment he [Benson] could find nothing at that time but the Office of Works to fall upon, so disguising himself under the pretence of an architect got himself made Surveyor General'. It was said that Benson: 'got more in one year (for confusing the King's Works) than Sr. Chris. Wren did in 40 years for his honest endeavours', but he soon proved his incompetence and in 1719 resigned his appointment after a Committee of the House of Lords reported adversely on his work. In about 1741 Benson lost his mind and lived in secluded retirement. That he never entirely recovered his reason is suggested by the fact that he considered that he performed a public service when he paid William Dobson a thousand pounds for translating Milton's *Paradise Lost* into Latin hexameters. As a 'professed admirer of Milton' Benson in 1737 erected the monument to Milton in Westminster Abbey upon which his own name is very prominently displayed, prompting Pope to satirise his literary pretensions in the *Dunciad* (Book 3, line 325) : 'On poet's tombs see Benson's titles writ!' .

Clouds and the Wyndhams

Clouds, a Victorian country house, was built on the hill to the north-west of East Knoyle as the home of the Wyndham family and the meeting place for large gatherings of their friends. During the late-19th and early-20th century Clouds was the venue for intensive political, literary and artistic activity. The political gatherings at Clouds were so significant that it was alleged that the government was conducted from this private house above East Knoyle.

In 1876 the Clouds estate was offered for sale and in 1877 it was bought by the Hon Percy Scawen Wyndham (died 1911). His wife Madeline Wyndham (died 1920) was an amateur painter of some renown and attracted to Clouds a host of well-known painters, including G F Watts and Burne-Jones. The presence of Camille Pissarro's son Lucien painting at East Knoyle in 1916–17 may be attributable to this lady. Other distinguished visitors to Clouds included Queen Mary, William Morris, John Singer Sargent, G K Chesterton, Hilaire Belloc, James Whistler, Arthur Balfour and Dylan Thomas.

Clouds was designed and built between 1876 and 1886 for Percy Wyndham by the Arts and Crafts architect Philip Webb (1831–1915), who was born almost exactly two hundred years after Wren and was a friend of William Morris. The house cost £85,000 and stood in grounds amounting to about three thousand acres which were shown as parkland on Andrews and Dury's 1773 map of Wiltshire. The new house was, after being burnt down in 1889, rebuilt to the same design by the same workmen in 1889–91. When the fire drove the Wyndhams from their house into the servants quarters Madeline Wyndham

was heard to comment wryly: 'It's a good thing our architect was a socialist because we are just as comfortable in the servants quarters as we were in our own'.

The Clouds estate then passed to Percy's son the Rt Hon George Wyndham (1863–1913) who died suddenly in Paris. From 1889 he was MP for Dover and he became a brilliant statesmen who would probably have become prime minister had he not died. His political influence was immense and he was 'one of the best loved men of his day, his kindness, his wise and great helpfulness and sympathy, his courtesy and nobility of character endearing him to everyone who knew him' (Edward Hutton writing in 1917). After his death he was remembered as: 'a first-class man of letters and a distinguished politician', and the fine stained glass in the east window of East Knoyle Church was designed by Ninian Comper and given in 1934 by members of both houses of parliament in his memory.

Five grandsons of Percy Wyndham died in the Great War, one being the Hon Edward Wyndham Tennant (1897–1916), the eldest son of Lord Glenconner. He had a sweet disposition that everyone loved, which was demonstrated when as a child he placed an apologetic notice on his tricycle: 'Sorry for the dust'. From late childhood he was a poet and at Winchester School he just missed the gold medal for English verse. At seventeen he went to Germany to study German with a view to joining the diplomatic service and when the Great War broke out he immediately joined up, and had served one year in France with the Grenadier Guards when he was killed in action on the Somme in September 1916. In *Home thoughts from Laventie* he wrote :

> Away upon the Downs
> I saw green banks of daffodils
> Slim poplars in the breeze,
> Great tan-brown hares in gusty March,
> A-courting on the leas;
> And meadows with their glittering streams, and silver scurrying dace,
> Home – what a perfect place!

This description of his home countryside around East Knoyle was enclosed in a letter to his mother and published in *Worple Flit* (1916) and in *Poems of To-day: Second Series* (1923).

The Clouds estate was inherited by Percy Wyndham's grandson Guy Richard Charles Wyndham, but between the wars the house became run down and by 1936 it was threatened with demolition. It escaped destruction, in 1944 became an institution, and later an establishment for 'drying-out' and treating alcoholics and drug addicts.

Wren's death and achievement

At the outset of his career as an architect, a profession not recognised in his day, Wren was an inexperienced amateur, and in his last years when he was very old and had been removed from his offices he may have become ineffective. Sarah Churchill, Duchess of Marlborough, certainly thought so when she employed him to design Marlborough House in St James, which was built between 1709 and 1711 when Wren was almost eighty. The tempestuous Duchess concluded that: 'the poor old man was being imposed upon by the workmen' and dismissed him. We should not however put too much reliance on her opinion as she was a turbulent lady who had quarrelled with her other architect John Vanbrugh, dismissed him from the works at Blenheim Palace, and refused to allow him to see his completed masterpiece.

Although Wren has had many buildings improbably attributed to him he appears to have designed little in his native county of Wiltshire. He travelled to France but never went to Italy, the home of classical architecture. There was perhaps no need, for Wren was as great as most of the master architects of the Italian Renaissance, as was emphasised by Wren's biographer Margaret Whinney when she wrote that: 'The extent and variety of the executed works of Sir Christopher Wren can hardly be rivalled by those of any other architect'. Wren's architectural achievements are too numerous to list here; it is sufficient to say that he is generally acknowledged to be the greatest British architect of all time, and is arguably the greatest of all Wiltshiremen.

In spite of the very limited number of houses which Wren is known to have designed his name has become associated with the sedate brick-built and Dutch-influenced houses which grace many country towns and villages throughout England. This is explained by two facts. Wren designed a number of institutional domestic buildings (such as Chelsea Hospital and probably the College of Matrons at Salisbury) which were very influential upon the design of houses. His official appointments left him with so little opportunity for domestic work that when approached by private clients he often passed such commissions to his colleagues at the Office of Works, and may consequently have influenced the design of these buildings. His influence on domestic design was therefore immense, and the style of the modest rectangular brick-built houses of the reigns of William and Mary and Queen Anne, in America as well as in England, has become known as the Wren style.

In February 1723 Wren died peacefully sitting before an open window at his home at Hampton Court. He was ninety-two and had behind him over seventy-five years of scientific and artistic activity, a working life that can seldom have been exceeded by any other artist. This many-faceted Wiltshireman died in his own words: 'worn out by a long life in the Royal Service, and having made some Figure in the world'. He was one of the very few cathedral designers who lived to see his creation virtually completed in his lifetime, and was buried in St Paul's where his epitaph, written by his son and carved on a column near his grave, reads: *Lector, si monumentum requiris, circumspice* ('Reader, if you seek his monument, look around').

The history of East Knoyle has been followed from its ownership by the Bishops of Winchester and through ownership by the great family of Seymour to the birth here in the 17th century of Sir Christopher Wren, and has concluded with the political, literary and artistic activities which took place at Clouds House in the late-19th and early-20th centuries. This is no mean history for a small village situated in a formerly remote and inaccessible position in the south Wiltshire Downs.

10   Stourhead and the Hoares

Most visitors to the 18th-century landscaped grounds at Stourhead appreciate them for their beauty and their aesthetic qualities but remain unaware of their significance in the history of world art. If the suggestion made by Professor Pevsner in *The Englishness of English Art* that 'the landscape garden is the most influential of all English innovations in art' is accepted, the importance of the grounds of Stourhead, as the best-preserved example of that style, cannot be over-emphasised. In these terms they are of world importance. There is also a hidden meaning behind the Stourhead landscape, in that these grounds were laid out as an allegory upon the classical story of Aeneas and his wanderings after the fall of Troy, as related by Virgil in the *Aeneid*.

The subjects of this chapter are Stourhead House and its landscape, the theories upon which both were founded, and the lives of their creators, the first three owners: Henry Hoare the Elder who bought the estate and built the Palladian house; his son Henry Hoare the Younger who created the landscape which is associated with the house; and Sir Richard Colt Hoare who extended the house, ensured the survival of the Stourhead landscape in its original form, and is recognised to be one of the founders of English archaeology.

The English landscaped garden

England's lowland rural landscapes have generally been created by man for the purpose of food production. In Medieval and Tudor times most of England consisted of wild landscapes, forests and wastes, interspersed with restricted areas of habitation and cultivation. Men abhorred and feared wild countryside for its inherent dangers and reacted by formalising their gardens into unnatural layouts incorporating geometrical parterres and knot gardens. As more wild landscapes were taken into cultivation to feed a growing population the value of what was being lost was recognised, and during the 18th century landowners began to deformalise their grounds and create more natural landscapes to compensate for the wild landscapes that had been lost. Stourhead is generally accepted to be the finest example of such informal landscape, evolved in the 18th century as part of the movement which created naturalised landscapes for entirely aesthetic reasons, and it is arguably the finest surviving example of this style.

The designers of these 18th-century landscaped gardens created idealised informal gardens that were sublime, beautiful and picturesque, sublimity in their terms meaning the evoking of mixed sensations of awe, wonder and disquiet – sometimes even of terror. Landscape designers at this time drew much of their inspiration from studying landscape painting, especially the paintings of Claude Lorraine (1600–82) and Nicolas Poussin (1593–1664), which rich estate owners had seen and collected on the European Grand Tours which were part of the education of every English gentleman. Consequently the movement became known as 'the Picturesque style', although it was also promoted by the concerted efforts of writers and poets such as Alexander Pope (1688–1744), who wrote:

> To build, to plant, whatever you intend,
> To rear the column, or the arch to bend,
> To swell the terrace, or to sink the grot,
> In all, let Nature never be forgot,
> But treat the goddess like a modest fair,
> Nor over-dress, nor leave her wholly bare;

Let not each beauty everywhere be spied,
Where half the skill is decently to hide.
He gains all points, who pleasingly confounds,
Surprises, varies, and conceals the bounds.
Consult the genius of the place in all:
That tells the waters or to rise or fall.

This extract from Pope's *Epistle IV to Richard Boyle, Earl of Burlington* (1732) lists most of
the essential constituents of the English landscaped garden, its buildings related to the
planting ('To build, to plant, whatever you in-
tend'), its naturalness ('let Nature never be
forgot'), subtlety in its consideration of viewpoints
('let not each beauty everywhere by spied'), the
element of surprise ('Surprises, varies and conceals the bounds'), and the extensive use of water
('That tells the waters or to rise or fall').

One of the usual characteristics of the picturesque English landscaped garden, particularly in
the later stages of the movement, was the extensive use of wide expanses of undulating turf
punctuated by strategically placed clumps of trees
dotted around the designed landscape, with architectural 'incidents' introduced as eyecatchers.
This is not the case at Stourhead, which is an
early and pre-Capability Brown example.
Stourhead has several architectural eyecatchers
and there were formerly more, but the confines
of the narrow valley in which the garden was
created did not allow the usual wide expanses of
grass punctuated with clumps of trees. Consequently Stourhead is a more intimate and less
wide-ranging landscape, with its planting and its
architectural features distributed in key positions
around the edge of a large three-armed lake,
which was artificially formed by damming the
river formed by the springs at the head of the
River Stour and flooding the steep valley.

The history of the manor of Stourton

The two families of Stourton and Hoare owned
the manor of Stourton from Saxon times until the
20th century. It was the home of the ancient family of Stourton from around the time of the
Norman Conquest until 1714, when the estate
was sold and acquired by the newly-rich Hoare
family. The Stourtons were said to be lords 'of

the River Stouer from its fountains [source] to the
sea' and a tradition recorded in 1697 suggested
that when William the Conqueror came west after his success at Hastings it was at Stourton that
he received the submission of the west of England.

At Stourton the Lords Stourton built their
ancient home. It was sketched by John Aubrey
who described their castle as: 'very large and very
old, but little considerable as to the architecture'.
This unassuming fortified house built around two
quadrangles was pulled down by Henry Hoare
the Elder in about 1720. The Stourtons had created a deer park over the coombe of Six Wells
Bottom which fed the source of the River Stour
and lay a little north-west of the house. Henry
Hoare invented the new name of Stourhead for
his Stourton estate in order to emphasise its
change in ownership from its ancient owners.

*Old Stourton House reconstructed from a sketch by
John Aubrey*

William Stourton, who was in the final year
of his life (1413) made Speaker of the House of
Commons, had in 1386 been granted by royal
patent custody of the castle and park of nearby
Mere. In 1427 Lord Stourton's own park at
Stourton was founded under a royal licence
granted to John of Stourton, and was recognised
as being no longer part of the royal Forest of
Selwood. The licence permitted him to enclose
and impark his manor of Stourton, a thousand
acres of land, meadow, pasture and wood. In
1441 John of Stourton also obtained a grant to
make 'certain deer-leaps' in the enclosure of his
park at Stourton, deer-leaps being gaps in a park-
pale to allow wild deer to leap into a park and
naturally replenish its stock.

John Speed's map made in 1610 shows a
park pale north-west of Stourton House which
would have included the coombe now called Six

Wells Bottom. A thousand-acre park would have covered an area extending approximately from Stourton village to the position on Kingsettle Hill later occupied by Alfred's Tower, and from Aaron's Hill and Castle Wood to Six Wells Bottom. This suggestion is consistent with Leland's description of the Stourton park in the mid-16th century:

> Ther is a parke among the hills joining the maner place . . . one castle towards the north-weste part within the parke, double ditched . . . The ryver of Stoure riseth ther of six fountaynes or springes, whereof three be on the Northe side of the parke, harde withyn the pale ; the other three by North also, but withoute the parke.

For those who wish to experience some of the character of the Medieval deer-parked and pre-landscaped estate of the Stourtons the National Trust have provided, as alternatives to the very popular walk around the lake in the landscaped grounds, a number of public walks to the north-west of Stourton through the ancient woodlands on either side of the source of the River Stour in Six Wells Bottom.

The last of the Stourtons at Stourton

A fine monument in Stourton church in the form of a tomb chest incorporating two recumbent effigies commemorates Edward, 5th Lord Stourton, who died in 1536, and his wife. Lord Stourton wears his armour and his wife Agnes Fauntleroy lies beside him. Some time after this the Stourtons suffered a series of disasters. The 8th Lord Stourton had, as he admitted to Protector Somerset in a letter in 1549, a fearsome temper, and as a member of the old nobility he despised his neighbour William Herbert, the newly-created Earl of Pembroke, and annoyed him whenever he could. A feud arose and Lord Stourton used to annoy Pembroke by ordering his attendants to blare upon their trumpets when they passed the gates of Wilton House. His temper was ultimately his undoing because in the reign of Queen Mary he was hanged in Salisbury market place for murdering at Kilmington church two local men, a father and son called Hartgill who had for long been in dispute with him over

some property at Kilmington. The 10th Baron went to the Tower for involvment in the Gunpowder Plot in 1605 and parts of the estate were forfeited. What survived suffered from the attentions of parliamentary armies during the Civil War, when Stourton House was used as a royalist stronghold and was attacked by Edmund Ludlow. The Stourtons suffered for being both catholics and royalists and by the early-18th century they were in severe financial difficulties which ultimately obliged them to put their Stourton house and estate on the market.

It is ironic that the proud and haughty family of the Lords Stourton should have lost their ancient estate to newly-rich men in the banking family of Hoare, because the Lord Stourton who was hanged in Salisbury market-place for the double murder of the Hartgills had taken such exception to the appearance of a 'new man' in William Herbert at Wilton.

Henry Hoare the Elder buys Stourton

In 1714 the 13th Baron Stourton sold his property at Stourton to Sir Thomas Meres who in turn sold it in 1717 for £14,000 to the trustees of Richard Hoare, the son of the founder of Hoare's Bank. Richard's younger brother Henry was then searching for a country estate and he bought the property in 1720.

Towards the end of the 17th century many banks were being opened in the City of London. Henry Hoare, known as 'the Elder' to distinguish him from his son another Henry, came from a London banking family. Hoare's Bank had been founded by Sir Richard Hoare (1648–1718), the son of a horse dealer, who was in 1666 apprenticed to a London goldsmith, and by 1672 was in business in London on his own account, having opened a bank in Cheapside where he practised as a goldsmith. At this time goldsmiths were evolving a system of banking and were achieving great affluence. Richard Hoare prospered and in 1692 he moved Hoare's Bank to Fleet Street to the sign of the Golden Bottle. He was knighted in the year (1702) that Queen Anne succeeded William III, from 1710 to 1715 he was MP for the City of London, and in 1712 he was Lord Mayor. Of his eleven sons only two became partners in the bank, one of these being Henry Hoare the Elder who bought and developed the Stourton estate.

Betwen 1718 and 1785 the Hoares built up their land holdings in Wiltshire, Somerset and Dorset, Stourton being situated near the meeting point of these three counties. The conveyance of the Stourton estate to Henry Hoare the Elder in 1720 refers to 'parks, Warrens and fairs', suggesting that more than one park then existed at Stourton. Some vestiges of a possible second deer park additional to the one associated with the house are traceable on White Sheet Downs east of Stourhead House. Henry Hoare then emphasised the change of ownership by changing the name of the house from Stourton to Stourhead.

Henry Hoare the Elder

Stourhead House
Between 1720 and 1725 Henry Hoare the Elder demolished the ancient mansion of the Stourtons and built on a nearby site his new house, which is one of the earliest examples of of the second

(18th-century) phase of English Palladianism. The name derives from the severe classical style of the Italian architect Andrea Palladio, which had for political reasons been re-introduced in 1714 to replace the gentle English baroque style practised by Sir Christopher Wren and his followers. Sir William Benson, who lived at Newton Tony east of Amesbury in Wiltshire and was a brother-in-law of Henry Hoare the Elder, was one of the instigators of the 18th-century Palladian revival and it may have been Benson who persuaded Henry Hoare to employ that style for his new house at Stourhead (for more information on Benson see Chapter 9, pages 140-1).

The new Stourhead House was a small Palladian villa which forms the central block of the present house. It was designed by Colen Campbell (died 1729), a Scotsman who first appears as the 'agent' of Sir William Benson, Wren's successor as Surveyor-General. Benson in 1718 arranged for Campbell to become Chief Clerk of the King's Works and Deputy Surveyor. After sharing Benson's fall from office in 1719 Campbell, who had in 1715 published the first volume of his influential *Vitruvius Britannicus*, was patronised by Lord Burlington and became a major practitioner of the revived Palladian style. He was probably recommended to Henry Hoare by Benson, and for Stourhead produced a design which was loosely based upon the central pavilion of the Villa Emo, which Palladio had built for Leonardo Emo at Fanzolo and illustrated in Plate 38 of his *Quattro Libri (Four Books of Architecture)*. The Villa Emo had exposed eaves as was usual with Palladio, but for Stourhead Colen Campbell provided lead parapet gutters concealed behind a balustraded parapet which were more appropriate in the English climate.

When his new house was practically complete Henry Hoare the Elder died in 1725. He was remembered as Henry the Good for his piety and the fact that he left large charitable bequests, including £2,000 for the distribution of Bibles to the poor. He was succeeded by his son Henry Hoare the Younger, then aged only nineteen, who completed the house for his mother, who was left in occupation of the house in which she lived until her death in 1741.

Stourhead House

Henry Hoare the Younger

Henry Hoare the Younger (1705–85) succeeded to the banking business at nineteen, having spent much of his youth at his father's house at Quarley in Hampshire, a little east of Wiltshire. He took charge of the bank and in 1726 married Anne, the eldest daughter of Lord Masham, and a descendent of Abigail Masham who had brought the Privy Purse account to Hoare's Bank when she replaced the Duchess of Marlborough as Queen Anne's favourite in 1710. Anne Hoare died in childbirth in the year following their marriage and Henry Hoare then married Susan Colt, the daughter and heiress of Stephen Colt of Clapham. In 1734 Henry Hoare became MP for Salisbury and about that time he bought Wilbury House in south-east Wiltshire (see Chapter 9, page 140) from Sir William Benson. He remained senior partner at the bank for fifty-six years and emulated his father by becoming Lord Mayor of London. He was also MP for Salisbury.

At his mother's death in 1741 Henry took up permanent residence at Stourhead. Although he had lost a daughter in 1735, and in 1740 his younger son had died, he was now at the peak of his fortunes. But in 1743 his second wife Susan died and he was left a widower with three children, a son of thirteen and two girls aged eleven and six. This series of family bereavements probably explains why he distracted himself from his family troubles by remodelling his grounds at Stourhead into a major English landscaped garden.

His grandson Colt Hoare recalled Henry Hoare the Younger as tall and elegant, a fine horseman and a good shot. He remained active into his old age and at seventy-six would still ride forty miles across Wiltshire from Stourhead to Savernake to visit his daughter Susanna, who had married Lord Bruce, the 1st Earl of Ailesbury, and lived at Tottenham House in Savernake.

A description of Stourhead Landscaped Garden

Having inherited his father's fine Palladian house following the deaths of his mother, two children, and his wife, the younger Henry Hoare began to develop the grounds at Stourhead and landscape them into the form that we see today.

In the library at Stourhead there are two plans for the garden, one a traditional geometrical plan and the other illustrating the informal garden as it was created. Both plans appear to be by the same hand but we do not know who drew them, and would like to know more on this subject, as well as how Henry Hoare decided upon which scheme to adopt. We are fortunate that he decided to proceed with the informal design that we see today at Stourhead, and thus transformed what must have been a sparsely planted Medieval deer park in a chalkland coombe into a picturesque elysium. His artificially formed lake, surrounded by profuse planting with a succession of high quality architectural incidents, have gained Stourhead its recognition as the best preserved-example of an 18th-century English picturesque landscaped garden.

Soon after he started this work Henry Hoare suffered another family loss when his son and heir died on the Grand Tour. Consequently Stourhead was inherited by Richard Colt Hoare, who mentions in his *Modern Wiltshire: The Hundred of Mere* (1822): 'I imagine the park was never kept up for deer after the purchase by Henry Hoare, though it retains the name', and continues: 'I myself pulled down a great part of the wall [of the deer park]. . . separating the six springs [in Six Wells Bottom]'.

The new landscaped layout obliterated the Stourton's deer park, with its mixture of *laundes* (lawns or clearings) and isolated copses which had provided refuges for the deer. An estate map of 1722 shows 'Deer Meadow' north-west of the house adjoining Six Wells Bottom, and the area which is now covered by the lake as then merely a chain of small fishponds. The dam built during the 1750s impounded the waters of the River Stour, drowned the valley, and created the large three-armed lake with its two small islands that is at the heart of the Stourhead landscape.

Soon after its creation Horace Walpole saw Stourhead and considered it to be 'one of the most picturesque scenes in the world'. Although he was uncomplimentary about the picture collection at Stourhead, William Hazlitt particularly liked the descent to the gardens through Stourton village:

. . . by a sharp winding declivity, almost like going under-ground, between high hedges of laurel trees, with an expanse of woods and water spread beneath. It is a sort of rural Herculaneum, a subterranean retreat. The inn is like a modernised guard-house; the village church stands on a lawn without any inclosure; a row of cottages facing it, with their white-washed walls and flaunting honeysuckles, are neatness itself. Everything has an air of elegance, and yet tells of other times. It is a place that might be held sacred to stillness and solitary musing.

The Spread Eagle Inn described by Hazlitt was built by Henry Hoare near the entrance to the gardens to accommodate the multitudes of visitors who came to view his Stourhead landscape, their numbers having become far too numerous to be accommodated in his house.

A series of plan and perspective drawings of the grounds of Stourhead made in 1779 by the Swedish artist F M Piper, significantly while Henry Hoare the Younger was still alive, provide a marvellous record of the gardens shortly after they were created, and also indicate the viewpoints and vistas that were considered in the original layout.

Sir Richard Colt Hoare, Henry Hoare's successor as the owner of Stourhead, suggested that Henry Hoare had designed the gardens unassisted, and fostered that belief when he wrote the often-quoted comment that his grandfather: 'had the good taste and, I may add, the good sense not to call in the assistance of a landscape gardener'. This is in fact improbable. In the 18th century leading architects often advised on landscape as well as building design, and their contribution was sometimes concealed by their rich patrons in order to obtain the credit. The Wiltshire & Swindon Record Office holds letters which establish that Henry Hoare was advised on many aspects of the layout of his grounds by the architect Henry Flitcroft, who from 1744 also designed several of the buildings which provided the architectural incidents in the grounds.

A walk around the lake at Stourhead is one of the great aesthetic experiences of Wiltshire, for the pleasure grounds survive today as the finest surviving example of an 18th-century landscaped garden to come down to us practically unaltered. It is however doubtful whether its 18th-century creators would have approved of the rhododendrons which attract so much admiration today. These controversial intrusions which have attracted the wrath of many critics were introduced around the margins of the lake by the 6th Baronet, Sir Henry Hoare (1894–1947). As evergreens they are acceptable, but when they are in bloom their vivid colours utterly disrupt the monochromatic Claudian character of the landscape envisaged by its designers. Ann Scott-James summed up the situation when she wrote in 1970:

The landscape at Stourhead is a masterpiece, but spoilt for some eyes, including mine, in the months of May and June, when modern plantings of rhododendrons come into fiery blossom and outrage the cool, clasical landscape of water and trees and stone.

The English are such enthusiastic gardeners that they usually update their gardens in accordance with current taste and as new species of plants become available. That Stourhead should have suffered this fate is a pity because as a major work of art it should have been maintained but left fundamentally unaltered and preserved from this fate. It is therefore best that anyone who wishes to experience the Stourhead landscape as Henry Hoare envisaged it should visit the grounds in autumn or winter when the rhododendrons are not in bloom, and misty or even rainy conditions enhance the subtlety of this atmospheric landscape. This is to a large extent disrupted in the bright sunshine of spring and summer, when this popular garden is overcrowded with both exotic flowering plants and summer visitors.

Henry Flitcroft

When enjoying a visit to this very important garden it is appropriate to remember not only its owner Henry Hoare the Younger, who has generally been credited with its creation, but also Henry Flitcroft, who advised on the layout of the lake and garden, and should probably be given much of the credit for the entire creation. The importance of this man as a Palladian architect should not be underestimated. Although he is less known than many architects of the 18th century Flitcroft was a very important figure in the development of 18th-century Palladianism. From comparatively humble beginnings he attained sufficient eminence to be chosen (in 1765) to be Sheriff of London and Middlesex, although he paid a fine to avoid serving.

Henry Flitcroft (1697–1769) was the son of Jeffery Flitcroft, William III's gardener at Hampton Court, the man who may have inadvertently changed the course of English history, by failing to level the molehill over which William III's horse stumbled and threw him, thus causing the pleurisy from which he died prematurely in 1702. As a royal head gardener's son Flitcroft presumably acquired some knowledge of gardening from his father, although he became a joiner. After breaking a leg falling from a scaffold when working on Burlington House, he was patronised by Lord Burlington, the major sponsor of Palladianism.

Burlington chanced to discover that Flitcroft could draw, and trained him to be his draughtsman and architectural assistant. Through Lord Burlington Flitcroft assimilated Palladianism, and early in his new career as architect often produced the drawings for his patron's designs. In 1721 he made the drawings for Lord Burlington's Palladian design for Tottenham Park in Savernake Forest for his son-in-law Lord Bruce, although they were signed 'Burlington ar.[chitect]'.

Lord Burlington also obtained for Flitcroft an appointment as Comptroller of Works at the Office of Works, where he became known as 'Burlington Harry', and became a nationally known architect who ran a flourishing private practice alongside his official duties. He designed the longest Georgian frontage in England at Wentworth Woodhouse in Yorkshire, and he designed for Henry Hoare at Stourhead the Temple of Flora (1745), The Pantheon (1753–6), the Temple of the Sun (also known as the Temple of Apollo) (c.1765), and also Alfred's Tower (c.1772) on an outlying part of the estate.

His introduction for this work at Stourhead probably resulted from his work on Lord Bruce's Tottenham House, for the Bruces of Tottenham in Savernake were friends of the Hoares of Stourhead, and in 1761 Lord Bruce married Henry Hoare's daughter Susanna. That Flitcroft also advised on the layout of the grounds is proved by his letter to Henry Hoare dated 25 August 1744 (before he designed any of the buildings), in which he refers to enclosing:

> . . . a sketch of how I conceive the head of the lake should be formed. 'Twill make a most agreeable Scene with the Solemn Shades about it and a variety of other agreeable circumstances.

It should be remembered that at the Office of Works Flitcroft was a colleague of William Kent (1684–1748), the great innovative designer of picturesque landscapes, who in the words of Walpole 'leaped the fence and saw all nature was a garden'. By the time that the Stourhead grounds were designed Kent had laid out extremely important gardens in the new informal picturesque style at Chiswick for Lord Burlington, at Stowe in Buckinghamshire, and at Rousham in Oxfordshire.

In addition to his work in Wiltshire at Stourhead and on Tottenham House in Savernake, Flitcroft is known to have surveyed the Amesbury Abbey estate and in 1726 added wings to the house.

Stourhead gardens as an allegory of Virgil's *Aeneid*

One of the distinctive features of the Stourhead gardens is the fact that they occupy a steep valley aside from the house, to which they are not directly related. We know precisely how these gardens appeared in 1779 soon after they were created because, in addition to written records, we have the drawings which are now in Stockholm made by the Swedish artist F M Piper.

It was I believe the late Kenneth Woodbridge in *Landscape and Antiquity: Aspects of English Culture at Stourhead* (1970) who first suggested that the grounds of Stourhead were deliberately laid out as a representation in three dimensions of the classical story of Aeneas as told by Virgil (70–19 BC) in his twelve-book epic poem the *Aeneid*. He narrates a legendary account of the imagined origins of the Roman nation after Aeneas escaped from the sack of Troy, and ultimately settled in Italy and founded the Roman state. There is a great deal of evidence which supports this theory, particularly as in the 18th century education was essentially classical and everyone with any pretensions to culture was familiar with the writings of Virgil. In the *Aeneid* Aeneas after the sack of Troy sailed to Thrace and then proceeded to Crete and Sicily. Driven by storm to North Africa, according to Virgil he met Queen Dido at Carthage, although in fact well over three hundred years elapsed between the fall of Troy in 1184 BC and the foundation of Carthage in 853 BC. In Virgil's story when Aeneas left her the love-lorn Dido committed suicide. He sailed on to Latium, part of ancient Italy and the country of the Latins situated south of the Tiber, married Lavinia the daughter of the king of Latium, and founded Lavinium, a town in Latium named after her. By uniting the native tribe which occupied part of Latium with the Trojans Aeneas became effectively one of the founders of Rome.

We have seen above (page 146) how Sir William Benson (1682–1754) of Newton Tony in east Wiltshire influenced the Palladian design of Stourhead House. It seems likely that he also influenced the Virgilian layout of the grounds because Benson was a great admirer of Virgil and wrote anonymously on the *Georgics* ('husbandry') in 1725. He also encouraged the Dorset poet Christopher Pitt (1699–1748), the rector of Pimperne, to translate Virgil's *Aeneid* between 1728 and 1738, a short time before the Stourhead grounds were landscaped. Pitt was a member of the family of the Pitts, Barons Rivers, who preceded the Pitt-Rivers family as owners of the Rushmore estate in south Wiltshire.

It is now recognised that many of the 18th-century English landscaped gardens were inspired by paintings acquired by their owners on their Grand Tours of the Continent. At Stourhead the influence of painting went a stage further, because the landscaping deliberately re-created specific scenes in the paintings produced by Claude Lorraine to illustrate the story of Aeneas. Henry Hoare's interest in the paintings of Claude is well established from his letters, and no one who compares Claude's *Coast View of Delos with Aeneas*, which illustrates an incident from Book III of the *Aeneid*, with the view of the Pantheon

Claude Lorraine's Coast View of Delos with Aeneas *showing distribution of buildings as at Stourhead*

at Stourhead as seen across the lake from near the Bristol Cross at the entrance to the grounds can have any doubt about this relationship. The Stourhead buildings with the Pantheon in the distance across the lake, the turf bridge to the left, and the Temple of Flora around the corner on the right, bear a close resemblance both in style and positioning to Claude's painting, with its Pantheon at its centre, a low-parapeted bridge on the left, and a Doric temple on the right. It cannot be proved that Henry Hoare knew this painting, although it was for sale in Paris in 1737 when he was travelling on the Continent, and it seems inevitable that with his known interest in the *Aeneid* he would have made a point of seeing the six paintings by which Claude illustrated the epic, of which this is one.

This suggestion that the layout of the Stourhead grounds was inspired by the *Aeneid* is supported by a number of quotations inscribed on its buildings. The Temple of Flora has the text *Procul, o procul este, profani* ('Hence, away, uninitiated ones') from Book VI inscribed on it, and the descent to the grotto represents the descent of Aeneas to Avernus (*Facilis descensus Averni*, meaning 'The way down to hell is easy') also from Book VI. In 1760 Henry Hoare bought from Richard Wilson a painting called *The Lake of Avernus* and he also wrote in a letter: 'I have made the passage up from the Sousterrain [the Grotto] Serpentine & will make it easier of access 'facilis descensus Averno'. The inscription *Intus aquae dulces, vivoque sedilia saxo, Nympharum domus* ('Within, fresh water and seats in the living rock, the home of the nymphs'), which was inscribed on the grotto, and is now embedded in a later extension, is taken from the description of the cave near which Aeneas landed in North Africa in Book I of the *Aeneid*:

> There is a cave directly in front at the foot of the cliffs. Inside it are stalactites and fresh water, and there are seats there, cut in the living rock, for nymphs have their home in the cave.

The Grotto at Stourhead, which is situated at water level as if 'at the foot of the cliffs', is designed as a circular domed chamber of rugged tufa rock ('living rock') with water gushing through ('fresh water'), there are stone seats ('seats there') recessed in its rock walls, a statue of a water nymph reclining on a pedestal, and a statue of Neptune – the Roman god of the sea – as a River God in a recess.

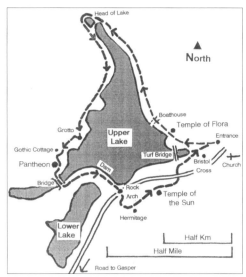

Stourhead Lake and Grounds

The progression around the lake

The gardens of Stourhead were laid out to provide a succession of vistas to be experienced as the visitor progresses around the three-armed lake, some of them focussed on the buildings which provide the architectural incidents, others illustrating episodes from the *Aeneid*. It is extremely important to be aware that the layout assumes that the walk is taken anti-clockwise around the lake. In the progression around the lake in this direction, which amounts to a walk of a little over a mile, the first building to be passed is the Temple of Flora, which stands above the Paradise Well and a grotto boathouse, marked by an elegant urn on a pedestal which was placed in this position in the early 20th century. The Temple of Flora is a single-roomed temple with a portico of four Tuscan columns, dedicated to Flora, the Roman goddess of spring and flowers. It was formerly known as the Temple of Ceres, this being the Roman name for the Greek Demeter, the goddess of the fruits of the earth, particularly corn. The Temple of Flora was the first of the architectural features to be added to the Stourhead landscape, being built in about 1745 to the design of Flitcroft.

Betwen the Temple of Flora and the head of the lake there was formerly the option of short-

Stourhead: the Temple of Flora

ening the walk by crossing the north arm of the lake by a long-span flat-arched timber bridge with open balustrades, which is shown in early drawings of the Stourhead grounds made in about 1770 by C W Bampfylde (1719–91), the Somerset landowner, painter and landscape designer. This bridge was generally known as the Chinese Bridge, although it was based upon a bridge illustrated by Palladio in his *Quattro Libri* (Book 3, Plate V).

This bridge is now gone, and it is perhaps as well that some of the more exotic and impermanent architectural elements in the Stourhead landscape have been removed, as the gardens may have become overbuilt. The present balance of buildings to planting seems to be ideal.

After continuing up the east side of the lake the lower end of Six Wells Bottom is reached at the head of the lake, the area referred to in Flitcroft's letter quoted earlier (page 149). This coombe was part of the wild landscape of the deer park of the Lords Stourton until it was tamed and landscaped. The River Stour rises further up the coombe at the point marked by St Peter's Pump, a 15th-century structure which is visible from the lakeside and was brought here from Bristol and re-erected in 1766 on a grotto base. As the head of the lake is crossed the basin-shaped pool on the left. Known as Diana's Basin as it was dedicated to the goddess of hunting and woodlands. After continuing down the west side of the lake the path forks. The left (lower) path leads to the Grotto, built in the years after 1748, and the higher path by-passes the Grotto.

The Grotto provides the most dramatic experience in this great garden. Its main chamber is approached through a preliminary grotto arch and down a dark, damp and canted tunnel of tufa rock. This tunnel entrance was added as an afterthought in about 1776. As the tunnel straightens a whitened lead statue of a Neptune-like River God is seen ahead through the main circular chamber of the Grotto, with its pebbled floor and a domed roof encrusted with tufa rock.

'Nymph of the Grot' in Stourhead grotto

View across the lake from the Grotto to the village church and the Turf Bridge

Although this statue of the River God has been attributed to Rysbrack it was in fact sculpted by John Cheere (died 1787), whose account dated 7 August 1751 survives in the archives of Hoare's Bank. The main chamber of the Grotto, built in about 1748, contains to the right another whitened lead statue of a reclining 'nymph of the grot' attributed to John Cheere, and isolated on a pedestal bench in a basin of water fed by one of the sources of the River Stour which splashes into it. On the edge of the basin is inscribed a translation by Alexander Pope from the Latin of Cardinal Bembo:

> Nymph of the Grot these sacred springs I keep
> And to the murmur of these waters sleep;
> Ah! Spare my slumbers, gently tread the cave,
> And drink in silence or in silence lave.

The domed roof has at its centre an open 'eye' which admits some daylight, although the light level is deliberately kept low and sombre in order to create the illusion that the Grotto is un-derground. It is also pervaded by the sound of continually splashing water. More daylight is admitted through a jagged opening in the grotto wall opposite the statue of the reclining nymph. This aperture provides perhaps the most stunning visual effect at Stourhead, superb views across the lake from water level towards the bridge which stands near the entrance to the gardens. The Stourhead Grotto represents a deliberate attempt to re-create Virgil's cave with 'Within, fresh water and seats in the living rock, the home of the nymphs'.

On each side of the nymph's basin a semi-circular headed stone seat is recessed into the tufa walls. The views from these two seats through the aperture across the lake were deliberately aligned on the Temple of the Sun on its hill and Temple of Flora and its grotto boathouse on the opposite side of the lake – although the latter has now unfortunately been obscured by the growth of later planting. Foliage now obstructs this view, which I believe to have been considered in the original layout. Having known and studied Stourhead for almost forty years and over this period observed the planting develop, I believe that it has in places become excessive and now screens out too much of the lake, particularly at its north end.

River God in the Grotto

Upon leaving the main chamber of the Grotto the whitened lead statue in its watery artificial cave is passed. This River God was modelled on *The Tiber* from Salvator Rosa's etching *The Dream of Aeneas*, another fact which supports the Virgilian theory for the layout of the grounds. The River God formerly held a trident in his right hand and with his left hand he holds the rim of an urn, from which issues water from a spring. In his *Visits to Country Seats* Horace Walpole recorded that in his time there were more lines from Virgil under this statue, which have been superseded by the rather banal couplet:

> This Stream like Time still hastens from my Urn,
> For ever rolling, never to return.

There can be no doubt that the Grotto is the most sublime element in the grounds of Stourhead, the word sublime being used in the 18th century for attempts to produce mixed feelings of astonishment, reverence and awe, feelings which were defined by the philosopher Edmund Burke (1729–97) in his *Philosophical Inquiry into the Origin of our Ideas of the Sublime and the Beautiful* (1757) as 'tranquillity tinged with terror'.

After leaving the Grotto up a flight of rugged winding steps the path after a short distance passes in front of a rustic gothic *cottage-ornée*, which was originally a utilitarian storage building concealed among trees. In 1806 Colt Hoare cleared some trees, made a feature of the cottage, and improved it by adding gothick elements including a porch and the decorative ogee-arched seat. The cottage was thatched until 1907 when the thatch was replaced with stone tiles.

Immediately after leaving the cottage the path swings right round a corner and suddenly reveals ahead the Pantheon with its Corinthian portico, which was distantly seen earlier from across the lake. In 1753 the celebrated English painter William Hogarth (1697–1764) published *The Analysis of Beauty*, a book on the theory of art in which he advocated 'the line of beauty' as a winding double curve, which he suggested led the eye 'a wanton kind of chase'. This was seized upon by designers of English landscaped gardens, and the manner in which the path curves right around the rustic cottage, suddenly reveals the Pantheon ahead, and then swings left in front of it, is a classic example of Hogarth's 'line of beauty'.

The Stourhead Pantheon is as its name implies a simplified and scaled-down version of the Pantheon in Rome. It is the largest, the grandest, and the most significant of the Stourhead temples, being strategically placed to be visible across the lake from the entrance to the grounds. It then disappears from view during the anticlockwise progression around the lake and suddenly re-appears as just described. Although the Pantheon in Claude Lorraine's painting *Aeneas at Delos* has a hexastyle Corinthian portico, the Pantheon at Stourhead is slightly different. Although it is in the Corinthian style the portico is hexastyle-in-antis, meaning six-columned with the colonnade set between flanking walls which are in line with the columns. Although the reason for this is not clear the change was probably for aesthetic reasons. The Pantheon was built in 1753-4 to a design by Flitcroft although, according to Walpole, it was altered in execution. It contains several statues, including an appropriately huge one of Hercules, signed by the sculptor Rysbrack and dated 1756, which explains its alternative name of the Temple of Hercules.

Stourhead: the Pantheon with the cottage (right)

In the round-headed niches on the front of the Pantheon are lead statues of Bacchus and Venus by John Cheere, the Venus being a scantily clad female who is studying her posterior over her shoulder. She is known as the *Venus Callipygos* (literally the 'Venus of the beautiful buttocks'), the classical story being that two sisters from Syracuse asked a passer-by to decide which of them had the prettiest bottom. The outcome was that this gentleman and his brother married the two sisters! It was probably this statue which prompted John Wesley, who may have known the story, to note in his *Journal* for 12 September 1776 that, although he admired the landscaping and scenery of Stourhead, he could not: 'reconcile statues with nudities either to common sense or common decency'.

After passing in front of the Pantheon the path crosses a small cast iron bridge supplied by Maggs and Hindley in 1860 with timber planked decking. The path then turns left through a dramatic tunnel of foliage, the drama arising from the fact that as the path gently rises up a short slope from below the water level the vast surface of the lake suddenly appears ahead at eye level above the dam. The path then emerges from this foliage

tunnel to run along the dam, which was constructed in about 1754 to impound the waters of the River Stour and create the principal lake. From this dam a lower lake with a water-wheel and a waterfall may be seen to the right, and a fine view of the Pantheon may be obtained by looking back.

At the Chinese Arch of rocky stone, built in about 1760–70 across the public road to Gasper, the options are either to continue following the path around the lake or to cross the road by climbing through the arch and then walk up Church Hill by the zig-zag path through the trees to the Temple of the Sun. Part of the way up this path on the right is the arched grotto recess known as the Hermitage, which was built in 1771 and was in Henry Hoare's time occupied by a hired hermit.

At the top of the hill is the Temple of Apollo (or the Temple of the Sun), a domed rotunda with a scalloped entablature and surrounding colonnade based by Henry Flitcroft on a temple at Baalbec and completed in about 1767. Apollo was the Greek god of order, art, and civilisation. In its prominent position on the high grassy plateau which offers splendid views over the lake, this building is another of the major architectural incidents in the Stourhead grounds.

Stourhead: Temple of the Sun

The continuation of the walk is downhill and through a dark damp tunnel under the public road to rejoin the lakeside path near the Turf Bridge with its low parapet walls. This was built about 1762 and was based on Palladio's bridge at Vicenza. The circuit of the lake is completed by passing left of the Bristol Cross, an authentic gothic cross which was was originally set up in Bristol in 1373, was later dismantled and stored, and lay neglected and unwanted until 1765 when it was acquired by Henry Hoare from the Bristol authorities.

Two architectural features that are not seen when walking around the lake are the Convent and the Obelisk. Deep among the woods to the north-west towards Alfred's Tower is the Convent, a fanciful picturesque turreted building with a thatched roof, built 1760–70 and now converted into a private dwelling and therefore not accessible. Only the top of the Obelisk is glimpsed from the walk around the lake. It stands axially

Stourhead: Temple of Flora (left) and the Temple of the Sun (centre)

to the house on the flat area above the valley to the north-east, beside the line of the old way through the estate which was diverted along Alfred's Tower Road. Crowned by a solar disk, the Obelisk was originally built in 1746–7, but was rebuilt in 1839–1840.

Upon reflection after a walk around the Stourhead lake we may agree with Professor Pevsner when he wrote in *The Buildings of England: Wiltshire* (1963):

> In thinking back of the whole of the grounds of Stourhead and especially the walk around the lake, the reader may agree with the writer that English picturesque landscaping of the C18 is the most beautiful form of gardening ever created, superior in variety and subtlety to the Italy of Frascati and the France of Versailles.

Sir Richard Colt Hoare

Henry Hoare the Younger died in 1785 having, in the words of John Britton in his *Beauties of Wiltshire*: 'at an advanced age had the heartfelt satisfaction of hearing his own creation universally admired and to see a barren waste covered with luxuriant woods'. Towards the end of his life, fearing for the stability of Hoare's Bank and apprehensive about the future of his house and garden, he decided to separate the succession of his Stourhead estate from that of the bank, and executed deeds conveying the bank to his nephew Richard and the Stourhead estate to his grandson Richard Colt Hoare, with a condition that he must never become a partner in the bank. When Colt Hoare married Hester Lyttleton in 1783 Henry Hoare retired to Clapham, and left Colt Hoare in occupation of the Stourhead estate.

Sir Richard Colt Hoare – his maternal grandmother was Susannah Colt (died 1743), the second wife of Henry Hoare the Younger – was descended from the Hoares on both sides of his family, his mother being Anne (1737–59), a daughter of Henry Hoare the Younger. He was an accomplished amateur artist and became a distinguished pioneer researcher and writer on archaeological and historical subjects. In 1784 his wife Hester gave birth to a son and in July 1785 another son called Richard was born. Colt Hoare then experienced a similar succession of family bereavements to those suffered by Henry Hoare the Younger. His wife Hester died in August 1785, and in September 1785 his grandfather also died, as did his infant son on the 20th of the same month. Afflicted by this succession of family misfortunes Colt Hoare travelled on the Continent for six years from late 1785 until the revolutionary disturbances in France put an end to Continental travel. During these six years he made only one brief visit to England.

Apart from being a very competent talent in his own right (he was described in 1811 by John Constable as 'no inconsiderable artist') Colt Hoare employed a number of artists. In the 1790s

Sir Richard Colt Hoare of Stourhead

he commissioned J M W Turner (1775–1851) to provide him with a series of twenty watercolours of Salisbury, to be engraved for a history of Wiltshire which was never published, ten being commissioned of the town and ten of the cathedral. Turner made the preliminary sketches in 1795 and worked on the watercolours until about 1802, but only seventeen were completed. They are now thought to be some of the best early work of Turner, who also painted a fine watercolour of Salisbury from Old Sarum with a shepherd and

his flock in the foreground, which was for a time in the collection of Ruskin. At Stourhead Turner painted a watercolour of the Bristol Cross and an unfinished painting of a sunrise over the lake in about 1800, and in 1825 he exhibited a watercolour entitled *Rise of the River Stour at Stourhead*. Colt Hoare also in 1804 employed Francis Nicholson (1753–1844), a founder member of the Water Colour Society in 1804 and a writer on landscape painting, to paint for him a number of views of the Stourhead landscape.

In 1791 Colt Hoare returned home from the Continent and for ten years he travelled extensively in England and Wales. At the age of forty-three he in 1801 finally settled down at Stourhead and soon became absorbed in the archaeology of his own neighbourhood, which he researched and excavated in collaboration with William Cunnington of Heytesbury. Colt Hoare later revealed that he became interested in archaeology entirely as a result of meeting Cunnington, when he wrote in *The Hundred of Mere* that from Mr Cunnington he 'became infected with the mania of Antiquarianism'.

Their joint immense contribution to pioneering archaeology was emphasised by Glyn Daniel when he wrote in *A Hundred Years of Archaeology* in 1950: 'Cunnington and Colt Hoare may very properly be called the fathers of archaeological excavation in England, just as John Aubrey was the father of field archaeology'. All three of these men had very strong associations with Wiltshire, Aubrey (see Chapter 6) as a native, Colt Hoare as the owner of Stourhead, and William Cunnington as a resident of Heytesbury for most of his life, from 1772 when he was eighteen to his early death in 1810.

William Cunnington (1754–1810) was the first of a celebrated succession of Wiltshire archaeologists to bear that surname. He was born in Northamptonshire and, after being apprenticed in 1772 to a woollen manufacturer near Warminster, he decided to remain in Wiltshire and set up business in Heytesbury where he lived. Warned by his doctors that for the sake of his health he must 'ride out or die' he understandably chose the former and began to ride over the downs around his home. Having always been studious, he at first interested himself in geology, but later became interested in the profusion of archaeological sites that he found in Wiltshire and began to investigate them. Inevitably he soon met Colt Hoare and in 1801 they began to collaborate, Colt Hoare providing the finance and William Cunnington undertaking the supervision of much of the field work. This arrangement worked well and William Cunnington deserves as much credit as Colt Hoare for the excavation work and the recording of the finds, because he often excavated when Colt Hoare was absent on other business. Cunnington died in 1810 and was buried at Heytesbury with a large memorial slab outside the south wall of the church.

After Cunnington's death Colt Hoare spent the remaining twenty-eight years of his life publishing the results of their joint researches and excavations. Although a competent topographical draughtsman in his own right he employed a local surveyor, Philip Crocker of Frome, as his illustrator. His principal publications are the two volumes of *Ancient Wiltshire* and the six-volume *Modern History of Wiltshire*, which covers all the hundreds of south Wiltshire as far north as Westbury. These histories of the hundreds were first published separately and were later combined into two large volumes. The earlier volumes are almost entirely the work of Colt Hoare, but as he became older he depended more upon collaborators.

Colt Hoare sensitively added symmetrical wings to Stourhead House to accommodate his books and pictures, and he also added the portico which had been envisaged in Colen Campbell's original design but was not built. In the grounds he augmented the planting with many indigenous trees, but he also added some exotics and extensively underplanted the woodlands with laurel. He also removed some of the more exotic minor buildings and by doing so probably enhanced the grounds which had become overbuilt.

From 1801 Colt Hoare suffered from gout and towards the end of his life was frequently unwell. He became increasingly more house-bound at Stourhead, writing in 1832 in his journal: 'Still home-bound, deaf and lame'. His son Henry was a disappointment to him and he worried about the succession at Stourhead, but in 1836 Henry predeceased his father and when Colt Hoare died aged eighty in May 1838 he left Stourhead to his seventy-six year old half-brother Henry Hugh, in whom ownership of the Stourhead estate and Hoare's Bank were re-united.

Stourhead House and gardens then continued to be owned by the Hoare family for about another century. At times the grounds were allowed to decline into semi-dereliction and in 1946, two hundred years after Henry Hoare began to create his garden, they were given with 2,300 acres of the estate to the National Trust. The Trust now administers and maintains them, and has re-instated the gardens to a condition approximating to their original conception as laid out by Henry Hoare the Younger in the second half of the 18th century.

Having frequently visited Stourhead over a period of almost forty years I find that I never tire of such visits, which invariably provide new experiences. Some people have expressed reservations about the principle of scattering buildings among the trees to create an 18th-century elysium. As for myself, I appreciate seeing high-quality classical buildings beautifully integrated into a man-made naturalised landscape, although I also suspect that the removal of some of the more exotic buildings such as the Turkish Tent and the Chinese Parasol which formerly existed has improved the Stourhead landscape.

Stourhead is generally recognised to be the finest surviving example of an 18th-century English landscaped garden, the art form that was described by Pevsner as: 'the most influential of all English inovations in art'. We are singularly fortunate that Henry Hoare, after suffering the misfortune of a succession of family bereavements, decided to alleviate his grief by transforming this formerly rather bleak southwestern corner of Wiltshire into a landscaped garden which became a major contribution to world art, a rare achievement which has enriched the lives of innumerable visitors to Stourhead over a period of more than two hundred years.

11   William Beckford
the Caliph of Fonthill

About a mile and a half east of Hindon in south Wiltshire the minor public road that runs south from Fonthill Bishop passes through a monumental classical arched gatehouse with massive flanking walls and urns into grounds which in the 18th century were landscaped as the setting for the former Palladian mansion known as Fonthill Splendens. Here the Beckfords, Alderman Beckford and his son William, successively created first a fine Palladian house in landscaped grounds and then a pseudo-gothic extravaganza. Although their respective houses known as Fonthill Splendens and Fonthill Abbey are now gone much of their landscaping survives.

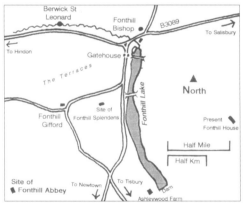

Fonthill Lake and Houses

After passing through the gatehouse the road runs down the west side of a linear lake about a mile and a half long which was formed by damming up a small stream at a mill site. A little beyond the point where the road diverges away from the lake a now-blocked semi-derelict pedestrian tunnel passed under the road and emerged at a grotto beside the lake. This tunnel (which is not acces-sible) allowed the Beckfords to walk unobserved under the public road which the elder Beckford had failed to get closed. The road then runs on to pass between some gateless gate piers near the Beckford Arms public house and a Victorian church which has replaced a classical church built here in 1748 by Alderman Beckford.

The history of Fonthill
As early as 901 AD the Bishop of Winchester held Fonthill Bishop which was consequently known as Bishop's Fonthill. By Domesday land at Fonthill was in the hands of Berenger Giffard, one of the Conqueror's henchmen, and it is from the Giffard family that the name Fonthill Gifford is derived. The manor of Fonthill later passed through the hands of the families of West, Mauduit, Hungerford, Mervyn, and Cottington, prior to its acquisition by the Beckfords in the 18th century.

The Cottingtons
The immediate predecessor of the Beckfords at Fonthill was Lord Francis Cottington (*c.* 1578–1652), the fourth son of Philip Cottington of Godminster near Bruton in Somerset. At the beginning of the reign of James I Francis Cottington became ambassador to Spain and served Charles I in the same capacity. He was knighted in 1623 and seems to have been a bold man, because when he quarrelled with the powerful royal favourite the Duke of Buckingham and Buckingham threatened to ruin him, Cottington calmly requested the return of hangings worth £800 which he had presented to the Duke to buy his favour. In 1631 Cottington was raised to the peerage as Baron Cottington. That year Charles Mervyn, 2nd Earl of Castlehaven, was denounced by his son and executed for

homosexuality, which was then a capital offence, and his forfeited estate at Fonthill was in 1632 given by Charles I to Francis, Baron Cottington, by then his chancellor, a post which he held when Civil War commenced in 1642.

At the outbreak of the war Lord Cottington seems to have decided to be cautious and pleaded gout as his excuse for not joining the king's forces in the north. It should be emphasised that he was then about sixty-four, an advanced age for a man at that time, and that ultimately he put up money for a troop of fifty horse and joined the royal cause in 1643. Clarendon described Cottington as being wise, having great self-control and a dry humour, but he also says: 'he left behind him a greater esteem of his parts than love of his person'. Lord Cottington shared Charles II's exile and died abroad in 1652. An example of his cunning occurred during their exile in 1649 when he was seventy-one. Cottington disapproved of a proposal of the young Prince Charles to appoint a soldier called Colonel Wyndham as his Secretary of State, and deliberately tricked Charles by begging a place for his falconer as a royal chaplain. Prince Charles fell into the carefully prepared trap by pointing out the unsuitability of a falconer as a chaplain, whereupon Lord Cottington pointed out that he was no less qualified than was Colonel Wyndham to be Secretary of State.

During the Commonwealth Cottington forfeited Fonthill and for a short time before the Restoration it was given to Lord President Bradshaw who had presided at the trial of Charles I. All of Lord Cottington's children predeceased him and at the Restoration the estate

was restored to Lord Cottington's heir, a nephew also called Francis Cottington, who was described by the republican Edmund Ludlow as 'a Papist and an idiot'. Fonthill then passed through the hands of his descendants, including Francis, Baron Cottington (died 1728) and his son, another Francis Cottington, who held it until 1745.

Alderman Beckford acquires Fonthill

In that year (1745) Francis Cottington sold the by then run-down Fonthill estate to the wealthy London Alderman William Beckford (1709–70) whose short biography will be found later in this chapter (page 163). His son was the celebrated but ill-reputed William Beckford.

Between 1745 and 1755 the Alderman developed and landscaped his new estate at Fonthill, which consisted of almost five thousand acres of former Medieval deer park. During the 18th century Fonthill was extensively planted with trees by the Beckfords and the lake was formed in the late-18th century by damming the little stream that feeds into the River Sem at Tisbury. This lake was not shown by Andrews and Dury on their 1773 map although it probably existed at that date. Between 1773 and 1796 the younger

Beckford's grotto ruins beside Fonthill Lake

William Beckford developed the park further and extended the lake southwards, until virtually all signs of the former deer parks had been erased. According to *The Place-Names of Wiltshire* (1939), part of Fonthill Old Park was known as *Nippard* and 'Nappern Mill' appears on Andrews and Dury at the south end of the area which was drowned when the lake was formed. Extensive signs of this former mill and its leats survive south of the dam and the cascade at the south end of the lake.

Typical Fonthill landscape near the site of the former Fonthill Splendens

Alderman Beckford's Fonthill Splendens

The houses at Fonthill

The story of the successive houses at Fonthill is complicated. Alderman Beckford's purchase included the gabled Elizabethan but part Georgianised house of the Mervyns and the Cottingtons situated west of the future lake. Lord Cottington was a celebrated sportsman and connoisseur of horses who, according to Colt Hoare, between 1631 and 1640 had added a stable block to his house which was said to be one of the largest in England. After making improvements to this house the Alderman lost it by a fire which was reported in the *Gentleman's Magazine* for 12 February 1755 :

> A sudden fire broke out at the seat of Wm. Beckford, Esq., at Fonthill, near Hindon, Wilts, which in three hours time consumed the greatest part of the building, and most of the rich furniture, together with the fine organ, which is said to have cost near £5,000. The whole loss is computed at £30,000, only six of which were insured.

Beckford now replaced this house with the magnificent Fonthill Splendens which was built on the same site and designed in the current Palladian style with a giant portico and linked quadrant wings, its design being based on that of Houghton Hall by Colen Campbell who had designed Stourhead. Fonthill Splendens has generally been attributed to an unknown architect called Hoare, although it was suggested by Sir Reginald Blomfield (1856–1942), a practising architect of some standing, an architectural historian, and President of the Royal Institue of British Architects, that the designer of Fonthill

Splendens was James Paine (c.1716–89), the late-Palladian architect who some years later designed nearby New Wardour Castle. When Fonthill Splendens was commenced in 1765 Paine was an established Palladian architect, who had been responsible for houses of national importance in Nostell Priory in Yorkshire (c. 1735–50) and Kedelston Hall in Derbyshire (1757–61). The possibility of Paine being the designer of Fonthill Splendens could explain the

Fonthill Lake. The urns survive from a grotto boathouse

attribution of the house to the unknown man called Hoare, who may have been either the builder or the site architect carrying out Paine's design. The picture gallery of Fonthill Splendens was designed by Sir John Soane in 1787, about the time that Paine became infirm in old age and retired to France. Another possible designer is Flitcroft, who probably designed Alderman Beckford's London house and died in 1769.

Paintings of Fonthill Splendens and its surroundings made in 1753 reveal that several elaborate garden buildings were associated with the house, and that the lake was then merely a narrow 'leat' or canal, spanned by a Palladian bridge.

After he inherited the Fonthill estate the Alderman's son William Beckford ultimately demolished most of Fonthill Splendens, while building his gothic extravaganza which he called Fonthill Abbey in the woods on the hill west of Fonthill Lake (at NGR 918309). The remote siting of his replacement house was decided by the reclusive William Beckford's wish for privacy, and his desire to get away from the public road down the west side of the lake which Alderman Beckford had attempted to get closed. To ensure this privacy, when he built Fonthill Abbey Beckford constructed a surrounding wall twelve feet high and inside it set man traps and released bloodhounds. The length of this wall has often been greatly overestimated, presumably on the assumption that it enclosed the entire estate. In fact it was only about three miles long and enclosed only the grounds around the Abbey some distance west of the lake. The enclosure was known as the Abbey Enclosure and amounted to only 524 acres, and its wall ran west of Beacon Hill (Stop Beacon), north up the road to Stop Lodge, and north-east to Stop Farm at Fonthill Gifford, from where it ran south-west then south, east of the Abbey and Bitham Lake, and then continued west passing a little south of Beacon Hill. Some of this wall survives although much reduced in places, and its existence heightened curiosity when Beckford was employing five hundred men to build his Abbey on a shift system that involved working at night by the light of *flambeaux*.

Having been built in the late 1790s and early 1800s, Fonthill Abbey collapsed in 1825. In 1829 the Fonthill estate was bought by James Morrison MP (died 1857) who occupied and improved the remains of Fonthill Splendens. This house then passed down the family to Alfred Morrison (died 1897), Hugh (died 1931) and the Barons Margadale. A new Fonthill House was designed in 1904 by Detmar Blow for Mr Hugh Morrison MP incorporating the former manor house of Berwick St Leonard at which William of Orange stayed in his advance east in 1688 to replace James II. In Colt Hoare's time in 1829 this manor

house was used as a barn and by 1905 it was a mere shell. Hugh Morrison bought it and Detmar Blow rebuilt it as part of the new Fonthill house at Little Ridge towards the east edge of Fonthill park.

Fonthill Lake with the present Fonthill House in the background

The Beckfords and their fortune

The Beckfords are believed to take their name from the village of Beckford ('Becca's ford') in Worcestershire, four miles north-east ot Tewkesbury. A Sir William Beckford who supported Richard III may have died at the Battle of Bosworth in 1485. Since they had supported the last Plantagenet against Henry Tudor the fortunes of the Beckfords declined under the Tudors until Peter Beckford (born 1643) emigrated to Jamaica after the Restoration of the monarchy in 1660. He founded the fortunes of the family by acquiring plantations and producing sugar on a large scale. Sugar had been a scarce commodity, but its availability from the West Indies at an economic price coincided with the introduction of coffee and tea into Europe. Fortunes were made from this eminently marketable commodity, although after the enslaved native population of the West Indies had been worked to virtual extermination the manufacture became dependent upon imported Negro slave labour transported from Africa.

An Alderman Sir Thomas Beckford of Maidenhead, mentioned by Pepys as an absentee proprietor, drew £2000 a year from his Jamaican estates. From 1660 a Richard Beckford also purchased plantations in Jamaica where the Beckfords prospered and became famous for extravagance. In 1692 William III appointed Peter Beckford Lieutenant-Governor and Commander-in-Chief over Jamaica. This

Beckford's prosperity was so great that his son was alleged in a 1740 history of Jamaica to have possessed property exceeding that of any subject in Europe. These Jamaican Beckfords were related to Alderman Beckford who was born in Jamaica in 1709, purchased Fonthill in 1745, and exerted a great influence upon his son despite the fact that the young William Beckford was only nine when his father died.

Alderman Beckford

Alderman William Beckford (1709–70) was sent to Westminster School and Balliol College at Oxford. In 1747 he was elected MP for Shaftesbury, he represented London in parliament from 1754 to his death, and was twice Lord Mayor of London, in 1763 and 1770. The considerable British interests in the West Indies were represented in parliament by Alderman Beckford, who was from 1756 one of the principal supporters of Chatham in the city. He supported Chatham and Wilkes in opposition to the court party of George III. As one of the newly rich Beckford was regarded as an upstart and often reminded that he was a slave-owner, but as the richest commoner of his time he had to be heard. He was a positive and combative person who attacked government of the state by a few aris-

Alderman Beckford

tocrats and advocated parliamentary reform. Horace Walpole described him as a 'noisy vaporous fool' and he was said to lack any charm or finesse. On one occasion in 1770 he outfaced the king when representing a Grand Remonstrance from the city, consequently became a popular hero, and at his death was commemorated by the striking of medals and by a statue in the London Guildhall, a distinction that he shares with the Duke of Wellington and the two Pitts.

Alderman Beckford had several illegitimate children before he married in June 1756 at the age of forty-seven the widow of Francis Marsh, another city man. This lady was particularly well connected, being a Hamilton and a grand-daughter of the 6th Earl of Abercorn. Alderman Beckford was notably impious but his wife was inclined to Methodism. Their only child William was born at Soho Square in London in September 1760.

William Beckford the Younger inherits Fonthill

When Alderman Beckford died in 1770 from a chill caught when travelling from Fonthill to London his nine-year-old son William inherited the huge estate of Fonthill, capital amounting to about one and a half million pounds, and an annual income of over £100,000 from the West Indian plantations. William Beckford, the only son of Alderman Beckford's late marriage and a child 'of a very tender and delicate constitution', has gone down in history as 'the Caliph of Fonthill', an eccentric author, and one of the most amazing Englishmen who ever lived.

Brought up by his mother at Fonthill Splendens with Lord Chatham and Lord Chancellor Thurlow as his guardians, William Beckford grew to loathe the 18th-century sporting pursuits of his class and was more interested in the arts, learning and languages. As a child Beckford was a good musician, and he recalled how at the age of eight he had received piano lessons from Mozart:

> My father was very fond of music, and invited Mozart to Fonthill. He was eight years old and I was six. It was rather ludicrous one child being the pupil of another.

There is some doubt about this claim as Mozart was in fact four years older than Beckford.

William Beckford, the Caliph of Fonthill

On the other hand, Mozart was eight in 1764 when Beckford was four, and did come to England in that year and stayed in England until 25 July 1765. It is therefore possible that Mozart came to Fonthill, for Alderman Beckford was then a very important person. Recognizing in his old age that he had frittered away all the advantages to which he was born, William Beckford fabricated an imaginary life backed by forged correspondence in which he claimed many improbable achievements, including writing parts of Mozart's opera *The Marriage of Figaro*, in particular the air for 'Non piu andrai'. This claim seems to be entirely spurious.

Beckford was taught architecture by Sir William Chambers (1726–96) and painting by the portrait painter George Romney (1734–82), who painted three portraits of him, the first a full-length when he was about twelve, the next a head-and-shoulders when he was a youth of seventeen, and the last a full-length of him in his prime leaning nonchalantly against a stone pedestal. Romney also painted Beckford's two daughters. From his art tutor, the painter Alexander Cozens (died 1786), Beckford acquired a love of the Orient and

the occult, and in view of his later life it is interesting to note that his godfather Lord Chatham disapproved of Beckford's liking for the Orient, and is said to have warned him on no account to read the *Arabian Nights*. William also became interested in genealogy and heraldry and, as his father had acquired a former John of Gaunt castle at Easton Bray in Bedfordshire, he attempted unsuccessfully to trace his descent from John of Gaunt.

William Beckford's early life

His father's death proved to be a decisive influence on the boy William's character. It left him as a nine-year-old only child in the hands of a very possessive and extremely wealthy mother (whom he called 'the Begum'), and he was probably spoilt. When he was sixteen his mother became worried about her son's effeminate nature, his consuming interest in the arts, and his lack of interest in the sporting pursuits of his class. On the advice of his guardians he was packed off to Switzerland to finish his education and there he acquired French and consequently wrote reasonable French. He also had an audience with Voltaire, developed a cosmopolitan outlook that was very susceptible to foreign influences, and began to write.

As a youth Beckford contemplated converting to catholicism because he felt that 'one must become half-catholic to enter fully the glories of Italian art', although this threat may also have been made to aggravate his Calvinist mother.

From November 1778 to June 1780 Beckford was back in England, and between August and October 1779, aged nineteen, he undertook an extensive tour of his home country. Early in this tour he stayed at Powderham Castle near Exeter and became infatuated with William Courtenay (1768–1835), the eleven-year-old son and heir of his host Viscount Courtenay. He nicknamed the boy 'Kitty' and wrote him passionate letters. This boy, who was in 1784 to be instrumental in Beckford's ruin, became 3rd Viscount Courtenay and 9th Earl of Devon. In 1811 he fled to France to escape arrest as a homosexual and died unmarried and in obscurity in Paris.

In about 1780 Beckford also met Louisa, a daughter of Lord Rivers of Rushmore in Cranborne Chase, and the wife of his cousin Peter Beckford, a landowner in Dorset and the writer of *Thoughts upon Hare and Fox Hunting*. Louisa had married Peter Beckford in 1773 but had never accepted life as the wife of a Dorset sporting squire. In six years she had five children of whom three died as infants. When she met her husband's young cousin she became infatuated with him and Beckford entered into a protracted romance with Louisa, who nevertheless became his willing accomplice in his pursuit of 'Kitty' Courtenay. Louisa Beckford was to die in Florence in 1791, aged thirty-five.

Scandal over the Courtenay affair became widespread and in 1780 Beckford was again sent abroad, this time on the Grand Tour of Italy which was a customary part of an English gentleman's education. In Italy Beckford associated with some disreputable people including the Countess Rosenberg, a friend of Casanova, and he developed passions for several attractive youths.

Beckford remained in Italy from June 1780 to April 1781 and also met Lady Hamilton, the wife of Sir William Hamilton, the British Minister to the Court of Naples, who became his friend and confidante. Lady Hamilton anticipated that Beckford's sexual predilections were likely to lead him into social ruin, advised him against his 'criminal passions', and made him promise to renounce his friendships with youths. Beckford then dallied at Paris, for having tasted freedom he was probably reluctant to return to his domineering mother. In Paris he became involved with the penniless Georgina Seymour, the daughter of a lover of Madame Dubarry, and then had to return to England to deal with legal complications over his inheritance.

Beckford was in England from April 1781 to May 1782, and in June retired to Fonthill to hide from Georgina Seymour when he heard that she was opportunistically coming to England in pursuit of him, and his fortune. At this time he was practising the harpsichord, preparing his diaries for publication, and writing and receiving passionate letters from Louisa Beckford, who readily accepted his preference for 'Kitty'

Courtenay. She wrote, 'I fancy that after Kitty I am the being you prefer to all others'. On intermittent visits to London Beckford was, despite his reputation, as a bachelor millionaire pursued by several dowagers as a prospective husband for their daughters.

At his coming-of-age celebrations in September 1781 Beckford was dismayed at the prospect of assuming adult responsibilities. He claimed: 'I'm still in my cradle!', and that Christmas he held his own private celebrations employing Philippe de Loutherbourg, the foremost stage designer of the time, to embellish Fonthill Splendens for the occasion. The decadent *Arabian Nights* nature of these celebrations was described by Beckford's biographer James Lees-Milne as 'an orgy of acting, music and love-making'. They caused a scandal in the district, but were an event of great significance as they triggered the writing of his Arabian story *Vathek*, which was originally written in French and was admired by Lord Byron, Stéphane Mallarmé, and Prosper Mérimée. The Caliph Vathek, the hero of the story who sells himself to the devil, was evidently Beckford himself. Lord Byron (1788–1824) expressed a high opinion of *Vathek*:

> For correctness of costume, beauty of description, and power of imagination, it far surpasses all European imitations, and bears such marks of originality that those who have visited the East will find some difficulty in believing it to be more than a translation. As an Eastern tale even Rasselas [by Dr Johnson] must bow before it.

Although Beckford was older by almost thirty years there are parallels between the lives of Byron and Beckford. Both were obliged to flee abroad to escape ostracisation for sexual misdemeanours, and there are marked similarities between the last couplet of Byron's *The Corsair* and the conclusion of Vathek.

In London in 1782 Beckford wrote the music for Lady Craven's operetta *The Arcadian Pastoral* in the style of Mozart, but his affair with his cousin's wife caused another scandal and that year (1782) he again left England. He also in 1782 lost by her death in Naples the wise counsel of Lady Hamilton. Later in that year

Beckford returned from Italy and wrote to Louisa Beckford confirming his affection for 'Kitty' Courtenay.

Beckford's character

The extreme wealth which he inherited when he was still a boy seems to have developed in Beckford a distant haughtiness that rendered him unattractive to a society which ostracised him and from which he always felt isolated. Consequently he tended to associate with artists and writers and became a dilettante. In a letter to Louisa Beckford written from Paris 19 January 1784 he suggested 'I fear I shall never be . . . good for anything in this world, but composing airs, building towers, forming gardens, collecting old Japan, and writing a journey to China or the moon'.

Although he abhorred oppression of the poor Beckford could not bring himself to condemn slavery upon which his wealth was founded, and he opposed the anti-slavery movement.

Excluded from society Beckford now commenced the activities that dominated the rest of his life – building, gardening and collecting. In 1782 he was patronising the artist Alexander Cozens who had been his drawing-master and continued to be a great influence upon him. In May 1783 he married Lady Margaret Gordon, the pretty twenty-year-old daughter of the fourth Earl of Aboyne. The Beckfords spent their honeymoon in Switzerland where they stayed until March 1784. Beckford became devoted to his new wife, by whom he had a still-born son and two daughters, Margaret (b. 1785) and Susan (b. 1786), who to improve their marriage prospects were brought up in London away from their disgraced father. As good-looking heiresses with distinguished relatives on their mother's side they were received into great houses such as Bowood, Wilton and Wardour. Margaret Beckford became against her father's wishes Mrs Orde when in 1811 she married the impecunious Colonel Orde, who ultimately became a general. Susan married the Duke of Hamilton in 1810. Both daughters continued to be devoted to their father, although Margaret predeceased him in 1818, aged 33.

Scandal and exile

The Courtenay family were now fully alert to the relationship between Beckford and young William Courtenay and in October 1784 Beckford was alleged to have been discovered by the boy's tutor in compromising circumstances with William who was now sixteen. It is possible that Beckford was framed, but society was outraged. The incident was described by the *Morning Herald* (27 November 1784) as 'a grammatical mistake of Mr B and the Hon Mr C in regard to the genders'. At that time the aristocracy retained sufficient power to hush up a scandal and (although homosexuality was then a capital offence, and a previous Mervyn owner of the Fonthill estate had been executed and forfeited his estates for it) Beckford was merely required to leave the country and remain for a discreet time abroad. Consequently in July 1785 Beckford and his wife fled to Switzerland, and there Margaret Beckford died after the birth of their second daughter in May 1786, aged only twenty-four. Despite his absences abroad Beckford was from 1784 to 1790 MP first for Wells in Somerset and subsequently for Hindon in Wiltshire.

For some time Beckford remained abroad, spending much of the time travelling in Portugal. This inspired some of his best writing, including his *Letters from Portugal*, which were published in 1834. As he was so much abroad and was ostracised in England Beckford considered settling in Portugal to escape the stigma and insults that pursued him at home, provided that he was given a title and would not be required to become a catholic. His letters nevertheless reveal his intense love for the landscape of England and the variability of her seasons. Loving England in general and particularly Fonthill he decided that he could never abandon either for good. In Portugal his romantic escapades became even more complicated as he became involved in several liaisons. These included the seventeen-year-old choirboy Gregorio Franchi, whose father had sent him to enter Beckford's service at Madrid in May 1788. Franchi, who died in 1828, later became Beckford's secretary at Fonthill and was the recipient of the thousands of letters in Italian which formed the basis of *Life at Fonthill, 1807–22*.

In 1789 Beckford was in Paris during the terror and is said to have snapped-up bargains from the possessions of guillotined aristocrats. He remained in Paris until the execution of the king, when, coming under suspicion himself, he returned to England. At Lausanne in 1792 Beckford bought Gibbon's library, and he stayed in Portugal for a second time from November 1793 to October 1795. His correspondence reveals that in 1797 he was, through his agent in Paris Nicholas Williams, attempting to arrange a peace between France and England. Then in 1798 his mother died.

Beckford develops the Fonthill Estate

After his return to England from Paris in 1790 Beckford's letters reveal him living a reclusive life at Fonthill Splendens as a lonely, ostracised and embittered man with a French dwarf as his servant-companion. He now began to landscape his grounds by planting thousands of trees, many of them the beeches that we see today. One of the objectives of his wall was to exclude poachers and hunters from his grounds, for one of the attractive sides to Beckford's character was his love of wild animals, in which respect he was far in advance of his time. He considered that:

> . . . we have no right to murder animals for sport. The birds in the plantations of Fonthill seemed to know me. They continued their songs as I rode close to them; the very hares grew bold. It was exactly what I wished.

Had Beckford not suffered social ostracism it is probable that two elements in his character would have led to him live a reclusive life at Fonthill: he had a profound contempt for his fellow men, who seldom shared his exotic tastes, and he also loved to escape into dreams, from which he was reluctant to return to reality by leaving 'the soft illusions of the night'.

Development of the idea for Fonthill Abbey

After reaching maturity William Beckford initially tried to improve his father's Fonthill Splendens, the house in which he was born but had never liked because of its damp situation west of the lake.

From about 1790 there was in England an increasing interest in gothic architecture as a reaction against the severity of classical Palladianism. Almost every number of the *Gentleman's Magazine* carried an illustration and description of a gothic building, and in 1792 a chapel was added to Winchester in the true gothic style.

The name 'Abbey' appended to the name of a mansion house is normally an indication that the property had been an abbey which was dissolved at the Dissolution of the monasteries, although this was not the case at Fonthill. In Fonthill Abbey we have an unusual case of a house that was called 'Abbey' by Beckford when he became interested in the revival of the gothic style, and decided to amuse himself by building at immense expense as a retreat a towered gothic house in the style of a Medieval abbey. He named it Fonthill Abbey in order to emphasise its Medieval character.

From his early years Beckford had been obsessed by towers. His interest may have originated with the tower built by his father as a landscape feature on Stop Beacon, now Beacon Hill in the woods half a mile south-west of the Abbey site, and he would also have known Henry Hoare's immense Alfred's Tower near Stourhead, which was completed in 1772 when he was thirteen. Beckford always regarded a tower in a painting as a virtue and sometimes bought inferior paintings simply because they included a tower. When he was eighteen he had written to Alexander Cozens:

> There we will execute those plans you have imagined, and realise in some measure the dreams of our fancy . . . we shall ascend a lofty hill, which till lately was a mountain in my eyes. There I hope to erect a Tower dedicated to meditation . . .

and in 1790 he wrote to Lady Craven: 'One of my new estates in Jamaica brought me home seven thousand pounds last year more than usual. So I am growing rich, and mean to build Towers . . .' In *Vathek* the caliph builds himself a tower of eleven hundred steps from which he could look down on the rest of the world, and many years later, after finally departing from Fonthill, Beckford in his old age built Lansdown Tower above Bath as his elevated study.

James Wyatt and the building of Fonthill Abbey

In 1791 Beckford attempted to engage James Wyatt (1746–1813) as the architect for his proposed gothic extravaganza. Wyatt was the principal architect of his day, who at the death of Sir William Chambers in 1796 became Royal Surveyor-General and Comptroller of the Works. As his official career coincided with the Napoleonic Wars Wyatt had few opportunities to design public buildings and developed a flourishing private practice. He was a man of great refinement, was on excellent terms with George III, and was President of the Royal Academy 1805–6. In Wiltshire from 1790–5 he designed Hartham Park near Corsham and he also 'gothicised' a number of houses for other clients. In 1787–93 he renovated – some say desecrated – Salisbury Cathedral and became known as 'the Destroyer' for his drastic work on a number of cathedrals.

In choosing James Wyatt Beckford appointed an architect who, like many architects of his time, designed in both the gothic and classical styles. He tended to be dilatory and initially be enthusiastic about his works, and then lose interest and neglect them. One of his exasperated clients wrote to Wyatt in 1793:

> It is near two years since you undertook a business for me neither requiring nor admitting of delay . . . I have written to you no less than five letters . . . and you have returned no answer.

Wyatt also had a reputation for finishing schemes late and at a cost very much above estimate.

The initial arrangements with Wyatt were interrupted by Beckford's travels on the Continent, during which his ideas for his house developed. When he returned home in June 1796 Wyatt was promptly engaged to design Fonthill Abbey, upon which work now commenced. The year 1796 was an important one for James Wyatt. Not only was he appointed Royal Surveyor, but he was already very busy in Wiltshire designing Bowden Park in the classical style on the hill above Lacock, and making designs for Longford Castle near Salisbury.

Wyatt once remarked that he hoped for a sudden death, and this was granted him in

Wiltshire on 4 September 1813 when his carriage overturned near Marlborough during his return journey to London after visiting a site in Gloucestershire. At the time he was reading a newspaper with his hat off, and his head hit the ceiling of the carriage, killing him instantly. Wyatt's career was then already in decline and Beckford upon hearing the news wrote unsympathetically to a friend: 'Alas my poor Bagasse had already sunk from the plane of genius to the mire: for some years now he has only dabbled in mud'.

One of Wyatt's early drawings illustrates Fonthill Abbey with a tall octagonal tower surmounted by a very narrow spire. Turner in 1799 painted it with a short spire with flying buttresses on a two-stage octagonal tower, but this spire collapsed during a storm in May 1800. The building was hastily reconstructed with a tall octagonal tower, which was in place, lacking a spire, in time for the visit in December 1800 of Horatio Nelson, whose funeral arrangements in St Paul's Cathedral Wyatt designed five years later.

Lord Nelson's visit to Fonthill

This visit represented a considerable achievement for Beckford who had been socially ostracised since the 1794 scandal. In inviting Nelson to Fonthill Beckford may have felt sympathy for a fellow flawed character, for the inadequacy of Nelson's private behaviour was recognised in his time. Although Nelson was a national hero of undoubted ability and courage, his superior the Earl St Vincent (John Jervis, 1735–1823) said of him: 'Animal courage was the sole merit of Lord Nelson, his private character most disgraceful'. After winning his decisive triumph over the French fleet at Aboukir Bay (the Battle of the Nile) in August 1798 Nelson had formed a liaison with Emma Hamilton (c. 1765–1815), a woman of great beauty and dubious past. From Naples in 1800 he disregarded an order to take his fleet to the defence of Minorca and was censured by the Admiralty for disobedience. He then resigned his commission and with Emma Hamilton and her husband Sir William made his leisurely way home across Europe. On his return he was ostracised by the king and the upper classes, because of his liaison with Emma. It was in these circumstances that Nelson was entertained at Christmas 1800 by the reclusive Beckford at Fonthill. On this visit he was accompanied by both Sir William and Emma who, despite being eight months pregnant by Nelson, demonstrated her famous 'attitudes'. They dined in the partly completed Fonthill Abbey on food 'unmingled with any of the refinements of modern culinary art', and it was perhaps as a result of the success of this visit by his celebrated guests that Beckford decided that he would live permanently in his new abbey.

The completion of Fonthill Abbey

In 1801 Beckford sold the rich contents of his father's house to finance his continuing building operations on the Abbey. When he returned to Fonthill from visiting France in 1803 the building of Fonthill was still proceeding, but as further materials were needed for his Abbey these were in 1807 obtained by demolishing Fonthill Splendens which he had never liked. Work continued on Fonthill Abbey until about 1820, although its architect Wyatt died in September 1813.

Beckford was particularly pleased with Bitham Lake, which was created by damming up a slight hollow a little distance south of the Abbey site. Of it he wrote: 'The lake looks as if God had made it, it is so natural, without the least trace of art'. The lake survives today in dense woods south of the Abbey site, but inaccessible to the public.

Opinions about the merits of Fonthill Abbey varied. Bishop Fisher of Salisbury described it as: 'a bad imitation of Salisbury Cathedral converted into a dwelling-house'. When passing the gate to Fonthill Abbey the painter John Constable noted: 'It is strange that such a place, so fairy-like and so filling by every standard of taste and elegance, should be standing alone in these melancholy regions of the Wiltshire Downs'. When he saw the interior of the house Constable considered it 'truly beautiful' and 'on the whole a strange, ideal, romantic place, quite fairy land'. He wrote: 'Imagine Salisbury Cathedral, or, indeed, any beautiful Gothic building, magnificently fitted up with crimson and gold, and ancient pictures, and statues in every niche . . .'

*Fonthill Abbey from the south-west, as drawn by
John Britton in 1823*

William Cobbett had in September 1811 corresponded with Beckford about an exchange of conifer seeds at the time when Cobbett was imprisoned in Newgate, and after visiting Fonthill Abbey on 29 August 1808 he wrote in glowing terms to Dr Mitford:

> Well, we saw Fonthill, but, even if I had the talent to do justice to it in a written description, ten such sheets as this would not suffice for the purpose. When I see you I will at times give you an hour's account of it. After that sight, all sights become mean until that be out of the mind. We both thought Wardour the first place we had ever seen, but Wardour makes but a single glade in Beckford's immense grounds and plantations.

Cobbett's liking for Fonthill did not however extend to its owner. Beckford claimed descent from the barons of England and his inclusion of a baronial hall in his Abbey prompted Cobbett to write in *Rural Rides*: 'Was there ever vanity and impudence equal to this: a negro-driver bragging of his lineage'. The critic William Hazlitt, who had trained as a painter, when visiting the art collection at Fonthill scathingly described the Abbey as:

> . . . a desert of magnificence, a glittering waste of laborious idleness, a cathedral turned into a toy shop, an immense museum of all that is most curious and costly, and at the same time most worthless in the productions of art and nature.

In the face of such adverse criticism Beckford became more reclusive, actively discouraged visitors from coming to Fonthill, and if they could not be deterred generally ensured that he was absent during their visits.

The sale of Fonthill

The protracted building of his immense Abbey proved to be too great a drain on even Beckford's immense resources. In 1820 he found himself in severe financial difficulties. His wealth was mostly tied up in Jamaican plantations which, for political and economic reasons, had become unsaleable, and his income plummeted as sugar sold at below the cost of its production. Outgoing interest on the mortgages on Fonthill and debts outstanding to his West Indies merchants added to his ever increasing difficulties, and in 1822 he had to accept that Fonthill and most of its contents, excepting only its library – for Beckford was said never to sell a book – had to be sold.

The sale of Fonthill was carefully organised. A pavilion was built in the grounds to provide overnight accommodation for prospective purchasers, as all beds were taken for miles around. Many celebrated visitors came to Fonthill to satisfy their curiosity, and the Duke of Wellington pronounced it 'The finest place in Europe'. The sale had been put into the hands of Christie's, but in 1822 Beckford sold the house and most of its contents by private treaty for £300,000 to Mr John Farquhar, who had made his fortune from gunpowder in India. Hazlitt scathingly suggested that his sale of Fonthill was 'the only proof of taste Mr Beckford has shewn'. He departed from Fonthill with few regrets, writing of the sale of his house and its contents: 'I am rid of the Holy Sepulchre which no longer interests me since its Profanation', this being the attendance of over seven thousand members of the public who paid to view the contents of his home.

The sale was effected only just in time, because three years later in December 1825 the immense tower of Fonthill Abbey collapsed. Later one of its masons confessed on his deathbed that the tower had been defectively built. Since it was placed at the crossing of the cruciform building, in falling it brought down much of the rest, but by this time Beckford was living at Bath. The rubble of Fonthill Abbey was sold as building materials and only the north wing of Fonthill Abbey remains today, and it is strictly private. John Farquhar in disgust divided the estate and

sold it off in lots, and it has never been re-united. Beckford had sold for a fortune a building that had in no time become a ruin.

Despite its early fall Fonthill Abbey had a profound influence upon English 19th-century architecture. Engravings of it were widely circulated, and it transformed gothic from being a picturesque fancy into a practical style of architecture. Its plan gave Barry the idea for his Houses of Parliament, and Sir Nikolaus Pevsner believed it to be 'the first neo-Gothic building to create sentiments of amazement . . . even of awe'.

Beckford moves to Bath

Beckford might have been expected to have been despondent after expending a fortune on his dream abbey and having then been forced for financial reasons to sell it at sixty-two, but this was not the case. He merely moved to Lansdown Crescent in Bath in 1822, bought two separate houses towards its western end, and added a linking bridge between them.

Although Bath stands a little outside Wiltshire it is appropriate to describe briefly Beckford's old age spent there. By 1825 he had acquired land extending up Lansdown Hill where at its summit almost a mile from his home he built Lansdown Tower. The intervening land was also purchased and landscaped by Beckford, who visited his tower daily to enjoy the views from his elevated study across Bath to his old home at Fonthill.

Beckford was on familiar terms – possible in those days – between master and servants. Beckford's French dwarf Pedro had accompanied him to Bath, and is said to have stood as a footman in the low niche in the entrance hall of his Lansdown Crescent house. At the tower his gardener Vincent was a man almost as old as Beckford himself, who at Bath retained an extraordinary vitality. He led an austere life, going to bed at ten and rising early at six, and when out walking he wore a long brown greatcoat and top boots. He walked extremely fast, and would suddenly stop when anything took his interest. He continued to ride his mare Deborah and in his extreme old age Beckford could be seen riding through the city of Bath, accompanied by Pedro on a grey pony, preceded by two grooms and followed by another.

Beckford's writings

Being born into immense wealth Beckford never needed to work, and during his reclusive life amused himself by writing. The book for which he is remembered is the fantastic oriental romance *Vathek*, an Arabian Tale originally written in French, but translated into English in 1786 by Samuel Henley, assisted by Beckford, who claimed to have written it in a single sitting of three days and two nights. This seems improbable and is generally disbelieved. Beckford's French is said to have been so inadequate that *Vathek* had to be translated into English and then back again into French to render the French version acceptable.

In his youth Beckford wrote the satirical *Memoirs of Extraordinary Painters*. He also wrote two travel books, *Dreams, Waking Thoughts and Incidents* (1783, and revised in 1834 as *Italy, with Sketches of Spain and Portugal*) and *Recollections of an Excursion to the Monasteries of Alcobaça and Batalha* (1835). Beckford's *Travel Diaries* were edited by G. Chapman in 1928.

Lansdown Tower

At Bath Beckford indulged his passion for towers by building between 1825–1826 the soaring Lansdown Tower on Lansdown Hill, employing the young Henry Goodridge (*c*.1800–63) as his architect. Lansdown Tower is in the classical style, which suggests that Beckford may have become disillusioned with gothic after the failure of his tower at Fonthill. Lansdown Tower was built to obtain the fine view which included Beckford's former home at Fonthill twenty-six miles away. It was topped by a timber octagonal lantern in classical Grecian style, from which the much-travelled Beckford claimed to enjoy 'the finest view in Europe'. In the rooms in the lower stages of the tower he kept his finest possessions, and daily he would climb the spiral staircase to contemplate the view and remember past days at Fonthill.

Surviving Remains at Fonthill

All that survives of Alderman Beckford's Fonthill Splendens is one wing near East Lawn Farm converted into two cottages. Of Fonthill Abbey there remains only its north end, the polygonal end of the Oratory, the walls of the Sanctuary, a corridor to its south, and a tower (the Lancaster Tower) at the end of Edward III's Gallery. These fragments are insignificant compared to the immense scale of Fonthill Abbey as built, and they remain inaccessible in the woods with no public footpath near, just as Beckford intended his Abbey to be almost two hundred years ago. The sites of neither Fonthill Splendens nor Fonthill Abbey are accessible by public footpath.

Gatehouse at Fonthill Bishop

Although Fonthill Splendens was destroyed by Beckford, its magnificent gatehouse still stands at Fonthill Bishop. It consists of a huge arch of ashlar stone with tufa stone dressings, surmounted by pediments and flanked by immense sweeping screen walls with huge urns, the whole ensemble being on a quite gigantic scale for a gatehouse. John Rutter, in his 1823 history of Fonthill, recorded the tradition that this gatehouse was designed by Inigo Jones, which would have made it pre-Beckford. This attribution appears to have first arisen in the sale particulars and may have been wishful thinking, although Sir Nikolaus Pevsner in his *Wiltshire* volume of *The Buildings of England* tentatively accepts this attribution to Inigo Jones. In style it appears to me to be 18th-century, and more likely to have been by James Paine when he designed Fonthill Splendens for Alderman Beckford. When designing subsidiary buildings Paine often used the monumental heavily rusticated Palladian style employed for the Fonthill Gatehouse, at for example the stables at Chatsworth designed in about 1760 shortly before Fonthill Splendens was built. At nearby New Wardour Castle Paine also employed a similar monumental style.

Through the Fonthill gatehouse passes the public road down the west side of Fonthill Lake. This is the road which Alderman Beckford tried to have closed to secure his privacy. A footpath follows part of the west side of the lake, and another crosses its south end, but the east flank of the lake is strictly private and its grotto boathouse is not accessible, although its large decorative flanking urns are visible from the footpath on the west side of the lake.

Beckford in old age

After in his later years reviewing his rather misspent life Beckford set about inventing a more glamorous one. He had been a talented musician and now claimed to have written parts of Mozart's *Marriage of Figaro*, and even fabricated a correspondence in which Mozart thanked him for the piece. Beckford certainly knew and was instructed in the piano by Mozart, whose opera *Don Giovanni* was probably based upon the escapades of the Italian adventurer Giacomo Casanova (1725–1798). Beckford knew Casanova's friend the Countess Rosenberg and it is interesting to speculate whether Beckford on his Continental travels met Casanova himself, who shared his interest in Islam and at one time visited England.

Beckford forged other letters to glamourise his earlier life and greatly exaggerated the influence of his *Vathek* on Byron's writings. Byron had admired the book and wrote of it: 'For beauty of description and power of imagination, this most eastern and sublime tale far surpasses all European imitation', but its influence on him was greatly exaggerated by Beckford.

Beckford's death and his burial at Lansdown

Beckford often contemplated death and twenty-nine years before he died wrote in 1815 to his major-domo Franchi:

The thought that the day is not far distant when all

that I have done or am doing will dissolve into thin air, fills me with the bitterest melancholy.

As he grew older Beckford sometimes suggested that death must have overlooked him, but in April 1844 he caught a chill, for a time struggled manfully against death, but died on 2 May 1844. A painting by Willis Maddox, the Bath artist who had been commissioned by Beckford to produce paintings illustrating the interiors of Lansdown Tower, shows Beckford lying on his deathbed, a narrow truckle bed, in a sparsely furnished room containing a minimum of furniture.

Beckford died a very old, lonely and embittered man, refusing to see either a priest or an Anglican clergyman. At this time when churchyards were becoming filled with graves the Victorians invented cemeteries for the burial of the dead. Beckford is buried beside Lansdown Tower in what had been his garden but is now a public graveyard, in an imposing pink granite tomb surrounded by a narrow dry-stone faced waterless ditch. It has been said that Beckford's stone sarcophagus was placed above ground because he did not relish the thought of coffin worms eating his body. In fact his body was moved to its present resting place at Lansdown after a period of interment elsewhere until the Lansdown cemetery was consecrated.

Beckford would not have relished occupying part of a public cemetery. He would probably have preferred to remain solitary in death as he had so often been in life. But with his tender feeling for animals and his love of natural history he would have been consoled by the fact that his garden, which became his burial place, has become a slightly derelict and delightfully overgrown nature reserve.

The Times was quite generous when, despite the scandals and ostracism which surrounded Beckford's long life, it noticed his death with the comment that he was: 'one of the few possessors of great wealth who have honestly tried to spend it poetically'.

12 The 'Three Wiltshire Bards'
George Crabbe at Trowbridge, Tom Moore at Sloperton, and Canon Bowles at Bremhill

In the early-19th century three poets who had become resident in Wiltshire became known as the 'three Wiltshire bards', although none of them had been born in the county. Two of them met soon after 1813 when George Crabbe, a man from the East Anglian coast, was as a recently widowed man of fifty-nine appointed to the living of Trowbridge. At the time of Crabbe's rather reluctant move to Trowbridge another poet, Canon Bowles, was already established in Wiltshire at Bremhill near Calne, to which he had been appointed rector in 1804. They were joined by the Irish lyricist Tom Moore when in 1817 he made his home at Sloperton Cottage near Bromham. Although George Crabbe and Will-

iam Bowles were Anglican clergymen and Tom Moore was the celebrated Irish catholic lyricist, all three men became firm friends. Of the three Crabbe, whose poetry had in his younger days received the approbation of Dr Johnson, was the finest poet, although Moore and Bowles are subjects of interest in their own right.

George Crabbe
Although he was nationally famous in his lifetime George Crabbe (1754–1832) is now, like his greater immediate predecessors Alexander Pope and Dr Johnson, little read. He is probably best known today for having written the story upon which Benjamin Britten based his opera *Peter Grimes*. He qualifies for inclusion in this book because, after being late in life appointed rector of Trowbridge in west Wiltshire, he remained at Trowbridge for his last nineteen years, leading something of a double life as a country parson at Trowbridge, and as a celebrity poet circulating in high society in London.

The poet and critic Edward Thomas emphasised Crabbe's essential relationship to his bleak native coastline at Aldeburgh, and referred to his 'amphibious fellow townsmen'. Crabbe loved his native east coast so profoundly that when living in Leicestershire he once leapt on a horse and rode sixty miles just to see the sea, and in his long poem *The Borough*, which included the story of Peter Grimes, Crabbe wrote a great deal about the sea and smuggling. The involvement of his family with the sea was revealed in 1830 when George Crabbe was seventy-six. On 17 April of that year his brother Robert, then living at Southwold a few miles south of Aldeburgh, wrote to the Admiralty pointing out that about eighty gallons of brandy that the lord of the

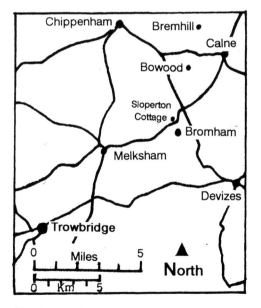

Plan showing the positions of Trowbridge, Sloperton Cottage, Bremhill and Bowood

manor was claiming as wrecked goods was in fact smuggled liquor and should be confiscated by the authorities.

The living of Trowbridge
In spite of his profound love of his native Suffolk coast Crabbe settled down quite happily at Trowbridge, which is far from the coast. The Seymour family held the manor of Trowbridge from 1536, when Henry VIII granted it to Sir Edward Seymour who became Protector Somerset, until 1750 when Algernon Seymour, 7th Duke of Somerset and 5th Baron Seymour of Trowbridge, died without male issue and his sister Francis took Trowbridge by marriage to John, 1st Duke of Rutland. When they sold the manor the Dukes of Rutland retained the right of alternately appointing its rector and it was the Duke as George Crabbe's patron who in 1813 offered him the living of Trowbridge.

In spite of his humble birth Crabbe had become used to moving in high society, and the prospect of moving to the apparently intellectual backwater of west Wiltshire caused him some concern, although when he finally took the plunge he found that the disadvantages of the move were compensated by the warm welcome offered by the gentry of the Trowbridge district. Greatly to his surprise he settled happily into his new living and soon succeeded in integrating himself into the society of the small west Wiltshire town. Not long after moving to Trowbridge he was pleased to enter the brilliant literary and artistic group that was centred at Bowood House near Calne, to which he was introduced by his fellow poets Thomas Moore and Canon Bowles. He also revived his London connections and there he basked in his reputation as a nationally recognised poet who had known and been praised by the great Dr Johnson.

Bowood and its political and literary associations
During the 18th century Bowood had become a centre of political and cultural activity, and this continued into the 19th century after Henry, Lord Lansdowne (Henry Petty Fitzmaurice, 1780–1863), in 1809 succeeded to the title as the 3rd

George Crabbe: a pencil drawing made while he was at Trowbridge

Marquis of Lansdowne. He had been Chancellor of the Exchequer in 1806-7, became Secretary of State for Home Affairs in 1828, and continued to hold high government office until his death in 1863, twice declining the premiership and once a dukedom. At Bowood Lord Lansdowne welcomed the company of literary men and his house became the great social and literary centre of Wiltshire. In his autobiography, which was privately printed in 1854 as a very limited edition of twenty-five copies for presentation (a copy exists in the library of Devizes Museum), John Britton included a section on 'Bowood and its Literary Associations at the end of the Eighteenth and to the middle of the Nineteenth Century, with anecdotes of the Rev. W. L. Bowles, the Rev. G. Crabbe, and Thomas Moore'.

Many individuals who were internationally celebrated in science, art, and literature visited Bowood which was in Crabbe's time a larger house than it is today. In the 1760s it was en-

Thomas Moore at the age of 40

larged to the designs of the famous Robert Adam, but in 1955–6 most of the Adam house was demolished and the house now consists largely of Adam's south range and the old stable blocks converted into flats.

An unanticipated benefit of Crabbe's move to Trowbridge was meeting Thomas Moore and Canon Bowles and it is therefore appropriate to include here short descriptions of the lives and achievements of Crabbe's two fellow 'Wiltshire bards'.

Thomas Moore at Sloperton

At the age of thirty-eight Tom Moore (1779–1852), then already regarded as the national lyricist of Ireland as a result of his *Irish Melodies*, came at the invitation of Lord Lansdowne to live in Wiltshire, at Sloperton Cottage near Bromham. The move prompted Moore's friend Lord Byron (1788–1824), himself a lord and in no need of a patron, to write unkindly of Moore's friendship with Lord Lansdowne : 'Tommy, . . . dearly loves a lord'. Byron, who had achieved literary success early in life and was said to have 'woke to find himself famous', also wrote a poem 'To Thomas Moore' which begins:

My boat is on the shore,
  And my bark is on the sea ;
But before I go, Tom Moore,
  Heres a double health to thee!

We do not know whether between 1817 when Moore moved in and Byron's death in 1824 he ever visited Tom Moore at Sloperton Cottage. This seems unlikely as Byron was almost continually abroad from 1816 until his death, ostracised because of scandal, and he would have been *persona non grata* at Bowood. For the rest of his life Moore rented Sloperton Cottage, which stands on the north side of the A3102 at Westbrook, about midway between Melksham and Calne, and a convenient few miles from Bowood House, the rent being forty pounds a year furnished. Since the famed *Irish Melodies* were written between 1807 and 1835 and Moore came to Sloperton Cottage in 1817 many of these essentially Irish songs must have been written in Wiltshire.

Sloperton Cottage, Bromham

Thomas Moore was born in Dublin in 1779, the son of a wine merchant and grocer described by his son as 'one of nature's gentlemen'. Moore was described by Sir Walter Scott as 'a little – very little – man, yet not without insignificance; his countenance plain, but the expression very animated, especially in speaking or singing'. In 1793 he went to Dublin University after an Act of Parliament opened it to Roman catholics and at nineteen he moved to London to become a student of law at the Middle Temple. Early in his career Moore in 1801 published some dubious verse under the title *The Poetical Works of the late Thomas Little*, his alias being presumably inspired by his small stature as described by Scott. These verses became extremely popular and remained in print for forty years. In 1803 he was appointed admiralty registrar in Bermuda, but having gone to Bermuda to take up his appointment he decided not to stay and appointed a deputy called John Goodridge to act for him.

When he was thirty Tom Moore met his wife Bessy Dyke (1793–1865) in Kilkenny when she was a sixteen-year-old actress playing Lady Godiva to Moore's Peeping Tom. They married in March 1811 and decided to live in the country, partly because as an actress Bessy was not acceptable to the exalted society circles in which her husband now moved. They tried several districts before settling in Wiltshire.

Moore's first great success was *Lalla Rookh* (1817), the name being that of the daughter of an emperor meaning 'Tulip Cheek'. For this book, which consists of a series of oriental tales in verse linked by a story in prose, Longmans offered three thousand guineas unseen, despite the fact that their author had absolutely no experience of the east. Their confidence was justified because by 1840 *Lalla Rookh* had gone into twenty editions. In spite of its success Hazlitt gave his opinion in *On the Living Poets* that: 'Mr Moore should never have written *Lalla Rookh*, even for three thousand guineas. His fame is worth more than that.' The book nevertheless gained its writer a European reputation and from the proceeds he was able to retire to his rural retreat at Sloperton.

At Sloperton Cottage Tom Moore worked in an upstairs study, and he referred to 'reposing on, or among, my laurels', a reference to the fact that his garden contained a raised walk bordered by laurels among which he would walk and think. At Sloperton the Moores were at first happy, although there domestic tragedy was to overcome the family. Tom and Bessy had five children, three daughters born before they came to Wiltshire and two sons born at Sloperton Cottage. Olivia Byron Moore had died at the age of one in 1815 and Barbara died aged five in 1817, and after they came to Wiltshire their other daughter Anastasia died in 1829 when sixteen of tubercolosis. The two sons attended Marlborough Grammar School but the boys were also destined to pre-

decease their parents. The second son John Russell Moore died aged nineteen in 1842 at Sloperton from a disease contracted in the tropics. The elder, Thomas Lansdowne Moore, was gazetted in the army in 1837. He caused his parents much distress by his wild behaviour, and having decided that he was unable to live on his army pay he sold his commission, joined the French Foreign Legion as its first British officer, and died in Africa in 1846, aged twenty-eight.

Although a Roman catholic Moore allowed his children to be brought up in the church of England, presumably at the wish of Bessy, who was a firm protestant and first attended a catholic service (incidentally in the chapel at New Wardour Castle) sixteen years after her marriage. In *The Fudges in England* (1835) Moore gently satirised an Irish priest who had turned protestant evangelist in England.

The year that the Moores moved to Wiltshire, 1817, was a momentous one for Tom Moore. In that year he published *Lalla Rookh* and this was followed by the defection of his deputy in Bermuda leaving him with a debt amounting to six thousand pounds. Moore fled to Italy but Lord Lansdowne generously helped him pay off the debt, which Moore ultimately repaid from profits from his writing. In order to raise money he turned in 1825 from poetry to prose and wrote a biography of the playwright Sheridan. His *Life of Byron* followed in 1830 and five years later he was granted a literary pension, which was in 1850 augmented by a civil list pension.

Tom Moore as lyricist

Shortly before his early death at Missolonghi from marsh fever Byron wrote to Moore asking him to 'remember me in your smiles and wine', this being a quotation from Moore's *Irish Melodies*. Many who are familiar with these haunting melodies are unaware that their composer was Moore, who believed that he had: 'an instinctive turn for rhyme and song'. He issued these one hundred and ten songs in batches of ten at irregular intervals for a payment of a hundred guineas per song or five hundred pounds a year. Some of Moore's songs remain popular to this day. Many people will know from their childhood *The Minstrel-Boy*,

Believe me, if all those endearing young charms, and *'Tis the last rose of summer.* And Moore's *Oft in the stilly night* (which is not in fact one of the *Irish Melodies*), is regularly played at the annual service of remembrance at the Cenotaph in London, as is *The Minstrel Boy.* Moore's *The Last Rose of Summer* became so popular that the German composer Friedrich von Flotow in 1847 'borrowed' it for *Martha*, probably assuming it to be a folk song, and Caruso died on stage of a haemorrhage when singing it.

Critics have with justification suggested that the *Irish Melodies* are of little value as verse when divorced from their music, but it must be recognised that they were never intended to be pure verse, being written as their title implies as lyrics to be set to music. Moore hated his lyrics being published dissociated from their music, although Longmans published the texts without their musical notation in 1846, and some have been included in anthologies of poetry.

His contemporary William Hazlitt (1779–1830) rather missed the point when he wrote dismissively of of Moore as a poet:

> His is the poetry of the bath, of the toilette, of the saloon, of the fashionable world . . . Mr Moore has mistaken the art of poetry for the cosmetic art . . . He can write verses, not a poem . . . All is flowery, all is florid to excess.

In spite of their shortcomings as poetry the *Irish Melodies* became extremely popular. One evening Moore and Lord Byron were discussing fame at Twickenham on the banks of the Thames when the strains of one of Moore's melodies was heard from a passing boat, whereupon Byron turned to Moore and exclaimed: 'There. That's fame!'.

As a musician Moore was self-taught, and although he had sufficient ear for music to enable him to accompany his fine light tenor voice at the piano when singing his *Irish Melodies*, he was assisted in setting them by two established composers, first by Sir John Stevenson (*c.*1760-1833), a Scot born in Dublin in about 1760, and later by the more famous Sir Henry Bishop (1786–1855), the first musician to receive a knighthood. On one occasion Moore remonstrated with his publishers that the payments made to Sir Henry Bishop for his arrangements were excessive.

The later life of Tom Moore at Sloperton

One of Tom Moore's endearing characteristics was his unobtrusive generosity. He would secretly arrange for his friends to send his own money to his wife for distribution among the poor of Bromham, explaining: 'It makes her happy, without the drawback of knowing that it comes from my small means'. Bessy consequently became very popular among the people of Bromham, although the local people seem to have ignored Tom Moore. They are said to have associated him with the Old Moore of the almanac and one villager is recorded as saying: 'Mrs Moore she wur a angel, but as for Mr Moore, thur he wur no good, vor he was allus in a brown study'.

The Wiltshire writer Edith Olivier recalled a family story of an incident that occurred when Tom Moore was visiting the Olivier family home at Potterne to hear her grandmother sing his *Irish Melodies*. After storming out of Wans House at Sandy Lane near Bowood at some imagined slight Tom Moore became lost on his way home to Sloperton Cottage and was found the next morning sitting patiently on a gate waiting for someone to come along and tell him where he was. On another occasion he was so appalled by the performance of one of his songs by a gentleman at a party that he approached the singer and enquired of him the name of the song and its composer, as he did not recognize it!

Three years after the death of his his last surviving child in 1846 Moore suffered a stroke which affected his memory. He lived out his last three years at Sloperton in a state of illness with short bouts of improved health, during which Bessy took him on walks from their cottage. In 1852 he died at Sloperton Cottage. He was seventy-three. Bessy continued to live at their cottage for her remaining thirteen years. In his will Thomas Moore instructed his executors to publish his *Journal* which ran from 1818 to 1841, the first part of his residence in Wiltshire, to 'afford the means of making some provisions for my wife and family'.

The spire of Bromham church is visible down the hill from Sloperton Cottage, and a public field path which must often have been followed by the Moores runs for half a mile south-east from near their cottage to Bromham. Edward Edgell, Moore's friend and the rector of Bromham from 1843 to 1904, agreed to bury him in the church-yard in a vault on the north side of the church, beside his two children Anastasia and John Russell Moore, where he was later joined by his wife.

After visiting Bromham church John Betjeman wrote a poem entitled *Ireland's Own*, commenting on the strange circumstance of Tom Moore, the ultimate Irish Celt, being buried far from his homeland in a remote Wiltshire church-yard. It includes the lines:

> I can but account you neglected and poor,
> Dear bard of my boyhood mellifluous Moore
> That far from the land that of all you loved best
> In a village of England your bones should have rest.

On 11 November 1906 a large Celtic cross which cost £232 was dedicated above the Moore vault in the presence of a number of dignitaries including many Irishmen. It bears verses by Moore and by his friend Byron incised on its base. In 1870 the east window in the chancel of the church was installed to the design of Burne-Jones to commemorate Bessy Moore, and nine years later the west window, financed by subscriptions from two hundred persons, was installed in memory of Thomas Moore, the Irish poet who chose to live out the last thirty-five years of his life in the Wiltshire countryside.

Canon Bowles

Canon Bowles of Bremhill

Crabbe's other particular Wiltshire friend was Canon William Lisle Bowles (1762–1850) who was rector of Bremhill near Calne from 1804 to his death in 1850. Bowles was in his time a con-siderable figure in the field of poetry. His standing as a poet now tends to be judged by the doggerel epitaphs which he provided for the tombs of his parishioners in Bremhill churchyard, and it has been said that it was 'ridiculous egotism' that led him to 'carve his bad verses even over his dead parishioners'. What is now usually forgotten is the fact that the poet and critic Coleridge, who had several associations with Wiltshire, was at the age of seventeen so impressed by Bowles's fourteen sonnets *Written chiefly on Picturesque Spots dur-ing a Journey* (1789) that, as he could not afford to buy them, he made forty copies of the entire volume by hand for his friends. These sonnets, which also impressed Wordsworth and Southey and were based on a tour made by Bowles the

Thomas Moore's cross in Bromham churchyard

previous year through Wales, Scotland, France and Germany, are a forerunner of the Romantic movement in English poetry. It was the influence of Canon Bowles that attracted Coleridge from theology to poetry, as Coleridge acknowledged in his *Biographia Literaria*, where he describes Bowles as: 'a poet, by whose works, year after year, I was so enthusiastically delighted and inspired'.

Although born at King's Sutton in Northants, Canon Bowles lived in Wiltshire for most of his adult life. He was the son of the Rev. William Thomas Bowles of Barton Hill House at Shaftesbury and his wife Bridget, the daughter of Dr. Richard Grey the archdeacon of Bedford. His brother, Charles Bowles, was a local historian who wrote *The Hundred of Chalke* (1830), which was incorporated in Colt Hoare's *Modern Wiltshire*, and in 1799 he became the steward of

Bremhill church

Tollard manor, and later recorder for Shaftesbury. William Bowles believed that he derived his interest in landscape gardening from his father and his musical interests from his mother. He was educated at Winchester and Trinity College, Oxford, and knew many writers including Coleridge and Richard Brinsley Sheridan. He quarrelled with Byron, and he also knew the composers William Linley and Sir Henry Bishop.

In 1788 Bowles was ordained deacon at West Knoyle in south Wiltshire and for nine years (1788–97) he resided at the cottage called Burltons, to the north-east of the road through Donhead St Mary. He also became rector of Chicklade and curate to Dr. Charles Wake the rector of East Knoyle. He courted the Reverend Wake's daughter Harriet and after she suddenly died in 1793 Bowles four years later married her sister Magdalen Wake, who remained his companion until she predeceased her husband in 1844. By this marriage Canon Bowles became distantly connected to the Beckfords of Fonthill, as, before he married at the age of forty-seven, William Beckford's father Alderman Beckford had several illegitimate children; the eldest of them, Barbara, married Parson Wake of East Knoyle.

Canon Bowles's garden at Bremhill

In 1803 Canon Bowles became a prebendary of Salisbury, and in 1805 rector of Bremhill where he remained for forty-five years. At Bremhill he tried to improve and unify the appearance of his architecturally rather undistinguished vicarage by running a 'picturesque' zig-zag pierced stone parapet around the roof. He had probably obtained the idea from Stourton, where Colt Hoare had added this treatment to the church and cottages which had been used as a landscape element at the entrance to the Stourhead grounds. From about 1800 Bowles was, significantly in view of his landscaping activities at Bremhill, acquainted with Colt Hoare, who also knew his brother Charles Bowles.

Bremhill vicarage has a fine view over the grounds of Bowood and the surrounding Wiltshire downland. In his *The Parochial History of Bremhill* (1828) Bowles enthusiastically described his 2½-acre grounds, which he developed in the tradition of the 18th-century landscaped garden and embellished with many fragments, many of them looted from the site of the nearby demolished Stanley Abbey :

The garden is on a slope, commanding views of the surrounding country, with the tower of Calne in front, the woods of Bowood on the right, and the mansion,

Bremhill vicarage from Britton's Beauties of Wiltshire

woods of Walter Heneage, esq., towards the south. The view to the south-east is terminated by the last chalky cliffs of the Marlborough Downs, extending to within a few miles of Swindon.

Bowles's garden contained a grotto, a small lake, an arched hazel walk, 'a kind of cave', and an inscribed urn, and was so littered with architectural features that his friend Moore wrote: 'He has frittered away its beauty with grottoes, hermitages and Shenstonian inscriptions . . . but he is an excellent fellow notwithstanding'. By con-

Canon Bowles's Bremhill vicarage

trast, in a letter written after a visit to Bremhill vicarage in 1815, Coleridge told Wordsworth that Bowles had 'a paradise of a place' at Bremhill.

It is typical of Canon Bowles that after he set up an obelisk in his garden at Bremhill to commemorate the end of the Napoleonic wars and inscribed it '1814', Napoleon escaped from Elba and resumed the war, which actually ended at Waterloo in 1815, immediately rendering Bowles's inscription innaccurate.

According to Geoffrey Grigson who knew it when he was young Bowles's garden at Bremhill also included a grotto converted into an outdoor lavatory, with: 'the stream running coldly under the seat'. When he visited Bremhill again at the end of the Second World War Grigson described it in *Places of the Mind* (1949) and reported finding: 'decay in possession'.

Maud Heath and her causeway

An episode of Wiltshire local history that attracted the attention of Canon Bowles was the story of Maud Heath and her causeway. More than four hundred years before Bowles came to Bremhill a 15th-century market woman called Maud Heath, who was born and lived at Langley Burrell and had frequently carried her produce through floods to Chippenham market, left funds for the construction and maintenance of a causeway to run for about 4½ miles from Wick Hill near Bremhill to Chippenham. Her causeway survives and is best seen near the point where it crosses the River Avon at Kellaways, carried on about sixty flat brick arches beside a length of road that remains subject to flooding. At Kellaways a pillar and sundial commemorating Maud Heath was set up in 1698 with a long inscription which ends with the exhortation: 'Injure me not'. Canon Bowles decided that this was insufficient recognition and in collaboration with Lord Lansdowne arranged for the construction on the Wick Hill escarpment of an imposing monument consisting of a tall stone column surmounted by a statue of Maud Heath, holding her basket and looking north over the plain. The monument is inscribed with verses provided by Bowles:

Thou who dost pause in this aerial height
Where Maud Heaths pathway winds in shade or
    light,
Christian wayfarer, in a world of strife,
Be still, and ponder on the Path of Life.

Beside a gateway at the side of the road on Wick Hill was also set up a commemorative stone inscribed with more lines by Bowles in the style of his epitaphs for his parishioners:

From this Wick Hill begins the praise
Of Maud Heaths gifts to these highways.

Maud Heath's monument on Wick Hill

Bowles in later life

Canon Bowles was of a particularly nervous and eccentric disposition. Robert Southey said that he was 'afraid of everything', and his nervousness and eccentricity often amused his friend Tom Moore. Canon Jackson's Wiltshire manuscript collection contains an account of the following amusing incident. In his old age Bowles became very deaf and obtained an ear trumpet, which so pleased him that he insisted on describing it to Moore. He explained how:

. . . I then went through the Barton, and what do you think – the very first thing I heard was – Cock-a-doodle-doo. I then went out past the cowhouse, and there I heard – the oxen low –! There, what do you think of that?

Moore, splitting with laughter, replied in a moment: 'Why, I'll tell you what, Bowles: if you had told this to anybody else, they would have said that it was a very cock and bull story'.

Bowles also wore stout outer clothing in case he was attacked by mad dogs, and once when dressing for dinner became annoyed because he could not find one stocking, and then found both on one leg!

Canon Bowles was so absent-minded that on one occasion he inscribed a bible that he was presenting to a child at a prize-giving 'With the author's compliments'. He became a canon of Salisbury and lived at 21 The Close in the North Walk to the north of the cathedral. This house, which was known in the middle ages as 'Aula-le-Stage', is a well-preserved Medieval canon's house which was refronted with a two-gabled Elizabethan facade with hood-moulded windows. Canon Bowles added the diminutive gothick porch, as well as new parapets in the style of the parapet that he had added to Bremhill vicarage. At Salisbury he became nervous about the stability of the cathedral spire and carefully measured the distance from his house to the cathedral to ascertain whether in the event of the spire falling he would be in danger. The spire is in fact 404 feet high and the distance from the centre of the cathedral crossing to the front of No. 21 The Close is about 450 feet, so that the margin of safety was about 15 yards.

Soon after taking up the living at Bremhill Bowles published his *Life of Pope* (1808). This was so inaccurate and controversial that it sparked a prolonged controversy between Thomas Campbell and Lord Byron which lasted for years from 1809 to 1824. His principal prose work was his two-volume *Life of Bishop Ken*, who had spent his last years at Longleat.

Canon Bowles's home in Salisbury Close (No. 21)

As a canon of Salisbury Bowles was buried in Salisbury Cathedral where he is commemorated by a memorial stone in the south choir aisle.

Crabbe's early life

Having described the two poets who introduced George Crabbe into the literary gatherings at Bowood, I shall now revert to George Crabbe, the principal subject of this chapter. He was born and spent the greater part of his early life at Aldeburgh in Suffolk on the bleak East Anglian coast, in a landscape that was utterly different from that of land-locked west Wiltshire in which he spent his last years. Although Edward Thomas made the point in *A Literary Pilgrim in England* (1917) that Crabbe 'did just as well to escape from the influence of Aldeburgh', he also suggested that: 'If a man spends his first twenty years in and about his birthplace, that is his country'. The Suffolk coast around Aldeburgh was indeed Crabbe's country and, although Thomas practically ignores the nineteen years of his life that Crabbe spent happily at Trowbridge, he half-relented when he suggested that in Wiltshire Crabbe: 'painted fields and houses among trees gently enough, but they were not Aldeburgh'. Thomas also conceded that: 'the more he [Crabbe] lived inland and in comfortable circumstances the more he saw calm beauty in the country'.

George Crabbe was the oldest of the six children of his father, another George Crabbe, and his wife who was a widow named Lobbock when he married her. In his *Life of George Crabbe* (1834) Crabbe's son wrote: 'The Crabbes of Norfolk have been, for many generations, in the stations of Farmers, or wealthy yeomen'. Crabbe's grandfather was a burgess of Aldeburgh who became collector of customs but seems to have made little money, because his son, the poet's father, was the schoolmaster and parish clerk. Although the younger George Crabbe had a very rudimentary education he overcame this deficiency by his extreme dedication to books. He was apprenticed to an apothecary near Newmarket, and from the age of sixteen to twenty-one assisted a surgeon at Woodbridge. Eventually after an eleven year engagement he married a local girl called Sarah Elmy, the Mira of his poems. In 1780 he borrowed a five-pound note and went to London, where he wrote poetry in the style of Alexander Pope but with a particular difference which was pointed out by Hazlitt, when he observed: 'Pope describes what is striking: Crabbe would have described merely what was there'. Hazlitt also expressed a poor opinion of Crabbe's work in his essay 'Mr Campbell and Mr Crabbe' (1825) in which he described Crabbe as 'a repulsive writer' and suggested that: 'Literary fidelity serves him in the place of invention'.

After failing to achieve any literary success Crabbe in desperation sent *The Candidate* (1780) to Edmund Burke, who immediately recognised its worth and persuaded Dodsley to publish it. Crabbe then stayed for a time with Burke at Beaconsfield, published *The Library* in 1781, and at Burke's suggestion took holy orders and went to Belvoir in Leicestershire as chaplain to the Duke of Rutland, a post which he held from 1782 to 1785 and ultimately led to his move to Wiltshire. In about 1783 Lord Chancellor Thurlow presented Crabbe with the two small livings of Evershot and Frome St Quintin in Dorset. He visited these in 1785 and much enjoyed the excursion, and this first experience of the west country may have influenced his decision to accept the living of Trowbridge when it was offered many years later, although he had surrendered his Dorset livings for better ones at Belvoir in 1789.

In 1783 Crabbe published *The Village*, a long poem in heroic couplets which had been subjected to revision by Burke. Its sombre realism was intended to counter the idealism of Goldsmith's *Deserted Village* with lines such as :

> Here joyless roam a wild amphibious race
> With sullen woe displayed on every face.

When this work was drawn to his notice shortly before he died in 1793 Dr Johnson wrote in a letter to Crabbe's friend Sir Joshua Reynolds: 'I read it with delight. It is original, vigorous and elegant . . . I do not doubt of Mr Crabbe's success.' Praise from such an eminent source secured both the success of *The Village* and Crabbe's reputation as a poet, although after *The Newspaper* in 1786 he published nothing more of any significance until 1807. During these twenty years he continued to write but destroyed all his work, until *The Parish Register* appeared in 1807 and re-established his reputation as an important narrative poet. In the same volume was included *Sir Eustace Grey*, Crabbe's powerful account of an asylum patient's fall from happiness and prosperity.

In about 1790 Crabbe suffered from vertigo and consulted a Dr Clubbe, who advised him: 'let the digestive organs bear the whole blame: you must take opiates'. From this time Crabbe took opium for medical reasons although several references to opium dreams in his verse suggest that he may also have used opium as a stimulant. Opium-taking was prevalent among many of Crabbe's contemporaries, although Crabbe's son in his biography of his father only admits to his father using opium for medical purposes.

The Parish Register (1807) was followed by *The Borough*, a poem based upon the coastal life at Aldeburgh which appeared in 1810, and in 1816 attained its sixth edition, despite Hazlitt's criticism of its 'sterile blighting lines'. Long after Crabbe's death *The Borough* provided the inspiration for one of the greatest operas of the 20th century. In 1941 Benjamin Britten, then living in America, was sent by E. M. Forster a copy of *The Listener*, which included an article on Crabbe and particularly referred to *The Borough*. Britten was like Crabbe a Suffolk man, born at Lowestoft in 1913, and he shared Crabbe's intense feelings for their native coast. He obtained a copy of *The Borough* and saw the potential of the fisherman Peter Grimes from ('The Poor of the Borough:

Letter XXII') as the basis for an opera. He commissioned Montagu Slater to write the libretto for the opera, which as *Peter Grimes* achieved huge success, although the Peter Grimes of the opera was a rather different character from that of *The Borough*, who was believed to have been founded on truth. Benjamin Britten considerably adapted Crabbe's plot, and one critic alleged that Crabbe's story had 'crabbed the opera'. Despite its great popularity in its time Crabbe's poetry is today little read; he is now perhaps best remembered for Britten's opera with its 'Four Sea Interludes' which so successfully evoke the atmosphere of the bleak Suffolk coast.

The Borough was followed by *Tales* in 1812 and *Tales of the Hall* containing stories that were both terrible and sombre. The latter, written 1817–18, is the major work that Crabbe wrote at Trowbridge. In it two elderly brothers reminisce in after-dinner discussions about their pasts.

Crabbe at Trowbridge

His son tells us that Crabbe had been depressed by the recent death of his wife and that, as being at home constantly reminded of her, he was keen to move. After some difficulties were resolved in an interview with the Bishop of Salisbury in London, Crabbe in 1813 moved to Trowbridge, a town which according to Crabbe's son was: 'remarkable for its diversity of sects and warmth of discussion'.

Soon after moving to Trowbridge Crabbe on a visit to Sidmouth in September 1814 became involved with a lady called Charlotte Ridout. His proposal of marriage was accepted but his sons seem to have convinced him that the proposal was ridiculous, and on reflection he withdrew from the commitment. He was visited at Trowbridge by an indignant Mr Ridout but the proposal fell through, although Charlotte remained keen on marrying the celebrated poet and her family considered that this incident contributed to her early death in 1831.

At Trowbridge there was a tradition that Crabbe was something of a ladies' man, and Jane Austen is alleged to have said that if she had any inclination to marry she could imagine herself as Mrs Crabbe. Crabbe's son recorded that his father was 'peculiarly fond of the society and correspondence of females' and that 'all his most intimate friends, I think, were ladies'. Francis Kilvert's father once met Crabbe at Trowbridge rectory and the diarist recorded (on 5 October 1874) his father's description of Crabbe as: 'a small plain insignificant-looking old man, bald with a whitish yellow complexion'.

Trowbridge parish church ('yon tall spire': Crabbe)

By 1817 Crabbe was widely recognised as a very distinguished man of letters. In 1819 he published while living at Trowbridge his last and greatest work *Tales of the Hall* which depicted the social life and the poverty that he often saw in his new parish. Since he was associating with the rich local clothiers of Trowbridge the book, for which John Murray paid him three thousand pounds, dealt principally with: 'people of superior classes, though not the most elevated'. That Crabbe was thoroughly unbusinesslike is illustrated by the story that after his publisher Murray paid him three thousand pounds in bills for the copyright of his poems and advised him to deposit the notes in the bank, Crabbe stuffed the notes into his pockets and set off for Trowbridge saying that he must show his son John his earnings from his writings.

Until his wife's death in 1813 Crabbe had been an enthusiastic botanist, but after his move to Trowbridge he became more interested in geology and spent many hours geologising in the Bath stone quarries in Wiltshire. Another of his

pleasures at Trowbridge was to sit writing under the still-existing mulberry tree in his rectory garden, of which he wrote:

> My garden, with its flow'rs of every hue,
> And yon tall spire that meets th'admiring view,
> My peaceful garden! sweetest of the kind,
> Should also bring thy goodness Lord, to mind,
> At all times cheerful, and at all times gay,
> It smiles in winter, as in genial May.

Nevertheless a Trowbridge friend, the cloth manufacturer Mr Norris Clark, recalled that when he complimented Crabbe on the beauty and seclusion of his rectory garden Crabbe told him that he: 'preferred walking in the streets, and observing the faces of the passers-by, to the finest natural scene'.

Life at Trowbridge

Crabbe was inducted at Trowbridge Church on 3 June 1814 by the Rev. Fletcher. His diary immediately after this event reveals that he very soon overcame his reservations about his move and accepted his new situation. It reads: '5 June – first sermon at Trowbridge', then on the 8th: 'Evening – solitary walk – night – change of opinion – easier, better, happier'. After Crabbe's death his son recalled that: 'after he mingled with the lively society of Trowbridge, he was subject to very distressing fits of melancholy', but that he: 'became contented and cheerful, and I hope I may add positively happy'.

There is no doubt that the newly-widowed Crabbe grew to enjoy the simple social life at Trowbridge, which was then a major woollen manufacturing town. On the night that he arrived at Trowbridge he was warmly entertained by Mr Waldron, a woollen manufacturer who lived at Westcroft House, a fine brick-built and pedimented Georgian town house which is dated 1744 and still (2002) stands in a semi-ruinous condition behind a high retaining wall in Frog Lane. Mention of Mr Waldron reminds me of an incident which reveals that the woollen mills were extremely dangerous places, particularly for child employees. My father's ancestors worked in the Trowbridge mills and during Crabbe's incumbency in September 1821 one of the Watts children, a boy of only eleven, was killed at Waldron's Mill when his clothes became caught in a drive belt, and every bone in his body was crushed when he was drawn between some metal rollers.

After recovering from the depression that he suffered after the death of his wife Crabbe regained some of his youthful vigour, and in the words of his son he 'had never looked so well'. He grew to like Trowbridge itself, although he disliked the fact that the River Biss was liable to flood. At that time quality food was difficult to obtain in Trowbridge and when he was about to entertain Crabbe would provide Miss Waldron with ten pounds to go to Bath and obtain for him the necessary provisions.

At the time when Crabbe became rector of Trowbridge the district was in a state of religious and political turmoil. The town had in common with much of the rest of west Wiltshire become a hotbed of nonconformity, as the weavers refused to conform to the orthodox religion. In the 1790s Trowbridge barracks had been built to house cavalry to police the area, and the Blind House prison, which had been built beside the town bridge in about 1758, was frequently in use. The

Westcroft at Trowbridge, now (2002) semi-derelict

stocks beside it were last used in 1817, four years after Crabbe's arrival. In 1826 there were riots over low wages and when the ringleader was incarcerated in the Blind House at the instigation of Crabbe's magistrate friend Mr Waldron the mob dismantled the roof of the little prison and released him.

The strength of nonconformity in his parish must have posed problems for Crabbe as the church of England rector, as did the fact that he supported a parliamentary candidate to whom the weavers of Trowbridge were hostile. He learned to work very amicably with the nonconformist ministers, but before he gained the respect of his Trowbridge parishioners Crabbe was twice abused at elections by mobs. He faced them down by intimating that nothing would persuade him to withdraw his support for Mr Benett. Crabbe's friend Canon Bowles left an account of the occasion when a mob besieged Crabbe's rectory to prevent him going to the poll, but he calmly emerged and 'told them that they might kill him if they chose, but, whilst alive, nothing should prevent him giving a vote at the election, according to his promise and principles'. This he did, and Mr Benett was duly elected.

Such resolution, his benelovence towards the poor, and his tolerance towards the many dissenters in Trowbridge, ultimately won the hearts of his parishioners, and Crabbe collaborated with the ministers of many denominations in good works, holding that:

> A man's opinion was his own, his due
> And just possession, whether false or true.

On one occasion when he met an old woman who explained her absence from his services being due to the fact that he spoke softly and she could not hear, Crabbe quietly slipped a halfcrown into her hand saying: 'Well my good friend, you do quite right in going where you can hear'.

Within a short time Crabbe was held in very high regard in the town. In 1816 one of his sons became his curate at Trowbridge and no doubt relieved him of much day to day work, for in 1816 Crabbe attained the age of sixty-two. His other son married into the Trowbridge family of Timbrell, which gave its name to Timbrell Street.

In 1816 Crabbe received the first of a series of letters from a Quakeress poet called Mrs Mary Leadbeater, whom he had first met in 1784 at the table of the Edmund Burke. His letters to this lady give insights into his life in Wiltshire, as when he wrote: 'I now dwell in the parsonage of a busy, populous, clothing town, sent thither by ambition and the Duke of Rutland. It is situated in Wiltshire, not far from Bath.'

Having settled at Trowbridge Crabbe began to return to the high society in London in which he had circulated earlier in his life. He knew Lord Holland (1773–1840) who was born at Winterslow near Salisbury, and in 1817 was welcomed to his literary gatherings at Holland House in Kensington. Lord Holland had a very high regard for Crabbe and placed his portrait in his library. A hundred years earlier Holland House had been owned by Joseph Addison (1672–1719), the statesman, poet, and writer of pure English prose who was also a Wiltshireman, born at Milston in the valley of the Salisbury Avon. Addison acquired Holland House in 1716 by his marriage to the widow of the 3rd Earl of Holland and Dowager Countess of Warwick, and died at Holland House three years later.

Crabbe's journal at this time contains succinct comment on some of his fellow poets, for example on 3 July 1817: 'Robert Bloomfield. He had better rested as a shoemaker, or even a farmers boy; for he would have been a farmer perhaps in time, and now he is an unfortunate poet.' Two days later his journal reveals that Crabbe attempted to write at least thirty lines of poetry every day. On 5 July 1817 he wrote: 'My thirty lines done; but not well, I fear: that daily is my self-engagement.'

Although his son admitted that Crabbe 'had no talent for speaking', and Tom Moore had such a poor opinion of his conversation that he wrote: 'I found that he had been, as usual, as dry as any land-crab that ever crawled', his publisher Mr Murray recorded that he said 'uncommon things in so natural and easy a way, that he often lost credit for them'.

Back at Trowbridge his duties must often have interfered with his writing, for he never allowed any parishioner who wished to see him to be turned away from his rectory. He always saw them and often gave them money, and a parishioner called Taylor recorded that Crabbe earned about eight hundred pounds a year, donated much of it to acts of charity, and that he was moderate in the collection of his tithes. If a parishioner in difficulties defaulted he would say: 'Let it be – Let it be'.

During Crabbe's last active season in London in 1822 he met Sir Walter Scott, who extracted from him a promise to visit him in London in the autumn. From 1823 Crabbe led a rather quiet life but still enjoyed annual excursions.

Crabbe's adjustment to living in an inland parish in west Wiltshire must have been difficult, for he deeply loved the east coast on which he had been brought up, and he loved to go back to it. In 1823 he went from Trowbridge on a nostalgic visit to Aldeburgh and found:

Much are we alter'd both, but I behold
In thee a youth renew'd – whilst I am old.
The works of man from dying we may save,
But man himself moves onward to the grave.

Places in Trowbridge associated with Crabbe

Crabbe's rectory at Trowbridge was an ancient multi-gabled building on the site of the modern rectory at the junction of Church Street and Union Street overlooking the parish church. It had massive stone walls, a stone tiled roof, and stone mullioned windows, and was smothered with climbing plants. A photograph of it appears facing page 337 of the 1950 edition of Arthur Mee's *Wiltshire* volume of 'The King's England' series, with coincidentally photographs of Canon Bowles's rectory at Bremhill and Tom Moore's Sloperton Cottage on the same page. After Crabbe's death his rectory and his library and bookcases were for long kept exactly as he left them, but the building became old and expensive to maintain and in the 1960s it was replaced by a modern rectory on the same site, although the mulberry tree under which he wrote *Tales of the Hall* survives.

The parish church of St James at Trowbridge is fundamentally of the Perpendicular style, although it underwent a heavy restoration in 1847–8, soon after Crabbe's death, which has left its interior, in the words of Pevsner 'distressingly new'. Its spire which Crabbe admired is the second highest in Wiltshire after Salisbury Cathedral.

Several places other than his rectory and the parish church in which he was buried are associated with Crabbe. He was frequently at Westcroft House in Frog Lane, the home of his friends the Waldrons who had so warmly welcomed him to Trowbridge. William Everett Waldron (1783–1833) then owned Westcroft and it was for a time thought that his daughter Maria Waldron might marry Crabbe.

Crabbe was also a welcome guest of the Mortimer family at Bellefield House, which was built in 1792 on the Hilperton Road. This house later became the home of the Clarks. In Crabbe's time they were at Polebarn House, which they had built in 1789 and surrounded with a tiny landscaped park. Other friends of Crabbe during his later life at Trowbridge were the Houltons at Farleigh House, just over the county boundary in Somerset. This family had during the 17th and 18th centuries made a fortune from woollen manufacture at Bradford on Avon and Trowbridge. Joseph Houlton had purchased Farleigh House from the Bayntuns of Bromham as his country retreat. They then acquired the manor in 1702 and the castle in 1730, and remained at Farleigh until they sold out to Lord Donington in 1891. They lived at the manor house which they remodelled early in the 19th century, and it was there that Crabbe was often entertained by John Houlton, who had succeeded his father Joseph in 1806. At Farleigh Crabbe met Canon Bowles and possibly also Tom Moore.

Early in the 18th century the Houltons built at the north edge of The Conigre at Trowbridge beside Westcroft House the now semi-derelict Conigre Parsonage, which derives its name from being given by the Houltons to the Trowbridge minister for church use.

Decline and death

During the summer of 1824 Crabbe spent several days with Tom Moore at Longleat where they walked in the grounds and Crabbe told Moore about an unpublished poem that he had in hand entitled, to the best of Moore's recollection, *The Departure and the Return*. By the mid-1820s Crabbe's health was in decline. In June 1825 he wrote: 'My time passes I cannot tell how pleasantly when the pain leaves me', and in 1827 he was complaining about the 'degradation caused by Trowbridge Fair' and rejoicing that 'quiet is now restored'. Trowbridge Fair for cheeses, cattle and pigs, and horses, was held in August. The fair was always well-attended and, because it sometimes became disorderly, Crabbe always kept an eye on the activities in the hope of keeping it respectable. In October 1829 Crabbe wrote in a rather bemused way to his son: 'I am in truth not well. It is not pain, nor can I tell you what it is.'

Near the end of his life Crabbe in 1830 preached a typically uncompromising sermon at the death of the little-lamented George IV, taking as his text, 'The sting of death is sin'. His own death took place at Trowbridge rectory on 3 February 1832. He died saying in response to the incessant enquirers after his health: 'What a trouble I am to them all'. When his death was announced the shutters of all the shops in Trowbridge were half-closed, and on the day of his funeral ninety-two of the leading townsmen, including all the nonconformist ministers, followed his coffin to his burial in Trowbridge church. When on the Sunday following Crabbe's funeral Mr Nightingale, the master of the Trowbridge Sunday School, explained to the children about the death of their rector, a little girl was heard to say: 'Poor Mr Crabbe will never go up in the pulpit any more with his white head'.

Crabbe's bones were not destined to lie undisturbed. For almost thirty years between 1847 and 1876 his skull was bizarrely unburied, having been misappropriated by some workmen when Trowbridge church was being reconstructed in 1847 about fifteen years after his death. The chancel floor was taken up and Crabbe's coffin was found to be decayed. His skull then somehow became separated from the rest of his bones and was not re-interred with the rest of his body. This omission was not discovered until the new floor had been laid, and the rector refused to dig up his new chancel floor. Crabbe's skull then languished unburied until 1876 when an oak casket was made for it and it was reburied as close as possible to the rest of his remains.

Crabbe's writings and reputation

The complete edition of Crabbe's works including his *Life* was published in eight volumes by his son in 1834. It included much previously unpublished work that added to his reputation. Although now entirely out of fashion Crabbe's poetry was in his time held in very high esteem and achieved wide circulation. Unlike many of the 18th- and 19th-century romantic poets Crabbe was a realistic portrayer of life as he saw it. As a parson Crabbe was well aware of the extreme poverty that then prevailed among the working classes, and his poetry was a protest against the idealised pastoral poetry of the 18th century. As a consequence of concentrating on often sordid realism Crabbe's poetry never attained the popularity reached by many of the more romantic poets. His uncompromising realism led Byron to describe him as 'natures sternest painter, yet the best'. Although he was often critical of his poetry Hazlitt admitted that Crabbe was: 'one of the most popular and admired of our living authors', but he was critical of the fact that:

> Literal fidelity serves him in the place of invention; he assumes importance by a number of petty details . . . he relies for the effect of novelty on the microscopic minuteness with which he dissects the most trivial objects . . .

and suggested that Crabbe: 'has no delight beyond the walls of the workhouse'. Then, after describing Crabbe as 'a repulsive writer', Hazlitt relented and wrote: 'Mr Crabbe gives us one part of nature: the mean, the little, the disgusting, the distressing, he does this thoroughly and like a master; and we forgive all the rest'.

Thomas Hardy in his autobiography admired Crabbe's realism and described him as: 'an apostle of realism who practised it in English literature three-quarters of a century before the French re-

alistic school had been heard of'. One wonders how much Crabbe's 'disgusting and distressing poetry' (Hazlitt) influenced the sombre style of the novels of Thomas Hardy, who was born in 1840 only eight years after Crabbe's death.

Although the critics had warned Crabbe against 'His frequent lapses into disgusting representations', and it was even suggested that 'the function of Poetry is not to present the truth if it is unpleasant', immediately after his death Tennyson (1809–92), who in 1850 succeeded Wordsworth as poet laureate, expressed his admiration for Crabbe's tragic realism and often read him aloud to his guests. After reading one of Crabbe's tales Tennyson on one occasion turned to his guests and reproached them saying: 'I do not see any of you weeping'.

Edward Thomas described Crabbe as 'the censor of mankind', and drew attention to the fact that just as when botanising he gave plants their proper names rather than poetic ones, when describing his fellow men and women he depicted them as they really were. Crabbe's realism, which was far in advance of his time, prompted Byron to write of Crabbe the epitaph that appeared on his monument in Trowbridge parish church. This monument consists of a high relief marble tablet, depicting Crabbe on his deathbed with a bible in his hands and angels hovering above him. It was designed by the fashionable Bristol sculptor E. H. Baily (1788–1867), who sculpted the figures for the National Gallery and worked at Buckingham Palace. It was financed by public subscription among his parishioners who, as a last mark of respect to their rector, refused to accept contributions from the poet's family. The inscription mentions that Crabbe was 'born in humble life', and makes only partial use of the epitaph that Byron had written for him, by quoting only its final lines:

> Yet Truth sometimes will lend her noblest fires,
> And decorate the verse himself inspires ;
> This fact, in Virtues name, let Crabbe attest,
> Though Nature's sternest painter, yet the best.

13 Coate and Richard Jefferies,

and Charles Hamilton Sorley

Anyone in 1875 visiting the heights of Liddington Hill, at the north edge of the Marlborough Downs and four miles south-east of Swindon, might have chanced upon a youth of about seventeen perched on the ramparts at the south-west corner of the hillfort enjoying the panoramic views over the valley of the Og. This would have been the young Richard Jefferies, the Wiltshire-born Victorian writer of the second half of the 19th century, the son of a small farmer who aspired to become a writer.

Although both sides of his family came from farming stock there were also printers on his father's side, and his mother's family included at least one artist. It was probably from his mother's side of his family that Jefferies inherited his literary aspirations. He began his writing career as a journalist, but finding regular work on newspapers not to his liking he became a freelance writer, unsuccessfully attempted to write novels, and achieved success only when he began to write about the subjects which he had known from childhood, the wildlife and landscapes of north Wiltshire.

Opinion varies about his standing. In his 1948 introduction to the 'Oxford World Classics' edition of *The Gamekeeper at Home* and *The Amateur Poacher*, David Ascoli suggested that Jefferies had 'suffered more than most controversial writers at the hands of his admirers', and had been 'subjected to something not far removed from literary canonisation'. As a writer on rural affairs and natural history Jefferies is almost unsurpassed, and is generally recognised to be the finest depicter in prose of the wildlife of Wiltshire, Surrey and Sussex; but as a writer of novels he is less highly regarded. Controversy about Jefferies has generally centred around his

emotive spiritual autobiography *The Story of My Heart*.

Richard Jefferies wrote unpretentious straightforward prose at a time when the elaborate prose of the pre-Raphaelites was in fashion. That he flirted with a more elaborate style is suggested by an undated letter in which Frederick Greenwood of the *Pall Mall Gazette* warned him against 'this tricky flashy manner', and strongly advised him to return to the straightforward prose style of *The Gamekeeper at Home*. Although we do not know to which piece Greenwood referred it is fortunate that Jefferies heeded this advice. In the next generation his simple direct prose style was to rescue his admirer and biographer Edward Thomas (see Chapter 14) from the unfortunate influence of the Aesthetic Movement of the 1890s.

In his introduction to his collection of Jefferies's essays *The Hills and the Vale* (1909), Edward Thomas wrote of the young Jefferies:

> He tried his hand at topical humour, and again and again at short sensational tales. But until he was twenty-four he wrote nothing which could have suggested that he was much above the cleverer young men of the same calling. There was nothing fine or strong in his writing. His researches were industrious, but not illuminated . . . Yet it is certain that in 1867 Jefferies was already carrying about with him an experience and power which were to ripen very slowly into something unique. He was observing; he was developing a sense of beauty in Nature, in humanity, in thought, and the arts . . .

When assessing Jefferies in an essay in *British Country Life in Autumn and Winter* (an anthology which he collected in 1907–8 and predated his biography of Jefferies) Thomas also wrote: 'Jefferies is a personality . . . at his best he was apt and direct but he could, and many times did, write abominably without caring at all', and then suggests that: 'admiration will compel them [his readers] to set a value upon his ordinary work which is sometimes not easily to be justified'.

Although as a literary stylist Jefferies is not of the very highest rank his failings are more than compensated for by his immense knowledge of the countryside, which he unobtrusively conveys to his readers, teaching them to see apparently inconsequential details of landscape or natural history which they might otherwise have missed. Readers of Richard Jefferies are instructed without being aware that a profound knowledge is being imparted, and it is arguable that the unevenness in his writings for which Jefferies has sometimes been criticised is one of his great attractions. His writings can be likened to country walks which are suddenly enlivened by interesting and unforeseen incidents.

A tendency to eulogise Jefferies was started by Walter Besant with his appropriately named *Eulogy of Richard Jefferies* (1888), a book which renders less than justice to its subject. Besant's adulatory approach to Jefferies was largely remedied by Edward Thomas with his authoritative *Richard Jefferies, His Life and Work* (1909). Although he had been since boyhood an ardent admirer of Jefferies, Thomas was severely critical and his book was in 1938 described as: 'a classic in critical biography, to stand with Lockhart's *Scott* and Mrs Gaskell's *Brontë* in point of intrinsic interest, and containing better literary criticism than many critical works.'

Jefferies's countryside

From an early age Jefferies wandered on foot over his home countryside around Swindon. In his Jefferies biography Thomas mentions: 'He visited places as far apart as Avebury, Huish, Aldbourne, Uffington, Ashdown, Highworth, Braden Wood, Cricklade, Fairford, Malmesbury, and Wootton Bassett'. There is no evidence that Jefferies ever rode and his wanderings were therefore restricted to the limits imposed by his walking range, and he seems never to have ventured far into the south of Wiltshire. If he did he

omitted to write about it. In *A Literary Pilgrim in England* (1917) Edward Thomas pointed out that Jefferies 'has his domain' in a special sense which he defined as:

> . . . part of North Wiltshire about his native Coate, which he created in his early books, his pure country books, and used afterwards for the texture of autobiography, fiction and meditation. To go over this country now with physical footsteps is an act of pure piety. But to explore the regions of Surrey where he roamed in his last healthy years, and of Sussex, where his five years of dying were chiefly spent, is legitimate curiosity.

Jefferies became familiar with all of the countryside of north-east Wiltshire and of the adjoining counties within his walking range, at first for sport with gun in hand and then, after abandoning his gun in his late teens, observing and studying nature. In his work as a reporter he assimilated knowledge of this countryside and its landscapes, its flora and fauna, both animal and human, which provided the material for his books when he ultimately became a writer.

Liddington Hill and Liddington Folly (right) from the west

The Story of My Heart

The Jefferies book which has always aroused the greatest controversy is *The Story of My Heart*, his spiritual autobiography which disconcerts many of its readers who find its frank and intense revelations of his innermost thoughts a disturbing read. Over a long period Jefferies felt a strong compulsion to write this book and yet seems to have done so reluctantly, for he introduced his preliminary draft which was written in about 1882: 'I am compelled to write these thoughts by

The view that Jefferies loved from the south-west corner of Liddington Hill past Liddington Folly (the tree clump on the right) across the Og Valley

an irresistible impulse which I cannot any longer disobey.' This draft is of particular interest as it contains more self-revelation than *The Story of My Heart* as it appeared in its final form after it had been polished for publication.

It might be expected that Jefferies's reserved and introspected biographer Edward Thomas would have disliked such an emotive book. In fact Thomas regarded it as a 'wonderful autobiography' and considered that:

> The book is a poem; I had almost said a piece of music . . . Prose has rarely reached such a length . . . and yet retained this absolute, more than logical, unity . . . The gift of words in the book is undeniable.

The difficult domestic relationship between his dreamy muddling father and his town-loving mother probably explains why young Richard Jefferies became a reserved boy with a love of solitude and remote places. On his solitary wanderings as a youth he often resorted to the high downs south of Swindon. *The Story of My Heart* is based upon his experiences in his late teens, when he would walk from his birthplace at Coate to the exhilarating heights of Liddington Hill.

Nowhere is his ecstatic enjoyment of the Wiltshire countryside more strongly expressed than in this often-quoted passage from the book:

> Moving up the sweet short turf, at every step my heart seemed to obtain a wider horizon of feeling; with every inhalation of rich pure air, a deeper desire. The very light of the sun was whiter and more brilliant here. By the time I had reached the summit I had entirely forgotten the petty circumstances and annoyances of existence. I felt myself, myself. There was an intrenchment on the summit, and going down into the fosse I walked round it slowly to recover breath. On the south-western side there was a spot where the outer bank had partialy slipped, leaving a gap. There the view was over a broad plain, beautiful with wheat, and inclosed by a perfect amphitheatre of green hills. Through these hills there was one narrow groove or pass, southwards, where the white clouds seemed to close in the horizon. Woods hid the scattered hamlets and farmhouses, so that I was quite alone. I was utterly alone with the sun and the earth.

The sustained ecstatic prose of *The Story of My Heart* renders it unique in English literature, apart perhaps from the *Centuries of Meditation* by Thomas Traherne (*c.* 1636–74), which Jefferies would not have known as they remained undiscovered until 1896. *The Story of My Heart* is an extended prose poem, and anyone who would understand Jefferies should pay a pilgrimage to Liddington Hill and visit the south-west corner of the hillfort 'where the outer bank had partially slipped' to experience the view described by him in the above passage.

Jefferies's early life

Richard Jefferies led an uneventful life that was succinctly summed up by Edward Thomas when he wrote that: 'He walked, and wrote and suffered'. In his early years he was utterly unsocial and preferred to wander alone in the countryside around Swindon rather than cultivate friendships. He married a neighbour, Jessie Baden, the daughter of Andrew Baden of Day House Farm. After he had achieved some recognition as a writer Jefferies remained impoverished and isolated from all fellow writers until he was struck down by the serious and progressive terminal illness from which he died at an early age in a state of extreme anxiety about the future of his family. Fame came to him posthumously.

Richard Jefferies's father, James Luckett Jefferies (1816–1896), was an eccentric and impractical small farmer born at Somers Town in London into a family that had formerly lived in north Wiltshire. As a young man he travelled in America but returned to farm for his father Coate Farmhouse, the small farm beside Coate Water at the south-east edge of Swindon. In London he had married Elizabeth Gyde, the daughter of a London bookbinder, a lady described by her niece as: 'a town-bred woman, with a beautiful face, and a pleasure-loving soul, kind and generous to a fault, but unsuited for country life'. She was of a nervous disposition and easily upset, and Richard described her as being 'nervous and liable to make herself miserable over the merest trifle'. The Gydes came from Gloucestershire where they had farmed. Elizabeth married James Jefferies in 1844, and John Richard Jefferies, who later 'dropped' his first name, was born at Coate Farm on 6 November 1848. He was the second of five children and his elder sister Ellen,

Richard Jefferies from the etching by William Strang

born in about 1845, was killed by a runaway horse at Coate when she was about six and Richard was three.

The Jefferies family had long been in this part of Wiltshire, Richard's great-grandfather having been born at Draycot Foliat in the 1730s. Both his parents outlived Richard Jefferies and his father after failing as a farmer gave up Coate Farm and moved to Bath, where he became a gardener and died in 1896, his wife having died the previous year.

Three letters written to Dr Theodore Rake by James Luckett Jefferies in 1896 when he was eighty suggest that Richard exaggerated his father's cultural interests when portraying him as Farmer Iden in *Amaryllis at the Fair*. These letters disclose a rather unattractive side to his character, when he revelled in the fact that before leaving Coate he had deliberately destroyed some of the trees that he had planted to beautify the place. He also resented his son's success as a writer, saying of his writing: 'I was quite in a rage. I knew it was words that I had spoken.'

Coate

In his introduction to the 1978 reprint of Edward Thomas's *Richard Jefferies* Roland Gant quoted from 'In the Footprints of Richard Jefferies', an essay by Edward Thomas printed in the *New Age* in 1896 when Thomas was a boy of eighteen. In it he implies that Richard Jefferies might become as great as White of Selborne:

> Coate is a name which has probably little significance for the mass of Englishmen; yet it may well be that this little hamlet will one day attain the celebrity, not to say sanctity, now enjoyed by the Hampshire village of Selborne. For Coate is the birthplace of Richard Jefferies.

Coate is a linear rather dispersed village now virtually attached to Swindon. In Jefferies's day it was more remote, being about two miles from the centre of the then much smaller town. It is thinly spread along the road (now the A419) that runs south-east out of Swindon towards Marlborough and Aldbourne, and its only claim to fame is as the birthplace of Richard Jefferies. In his last years, when he was housebound in Sussex – a time described by Edward Thomas as 'his five years of dying' – Jefferies nostalgically reminisced about his life at Coate in a poignant essay 'My Old Village'. The changes that have now brought a motel, the inevitable development of the road system, and the expansion of Swindon which has made Coate virtually a suburb, began before Richard Jefferies died but after he had left Coate.

In 'My Old Village', after describing at length the sudden death of his father's milker John Brown, and assessing the man's unrecognised achievements in a long labouring life (during which he incidentally had nineteen children), Jefferies lovingly describes Coate and its inhabitants cottage by cottage, and then writes at length about the changes that had occurred since his childhood in sentences beginning:

> I think I have heard that the oaks are down . . . The brooks have ceased to run . . . There used to be footpaths . . . The walnut trees are dead at home . . .

He also recalls how in his youth he had loitered;

> . . . everywhere under the trees in the fields and footpaths, by day and by night, and that is why I have never put myself in the charge of the many wheeled

creatures that move on the rails and gone back hither, lest I might find the trees look small, and the elms mere switches, and the fields shrunken, and the brooks dry, and no voice anywhere.

Coate Farm had been bought in 1800 by an earlier Richard Jefferies, who was a miller and baker at Swindon. For eleven hundred pounds he purchased a 36-acre freehold which included a rambling 18th-century cottage. In 1825 the property passed to the author's grandfather John Jefferies who worked in London for a printer and publisher called Taylor, but returned to Swindon to run the family mill and bakery. One of his specialities was the larded layered Wiltshire cake called lardy-cake, which explained his nickname of 'Lord Lardy Cake'. He enlarged the cottage at Coate into a farmhouse and his eldest son James Luckett Jefferies, Richard's father, when he married in 1844 gave up his employment with a London printer in order to farm Coate Farm. In a letter James Luckett Jefferies wrote: 'Snodshill was the name on my Waggon and cart, he [Richard] styled it Coate Farm it was not worthy of the name of Farm it was not Forty acres of land'. Richard Jefferies seems to have designated his home 'Coate Farm' to give a better impression than Snodshill when he wrote his letters to *The Times* in 1872.

When Richard was twenty his father inherited the farm at Coate which he had already farmed for twenty-four years, but the inheritance was encumbered by legacies amounting to thirteen hundred pounds for his two married sisters. It may have been these legacies, together with the fact that James Luckett Jefferies was more of a dreamer than a farmer, that ultimately led to the sale of Coate Farm by auction to the Dean and Chapter of Westminster in 1877, the year that Richard Jefferies left Wiltshire. We do not know whether Richard felt any pangs of conscience about the sale of the farm in which he was born and where he had resolutely refused to assist his father. When revisiting Coate some time later he noted sadly: 'the old house deserted. Wall scribblings. The swallows building there inside the broken window, attaching their nests to the ceiling.'

Coate Reservoir

This extensive lake which lies south-west of Coate Farm was artificially formed in 1822, after the Jefferies family had bought the farm, by damming the tiny River Cole (or Dorcan) to form a feeder reservoir for the now defunct Wilts and Berks Canal. The lake is therefore known as both Coate Reservoir and Coate Water. In plan it resembles a fish with its head at its south-west end, its tail at its north-east towards Coate Farm, and its ventral fin towards the east. The lake is about three-quarters of a mile long and it fed the canal system by way of an open ditch which ran north across the fields of Walcot. Coate Reservoir was therefore a comparatively new lake in the 1850s when Richard Jefferies enjoyed the boyhood experiences on and around it that he so memorably described in *Bevis: The Story of a Boy*.

Coate Water from its west end

At the instigation of a former Swindon mayor, Mr Reuben George, Coate Farmhouse was bought by Swindon Corporation in 1926 and converted into the Richard Jefferies Museum, a function which it still serves today. Shortly after the Second World War Coate Reservoir became a place of public recreation and the area has progressively become more urbanised as Swindon has expanded towards it. Anyone wishing to experience the reservoir as it was in the past should visit its south-western end where, despite the adjoining golf course, its reed-choked bird sanctuary provides something of its atmosphere that Jefferies knew.

Education and youth

Richard Jefferies spent some of his formative years from about the age of four to nine staying with his Uncle and Aunt Harrild at Sydenham, and was for only part of these years with his parents at Coate. At seven he was sent to a preparatory school at Sydenham and after he returned to Coate at the age of ten his education continued at several Swindon schools. His surviving notebooks contain drawings which reveal that, having been taught to draw by his artist uncle Fred Gyde, he was proficient at sketching.

Upon leaving school Richard refused to enter farming. For a time he 'mooned' about the local countryside, acquired the nickname of 'moony Dick', and became friendly with Edward Haylock, the Burderop Park gamekeeper who lived in the gamekeeper's cottage (the only cottage to the west of the road) at Hodson, a tiny hamlet in a wooded coombe towards Chiseldon. On Keeper Haylock he was to base his first really successful book *The Gamekeeper at Home*. The gamekeeper's cottage survives today very much as Jefferies described it at the start of the book:

> The keepers cottage stands in a sheltered 'coombe', or narrow hollow of the woodlands, overshadowed by a mighty Spanish chestnut, bare now of leaves, but in summer a noble tree. The ash wood covers the slope at the rear; on one side is a garden, and on the other a long strip of meadow with elms. In front, and somewhat lower, a streamlet winds, fringing the sward, and across it the fir plantations begin, their dark sombre foliage hanging over the water.

Early writings

When he was eighteen the matter of employment was discussed, for Richard could no longer be allowed to idle away his time apparently aimlessly wandering about the countryside. He decided upon journalism and as the result of a chance meeting with a Mr Frampton of the *North Wilts Herald* in March 1866 he obtained a full-time post as a reporter on that paper.

Jefferies worked in Swindon with the *North Wilts Herald* editor, a Mr Piper, and in addition to normal journalistic work he wrote a great deal of local history. By mid–1867 he had written for the *North Wilts Herald* twenty pieces on 'The History of Malmesbury' but later in that year he

Hodson cottage, the home of The Gamekeeper at Home

suffered a serious illness which terminated his full-time employment with that paper. He continued however to contribute to the *North Wilts Herald* and from 1867 to 1872 wrote a series of articles on the history and topography of Swindon and its neighbourhood. In 1873 he published at his own expense *A Memoir of the Goddards of North Wilts*, and in September of that year he read a paper on 'Swindon and its Antiquities' before the Wiltshire Archaeological and Natural History Society.

By 1867 Jefferies was working for the *Wiltshire and Gloucestershire Standard* under its editor, a Mr Harmer. He stayed with this paper for two years and in 1872 again returned to its staff. He was however unsuited to regular work as a newspaper reporter and in 1873 he finally gave up full-time reporting to become a freelance writer. Although he had found regular journalistic work arduous it had brought him into contact with all classes of people and provided him with most of the material upon which he later based *Hodge and His Masters*.

In 1868 Jefferies considered applying for a Civil Service clerkship (letter 5 June 1868) but in a later letter dated 12 July 1868 he reveals that he was attempting short story writing. In spite of severing his connection with the *Wiltshire and Gloucestershire Standard* Jefferies continued for a time to be a part-time journalist. As a freelance writer he wrote many technical articles for agricultural magazines including the weekly *Live Stock Journal*, while simultaneously undertaking more congenial writing for periodicals including *Frasers, Longmans*, the *New Quarterly, Cham-*

bers, *The Standard, The Graphic*, and the *Pall Mall Gazette*.

In 1870 Jefferies attempted verse with an unpublished poem on the 'Exile of the Prince Imperial' and then in 1872 he wrote three letters to *The Times* on the subject of the Wiltshire farm labourer and the allotment system. Although the authority with which he spoke on rural subjects was instantly recognised, Jefferies still regarded himself as a novel-writer, did not pursue this success, and embarked on three large-scale novels, *The Scarlet Shawl* (1874), the 'three-decker' *Restless Human Hearts* published 1875, and *World's End*, another 'three-decker' which came out in 1877. He had high hopes for his fiction which he published partly at his own expense, but having lived an utterly unsocial life in a remote part of rural Wiltshire he lacked the background that would have enabled him to write novels about society life with much authority, and these early novels achieved very limited success.

Marriage and move away from Wiltshire

Jefferies and Jessie Baden were married at Chiseldon church in 1874 and set up house at 22 Victoria Street, Swindon. They ultimately had several children and Mrs Jefferies outlived her husband by many years. One of their sons lived into the 1940s.

In 1877 the family moved away from Wiltshire to live at Surbiton in Surrey on the outskirts of London, in order to improve Jefferies's prospects by being nearer the London publishers. The move away from Wiltshire was probably unnecessary as rail communications between Swindon and London were by that time extremely good. Five years after moving Jefferies's health broke down and from that date he suffered intermittent illness until his death in 1887.

It is a matter of debate whether Jefferies was wise to leave Wiltshire and spend his later life in exile from his native county. His town-bred mother had never really settled in rural Wiltshire but Jefferies conversely probably never adjusted to life away from Wiltshire. After leaving he frequently reminisced in his writings about Coate and his Wiltshire experiences, and these recollections provided the material for most of his best books.

The stress of exile from his native Wiltshire may also have contributed to his illness and early death. It is perhaps significant that after leaving Wiltshire he was often intensely nostalgic about his earlier life, for example in his moving late essay 'My Old Village':

> I think I have heard that the oaks are down. They may be standing or down, it matters nothing to me; the leaves I last saw upon them are gone for ever-more, nor shall I ever see them come there again ruddy in spring. I would not see them again even if I could; they could never look again as they used to do. There are too many memories there. The hap-piest days become the saddest afterwards; let us never go back, lest we too die . . . No one else seems to have seen the sparkle on the brook, or heard the music at the hatch, or to have felt back through the centuries; and when I try to describe these things to them they look at me with with stolid incredulity. No one seems to understand how I got food from the clouds, nor what there was in the night, nor why it is not so good to look at it out of the window. They turn their faces away from me, so that perhaps after all I was mistaken, and there never was any such place or any such meadows, and I was never there. And perhaps in course of time I shall find out also, when I pass away physically, that as a matter of fact there never was any earth.

Two months before this essay appeared in *Longmans Magazine* in October 1887 Jefferies died, on 14 August 1887. It later appeared in his widow's collection of his essays *Field and Hedgerow* (1889).

Despite living for three-quarters of his life in and around Swindon, at first at Coate and after his marriage in Swindon, Jefferies although es-sentially a Wiltshire writer was not exclusively so. He left his native county at the age of twenty-nine, spent his last ten years far away, and wrote a good deal in his later years about the Surrey and Sussex countrysides; but his formative years and his early working life were spent in Wiltshire with which he always strongly identified. Although most of his significant work, starting with *The Gamekeeper at Home*, was published in book form after he had left Wiltshire, many of his best books were based on his Wiltshire experiences.

He appears to have had the gift of absolute re-call which was no doubt assisted by the notebooks that he had habitually kept.

The Gamekeeper at Home

After the limited success of his early novels Jefferies recalled the favourable reception given to his letters to *The Times* and radically changed the direction of his writing. In 1876 he wrote rather diffidently to the editor of the *New Quar-terly* indicating that he was planning a book based on his experiences as a countryman. *The Gamekeeper at Home* appeared in 1878 having earlier in that year appeared as a series of articles in the *Pall Mall Gazette*. In his short preface Jefferies emphasised that: 'the facts here collected are really entirely derived from original observa-tion', and the book was based on the working life of his friend Keeper Haylock at Hodson.

The Gamekeeper at Home was illustrated by the celebrated artist and mountaineer Edward Whymper (1840–1911), as were several other books by Jefferies. When Whymper was ap-pointed to illustrate *The Gamekeeper* Jefferies expressed his satisfaction by writing to the pub-lisher: 'I should imagine that no better artist could have been selected', although later he criticised the reproduction of the engravings in the first proofs.

The Gamekeeper at Home was followed by *Wild Life in a Southern County* (1879), *The Amateur Poacher* (1880), *Greene Ferne Farm* (1880), the two-volume *Hodge and His Masters* (1880), and *Round About a Great Estate* (1880). *Bevis: The Story of a Boy* appeared in three vol-umes in 1882, and in 1883 he wrote *Nature near London* and the controversial *The Story of My Heart*. Although they were written after Jefferies left Wiltshire in 1877 these books were, with the obvious exception of *Nature Near London*, es-sentially Wiltshire books which recalled the experiences that he had obtained in his native countryside around Coate.

Wild Life in a Southern County

Within easy walking distance of his home at Coate Richard Jefferies had access to a variety of landscapes – the downs of Liddington Hill, the reservoir at Coate, and the woods of Burderop, three distinctly different habitats which recur in *Wild Life in a Southern County*. The book consists of twenty chapters of somewhat random description mainly of the Wiltshire countryside and its wildlife, although parts describe nature nearer London. It describes with great authority the wildlife that was to be seen in the various habitats which are indicated at the head of its chapters. The book contains a description of The Ridgeway, which crosses Jefferies's countryside of north-east Wiltshire northwards, from the Vale of Pewsey along Hackpen Hill, before swinging north-east to run under the twin Iron Age hillforts of Barbury Castle and Liddington, on its way into Berkshire, now officially Oxfordshire:

The Ridgeway on Hackpen Hill, looking north

A broad green track runs for many a long, long mile across the downs, now following the ridges, now winding past at the foot of a grassy slope, then stretching away through cornfield and fallow. It is distinct from the waggon-tracks which cross it here and there, for these are local only, and, if traced up, land the wayfarer presently in a maze of fields, or end abruptly in the rickyard of a lone farmhouse. It is distinct from the hard roads of modern construction which also at wide intervals cross its course, dusty and glaringly white in the sunshine. It is not a farm track – you may walk for twenty miles along it over the hills; neither is it the kings highway . . . The origin of the track goes back into the dimmest antiquity . . . Plough and harrow press hard on the ancient track, and yet dare not encroach upon it. With varying width, from twenty to fifty yards, it runs like a green riband through the sea of corn – a width that allows a flock of sheep to travel easily side by side, spread abroad, and snatch a bite as they pass.

The Amateur Poacher

In his next book Jefferies pursues subjects similar to those of *The Gamekeeper at Home*. *The Amateur Poacher* demonstrates the accuracy of his powers of observation and his ability to present them in memorable prose, and like its predecessors is firmly rooted in the Wiltshire countryside. *The Gamekeeper at Home*, *Wild Life in a Southern County* and *The Amateur Poacher* all first appeared in serial form in the columns of the *Pall Mall Gazette*. With his next book, *Greene Ferne Farm*, Jefferies reverted to novel writing by setting a book in the Wiltshire countryside which is an advance on his earlier novels.

Hodge and His Masters

Hodge and His Masters (1880) is a two-volume in-depth study of the English farm worker and the people who influenced and controlled his life. Hodge is derived from the name Roger, an old-fashioned name for a country labourer. The book was initially written as a series of articles which appeared serially in a London paper (*The Standard*), and were then collected and published in 1880 by Smith Elder. Most of his material was obtained by Jefferies during his time as a journalist in north Wiltshire in the 1860s and early 1870s.

At the time when *Hodge and His Masters* was written English agriculture had experienced the depression of the early part of the 19th century, the high farming of the mid-century, and was now beginning to feel the effects of the depression in agriculture that was to extend almost up to the Great War. From his experience of his father's struggling farm at Coate Jefferies was well aware that behind the beauty of English landscape lay the harsh realities of the farmer's struggle and the grimness of the farm labourer's lot. Hodge describes the circumstances of many members of late-Victorian rural society, from Hodge at the bottom to the men – his 'Masters' – who controlled his life. Jefferies generally expressed his sympathy for all and indicated at the end of his preface: 'all I claim for the following sketches is that they are written in a fair and impartial spirit'.

Hodge provides an invaluable source of authentic information for anyone researching the agricultural scene in southern England towards the end of the 19th century. It ends with a poignant passage quoted later in this chapter (pages 199-200), describing the last days of an old labourer after he had been forcibly taken from his cottage to the workhouse.

Round About a Great Estate

In his introduction to a 1948 edition of *Round About a Great Estate* (1880) C. Henry Warren suggested that in this book: 'There is a buoyancy, a geniality . . . such as Richard Jefferies did not often achieve' and described it as being 'packed with information and inimitably told'. The book's genial qualities are probably explained by the fact that it is based upon Jefferies's recollections from the time when he courted his wife Jesse Baden at Coate. The 'Okebourne Chace' of the book and the 'Great Estate' of its title were Burderop Park south of Swindon. 'Luckett's Place' seems to be Day House Farm, the home of Jessie Baden, which stands a short distance south-east of Coate Farm down Day House Lane.

Round About a Great Estate was followed by the two-volume *Wood Magic: A Fable* in 1881, and in 1882 by *Bevis: The Story of a Boy*.

Bevis

As a boy Richard Jefferies's favourite haunt was Coate Water beside his home at Coate Farm near Swindon. Here he enjoyed a happy boyhood with his brothers, which he nostalgically recalled in *Bevis: The Story of a Boy*, the book of which E. V. Lucas wrote:

> As a book for boys Bevis I think stands alone in its blend of joy in the open air, sympathetic understanding of boy nature, and most admirable writing . . . It is a boy's book from the first word to the last – a book for boys who are still boys, and also for boys who are masquerading as boys and fathers.

Bevis was with some justification criticised by the Jefferies enthusiast Samuel Looker for being 'rather over-long', and it is true that its length might deter a child, but the book is written with an ease and maturity that is absent from the more fanciful *Wood Magic*. It is a book written from the heart by a man recalling an exceptionally happy childhood at a time when, aged thirty-four and

exiled from his beloved Wiltshire, he was perhaps aware that his health was on the verge of terminally breaking down.

Essays

With these books Richard Jefferies's works on Wiltshire subjects ended except for many of the essays which, having been originally published in magazines and periodicals such as *Longmans Magazine*, *Frasers Magazine*, *The Graphic* and *The Standard*, have been collected and published in eight volumes.

His essays contain some of Richard Jefferies's best work and many of them are devoted to Wiltshire subjects. During his lifetime Jefferies arranged the reprinting of many of them in three collections entitled *Nature Near London* (1883), *The Life of the Fields* (1884) and *The Open Air* (1885), and after his death five more volumes of essays appeared as *Field and Hedgerow* (1889), *The Toilers of the Fields* (1892), and *The Hills and the Vale* (1909), the last a collection made by his biographer Edward Thomas. Much later Samuel Looker collected *Chronicles of the Hedges* (1948) and *Field and Farm* (1958).

In 1896 Grace Toplis gathered some of Jefferies's early writings on local history subjects, pieces which might otherwise have remained interred in the files of the local newspapers, and published them in *Jefferies Land: A History of Swindon and its Environs*.

Later life in exile from Wiltshire

Upon leaving Wiltshire in 1877 at the age of twenty-nine Jefferies took a house at Surbiton in Surrey. After five years in 1882 he moved his family to West Brighton. Their subsequent homes were at Eltham in Kent (1884-5), Crowborough in Sussex (1885-6), and Goring-on-Sea at Worthing (1886-7). His later books included *Red Deer* (1884), *The Life of the Fields* (1884), a novel in two volumes called *The Dewy Morn* (1884), *After London* (1885), *The Open Air* (1885), and *Amaryllis at the Fair* (1887).

Red Deer was written in 1882 when Jefferies was convalescing on Exmoor. It is an unsentimental and factual book about red deer, their environment, and the men who hunted them. In both *The Dewy Morn* and *Amaryllis at the Fair* Jefferies reverted to the novel form and produced two fine books. They are a great advance on his earlier novels, which suffered from weak plots and characterisations. *The Dewy Morn* (1884) was a seminal work in which the formerly Conservative Jefferies turned radical by suggesting that rural cottagers were being turned into nomads by the oppressions of the landowners, and he significantly offered it to Longmans with a request that it should not be given to a Tory reader. *The Dewy Morn* had been first offered to a publisher shortly after *World's End* was published in 1877, but was refused, and when it re-appeared in 1884 it was in a revised form. Edward Thomas wrote of 'the glory of *The Dewy Morn*' which revolves around the character of Felise, a girl of twenty with two lovers, one a struggling farmer and the other an estate bailiff who has secretly admired her since her childhood. He writes of Felise's profound appreciation of nature 'as she roamed about the hills'.

In *Amaryllis at the Fair* the characters are based upon Jefferies and his immediate family. The book can be described as a novel in only the loosest terms as it is really an extended short story, an evocation of its author's life at Coate Farm with no plot and no end. Iden and his wife are the author's father and mother, Old Iden his grandfather, Alere Flamma is his artistic uncle, and the lonely sensitive girl Amaryllis appears to be an amalgam of Jefferies and his sister. Edward Garnett considered *Amaryllis* superior to Hardy's *Tess* and *The Mayor of Casterbridge* and it is regarded by many people as Richard Jefferies's masterpiece.

Illness and death

After a short but prolific life of writing Richard Jefferies in December 1881 fell ill at the age of thirty-four, and for the rest of his life was a partial invalid suffering periodic bouts of severe illness. In April 1885 his health finally broke down and from that time he was continually ill until his death, which occurred at his house at Goring-on-Sea on on 14 August 1887 when he was only thirty-eight.

In his terminal illness this man who had delighted in contact with nature wrote poignantly

of seeing but not hearing the birds through the glass of his window, and speculated: 'What will they do without me?' His early death may have been precipitated by the fact that his severe illness prevented him from maintaining his lifelong need to wander in the countryside. He lingered dictating from his sick bed his last writings to his wife in a desperate last attempt to provide for his family, and died in great pain and anxiety for the future of his dependants. His death was certified as being due to 'chronic fibroid phthisis – exhaustion'.

In describing the tragic death of Richard Jefferies I am reminded of his moving account of the death of the old labourer with which he concluded *Hodge and His Masters* seven years before he fell ill:

> At the workhouse the monotony weighed upon him. He used to think as he lay awake in bed that when the spring came nothing should keep him in this place . . . The spring came, but the rain was ceaseless. No work of the kind he could do was possible in such weather. Still there was the summer, but the summer was no improvement; in the autumn he felt weak, and was not able to walk far. The chance for which he had waited had gone. Again the winter came, and he now rapidly grew more feeble . . . The end came very slowly; he ceased to exist by imperceptible degrees, like an oak tree. He remained for days in a semi-unconscious state, neither moving nor speaking. It happened at last. In the grey of the winter dawn, as the stars paled and the whitened grass was stiff with hoar frost, and the rime coated every branch of the tall elms, as the milker came from the pen and the young ploughboy whistled down the road to his work, the spirit of the aged man departed . . . Hodge died, and the very gravedigger grumbled

Liddington Hill (left) from Burderop Down with the Richard Jefferies memorial stone (centre)

as he delved through the earth hard-bound in the iron frost, for it jarred his hand and might break his spade. The low mound will soon be level, and the place of his burial shall not be known.

Jefferies was buried in Broadwater Cemetery at Worthing, his gravestone being inscribed: 'To the Prose-Poet of England's Fields and Woodlands'. In Wiltshire Jefferies and his fellow north Wiltshire writer Alfred Williams are commemorated by a standing sarsen stone memorial, which was set up in 1939 on Burderop Down, a little east of Barbury Castle car park and overlooking Burderop Park. His birthplace and early home at Coate Farm beside Coate Water is now the Richard Jefferies Museum administered by the local authority. The farmhouse remains much as Jefferies knew it except that its thatch has been replaced by slate.

Jefferies Memorial Stone, Burderop Down

The influence of Richard Jefferies
Dying as he did in comparative obscurity and considerable poverty Richard Jefferies would not have believed that more than a hundred years after his death his work would be widely read and admired. His posthumous influence upon writers on the natural history and landscapes of Wiltshire first appeared in the writings of a number of writers with strong Wiltshire associations, including his biographer Edward Thomas (Chapter 14), W. H. Hudson (1841–1922), Alfred Williams (1877–1930) and H. W. Timperley (1890–1961). Edward Thomas freely acknowledged his immense debt to Jefferies, and Hudson

emulated him by writing about Wiltshire and choosing to be buried near him. Alfred Williams came like Jefferies from the neighbourhood of Swindon and wrote both prose and poetry about the Wiltshire countryside, and H. W. Timperley came to live in Wiltshire at Bishopstone and wrote authoritatively on the Jefferies countryside. But perhaps the most surprising among devotees of Jefferies, because he was a Scotsman, was Charles Hamilton Sorley.

Charles Hamilton Sorley
Unlike Jefferies, who wrote almost invariably in prose and only flirted with poetry, Charles Hamilton Sorley (1895–1915) always aspired to be a poet, although his published letters are well worth reading as they reveal much about his attitude to his writing. He was born in Aberdeen and when he was five the family moved to Cambridge where his father became a professor of philosophy. After coming to Marlborough College in 1908 Sorley grew to love the Marlborough Downs in all weathers including the wind and the rain. He discovered the writings of Richard Jefferies and reading them intensified his growing attachment to the landscape of north Wiltshire. He celebrated the Marlborough countryside in verse and identified with it as 'my land' in a poem he sent home from the Western Front.

Out of admiration for Jefferies Sorley spent time on Liddington Hill and was there inspired to write his poem to 'Richard Jefferies'. He also celebrated the area in his poem 'Marlborough':

I, who have walked along her downs in dreams,
And known her tenderness and felt her might,

Liddington Hill from the west

The view that Sorley loved, west from Four Mile Clump across the Marlborough Downs to Hackpen Hill (left) and Barbury Castle (right)

And sometimes by her meadows and her streams
Have drunk deep-storied secrets of delight.

His best-known and much-anthologised poem 'The song of the ungirt runners' recalled long-distance runs he had taken from Marlborough to Four Mile Clump, a vantage point on the Marlborough to Swindon turnpike four miles from Marlborough, which he also celebrated in verse as 'Four Milers heights'. On these cross-country runs he sometimes took the route followed by generations of Marlborough boys between the founding of the college in 1843 and the opening of the Midland and South Western Junction Railway through the Ogbourne villages in the 1870s. At the beginning and end of term the boys would travel between Swindon and Marlborough across the downs past Four Mile Clump on Jerry Hammond's horse-drawn bus, Jerry Hammond being the proprietor of the *Castle and Ball* inn at Marlborough.

Sorley loved the Marlborough Downs so profoundly that on his return to school at Marlborough from his home at Cambridge he sometimes left the train at the remote station of Fenny Stratford in the Berkshire Downs, walked the Ridgeway into Wiltshire, and then passed south of Liddington Hill and swung south over Whitefield Hill and Poulton Downs to Marlborough. He regretfully left Marlborough

early in 1914 to pursue his studies in Germany, and after spending six months at the University of Jena he was in Germany at the outbreak of the Great War in September. He escaped internment by crossing into Belgium and upon reaching England immediately volunteered for the army in which he was commissioned.

In spite of his youth Sorley went to the war with great reservations. His attitude was in marked contrast to those of his fellow poets Rupert Brooke and Siegfried Sassoon who went idealistically to the war as a sort of crusade. Sorley demonstrated an awareness of the horrors of mechanised warfare which was far in advance of the general perception in the country. He deplored the jingoistic fervour which was then rife in Germany as well as in England, writing in a letter home in 1914 how, having witnessed a German patriotic demonstration, he: 'felt that perhaps I could die for Deutschland'. Jon Silkin suggested in *Out of Battle* (1972) that Sorley was: 'the most interesting of the poets killed in the early part of the war, and from his letters seems to have had a more acute intelligence than any in that period'.

Sorley's promise as a poet was only beginning to be recognised when he went to the front. Behind the lines in France he read Richard Jefferies: 'to remind me of Liddington Castle and the light green and the dark green of the Aldbourne Downs in summer', and he died at the

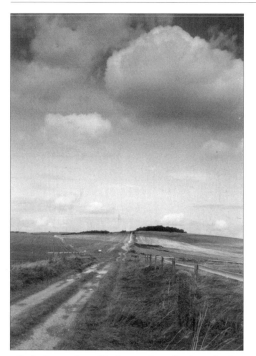

Sorley's way from Marlborough up the turnpike to
Four Mile Clump on the horizon

age of only twenty, shot by a sniper when leading his platoon near Loos after being only nine
weeks at the front. In 1976 he was commemorated by a small sarsen boulder inscribed 'C. H.
S. 1895–1915' set beneath 'that crazy signpost
arms askew', which he knew and loved. It stands
at the intersection of trackways a little north-east
of Rabley Wood, a mile and a half north of
Mildenhall, and has been maintained and restored by Marlborough College in his memory.

Conclusion
Throughout his life until he was struck down by
his terminal illness Richard Jefferies was essentially
a solitary outdoor man who found solace in wandering alone in remote countryside. The prolonged

final illness during which he was housebound and
only saw the countryside through window-glass
must have been purgatory to the man who had
lived so much of his life out of doors, had said that
he would prefer to continue to see beautiful things
than to write, and had written: 'The sunlight puts
out books as it puts out the fire'.

At the end of *The Amateur Poacher* Richard
Jefferies wrote the exhortation that inspired his
biographer Edward Thomas, and today chimes
with the needs of the many people who look to
the countryside and natural things to provide
them with some relief from the artificiality of
modern living:

> Let us get out of these indoor narrow modern days,
> whose twelve hours somehow have become short-
> ened, into the sunlight and the pure wind. A
> something that the ancients called divine can be
> found and felt there still.

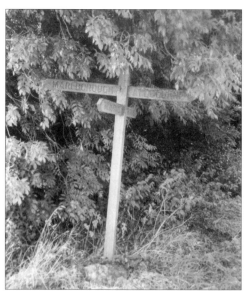

Sorley's signpost on Poulton Downs north-east of
Marlborough

14 Edward Thomas in Wiltshire

Towards dusk on the evening of the 28th of January in the particularly bleak winter of 1916–17 a tall lean man who was once described as 'absurdly thin', with hair bleached gold and complexion bronzed by prolonged exposure to the elements over many years spent wandering in southern England, rode a bicycle across the south Wiltshire Downs between Tisbury and Codford. He wore the uniform of a second lieutenant in the Royal Garrison Artillery. Edward Thomas, the critic and prose writer who soon after the outbreak of the Great War had become a poet, was making the last of his innumerable journeys in his favourite county of Wiltshire, having visited his young daughter Myfanwy then staying at East Hatch farmhouse near Tisbury. He was returning to Camp 15 at Codford. Early next morning he embarked at Codford station for France, where on Easter Monday 1917 he was killed by shell blast at the Battle of Arras at the age of thirty-nine. His friend Walter de la Mare wrote in his foreword to *Collected Poems* by Edward Thomas : 'When Edward Thomas was killed in Flanders, a mirror of England was shattered of so pure a crystal that a

Edward Thomas in 1913

clearer and tenderer reflection can by found no other where than in these poems'.

No particular location has been indicated in the heading to this chapter because Edward Thomas is identified with virtually the whole of Wiltshire, especially its byways, footpaths, and its remote places, particularly when they bore intriguing names such as Glory Ann beside the Ridgeway on Hackpen Hill, about which he speculated when writing the introduction to the 1911 Everyman edition of Isaac Taylors *Words and Places*. His early experiences of Wiltshire were obtained as a schoolboy spending holidays

Glory Ann Pond, a name that intrigued Thomas beside the Ridgeway on Hackpen Hill above Avebury

with relatives in the railway village at New Swindon. At this time he wandered over the countryside around Swindon with an old man called David Uzzell, whom he called 'Dad' and was to immortalise in several prose essays and in his poem 'Lob' (see later, pages 205-6).

Since he was born and raised in London, Thomas was neither a native nor a resident of Wiltshire, although he reacted against his London birth and upbringing and became a man who loved to wander in the rural parts of southern England. He became a frequent visitor to Wiltshire, particularly its chalk downland ways ('the loops over the downs').

After his former working-class Welsh father allowed him to go to Oxford on a scholarship Edward Thomas left university resolved to become a freelance writer, and in spite of strong parental opposition began earning a meagre living from commissioned writing and reviewing. He aspired to write prose in the precious style of Walter Pater, but having married young and become a father the necessity of earning a living for his family prevented him from writing poetry, until the outbreak of the Great War in 1914 put an effective end to paid work. Between 1914 and 1916 he produced the low-key musing poetry which has posthumously earned him his enduring recognition as one of the major poets in English of the 20th century.

Thomas became a reserved and introverted man who throughout his life was at his happiest wandering in search of solace from his unfulfilled life as a writer of commissioned books and reviews. In the English countryside he sought some unrecognised and perhaps unattainable need that he was destined never to find, although late in his short life he achieved some self-fulfilment as a poet, and it is as a poet that he has achieved widest recognition. That he acknowledged he would never attain the indefinable something that he sought is revealed in the second line of his long Wiltshire poem 'Lob' which begins:

At Hawthorn-time in Wiltshire travelling
In search of something chance would never bring.

The strangely evocative nature of Edward Thomas's landscapes in prose and poetry is

largely explained by the fact that they are more than visual. He experienced landscapes with all of his senses and often introduced into his literary landscapes the senses of sound, smell and occasionally touch, as demonstrated in his most-anthologised poem 'Adlestrop', with its several references to sound, 'the steam hissed', 'someone cleared his throat', 'a blackbird sang', all in a short 16-line poem. In his poem 'The Source' Thomas refers to the wild weather: 'Drowning the sound of earth', and he acknowledged this characteristic of his poetry when he ended 'The Brook':

And what I felt, yet never should have found
A word for, while I gathered sight and sound.

His friends were bemused when he suddenly volunteered for the army in 1915, and Eleanor Farjeon recorded that when she asked him why he reached down, picked up a handful of earth and said: 'Literally for this'.

The young Edward Thomas at Swindon
In spite of its celebrity as an early planned housing estate the Great Western railway village at New Swindon was an unlikely place to have fostered one of the most significant poetic talents in English of the 20th century. During his childhood Edward Thomas was often at his grandmother's railway company house in the railway village at New Swindon, the town which as a boy escaping from London he thought 'paradisal'. Many years later he in 1913 evocatively described his boyhood times spent at Swindon: 'Toward the end of these days I spent the greater part of a summer term [probably 1888] in a Board School in Swindon . . . I became a Wiltshire boy in accent.' Wiltshire gradually replaced the Wales of his ancestors in young Edward's affections, and he took every opportunity to come to Wiltshire. Later he became familiar with the entire county when researching the endless succession of prose works which he wrote over the period 1894–1914. It is noticeable that throughout his life Edward Thomas cultivated Wiltshire-based friends who would provide him with opportunities to visit the county, from 'Dad' Uzzell when he was in his teens to Clifford Bax after 1911. Between these the solicitor J. H. Morgan and the

writers Stephen Reynolds and Arthure Ransome come to mind.

Among the immigrants to Swindon railway village were Edward's paternal grandparents, a Welsh engine fitter named Henry Thomas and his wife Rachel who was born in 1823. At Swindon they produced a family and Henry's Welsh-speaking widow Rachel continued to live in the railway village until her death in 1909. The 1881 census schedules Rachel Thomas, born at Tredegar in Wales and then a widow aged fifty-eight, living at 19 Cambria Place, so-named because it was colonised by the Welsh immigrants to Swindon. Cambria Place survives, although both the number and the street name of Rachel Thomas's house are now changed and I have established that her house is now 171 Faringdon Road, opposite the park and now a Chinese restaurant. Edward Thomas would have had this house in mind when in 1886 at the age of nine he wrote in his exercise book that the houses of Swindon were: 'like bulldogs, small but strongly built'.

The eldest son of Henry and Rachel Thomas was Philip Henry Thomas (1854–1920), who became a pupil-teacher at Swindon before passing the Civil Service examinations, moving to London and taking an appointment at the tramways division of the Board of Trade. Philip Thomas was a 'practical, self-made man . . . a short, stocky Welshman', a dark, good looking man, particularly proud of his achievement in having worked his way up from his origins in a humble Welsh working-class family to a position in the Civil Service. In London he married a Welsh wife Mary Elizabeth Townsend, and they had six children, all of them sons. The eldest, Philip Edward, born at Lambeth in 1878, emulated John Richard Jefferies by 'dropping' his first name and becoming known as Edward Thomas. To the family he was 'Edwy'.

Friendship with 'Dad' Uzzell

When staying at Swindon as a boy Edward Thomas made friends with David Uzzell (1841–1919), an elderly and slightly disreputable bushy-bearded Swindon resident with three grown-up sons, whom he met when fishing the former Wilts and Berks Canal where it passed

Cambria Place. David Uzzell was born at Kemble when it was still in Wiltshire, prior to being transferred to Gloucestershire in 1897. During a varied life Uzzell had acquired much knowledge of the countryside and at this time was trying to live down his rather colourful past as a poacher by becoming tee-total and an ardent Salvationist. A faded photograph survives of David Uzzell and his wife in 'army' uniform holding their pension books on the day that they qualified for the old age pension, probably in 1911 when David Uzzell became seventy.

David Uzzell in Salvation Army uniform on the first day of his Old Age Pension

The old countryman and the London boy became friends and began to roam over the Wiltshire countryside around Swindon. On these walks David Uzzell imparted much country lore to young Edward Thomas, who wrote of him in an unpublished essay headed 'Dad', written when he was seventeen, that he: 'had a whole store of out of door knowledge which he was quite prepared to impart'. Much later Thomas immortalised 'Dad' Uzzell in his favourite poem 'Lob' which opens with a description of his friend:

> At hawthorn-time in Wiltshire travelling
> In search of something chance would never bring,
> An old mans face, by life and weather cut

And coloured, – rough, brown, sweet as any nut, –
A land-face, sea-blue-eyed, – hung in my mind
When I had left him many a mile behind . . .

This word portrait of 'Dad' Uzzell is succeeded by 150 lines of poetry woven together of
threads from a variety of sources – including landscape, natural history, folklore, colloquial
language, and local history – to create the poem
that has been described as 'one of the finest evo-
cations of country life in English literature'. The
place-names which are introduced (the
Manningfords, Alton Barnes, Alton Priors, and
'Adams Point' for Adams Grave long barrow on
Walkers Hill) establish that Edward Thomas had
Pewsey Vale in mind when he wrote 'Lob'.

Adam's Grave on Walker's Hill, the 'Adam's Point' of
the poem 'Lob'

The landscape of north Wiltshire provided the
young Edward Thomas with his introduction to
English countryside, and he was thrilled to visit
places such as Burderop Woods, Barbury Castle,
and particularly Liddington Hill and Coate, for
their associations with Richard Jefferies. Many
years later he was to write *Richard Jefferies, His
Life and Work* (1909), a fine biography with an
introductory chapter which contains detailed descriptions of the north Wiltshire countryside.

In the second volume of her memoirs (*World
Without End*) Edward's wife Helen wrote of her
husband: 'The downs country about Swindon he
knew and loved as no other part of England, and
the introductory chapter ('The Country of Richard Jefferies') of Thomas's biography of Jefferies
prompted the *Swindon Advertiser* for 4 May
1917 to announce in its obituary notice: 'No man
has in more capable language painted the beauties of the environs of our town'.

Throughout his life Edward Thomas continued to visit Wiltshire. He matured into a tall

Helen Thomas

handsome man and while at Oxford he married
Helen Noble, a daughter of the literary critic
James Ashcroft Noble, who had encouraged him
in his early aspirations to become a writer and
had helped him place his first book *The Woodland Life* (1897) which was to a great extent
based upon his Wiltshire experiences.

Hodson Cottage

One of the Wiltshire places most associated with
Edward Thomas is the gamekeeper's cottage at
Hodson in Burderop Woods a few miles south
of Swindon, the only cottage to the west of the
road through this tiny hamlet. This association
arises from Helen Thomas's description in *As It
Was* (1926) of her 'tiny honeymoon' with Edward
at 'a little place he knew very well among the
Downs just outside S – – ', and her statement
that they 'put up at the home of his old gamekeeper friend'. Helen's description is undoubtedly
of Hodson Cottage, but it is unlikely that 'Dad'
Uzzell ever lived at Hodson. My researches over
many years have found no evidence that he was
ever the gamekeeper at Hodson, and much evidence to the contrary.

Helen and Edward Thomas would have
known and visited this cottage in 1909 when
Edward was researching Richard Jefferies and

Helen stayed with him nearby at Broome Manor Farm in Broome Manor Lane. Edward would also have known Hodson Cottage earlier when staying as a boy at Swindon, for it had been the home of the keeper who inspired Richard Jefferies to write *The Gamekeeper at Home*.

Despite the old expression 'poacher turned gamekeeper' it seems unlikely that David Uzzell would have became the Burderop keeper and the Swindon directories list other keepers at Hodson at this time. They also suggest that David Uzzell always lived in Swindon, and Edward's descriptions of their friendship also positively place him in New Swindon ('At that time he lived with his wife under the roof of a son who was in the [Swindon railway] factory'). Edward and Helen's daughter Myfanwy has also informed me that when she visited Hodson cottage after her mother's death in 1967 she closely examined the gamekeeper's book (now apparently lost) and it contained no mention of David Uzzell. Two decisive facts are contained in a letter dated 22 May 1898 from Edward Thomas to 'Dad' with which he enclosed an order for two shillings and explained: 'You must change the order at the post office in new town' [New Swindon], and in the wedding certificate of Uzzell's daughter dated 1899 about the time that Edward and Helen stayed at Hodson. On that certificate David Uzzell gave his address as 6 John St. Terrace at New Swindon, an address which was significantly very near the Salvation Army citadel in Fleet Street, and was also the address at which he died in 1919.

Helen Thomas was a great romantic and she never claimed to be writing accurate biography. She wrote *As It Was* and *World Without End* with

Hodson Cottage, near Chiseldon, where Helen claimed to have spent her honeymoon with Edward Thomas

no thought of publication, as a therapeutic exercise some time after the death of her husband. She would therefore be entitled to romanticise her honeymoon by translating it from urban Swindon, where 'Dad' lived, to Hodson Cottage. My own opinion is that they probably stayed at the cottage and that Helen accidentally or intentionally blended two persons, the gamekeeper at the time – a man called John Staniforth (*North Wilts Directory*) – and 'Dad' Uzzell, into a single person. It should also be remembered that Helen was writing at a time when she was still in shock over her husband's death and almost thirty years after the event which she was describing, long enough for her to admit: 'I do not remember the hamlet to which our cottage belonged'. Whatever the facts of this matter, Hodson Cottage is now one of places most closely associated with Edward Thomas in Wiltshire.

Thomas resolves to become a writer

Upon leaving Oxford in 1901 with a disappointing second in history Thomas ignored the strong opposition of his father who wished him to take a steady job in the Civil Service. He decided to become a writer and live in the countryside, and the consequence of this decision was that Edward Thomas found himself between 1901 and 1914 on a treadmill writing an endless succession of prose works – topographical books, biographies, books of literary criticism, and innumerable reviews – in an endless endeavour to earn a moderate living for his family. He once suggested in a letter to 'Dad' Uzzell that if they ever decided to list his books on his gravestone he would need a stone as large as one of those at Stonehenge.

Thomas acknowledged that he was not an imaginative writer, that he lacked the ability to imagine a plot, create characters, and construct a novel. An early attempt at novel-writing failed and he also freely admitted his inability to write 'long things'. In his one unconventional novel *The Happy-Go-Lucky Morgans*, although the book is immensely successful in creating the atmosphere of suburban London in the late–19th century, most of the characters are to a large extent autobiographical. Thomas's strength as a writer lay in his ability evocatively to re-create events and places that he had known, often long after the experience. For most of his life this was achieved in an often beautiful but sometimes over-elaborate prose, and ultimately in about a hundred and forty consistently fine poems which were the fruits of his long apprenticeship in prose and were written during the last three years of his life. In 1923 Aldous Huxley described how Thomas had : 'devised a curiously bare and candid verse to express with all possible simplicity and clarity his clear sensations and emotions', and described his verse as containing: 'quiet happiness shot with melancholy'.

An example of his ability to depict a landscape in a few words of prose appears in Chapter 11 of *The Heart of England*, (1906):

> Yonder the road curves languidly between hedges and broad fringes of green, and along it an old man guides the cattle in to afternoon milking. They linger to crop the wayside grass and he waits, but suddenly resumes his walk and they obey, now hastening with tight udders and looking from side to side. They turn under the archway of a ruined abbey, and low as if they enjoy the reverberation, and disappear. I never see them again; but the ease, the remoteness, and the colour of the red cattle in the green road, the slowness of the old cowman, the timelessness of that gradual movement under the fourteenth century arch, never vanish.

Thomas's temperament

The often-discussed melancholic temperament of Edward Thomas has usually been attributed to his Celtic ancestry. The fundamental problem around which his entire life revolved was the fact that, having married and assumed family responsibilities when very young, his chosen occupation as a freelance writer was compromised when he had to take on uncongenial commissioned work and reviewing in order to support his family. This left him little time to indulge in the creative work that he longed to write, he grew to resent this, and probably gradually came to the unpalatable conclusion that his father had probably been right in opposing his decision to commit himself to a full-time writing career. These circumstances caused him to lose his self-respect and refer to himself as a 'doomed hack' and as a 'writing animal'.

Although writing to order constantly interfered with his wish to satisfy his creative ambition of writing essays and books on subjects of his own choice, Thomas was occasionally commissioned to write books on congenial subjects, such as his *Richard Jefferies*. He particularly disliked writing his so-called 'colour' books – *Oxford*, *Beautiful Wales*, *The Isle of Wight* and *Windsor Castle* – in which the text provided a mere accompaniment to the coloured plates and the writers names were subordinated to the names of the illustrators.

Despite his father's 'remarkable skill for public speaking' mentioned in his obituary, Edward Thomas was an extremely reticent man who dreaded addressing an audience, although he was a brilliant conversationalist in small gatherings of his friends. A number of those friends have testified that Thomas was essentially humorous and have insisted that he was seldom melancholy in their company. It seems that his demon of melancholy overcame him when he was working in isolation and to order on uncongenial subjects, while longing for the opportunity to write more creative work.

Helen and Edward's three children were all given Welsh names. The first was Merfyn (born 1900) whose interest in mechanical things was utterly alien to the interests of his father, then came Bronwen (born 1902) who was very close to her father, and Myfanwy (born 1910) who was very similar in temperament and appearance to her mother Helen. Their father struggled endlessly to support his young family on the proceeds from commissioned writing, his consolation being that his writing provided him with ample opportunities to wander in Wiltshire and the rest of southern England obtaining material for his books. As an adult he became familiar with the landscapes of the whole of Wiltshire about which he wrote, at first in prose but later in poetry, with a sensitivity that has been achieved by few writers.

Being thoroughly Welsh on both sides of his family and brought up in London, there is little doubt that Thomas initially felt a little ill at ease when writing about English countryside. It is noticeable that he tended to associate with writers such as Hilaire Belloc, Joseph Conrad, and Robert Frost, all of whom were at least partly alien to England, and he was very fond of the Argentinian-born W. H. Hudson. It is probable that Thomas was justifying his own position when he came to the conclusion that Belloc's alienness gave him: 'a special sense of England, heightened, perhaps, beyond what is in other Englishmen by his birth in France'. Of William Morris who was born in the London suburbs and lived in London he wrote: 'For most of his life he was a somewhat dismayed countryman, but an imperfect Londoner', and then speculated that Morris was (like himself?): 'probably one of those survivors who cannot accept the distinction and division between town and country which has been sharpening . . . '.

For a short time after their marriage Edward and Helen lived at a number of dingy homes in London and then decided on the country at any price, and moved to Kent where they had a succession of homes, all of them rented, for Edward Thomas never owned a house. During this period from 1901 to 1906 opportunities for Edward Thomas to visit Wiltshire were few, although he occasionally visited Wiltshire friends, one of these being John H. Morgan (1876–1955), a journalist and lawyer from Wootton Bassett who later defended Roger Casement and became Professor of Constitutional Law at London University. Morgan befriended Alfred Williams in his struggles and after the Second World War took part in the Nuremberg trials.

From 1906 Thomas's great confidant in personal and literary matters was the north-country poet and verse dramatist Gordon Bottomley (1874-1948), who visited Wiltshire for the first time in 1948. He stayed at the thatched house then

Edward Thomas drawn in his walking clothes by Robin Guthrie

known as Martinscote on the north side of Chapel Lane at Oare, under the looming Giant's Grave promontory of Martinsell Hill. He would probably have recalled that Martinsell was one of the favourite hills of Edward Thomas, whom he had last seen when he was on embarkation leave in 1916. There at Oare under Martinsell Hill Bottomley suddenly died. The house in which he died is also associated with the composer Vaughan Williams, who had stayed there in 1924 when composing his suite *Flos Campi* ('Flower of the Field') based on the *Song of Solomon*.

In 1906 Thomas moved his family to Steep, near Petersfield in Hampshire, to enable his children to attend the progressive Bedales School. In this area they lived in three successive homes while their children were educated. From his Hampshire homes access to Wiltshire was easier and from Steep he travelled frequently over southern England, at first tramping on foot, for he was an extremely strong walker, and after about 1910 riding a bicycle which enabled him to travel more rapidly and cover greater distances.

If in writing of his early associations with the Swindon district I have given the impression that Edward Thomas knew only the north of Wiltshire, this was by no means the case. As a boy Edward had identified strongly with Wales and the Swindon area where his father had lived and he wandered with David Uzzell, but as an adult he took every opportunity to get to know the other parts of the county. After his move in 1906 from Kent to Hampshire he often walked over all parts of Wiltshire and in its countryside where he found great solace from walking and escaping from the stress and drudgery of being a 'doomed hack' writing commissioned work in order to support his family. By the time he was thirty-one Thomas was sufficiently familiar with all of Wiltshire to be asked to write a guide to the county. In December 1909 he mentioned in a letter : 'In fact I have consented to do a guide – pure guide – to Wiltshire, but it is not settled & I shall cry off if I possibly can'. Evidently not enthusuiastic about doing a 'pure guide' he did 'cry off' and Wiltshire lost what might have been a superb guide to the county.

Visits to Stephen Reynolds at Devizes

From 1907 Edward Thomas was often in Wilt-shire researching *Richard Jefferies, His Life and Work* (1909) and *The South Country* (1909). On two of these visits he stayed at Devizes with the Wiltshire writer Stephen Reynolds (1881–1919) and explored the countryside of mid-Wiltshire.

Reynolds – who has been described as 'the lost voice of Edwardian literature' – was born in Devizes in a brick-built cottage, 63 New Park Street. In the 1890s he studied at Devizes College, now a stationer's shop at the north end of the Market Place. He became a good musician and in 1899–1902 studied chemistry at Owens College at Manchester, then went to Paris (1902–3) and returned to live intermittently at Devizes, having resolved to go against the wishes of his father and become a writer. In 1906 he wrote in three weeks for ten guineas a controversial town guide *Devizes and Roundabout*.

Reynolds then attempted to live by writing while lodging at Sidmouth in Devon at the home of a fisherman called Bob Woolley. Having written his first book, *The Holy Mountain* (published 1909) 'at a little window overlooking the wide western edge of Salisbury Plain', apparently near Warminster, Reynolds achieved a notable success with *A Poor Man's House* (1908), based upon the lives of the fisherman's family. In 1908 he was asked by Nelson to write a guide to Wiltshire but rejected it because the research would take him away from Sidmouth. Now well-known in literary circles Reynolds lived for a time in London, but disillusioned with the lack of recognition of his later books he turned to politics and administration, and at the outbreak of war in 1914 became Resident Inspector of Fisheries for the South-Western Area. He was contemplating becoming the Socialist candidate for St Ives when in February 1919 he was taken ill in the great post-war influenza epidemic when driving to London for a meeting. He reached London despite deep snow but became so unwell that he rushed back to Devon by train where he died and was buried. Hilaire Belloc described him as: 'that strongest-souled and most sincere of men, who desired and did good all his life'.

When Edward Thomas first met Stephen Reynolds on 12 March 1907 at a literary gather-ing at the Mont Blanc restaurant in London the two men found that they had much in common. Both were struggling to establish literary reputations, were keen walkers, and were at odds with their fathers. Reynolds invited Thomas to visit him at Devizes. The Reynolds family homes had been 11 and 12 Maryport Street 1800–87, the *Bear Hotel* where his father had been the landlord 1887–93, and Beech Cottage in the Castle Grounds 1893–9, but from 1905 to 1908 Stephen lodged in a furnished bed-sitting room at the front of the now-modernised 2 Stanley Terrace in Pans Lane at Devizes. A haven to which Stephen Reynolds often took his literary visitors was his Aunt Jane's home, the villa called Prospect Rise at Rowde near Devizes.

It was to Pans Lane that Thomas came to visit Reynolds for a walking weekend on 18 March 1907. That day they set off on Reynolds's favourite fifteen mile walk, west to east over Tan Hill, down to All Cannings, through Coate and west along the track (the Broadway) to Devizes Green. The next day they covered thirty miles, from Devizes through Marlborough and Savernake Forest and back, and Thomas wrote in his notebook: 'Reynolds good company'. On their last day they strolled through Urchfont, the Ridgeway, and Easterton.

In April 1907 Reynolds spent a few days (25-29 April) staying with Edward and Helen Thomas at their home at Berryfield Cottage near Petersfield in Hampshire and explored Thomas's home district. A few months later, in December 1907, the two men travelled to Devizes by train from Paddington for a third walking weekend together. On the Saturday they again walked through Coate and Horton to Tan Hill and back through All Cannings and Coate, and on the Sunday morning they took a shorter walk through meadows to Drew's Pond and Potterne. Thomas departed on foot on the Monday morning by way of Marlborough and Savernake Forest.

The following year (1908) Reynolds finally broke with his father, went to lodge with the Woolley family and seldom visited Devizes. With Reynolds now in remote Devon his short-lived friendship with Edward Thomas waned and was never renewed; although when he was invited, with others including Alfred Williams, to speak in June 1911 at a Workers Educational Association meeting in honour of Richard Jefferies at Coate Farm , Swindon, Edward Thomas, who dreaded public speaking, persuaded Stephen Reynolds to deputise for him, and Reynolds opened his address:

> I ought to acknowledge at once that I am here as a substitute for one who would have discharged the duty much better than I can. I refer to Edward Thomas, the last and most exhaustive biographer of Richard Jefferies.

Richard Jefferies and The South Country

Richard Jefferies, His Life and Work, which had necessitated long stays and much research in the Jefferies country around Swindon, was published in 1909. In his first chapter headed 'The Countryside of Richard Jefferies' Thomas, after describing the area as: 'a beautiful, a quiet, an unrenowned, and a most visibly ancient land', sometimes became lyrical about his favourite places such as Shipley Bottom which lies east of Sugar Hill:

> . . . then through Shipley Bottom, where stand a barn and stacks under ash and sycamore and elder, in the midst of corn, and walled on every side by down and sky. There the painted lady butterfly comes to the scabious flower and the bee to the sweet basil in perfect solitude.

Shipley Bottom west of Sugar Hill, a favourite place of Edward Thomas

The Jefferies book, which has been described as : 'a classic in literary biography . . . containing better literary criticism than many critical works', was immediately followed by *The South Country* (1910), containing many descriptions of generally unidentified Wiltshire landscapes. The breadth of knowledge which he had assimilated by 1910 about Wiltshire is revealed by Thomas early in this book in which he lists the Wiltshire rivers he 'remembers best' as: 'the Kennet, the Ray, the Winterbournes, the Wiltshire Avon, the Wylye, [and] the Ebble'. Later when listing his favourite place-names the Wiltshire ones included the Bassetts, the Winterbournes, the Deverills, the Manningfords, the Lydiards, Clevancy, Amesbury, Melksham and Draycot.

Arthur Ransome at East Hatch

In the winter of 1910 Edward Thomas visited his writer friend Arthur Ransome (1884–1967) then staying at Peake's Farm on the Dorset boundary west of Semley in south-west Wiltshire. Thomas first met Ransome in 1904 and formed a rather strained relationship with him, envying him his early successes while he remained largely dependent upon reviewing. Ransome was now searching for a house in Wiltshire and Edward helped him to find Manor Farm at East Hatch near Tisbury. At this time Ransome was a successful essayist and journalist. He had experienced an unhappy childhood and his father died when Arthur was thirteen, convinced that his son would be a failure. His children's books were an attempt by Ransome to create for himself a happy childhood such as he had never enjoyed. I have also heard it suggested that Ransome used to stay at a farm at Seend, between Seend and Sells Green, which if correct would explain his mention in his autobiography of 'Warminster and the country I knew and liked about Devizes'.

From 1911 Ransome rented East Hatch Farm, the stone-mullioned farm at the road junction at East Hatch, and there settled down with his flamboyant wife Ivy and their daughter Tabitha, but their marriage was troubled. In 1913 Ransome finally left his family at East Hatch, went to Russia as a correspondent, and there stayed for some years with occasional visits to East Hatch. He finally divorced Ivy in 1924 and married Trotsky's secretary Evgenia Shelepina.

The Icknield Way and breakdown

During 1911–12 Edward Thomas was again in Wiltshire researching his book on *The Icknield*

Way (1916), the ancient traffic route which runs south-west from Norfolk into north Wiltshire. This book, which has generally been harshly castigated by critics, contains many descriptions of Wiltshire, particularly in its fine introductory chapter 'On Roads and Footpaths' and its final chapter, in which Thomas reaches Wiltshire having followed the Icknield Way all the way from Norfolk. As he neared Wiltshire the sombre mood of the book lightened, perhaps because Swindon held happy memories of childhood holidays and there his old friend 'Dad' Uzzell still lived. At Chiseldon and Coate he was turned away and had to walk 'four unexpected miles' to Swindon for a bed.

The Icknield Way reflected the low psychological state which Thomas had reached, and later in 1911 he suffered a serious nervous breakdown. For a time he contemplated suicide, as described in his essay 'The Attempt' in *Light and Twilight* (1911) and confirmed by his wife in her account of their lives. At this time of crisis he frequently stayed away from his family for their mutual benefit and according to Robert Frost's biographer Lawrance Thompson: 'in the spring of 1913 he became obsessed with the notion that he should divorce his wife'. He was rescued by a group of new and stimulating friends met at Broughton Gifford in Wiltshire, and by an important new friendship with the American poet Robert Frost (1874–1963).

Thomas stays at Broughton Gifford

In 1911 Edward Thomas became friendly with the writer Clifford Bax (1886–1962), then living at the fine Jacobean manor house at Broughton Gifford near Melksham which he had taken in the spring of 1911. This house, which stands towards the south end of the village at the bend in the road, had been renovated by an architect called Schmidt who died as soon as the work was completed. Clifford Bax was a writer with private means, a brother of Sir Arnold Bax the composer. They were the well-to-do sons of Ernest Belfort Bax (1854–1926), a founder of English socialism, and with William Morris of the Socialist League. Clifford was a cultured man who trained as a painter and had a compulsive interest in literature and the stage.

Bax first met Edward Thomas in 1911 and often invited him to stay at his manor house at Broughton Gifford. There Thomas enjoyed the stimulating company and conversation of Bax's circle of literary and artistic friends and made new friends in the writers Herbert Farjeon (1887–1945) and his sister Eleanor Farjeon (1881–1965). Clifford Bax recalled his friendship with Edward Thomas in *Inland Far* (1925) and *Some I Knew Well* (1958).

At Broughton Gifford Thomas joined Bax's 'Old Broughtonian' literary cricket team, which every August played matches against local teams in west Wiltshire, at Corsham, Box, Lacock, Bradford on Avon and Trowbridge. At first he was merely the team's scorer but in 1912 he was persuaded to play. The sporting columns of the *Wiltshire Times* reveal that he was an indifferent cricketer. He batted at number eleven, never seems to have bowled, and was generally 'hidden away' in the field. He once signed a letter to Bax as 'Third Man'.

Broughton Gifford Manor where Thomas often visited Clifford Bax

Clifford Bax describes in *Inland Far* how on one occasion: 'Thomas and I set out for a stroll, and, following a grass-track that meandered through buttercup meadows and under a series of stiles, came at length to an unfrequented stretch of the River Avon'. He later mentions how: 'It was pleasant to walk through the fields to the river . . . to a fifteenth century bridge of stone'. This walk was south from Broughton Gifford manor house across the fields east of the church to the packhorse bridge between Monkton House and Whaddon. There Thomas sometimes fished

Packhorse bridge over the Avon where Thomas bathed and fished when at Broughton Gifford

and bathed, and also tried his hand at water-divining at one of Bax's riverside picnics.

In 1912 Thomas, 'thinking that he could not stay any longer at the Manor House' (Bax), took for three months the top rooms of Dillybrook Farm near Southwick and there recovered from a nervous breakdown while writing a severely critical book on Swinburne! During this stay at Dillybrook Thomas discovered one of his favourite places in Wiltshire, the remote village of Tellisford below Dillybrook Farm in the steep-sided valley of the River Frome, which he described in such loving detail in his 'book of the journey', *In Pursuit of Spring*.

In Pursuit of Spring

Edward Thomas was always fascinated by the subtle way in which spring gradually emerges out of winter. *In Pursuit of Spring* describes a single long cycle ride undertaken in early 1913 from London to the Quantock Hills, although in fact it was researched in a number of cycle rides. *In Pursuit of Spring* is a fine book written by an experienced prose writer on the verge of becoming a poet, and it includes several prose passages that were later rewritten by Edward Thomas as poetry. In his first chapter headed 'In Search of Spring' Thomas, while deliberating at home in Hampshire about the route he should follow, demonstrates his considerable knowledge of Wiltshire:

> That evening, without thought of Spring, I began to look at my maps . . . Whatever I did, Salisbury Plain was to be crossed, not of necessity but of choice; it was, however, hard to decide whether to go reasonably diagonally in accordance with my western purpose, or to meander up the Avon, now on one side now on the other, by one of the parallel riverside roads, as far as Amesbury. Having got to

Amesbury, there would be much provocation to continue up the river among those thatched villages to Upavon and to Stephen Duck's village, Charlton, and the Pewsey valley, and so, turning again westward, in sight of that very tame White Horse above Alton Priors, to include Urchfont and Devizes.

> Or again, I might follow up the Wylye westward from Salisbury, and have always below me the river and its hamlets and churches, the wall of the Plain always above me on the right. Thus I should come to Warminster and to the grand west wall of the Plain which overhangs the town.

> The obvious way was to strike north-west over the Plain from Stapleford up the Winterbourne, through cornland and sheepland, by Shrewton and Tilshead, and down again to other waters at West Lavington. Or at Shrewton I could turn sharp to the west, and so visit solitary Chitterne and solitary Imber.

> I could not decide.

This passage, with its 'I could not decide', demonstrates Thomas's usual indecision when confronted with alternative routes. After some hesitation he would choose one way, but his enjoyment would be marred by anxiety over what he had missed on the other one. He finally decided on the last of these options, except that he avoided Chitterne and Imber. Having written: 'Above all, I wanted to ride along under Dean Hill, the level-ridged chalk hill dotted with yew', he entered Wiltshire at East Dean east of Salisbury and continued through Salisbury, Shrewton, Tilshead, West Lavington, Erlestoke, Edington, North Bradley and Southwick, to Tellisford. As I write I have in my hands Edward Thomas's own copy of the Sheet 299: Winchester 1904 map which he used on this journey.

Dillybrook Farm and Tellisford village below it in the valley of the River Frome are places particularly associated with Edward Thomas because of the affection he revealed for them when writing *In Pursuit of Spring*. He describes Tellisford as:

> a hamlet scattered along half a mile of by-road, from a church at the corner down to the Frome. Once there was a ford, but now you cross by a stone footbridge with white wooden handrails. A ruined flock-mill and a ruined ancient house stand next to

it on one side ; on the other the only house is a farm [Vaggs Hill Farm] with a round tower embodied in its front. Away from the farm a beautiful meadow slopes between the river and the woods above.

He mentions having run in the sun in this meadow 'after bathing at the weir', and a service tree ('in that tree sang a thrush all through May'), two nostalgic memories recalled from his stay at Dillybrook the previous year.

Tellisford is very little changed since Thomas was here, and his service tree may still be seen beside a farm gate at the top of the hill between Dillybrook and Tellisford. There is a tradition that W. G. Grace (1848–1915) used to visit Vaggs Hill Farm when fishing on the Frome, and he could have been here at the same time as Edward Thomas in 1913. Thomas then reluctantly left Wiltshire, crossing the footbridge and carrying his bicycle up the steep flight of stone steps, 'between walls that were lovely with humid moneywort' (they still are), which took him away from Wiltshire into Somerset.

Tellisford packhorse bridge

In describing his journey *In Pursuit of Spring* Thomas gives us an interesting account of Wiltshire in the years just prior to the Great War. Fearing that if he named his places his books might be regarded as mere guide books he had previously been reluctant to be precise about his locations, but by this time he was fulfilling his publisher's demands to be more exact about his places and *In Pursuit of Spring* contains much precise topographical material. Some of the incidents are memorable, for example at Edington where some children derisively called 'Longlegs' after Thomas as he cycled away. A little later Thomas related the incident to his friend Walter de la Mare (1873–

1956) when he visited him at Dillybrook and they were sitting beside the weir at Tellisford. De la Mare remembered this and made it the basis of his poem 'Longlegs' in his *Peacock Pie* (1913) with its : 'Longlegs – he yelled 'Coo-ee'.

In Pursuit of Spring contains some of Edward Thomas's finest prose. Upon reading it Robert Frost suggested that it contained poetry expressed as prose and pointed out paragraphs that would make excellent poetry if written in verse in exactly the same cadence.

The Great War and the poetry

Edward Thomas was at Swindon in August 1914 bicycling to meet Robert Frost in Herefordshire, when he heard the hooter at the railway factory hoot ten times to announce the war that was to turn him into a poet and take his life. With the outbreak of the Great War the commissioned work by which he supported his family was drastically reduced and, lacking paid work, Thomas began to indulge in writing poetry. Between December 1914 and December 1917, the month before he embarked to France, he wrote a hundred and forty four poems of outstanding quality upon which his reputation as a writer now stands.

One of the most interesting aspects of Edward Thomas's poetry is the fact that he often drew his subjects from his many notebooks and his prose, and occasionally from the prose of other writers. Many of his poems were based on passages from *In Pursuit of Spring*, an example being an incident which took place near Trowbridge, between North Bradley and Southwick, which he reworked into his fine early poem 'March'. The prose passage reads:

> I went down this road, past farms called Ireland and Scotland on the left . . . Venus, spiky with beams, hung in the pale sky, and Orion stood up before me, above the blue woods of the horizon. All the thrushes of England sang at that hour, and against that background of myriads I heard two or three singing their frank, clear notes in a mad eagerness to have all done before dark; for already the blackbirds were chinking and shifting places along the hedgerows.

A little over a year later Thomas used this passage as the basis for 'March', his third poem written on 5 December 1914. The poem starts

'Now I know that Spring will come again', a reference to the theme of *In Pursuit of Spring*, and continues:

> What did the thrushes know? Rain, snow, sleet, hail,
> Had kept them quiet as primroses.
> They had but an hour to sing. On boughs they sang,
> On gates, on ground ; they sang while they changed
>   perches
> And while they fought, if they remembered to fight:
> So earnest were they to pack into that hour
> Their unwilling hoard of song before the moon
> Grew brighter than the clouds . . .

The 'unwilling hoard of song' was the poetry that had lain dormant in Edward Thomas until the outbreak of war provided the excuse to write his verse. It is often peopled by elderly country characters of the 'Dad' Uzzell type encountered in his many years of wandering in southern England. Birds, too, often feature in his poetry, a fact which prompted the eminent ornithologist James Fisher to describe Thomas as a 'near genius', in his view 'the major English bird poet of our century', and to suggest that he: 'understood birds as symbols of rural history and continuity more deeply than any other poet I know of'.

At first Edward Thomas's poetry was generally written in his study on the hill above his home at Steep in Hampshire, but after he joined the army in July 1915 it was often hurriedly written in adverse circumstances, on trains travelling to and from camp, or in crowded barrack rooms. Sometimes he wrote verse disguising it as prose with capitals to indicate the lines in order that his fellow soldiers should not be aware that he was writing poetry.

Thomas volunteers for the army

At the outbreak of the Great War Thomas anguished long over whether he should volunteer for the army. As a family man of thity-six there was no compulsion, and the need for a decision was deferred when he badly sprained an ankle in January 1915. By July he was fully recovered and he then suddenly volunteered for the army and was enlisted into the Artists' Rifles. The impulse which led to this sudden decision has never been conclusively explained. It is possible that he finally decided as a result of writing an obituary

for his young friend Rupert Brooke (1887–1915), although his financial position had become precarious from lack of work and the decision to enlist may have come about from a combination of both. There is in fact evidence from his letters that his decision was prompted by his dire need for regular earnings, and when asked by his friend Eleanor Farjeon why he had volunteered he replied: 'To get a pension for Helen'.

Edward Thomas's soldiering led to a renewal of his contacts with Wiltshire. After undergoing basic training at several camps in London and Essex, and becoming an instructor in the map-reading that he had practised from childhood, he volunteered for officer training in the Royal Garrison Artillery.

Trowbridge Barracks

For his officer training Thomas was sent for several weeks in October–November 1916 to Wiltshire as an officer cadet at the former Trowbridge Barracks, which was situated on land now occupied by commercial premises and a garage at the junction of the A361 Frome Road and the A363 Bradley Road. Here Thomas, after living under canvas at the rear of the barracks – where today we find a road poignantly called Arras Close (he was killed at Arras) – was gazetted as a second lieutenant in November 1916. From Trowbridge he mentions in letters, some written from Tabernacle Men's Institute: 'This is country I know & have seen something of it'. He described the countryside as having:

> two good little rivers, one in a shallow level valley [the Biss near Southwick], the other in a steepsided narrow one [the Frome at Tellisford]. There is a castle [Farleigh], and many fine old houses near, and Salisbury Plain just too far off for our short afternoons, but its old White Horse plainly visible all day.

He introduced the White Horse into his poem 'The Child in the Orchard' as : 'Westbury White Horse, Over there on Salisbury Plain's green wall'.

Codford Camp

It is remarkable how events beyond his control continued to bring Edward Thomas to Wiltshire. After leaving Trowbridge Barracks in November

1916 he was in January 1917 posted to embarkation camp, Camp 15 at Codford situated on the north-west side of New Road at Codford St Peter. There the guardroom hut where he was orderly officer survived, used as a farm called Mayflower Farm, until 1995 when it was destroyed to make room for a modern house. His

Guardroom of Camp 15 at Codford (now destroyed) where Edward Thomas was orderly officer in January 1917

War Diary reveals that at Codford from 15-30 January 1917 Thomas enjoyed some long walks, including visits to the village pubs at Chitterne and Chilmark, and long route marches in and around the Wylye Valley He walked to Netherhampton along the south edge of Grovely Woods to visit the Newbolts at Netherhampton (see Chapter 15, page 229), and on the way noted: 'Beautiful Downs, with one or two isolated thatched barns, ivied ash trees, and derelict threshing machine. Old milestones lichened as with battered gold and silver nails.'

At the end of January 1917 he embarked with his unit to France, and on Easter Monday 9 April 1917, he was killed by shell blast at his forward observation post near Arras.

Helen Thomas lives near Chippenham
From Codford in January 1917 Edward wrote to his wife: 'Some day I hope we shall live in Wiltshire' and after his death Edward's widow Helen, who survived her husband by exactly fifty years and three days, went to live in Wiltshire. In her widowhood she had first lived at a number of places and after becoming a successful writer in the early 1930s she decided that she wanted to live in the country again. With the help of two young artist friends, Robin Tanner (see Chapter 17) and Cyril Rice from near Chippenham, she found accommodation at a stone-built and stone-

tiled farmhouse between Biddestone and Chippenham, which the farmer Harold Tucker and his wife Adeline agreed to share with her. And so in 1932 Helen Thomas moved into Starveall Farm which she called Starwell, and there in her husband's favourite county she lived a full and contented country life for twenty years until 1954, when she moved to Eastbury in Berkshire to be near her daughters Bronwen and Myfanwy. There she died and was buried at the top of the churchyard in April 1967.

Edward Thomas and his countryside
The unbalanced nature of Edward Thomas's literary life is emphasised when it is realised that he spent fourteen years from leaving university in 1900 to the outbreak of the Great War in 1914 writing prose, often of an impermanent nature in reviews now buried in the files of newspapers, and merely two years from December 1914 to December 1916 writing the verse upon which his reputation as a writer is now founded.

Edward Thomas died having achieved little general recognition. Walter de la Mare lamented: 'how comparatively unheeded in any public sense was his coming and going', and Clifford Bax recorded (in *Inland Far*: 1925) a casual meeting with Thomas in Shaftesbury Avenue a few weeks before he went to the front, at which Edward confided to him: 'It's too late for me now to hope – as a writer. I'm nearly forty, and its clear that I've missed the mark.'

Thomas would never have dreamed that, largely as a result of the exertions of his wife Helen and his daughter Myfanwy, several memorials would be raised to him by public subscription. Such general acclaim would have meant little to him. In one of his last letters to his American friend Robert Frost he indicated that the thing that meant most to him was his reputation as a poet. He would have welcomed his posthumous reputation as a prose writer of rare quality, but the recognition that he would have cherished most is his now-assured reputation as a poet, as one of the major poets in English of the twentieth century, in the tradition of Chaucer, Shakespeare, Clare, Barnes and Hardy. By inserting 'Haymaking' and 'The Manor Farm' under a pseudonym into his anthology *This England: An Anthology of Her Writers* (1915) Thomas had placed himself in the succession of these writers who celebrated in verse the landscape of England, and in his fine essay 'The Stile' from *Light and Twilight* (1911) he wrote:

> And in that company I had learned that I am something which no fortunes can touch, whether I be soon to die or long years away. Things will happen which will trample and pierce, but I shall go on, something that is here and there like the wind, something unconquerable, something not to be separated from the dark earth and the light sky, a strong citizen of infinity and eternity. The confidence and ease had become a deep joy ; I knew that I could not do without the Infinite, nor the Infinite without me.

In his deep concern for the future of the English countryside Edward Thomas was sometimes prophetic, as when he wrote as early as 1909 in *The South Country*:

> The landscape retains the most permanent marks of the past, and a wise examination of it should evoke the beginnings of the majestic sentiment of our oneness with the future and the past, just as natural history should help to give the child a sense of oneness with all forms of life. To put it at its lowest, some such cycle of knowledge is needed if a generation that insists more and more on living in the country, or spending many weeks there, is not to be bored or to be compelled to entrench itself behind the imported amusements of the town.

Many people find themselves drawn to places with known associations with people of the past which adds another dimension to their enjoyment of landscape. This attraction provides the subject of this book and many writers, including Thomas, have attempted to explain the fascination that such places provide for them. In describing the Wiltshire countryside of Richard Jefferies in *A Literary Pilgrim in England* he wrote: 'To go over this country now with physical footsteps is an act of pure piety' (see also the quotation from Thomas in my Introduction, page vii).

A number of writers have sensed the spirit of Edward Thomas surviving in the countryside. Thomas wrote in a letter to his friend Duncan

Williams: 'I was born to be a ghost', and as early as the 1920s Henry Newbolt said perceptively of him: 'he did not so much inhabit England as haunt it'. In the introduction to his 1948 collection of Edward Thomas's prose Roland Gant wrote: 'for me, and for many others, his spirit is as living as the countryside of which he wrote', and Elizabeth Jennings in 1977 wrote a poem ('I have looked about for you many times') in which she expressed her feelings of the presence of Edward Thomas at his special places in the countryside. In a radio broadcast in December 2001 the poet-laureate Andrew Motion admitted to being 'haunted by Thomas', and having walked a great many of his walks and related them to his writings and his personality I too am aware of many places which I strongly associate with him, in Hampshire, Gloucestershire, and particularly in Wiltshire.

Lesley Norris noted how Thomas was: 'strikingly exact and evocative about his places' and for me his presence is still felt at many places in Wiltshire. Around Barbury Hill at the north edge of the Marlborough Downs the young Edward Thomas is easily imagined wandering with his elderly Wiltshire friend 'Dad' Uzzell. Thomas's spirit haunts both the Icknield Way, along which he wearily plodded his solitary way researching his book of that name, and the Ridgeway which

The way along the turnpike to Barbury Hill followed by the young Edward Thomas and 'Dad' Uzzell

he described as the 'best of all the downland ways'. In that area stands the gamekeeper's cottage in Hodson Bottom near Swindon which became, as the former home of the gamekeeper of Richard Jefferies's *The Gamekeeper at Home*, a kind of shrine to Edward Thomas. It is also associated with Edward Thomas as a result of

Helen's moving description of their 'tiny honeymoon' in *As It Was* – although this may have been a fiction (see earlier, pages 206-7). The Harrow Way as it climbs Kingsettle Hill out of Somerset into Wiltshire, its continuation over White Sheet Downs (where 'cows do not often see a pencil sharpened'), and 'under Grovely', where Edward and his son Merfyn watched hares playing follow-my-leader, invariably evoke for me recollections of Edward Thomas, as does Broughton Gifford 'of happy memory' where he enjoyed the stimulating company of Clifford Bax and his literary and musical friends.

Not far from Broughton Gifford is Dillybrook Farm near Southwick where Thomas stayed in the summer of 1912 recovering from a serious nervous breakdown, with below it the River Frome running through Tellisford where Thomas bathed at the weir, talked with de la Mare, who later wrote the foreword to the *Collected Poems of Edward Thomas*, and returned in 1913 when he was so obviously reluctant to tear himself away from Wiltshire to resume his journey westwards *In Pursuit of Spring*.

East Hatch Farm near Tisbury

Pewsey Vale provided the 'roll call of country names' for Edward's longest and favourite poem 'Lob'. But perhaps the two most evocative of his places in Wiltshire, far more than his grandmother's house at New Swindon which is now a Chinese reataurant, are the site of the Great War Camp 15 at New Road at Codford, and Manor Farmhouse at East Hatch near Tisbury, where Edward parted from his 'daughter the younger' Myfanwy on that bitter evening in January 1917 before he embarked for France. For readers of Edward Thomas such places have a particular poignancy.

The instinctive feelings for open landscapes of ancient man who lived most of his life in the open air remain with us still. One of the most effective ways of satisfying our need for the countryside is by visiting the landscapes associated with country writers such as Jefferies, Hudson, Hardy and Edward Thomas, who celebrated them in their writings. Anyone who sets off in pursuit of the places described by Thomas in his prose and poetry will be richly rewarded. They will find that although he died almost ninety years ago Thomas will introduce them to some of the finest and remotest parts of the English countryside. Walking over this land Edward Thomas found solace from the literary and domestic problems which plagued him throughout his adult life, and here we too may find relief from the petty pressures of modern living which tend to detach us from all natural things. This countryside Thomas described in *The Heart of England* as exercising:

> a soft compulsion upon the passer by, a compulsion to meditation . . . And yet it is a land that gives much. Companiable it is, reassuring to the solitary ; he soon has a feeling of ease and seclusion here.

From childhood Edward Thomas shared the feelings for the English countryside expressed by Richard Jefferies at the end of *The Amateur Poacher*:

> Let us get out of these indoor narrow modern days, whose twelve hours somehow have become shortened, into the sunlight and the pure wind. A something that the ancients thought divine can be found and felt there still.

These words Edward Thomas as a London schoolboy copied into his exercise books and held to them throughout his life. In *The South Country* he described how some landscapes had a 'rich symbolical significance' for him, and of how 'Something in me belongs to these things'. Edward Thomas found his true home in the landscapes of southern England, and particularly in Wiltshire, of which he wrote in *The South Country*:

> Yet is this country, though I am mainly Welsh, a kind of home.

15 Poets of Empire

Newbolt at Netherhampton,
and Rudyard Kipling and Sir John Davies at Tisbury

A short distance west of Salisbury stands a house that was for many years the home of a poet who lived to see his patriotic poetry go entirely out of fashion. Standing on a loop of road north of the A3094, Netherhampton House is an old rambling house which in the late–17th or early–18th century was given a distinctive baroque facade of a character which prompted Pevsner to describe it as 'A most amazing facade'. Its two-storeyed centre is flanked by single-storeyed ends with parapets which sweep up to meet the central block. The centre bay contains a doorway with above it a semi-circular headed niche and above that a blind window recess. The façade is crowned by three large urns and its sash windows are set in segmental-headed openings.

Netherhampton House, the former home of Sir Henry Newbolt

The principal subject of this chapter is Sir Henry Newbolt (1862–1938), a writer whose poetry enjoyed immense popularity in the early part of the 20th century and during the Great War, which made his patriotic verse more popular than it might otherwise have become. Although not a Wiltshireman Newbolt chose to spend most of the latter part of his life, from 1907,

living at Netherhampton House. He grew to love his Wiltshire home and its surrounding countryside, to which he moved at the time when his writings had reached the summit of their popularity. He stayed to see his work go out of favour as the British Empire declined, but did not live to see its final collapse in popularity after the Second World War.

The British Empire
The standing of Newbolt's poetry coincided with the prosperity of the Empire. During the first half of his life the British were immensely proud of their Empire which was acknowledged in 1900 to be the greatest ever known. It covered a quarter of the world's land surface, had a population of four hundred million, and was so far flung that it was referred to as 'the Empire on which the sun never set'. The dispersed nature of the Empire and its support by the Royal Navy enabled Britain to dominate world trade, but warning cracks began to appear during Newbolt's life, and at the turn of the 19th century, when he was thirty-eight, the Boer War heralded its end.

The British Empire began in Elizabethan times, when England aspired to become more than a minor offshore European state by expanding her territories abroad. Elizabethan gentleman adventurers such as Sir Philip Sidney (Chapter 5) and Sir Walter Raleigh began to claim newly-discovered territories and exploit them in search of gold and fortunes. After he was ordered by the queen to draw up a chart (now in the Britsh Museum) of lands discovered by Englishmen, the queen's astrologer and geographer John Dee (1527–1608) originated the term 'British Empire'.

The attitude of exploitation persisted, until the abolition of slavery by parliament in 1807 initiated a change, and it was decided that Britain should in future be more benevolent and would civilise and evangelise its colonies rather than exploit them. This policy was maintained until late in Queen Victoria's reign when an undignified scramble for colonial wealth and possessions by some unscrupulous adventurers took place and led to war with the Boers.

As early as 1878 passionate national feeling had been aroused when a Russian proposal to annexe Constantinople prompted G. W. Hunt to write the music hall ditty which began:

> We dont want to fight, but, by Jingo if we do,
> We've got the ships, we've got the men, we've got the money too.

The Empress Jingo was a legendary ruler of Japan who was reputed to have invaded Korea about eighteen hundred years ago. The word 'jingo' survived throughout the 1890s, when immense national pride in Empire was encouraged by the 1897 Diamond Jubilee.

The public schools fostered the 'queen and country' Imperialistic ideal and the extremely popular *Boys' Own Paper*, founded in 1879 (significantly the year after the invention of the term jingoism), published extremely patriotic pieces and illustrations, a typical example being a picture captioned 'For School and Country' depicting a rugby player running with the ball, whose shadow was that of an infantryman with rifle and bayonet. That same year (1879), when Newbolt was seventeen and Kipling (see later, pages 229-31) was fourteen, a large well-armed British column was annihilated by poorly-armed Zulus at Isandhlwana, and the subsequent heroic but minor defence of Rorke's Drift was widely publicised to distract public attention from the Islandhlwana disaster. Six years later when General Gordon died at Khartoum prime minister Gladstone significantly resisted relieving him because he felt that the Empire had grown too large.

Another positive warning of the end of the Empire occurred in South Africa when Newbolt

Henry Newbolt

was thirty-three in December 1895. Frustrated by the obstruction caused by Kruger's Boer Transvaal republic to the expansion of British South Africa, Cecil Rhodes (1853–1902) instigated the ill-fated armed Jameson Raid into the Transvaal. This ended his political career and ultimately led to the Boer War, in which the British army was for a time humbled by the vastly outnumbered but well-armed Boer farmers. Britain ultimately won the war but Kipling's verdict was : 'We have had no end of a lesson : it will do us no end of good.' Although everyone read this warning few took any heed, and it was Kaiser Wilhelm's envy of the British Empire and the Royal Navy which supported it that was one of the major factors in bringing about the Great War in 1914.

The Newbolts move to Wiltshire

In London in 1902 the Newbolts became friendly with the well-known young portrait painter Charles Furse (1868–1904) and through him with the rest of the artistic Furse family. They often stayed with Charles Furse at his home in Surrey and after his early death they entered in 1907 into a joint tenancy of Netherhampton House with Charles Furse's father, the crippled sculptor Henry (J. H. M.) Furse, who executed a bronze bust of Henry Newbolt's wife Margaret. By 1915 Henry Furse had departed to live in Devon and the

Newbolts were left as the sole tenants of Netherhampton House.

Of his move from London to Netherhampton Newbolt wrote: 'On a chart of my life the course of the year 1907 would be marked as a very sharp turn', and:

> The house itself had fascinated me ever since I first saw it, a year before we came to live in it. At the first sight I remember that I was a little disappointed: it was so retiring, so successful, as I afterwards discovered, in hiding the bulk of itself behind one wing.

The move to Netherhampton was intended to be temporary, but the Newbolts so loved the house that they stayed on until 1934 when Newbolt was seventy-two. Of this long stay Newbolt wrote in his autobiography in 1932:

> Could anything give a better example of the dimness with which we see the road immediately ahead of us? We went to Netherhampton for a year; the experiment [sharing the house with Henry Furse] lasted for seven, and here we are still at Netherhampton after more than a quarter of a century. That was a very unexpected result; but it is even more surprising to realise now that in this temporary visit we have had our life and spent it.

Five years earlier in June 1927 Newbolt had written to his wife:

> Certainly we shall be haunted to the end of our days by the remembrance of our summers at Netherhampton – and the beauty of it, and the flow of friends, and the wild dream of the War, and the little church with its two memorials . . .

The 'two memorials' were the war memorial, and the memorial in Netherhampton Church to his parents, both of which have inscriptions written by Newbolt. His study at Netherhampton, which he called The Ark, was a room situated on an upper floor on the east side of the house, with a view towards Salisbury through a small oval window.

During his early career as a writer Newbolt was at the centre of literary activity in England, and while he lived at Netherhampton many celebrated literary figures visited the house including Walter de la Mare (1873–1956) and Virginia

Woolf (1882–1941). The house however had an earlier literary association.

Shelley's connection with Netherhampton House

Almost a hundred years before the Newbolts came to Netherhampton House it was associated with the poet P. B. Shelley (1792–1822) as a result of its ownership by the Groves of Ferne House near Shaftesbury in south Wiltshire. Netherhampton House was the home of the 'Aunt Grove' of Shelley's cousin and first love Harriet Grove. Charlotte Grove, the sister of the poet's mother Lady Shelley, had in 1781 married Thomas Grove of Ferne. Their daughter Harriet became engaged to Shelley, and since Harriet is known to have often visited her aunt at Netherhampton House it is likely that Shelley accompanied her on some of her many visits in 1810, the year in which she collaborated with him in writing the novel *Zastrozzi*. When Shelley was expelled from Oxford in 1811 for his pamphlet *The Necessity for Atheism* a coolness developed between him and the Grove family. In the autumn of that year Harriet was taken to stay with the Helyars of Coker Court, a few miles south of Yeovil in Somerset, and in November 1811 she

Netherhampton House with Gauntlett gates (left)

married William Helyar. Shelley's anguished re-action was: 'She is gone! she is lost to me forever! She married! Married to a clod of earth, she will become as insensible herself.'

During their long residence at Nether-hampton the Newbolts often recalled the association of Harriet Grove with their home. Newbolt wrote:

> But Harriet still haunts us in a very different fashion. We can call her back on any quiet day in June or September – the scene is still set for her much as she knew it. The lawn is there (the 'shrubbery' of her day) and the tall limes, and the hornbeams in the wilder-ness: the drawing-room is still the drawing-room, and the white portico [to the side of the house], freshly repainted, looks as new and cool as it did when it furnished the portrait for Aunt Grove, now at Ferne.

Netherhampton House and the Gauntletts

Netherhampton House had formerly been owned by the Gauntlett family of Wiltshire clay pipe makers, which included Edward Gauntlett the Mayor of Salisbury in 1560. After tobacco smoking was brought into England from the New World in about 1565 this man started the manu-facture on a large scale of clay tobacco pipes, which were stamped on their heels with his em-blem, a long sleeved glove known as a gauntlet. His pipes were also sometimes ornamented and stamped with the wording 'AMESBVRY PIPES', because the pipe clay was excavated from pits between West Amesbury and Normanton, at a place on Normanton Farm called in a 1772 per-ambulation Wrosley's Gate .

Although the Gauntletts lived at Netherhampton, where their monuments in the church date from 1672 to 1713, their pipe-mak-ing continued at Amesbury for several generations, and by it they achieved great pros-perity. In July 1670 Mr Gauntlett registered his coat of arms which is incorporated over the gate in the ironwork screen. This dates from about 1750 and separates the forecourt of Netherhampton House from the road. John Aubrey mentions several of the Gauntletts, whose success presumably explains the wings which

were added to Netherhampton House, probably soon after 1700. When the Gauntletts died out in about 1770 Netherhampton House was bought by Thomas Grove of Ferne near Shaftesbury as a dower house, which explains the presence here of Aunt Grove.

The Wiltshire associations of the Raleighs

Tobacco smoking was first introduced into En-gland in the 1560s by sailors who had acquired the habit from American indians, and it was Sir Walter Raleigh (1554–1618), the poet, soldier, courtier, and explorer, and also one of the sub-jects of Newbolt's *Admirals All*, who brought the smoking habit to court. Raleigh, who has several Wiltshire associations, also introduced into En-gland the potato, although it was not at first recognised to be a food plant. In addition to be-ing a major Elizabethan poet, Raleigh was a major contributor to the foundation of the Brit-ish Empire when he founded Virginia and named it after Elizabeth, the virgin queen. In 1583 his half-brother Sir Humphrey Gilbert (1537–83) had, when provided with a commission by Queen Elizabeth to annexe any available lands, laid the foundations of the British Empire when he claimed Newfoundland for England, although he was drowned when his ship foundered on the return voyage.

Raleigh was a west-countryman, a Devon man who had several personal and family con-nections with Wiltshire. He lived at Sherborne in Dorset, and although his own associations with Wiltshire are few his brother Carew settled at Downton where his family remained for many years (see later, pages 223-4). In 1577 Sir Walter and Carew Raleigh were jointly appointed 'Keep-ers of Her Highnesses Park of Meere' (Mere in south-west Wiltshire), although in 1586 they were deprived of Mere after Sir Walter had been re-placed in the queen's affections by the younger Robert Devereux, Earl of Essex (1567–1601). Of Raleigh Aubrey wrote, in addition to a scurrilous incident involving a maid of honour:

> Sir Walter was the first that brought Tobacco into En-gland and into fashion. In our part of North Wilts,

e.g. Malmesbury hundred, it first came into fashion by Sir Walter Long.

I have heard my grandfather Lyte say that one pipe was handed round from man to man about the Table. They had first silver pipes, the ordinary sort made use of a walnut-shell and a strawe.

It [tobacco] was sold then for its wayte in silver. I have heard some of our old yeomen neighbours say, that when they went to Malmesbury or Chippenham market, they culled out their biggest shillings to lay in the Scales against the Tobacco.

Sir Walter Raleigh, about 1588

A persistent Wiltshire tradition suggests that tobacco was first smoked in England by Sir Walter Raleigh and Sir Walter Long at South Wraxall manor house near Bradford on Avon. By the end of the 16th century tobacco smoking had become widespread, despite the opposition of King James who published his *Counterblaste to Tobacco* (1604) in the second year of his reign, and considered smoking to be: 'A branch of the sin of drunkenness, which is at the root of all sins':

Herein [he wrote] is not only a great vanity, but a great contempt of Gods good gifts, that the sweetnes of a man's breath, being a good gift of God, should be wilfully corrupted by this stinking smoke.

The career of Sir Walter Raleigh as an Elizabethan adventurer and royal favourite at the court of Elizabeth is well-known. He colonised Virginia and owned 42,000 acres of Ireland in Munster which he peopled with English settlers. He was also a major poet who associated with the principal poets of his time, and his friendship with Marlowe led to him being suspected of atheism.

Towards the end of Elizabeth's reign Raleigh lost his position as royal favourite, and his rivals undermined his position with James I by alleging that he had opposed his succession. In 1604 he was accused of 'being guilty of compassing the death of the King and intriguing to set Arabella Stuart on the throne'. After being tried at Winchester and sentenced to death for treason he was reprieved on the scaffold and then spent thirteen years in the Tower, writing his *History of the World* (1614). He hoped that he would be released as a result of his friendship with Prince Henry, who was said to have promised him his freedom and the return of his estates. The prince however died in 1612 and in 1616 Raleigh was granted by King James a chance to obtain reinstatement by undertaking a voyage to Guiana in search of a gold mine. He was given a crew which he described as 'the worlds scum', the enterprise failed, and against orders he attacked a Spanish town. Upon his return in 1618 Raleigh was arrested at Plymouth, and on his way to London in the charge of his cousin Sir Lewis Stukeley he remained for some time at Salisbury. There he feigned illness and gained a few days respite, during which he wrote his *Apologie for the Voyage to Guiana* justifying his actions. According to Aubrey: 'by his great Skill in Chimistry, he made himself like a Leper: by which meanes he thought he might retard his journey to a Prison: and study his escape'. This stratagem failed to save Raleigh from the king's wrath and he was executed at the insistence of the Spanish ambassador, under the old 1603 Winchester sentence which had been commuted to life imprisonment.

Raleigh's older brother Sir Carew Raleigh (*c.* 1550–1626), who had also taken part in voyages to the West Indies, lived in south-east Wiltshire at Downton on the River Avon south of Salisbury. After being Sir John Thynne's Gentleman of the Horse at Longleat he married Sir John's widow Dorothy, who lived at the Longleat dower house, the manor house at Corsley, sold

Manor House, Corsley

up his Devon properties, and settled at Downton. He leased Downton manor house, the northern part of the Parsonage Manor House which dates from the 14th century, and is situated a little north of the church on the west side of Barford Lane. There was formerly hung the portrait of Sir Walter Raleigh by Zuccaro, reproduced earlier (page 223), which is now in the National Portrait Gallery.

Carew Raleigh was knighted at Basing House in 1601 and sat as MP for Wiltshire from 1584 until 1621. At Downton Carew and Dorothy Raleigh had three sons, nephews of Sir Walter. Their eldest son Gilbert in 1626 succeeded his father and was MP for Downton, but died in 1628. He also married a Wroughton – Lucy, a daughter of Sir Giles Wroughton of Broad Hinton – and was followed at Downton by his son, another Gilbert (died 1675). Sir Charles Raleigh (died 1698) and another Carew Raleigh served as Downton's MP from 1698 until the latter's death in 1701. The Raleigh presence at Downton finally ended in 1713.

During the Civil War most of the Raleighs of Downton suffered as royalists, although Carew Raleigh, no doubt remembering how his brother Sir Walter had been judicially murdered by James I, was as an anti-royalist granted £500 a year from the estates of the Digbys, who now owned Sir Walter's former manor at Sherborne in Dorset. Carew Raleigh's second son, Dr Walter Raleigh (1586–1646), entered the church and became chaplain to William, Earl of Pembroke. He was granted many preferments including the

Wiltshire livings of Wilton St Mary and Wroughton, and became chaplain to Charles I and Dean of Wells in 1642. As a royalist during the Civil War he was captured at Bridgwater and imprisoned. On 10 October 1646, when under confinement in his own house at Wells, he was stabbed for refusing to show a letter he had written to his wife by a shoemaker called David Barrett, who was responsible for his welfare. He died from the wound but his murderer was acquitted by a sympathetic court. Dr Raleigh had five sons and six daughters. Carew Raleigh's third son George is believed to have died young.

Sir John Davies of Chicksgrove

A Wiltshire-born poet, lawyer and politician who contributed to the foundation of the British Empire, by administering from high office the plantation of Ireland, was Sir John Davies (1569–1626). He is not to be confused with his contemporary namesake who, after joining the rising of the Earl of Essex against Elizabeth, was condemned to death as a traitor but was reprieved.

The Wiltshire John Davies was born at Lower Chicksgrove Manor, the Elizabethan house with a two-storeyed porch which stands on the north side of the road to Dinton a short distance east of Tisbury. He was the third son of John Davies by his wife Mary, a daughter of John Bennett of Pyt House, which lies four miles west of Chicksgrove. His father died early and the three boys were brought up by their mother. He went to Winchester School, at sixteen entered the Queen's College at Oxford, and in 1595 qualified as a lawyer at Middle Temple. After acquiring a considerable reputation as a wit by publishing a volume of epigrams, in 1595 he began to write poetry. In 1596 he wrote his finest work, *Orchestra: a Poem of Dancing*, which discusses the universality and antiquity of dancing. The world was exhibited as a dance, the 'orchestra' of the title being the area in the Greek theatre where the chorus danced and sang.

Having dedicated *Orchestra* to Richard Martin his friend and fellow at Middle Temple, Davies in 1598 lost his temper with Martin in a dispute over literary matters and cudgelled him about his head in the hall of the Middle Temple; for this violence he was banished. He returned to Oxford and in 1599 wrote his poem *Nosce Teipsum* (Know Thyself), a long didactic poem on human learning and immortality, which he dedicated to Queen Elizabeth. This poem is now forgotten although it was admired by Coleridge, but the queen liked it and in 1601 she promised Davies preferment and had him reinstated to the Middle Temple after he had apologised to Richard Martin.

From this time Davies pursued a very successful career as a lawyer and politician. After becoming in 1601 MP for Corfe Castle, at the death of Queen Elizabeth he had the foresight to accompany the official commissioners to the Scottish court and so gained the favour of James I. In 1603 he was made Solicitor-General for Ireland, where he did everything possible to promote the protestant religion. Three years later he was knighted and made Irish attorney-general. He then entered the Irish parliament, became its Speaker, and made his contribution to Empire by taking part in the plantation of Ulster.

After many years in Ireland John Davies in 1614 returned to England and in 1621 became MP for Newcastle-under-Lyme. His married life was unhappy because his wife Eleanor Touchet, a daughter of Baron Audley, believed that she was a prophetess and became insane. When at the start of Charles I's reign Chief Justice Crew was in 1626 dismissed from office for refusing to recognise the new king's forced loans as legal, Davies was rewarded for maintaining the legality of the loans by being nominated to succeed Crew as Chief Justice. He never succeeded to the office because, having become very cor-

pulent, on the morning of 8 December 1626 he was found dead in his bed of apoplexy. He was fifty-seven. His wife married again and according to John Aubrey she: 'was confined in the Tower before the late troubles [the Civil War] for her prediction', but she survived until 1652, when she died still believing herself to be a prophetess.

A few years before his death Sir John Davies collected into a single volume his three most successful poems *Orchestra* (1596), *Nosce Teipsum* (1599) and *Hymns to Astraea* (1599) – the last being a collection of acrostics on the name Elizabeth Regina.

Newbolt's early life

Having digressed into the subjects of the part played by the Wiltshire Gauntletts in the introduction of pipes and tobacco smoking into Wiltshire, and two men (Raleigh and Davies) connected with Wiltshire who took part in the Elizabethan expansionism from which the British Empire developed, I shall now return to the principal subjects of this chapter, the two later poets of Empire, Newbolt and Kipling.

Henry Newbolt was born on 6 June 1862 in St Mary's Vicarage at Bilston near Walsall in Staffordshire, the eldest child of the Rev. Henry Francis Newbolt (1824–66), the vicar of Bilston, and his wife Emily, née Stubbs (1838–1921). Emily was the Rev. Newbolt's second wife. She was the daughter of a prosperous Stafford businessman with Jewish connections. There were three children, Henry, a younger brother Francis, and a young sister Emily. In 1866 the Rev. Newbolt died at the early age of forty-two and Mrs Newbolt moved with her three young children to Walsall to be near her family. She outlived her husband by fifty-five years. At Walsall the dominating influence on Henry Newbolt was his Grandfather Stubbs, until his death in 1873 when Henry was eleven. Mrs Newbolt was left tolerably well off and the family took regular holidays in the Malverns, Yorkshire and North Wales, during which Newbolt developed his lifelong hobbies of birdwatching and fishing. Henry and his younger brother were also sent to the grammar school at Caistor in Lincolnshire.

Lower Chicksgrove Manor, the birthplace of Sir John Davies

Newbolt at Clifton College

Pivotal to Newbolt's entire life was his education at Clifton College in Bristol, where he was impressed by the late-Victorian public school imperialistic ethics of Empire. Clifton College had been opened in 1862 by the efforts of a group of Bristol businessmen who wished to provide a public school for their city. From Lincolnshire Newbolt in 1876 travelled west to sit the scholarship examination at Clifton. He was very much impressed by the 'rich warm radiance' of the west, passed the examination, and particularly liked the college. His later claim that he: 'was born in June 1862', that is the same year and even the same month in which the school itself came into existence was not strictly true. In fact Clifton was officially opened on 30 September 1862.

Mrs Newbolt was also impressed by Clifton and purchased a house in Worcester Crescent with a view of the College, in order that Henry and Francis could be day boys and their younger sister Emilly could attend Clifton High School for Girls.

The significance of Clifton College in forming the character of Henry Newbolt cannot be over-emphasised. There, from the age of fourteen to nineteen (1876–81), his entire philosophy of life was formulated under a staff which taught strict Victorian standards of religion, gentility, manliness, and sacrifice.

At Clifton Newbolt was never a member of the cricket or football elevens, but he became a good cross-country runner and was persuaded to join the Cadet Corps, in which he rose to be captain and won the challenge cup for marksmanship in 1880. Serving in the Clifton Cadet Corps was his first and last experience of being in uniform. Newbolt always remained so immensely proud of his old school that his friend H. G. Wells wrote to him on 2 May 1904: 'your heart is with Clifton and the accidents of your own life'. Many years later Newbolt in 1922 became President of the Old Cliftonian Society. He was saddened when many of the close friends he had made at Clifton died young in the Great War, although one friend who survived the war was Douglas Haig (1861–1928), who had become commander-in- chief on the Western Front.

Corpus Christi, Oxford

After failing a scholarship to Balliol Newbolt in December 1880 sat the examination for Corpus Christi and obtained a scholarship. He was at Oxford from 1881 until 1885, living in the rooms with a view across Church Meadow which had been occupied by Ruskin as Slade Professor, Ruskins carpet and wallpapers being still *in situ*. Rowing was all-important at Oxford but Newbolt never rowed, being at 9½ stones too light to be an oarsman and too heavy to be a cox. He concentrated on his studies and after five years at Oxford was disappointed when he obtained only a second, which he described as: 'more than a disappointment, a catastrophe'. Many years later he was made an honorary fellow of Corpus Christi.

Upon leaving Oxford in 1885 Newbolt went to London to Lincoln's Inn and was called to the bar in the summer of 1887. At this time he met at social gatherings many influential people including Oscar Wilde. He also 'helped-out' at boys clubs and grew to admire the independent qualities and resourcefulness of working-class boys, an admiration which he felt enlarged his 'idea of patriotism'. He practised law for twelve years but began to write, and in 1899 finally abandoned law in order to devote himself to writing.

Newbolt's marriage to Margaret Duckworth

His brother and sister having married, Henry was by 1888 the only unmarried Newbolt. He had become friendly with a family called Chilton who lived in Surrey and had a villa at Lynton in North Devon, and in the summer of 1887 he joined them for a holiday at Lynton. At Yeovil Miss Margaret Duckworth, the fourth daughter of the Rev. W. A. Duckworth, who owned Orchardleigh House, joined the train and during the holiday Newbolt resolved to marry her. After returning to London Newbolt received from the Rev. Duckworth a letter enquiring about his prospects, but it was not until the following year that Margaret accepted his proposal of marriage.

Newbolt's *The Old Country* (1906) was based on his wife's family home at Orchardleigh, a few miles outside Wiltshire towards Frome. It was here in 1899 at the little church on the island in Orchardleigh Lake (accessible to the public by a footbridge) that Newbolt married Margaret Duckworth (1867–1960), who agreed to marry him on condition that she would be allowed to continue her friendship with her cousin Ella Coltman. That the marriage was opposed by Margaret Duckworth's family is suggested by a phrase in Newbolt's dedicatory introduction to *The Old Country* (1907): 'Gardenleigh [Orchardleigh] alone has some resemblance to a sketch from nature, and there I put my trust in the generosity of its possessors, remembering that they have before now forgiven me a far costlier theft.' The newly-married couple set up house in west London, and during the eight years that they lived at 14 Victoria Road Newbolt liked to spend the afternoons in the company of his wife and her two close friends, Ella Coltman and Mary Coleridge.

Early writings

Newbolt's first book was a novel set in 1821 called *Taken from the Enemy* (1892), which had as its plot an attempt to rescue Napoleon from St Helena by submarine, which was thwarted by Napoleon's death. It was followed in 1895 by a tragic drama entitled *Mordred*, a five-act drama in blank verse on an Arthurian theme which was not so well received. Newbolt at this time often visited Robert Bridges (1844–1930) at his house at Yattendon in Berkshire, and when Bridges passed some of Newbolt's manuscript poems to Laurence Binyon he offered to publish them.

His collection *Admirals All*, which was published in *Longman's Magazine* in 1895, immediately established Newbolt's reputation as a patriotic poet. As the title implies many of the poems were on nautical themes, with the 'Admirals all, for Englands sake' listed as Effingham, Grenville, Raleigh, Drake, Benbow, Collingwood, Byron, Blake, and the 'peerless' Nelson. Some of the poems were on other subjects and these included *Vitaï Lampada*. The allusion is to a quotation from the Latin poet Lucretius, which may be translated as, 'and like relay runners they pass on the torch of life'; it contains some of Newbolt's best-known lines. The poems were enthusiastically received, in one year *Admirals All* sold twenty-one editions of one thousand copies, and

they retained their popularity throughout the Great War.

With his literary reputation now established Newbolt followed up his success with *The Island Race* (1898), twenty-eight new patriotic poems added to the twelve poems of *Admirals All*. The new book, which included 'Clifton Chapel', was also extremely successful and persuaded Newbolt to abandon the bar and become a full-time writer, no doubt influenced by Robert Bridges, who suggested to him that: 'Ten years is quite long enough to be in any profession'.

As a result of these successes Newbolt was in 1900 appointed by John Murray to edit his new literary magazine which they decided to call *The Monthly Review*. During the four years that he remained editor Newbolt considered that his life was radically changed as a result of his friendship with H. G. Wells. He also discovered Walter de la Mare, and and became a friend of Thomas Hardy, after being one of the critics who enthusiastically reviewed his epic*The Dynasts*. During Newbolt's years as editor of *The Monthly Review* the Boer War was fought. This conflict prompted many patriotic poems from Newbolt and in *The Monthly Review* in 1904 Newbolt defended Lord Methuen (1845–1932) of Corsham Court, who had been blamed for the severe defeat at Magersfontein in December 1899. He also became Vice-President of the Royal Society of Literature, Member of the Academic Committee, and Professor of Poetry and Chairman of the English Association. In the summer of 1904 he left *The Monthly Review*.

Having now acquired a profound knowledge of history Newbolt was commissioned in 1911 by the Oxford University Press to provide annotations to an edition of Shakespeare's *Richard II*, which were considered by the publishers to be 'first rate'. From 1911 to 1921 he was also Professor of Poetry at the Royal Society of Literature.

Newbolt's patriotism

Although he never served in the armed forces Newbolt was intensely patriotic, a characteristic that may be attributed to the fact that his grandfather Captain Charles Newbolt had served in Nelson's fleet and a great-uncle had been a colonel in India. He assembled a family history of his Newbolt forbears of which he wrote in 1925:

> I am haunted by a fear that all the little family history I have acquired in fifty years nosing around, will perish with me unless I get it down on paper before my time is up.

At the centenary of Trafalgar in 1905 Newbolt published *The Year of Trafalgar*, a book which included a controversial analysis of the strategy used by Nelson and Collingwood at that battle. His views were vindicated after an enquiry into the subject by a panel of three, which included two admirals. This recognition firmly established his reputation as a naval historian.

His constant adherence to his concept of England and Englishness throughout his life and his pride in his military ancestors prompted Newbolt to write the verse that is today regarded as jingoistic. His early patriotic style is typified by his analogy between the game of cricket and warfare in his poem *Vitaï Lampada*. After a British square is broken in an eastern desert war a young subaltern 'rallies the ranks' with a cry of 'Play up! play up! and play the game!' Such patriotism motivated British men to volunteer in hordes to go blindly into the carnage of trench warfare in the Great War. Newbolt perceptively anticipated the war as early as 1908, when he wrote a letter expressing his opinion that Kaiser Wilhelm was mad, and his anxiety that such a man should be in command of the most powerful army in the world.

Newbolt's war service

When war broke out in 1914 Newbolt was too old to serve in the forces, although later in the war he wrote in a letter dated 22 December 1917:

> . . . I am glad that the Great War came in my time and not after me ; it is good to find so much courage in our countrymen and good to find so much in our class and ourselves . . . I used to think courage a common thing, and supposed most men had more than I . . . It is a real joy to me to see F. [his son Arthur Francis Newbolt who survived the war] go off so cold and cheerful to his horrid huts and trenches . . .

The war transformed Newbolt from being a professional writer who served on several com-

mittees and advisory boards into a government adviser serving the Admiralty, the Foreign Office, and the Ministry of Information, where he became Controller of Wireless and Cables. His services were recognised by a knighthood in 1915. His official activities continued after the armistice and he became a Companion of Honour in 1922. In 1923 he was appointed to complete Sir Julian Corbett's official naval history of the First World War and he also wrote his own unofficial naval history. As a result of becoming chairman of the Departmental Committee on English Education he became educational editor to the publishers Nelson.

Newbolt's *Collected Poems, 1897–1907* contains many nautical poems, including the well-known 'Drakes Drum' with its famous opening lines:

> Drake he's in his hammock an' a thousand mile' away,
> (Capten, art thou sleepin' there below?)

Of this poem the poet-laureate Robert Bridges wrote to Newbolt: 'It isn't given to a man to write anything better than that. I wish I had written anything half so good.' Newbolt's other poems on historical naval subjects include 'The Fighting Téméraire', 'Hawke' and 'The Old Superb'. Although these nautical poems gained him much of his fame they were merely a phase which he left behind, and his best-known poems are probably 'Clifton Chapel' and *Vitaï Lampada* with its recurrent chorus of 'Play up! Play up! and play the game!' which opens with equally well-known lines:

> There's a breathless hush in the close tonight –
> Ten to make and the match to win –
> A bumping pitch and a blinding light,
> An hour to play and the last man in

Newbolt's admitted Imperialism is evident in the tone of much of his poetry, which for a long time chimed with the mood of a nation determined to cling to its Empire. He expected his books to sell thirty thousand copies, but it was Newbolt's tragedy that he became identified as the poet of Empire at the time that the British Empire was declining, and that he lived long enough to see his patriotic verse go completely out of fashion.

Newbolt's actress grandaughter Jill Furse

A year before the Great War broke out Captain Ralph Furse arrived with a detachment of his men to bivouac in the garden at Netherhampton House. They picketed their horses in the field opposite the house and during this stay Ralph Furse courted Newbolt's daughter Celia who later became a minor poet. In 1919 Constable published her book of poems *The Gift* from which 'The Lamp-flower' was published in the second volume of *Poems of To-Day* (1923). Ralph Furse and Celia Newbolt became engaged in October 1913 and were married at Netherhampton in June 1914. Their daughter Jill Furse became the actress who married Laurence Whistler (1912-2000), the younger brother of the artist Rex Whistler, who regarded Netherhampton House as the most beautiful house he knew. After starting life as a poet and architectural historian Laurence Whistler became the illustrious glass-engraver and was knighted in the last year of his long life for his services to art.

On 21 January 1917 2nd Lieutenant Edward Thomas walked from his embarkation camp at Codford over the downs to visit the Newbolts (the visit is described in Chapter 14, page 216). Newbolt was then away from home and Thomas was entertained by Margaret Newbolt and her daughter Celia Furse. In his letter to his wife Helen describing this visit Edward Thomas referred to Netherhampton House as being 'grandish but small in front, but it is long behind, really big'. Thomas would as a connoisseur of clay pipes have been interested in the connection of the Gauntlett pipe makers with the house.

Although they were acquainted from having served on various prize committees Newbolt and Thomas appear to be an ill-assorted pair, the one a celebrated poet of Empire, the other a reserved writer of quiet musing verse which so sensitively evoked the subtleties of the English countryside. Edward Thomas was not then a recognised poet, his reputation at that time being that of a hack prose writer and reviewer. He seems to have been rather coolly received by the Newbolts as in the letter quoted above he also wrote in, reference to an invitation to visit again: 'I would rather end up at any old pub'.

The Kiplings at Tisbury

During Newbolt's long residence in south Wiltshire Rudyard Kipling (1865–1935) was also sometimes in south Wiltshire, at Tisbury in the Nadder valley about eleven miles west of Netherhampton. Kipling had always been interested in ships, and during the latter part of the Great War he often visited the Grand Fleet in Scotland and at Dover and Harwich, and he sometimes designed crests and badges for ships. His poetry was also frequently about ships, 'Big Steamers' and 'The Coastwise Lights' being examples. Their mutual nautical interests provide a link between Kipling and Newbolt, although in spite of these and the fact that they were almost contemporaries there seems to have been surprisingly little direct contact between the two men. Kipling was complimentary about Newbolt when he wrote in 1910: 'Newbolt in two priceless lines has just hit the whole situation. It is splendid.' And Newbolt mentions in a letter dated 4 April 1919 sitting beside Kipling at a meeting at the *Athenaeum* and having 'my first talk with him : which is odd, for we've corresponded time and again'. Newbolt also recorded that 'he [Kipling] was good company'. He also mentioned Kipling familiarly as 'Rudyard' in a letter to John Buchan written on 5 October 1923.

The coincidence that Kipling as the second of England's two great early-20th century poets of Empire should like Newbolt be associated with south Wiltshire came about as follows. After returning from India Kipling's methodist parents retired to Diane Lodge in Hindon Lane at the north edge of Tisbury which they renamed The Gables, the name by which it is still known. Their son Rudyard and his wife Carrie in 1894 rented Arundell House on the east side of the top of Tisbury High Street to be near his parents. Kipling joined Tisbury cricket club and took an active interest in the local history of Tisbury. He and his wife were again at Tisbury in 1900–01 at about the time that *Kim* was published.

Kipling's father John Lockwood Kipling (1837–1911) was a Yorkshire-born artist and craftsman in the Arts and Crafts style of William Morris. He had gone to India in 1865 as Professor of Architectural Sculpture at Bombay

University and became principal of Lahore School of Art (1875–93). He remained in India for almost thirty years and advised Queen Victoria on the Indian style of the Durbar Hall at Osborne House on the Isle of Wight. Rudyard was born at Bombay and was particularly close to his father, who became both his literary adviser and the illustrator of some of his books including *The Jungle Books* (1894–1895), which were part written by Rudyard at Tisbury. While living at Tisbury Lockwood Kipling was a frequent guest of the Arundells at Wardour, the Wyndhams of Clouds at East Knoyle, and the Morrisons at Fonthill. The fact that Kipling was named after Lake Rudyard in Staffordshire, where his parents met at a picnic party, is of interest in that Henry Newbolt was the son of a Staffordshire vicar.

During 1900 Kipling was often at Tisbury to consult his father about *Kim* (1901), for which Lockwood Kipling provided the illustrations using a local schoolboy as the model for Kim and local tradesmen for the other characters. Kipling also took the drafts of *The Jungle Books* and *Puck of Pook's Hill* (1906) to Tisbury to be discussed with his father who was always his most trusted critic.

Kipling's mother Alice (1837–1910) was the eldest of four daughters of a methodist minister called Macdonald. All four sisters became interested in art and were writers who had their work published. Georgiana married the painter Burne-Jones, Agnes married another painter Edward Poynter, Louise painted with Burne-Jones and

Tisbury church. The Kipling graves are the flat slabs near the centre of the picture

William Morris but married an iron-founder, and Alice married Lockwood Kipling. In November 1910, having aged rapidly due to the stress she suffered in caring for her beautiful but disturbed married daughter 'Trix', Alice Kipling died and was buried at Tisbury. Within two months of her death her husband Lockwood also died on a visit to the Wyndhams at Clouds and was buried in an adjoining grave. Their graves are marked by two large slabs near the south-east corner of the church.

Although born at Bombay Rudyard Kipling was educated in England. He was lodged by his parents from 1871 to 1877 at the house of a retired naval captain ('Uncle Harry') at Southsea where he was extremely unhappy. He then spent four happy years (1878–82) at the United Services College at Westward Ho! in North Devon. From there at the age of seventeen he returned to India, worked as a journalist on the *Lahore Civil and Military Gazette*, and wrote books of verse, at first on the Indian Civil Service (*Departmental Ditties*: 1886) and then on soldiers of the army in India (*Soldiers Three*: 1889). These gained him some reputation in England to which he returned in 1889 and there wrote his first novel, *The Light that Failed* (1890). In England Kipling became a prolific writer, met the American publisher Wolcott Balestier (1861–91), and after his death married his sister Caroline Balestier (1862–1939) in 1892. For a time they travelled abroad. After paying a visit to his in-laws in America Kipling visited South Africa during the Boer War, and this visit was followed by a visit to Australasia. After this although he continued to travel extensively Kipling's home was in England.

In 1892 Kipling achieved a huge success with *Barrack Room Ballads* but continued to write very successfully on Indian subjects such as *Kim* (1901) and *The Jungle Books* (1894 and 1895). His books on English history included *Puck of Pook's Hill* (1906) and *A History of England* which he wrote in 1911 in collaboration with C. R. L. Fletcher.

Kipling's writings were often far from Imperialistic, as when he wrote of: 'killing Kruger with your mouth', and when writing on Imperial subjects Kipling often expressed considerable reservations about the principle of Empire. He

Carrie and Rudyard Kipling

circumstances and with little help or reward'. He never hesitated to associate with private soldiers, he frequented music halls, and long before John Masefield was credited with introducing collo-quial speech into poetry with *The Everlasting Mercy* (1911) and *The Widow in Bye Street* (1912) Kipling had used such speech in his very successful *Departmental Ditties* (1886) and *Barrack Room Ballads* (1892). The huge popularity of these volumes of verse was due largely to their use of the everyday language of the working classes, and it is a fact that today many people remain familiar with Kipling's writings in both verse and prose. In 1995 his poem 'If', included in *Rewards and Fairies* in 1910 and said to have been inspired by Dr Jameson of Jameson raid notoriety, was voted England's most popular poem.

Kiplings daughter had died when she was only six, and when his young son John (1897–1915) was killed in the Great War his body was not found and Kipling spent much time after the war trying to find his grave, and writing *The Irish Guards in the Great War* (1923). He also became an Imperial War Graves Commissioner, an appointment that he performed with great diligence for the rest of his life. He wrote the inscription that was often used on war memorials: 'Their name liveth for evermore', and the phrase: 'Lest we forget'.

sometimes satirised its less admirable aspects, believing that the duty of Britain ('the White Man's Burden') towards its Empire was a duty of service and obligation. In a letter written in 1895 he expressed his objection to missionaries:

> . . . it seems to me cruel that white men, whose governments are armed with the most murderous weapons known to science, should amaze and confound their fellow creatures with a doctrine of salvation imperfectly understood by themselves and a code of ethics foreign to the climate and instincts of those races whose most cherished customs they outrage and whose gods they insult.

Kipling often expressed his admiration for the unacknowledged men who dedicated their lives to developing and administering the Empire, and described how they 'cursed their work, yet carried it through to the end, often in difficult

Newbolt's decline and death

Towards the end of his life Newbolt entertained hopes of becoming poet laureate, although his style had already become unfashionable and he was profoundly disappointed when in 1930 the appointment went to John Masefield. By 1933 his health had begun to decline and he suffered from an illness described by his wife as 'some insidious enemy microbe'. In October 1934 after a residence of twenty-seven years the Newbolts reluctantly left Netherhampton to move into Ella Coltman's house at Campden Hill in London. Lady Newbolt later wrote:

> The pulling up of deep laid roots and the cutting away of attachments to village and neighbourhood and to our lovely water-meadows and downs, to say nothing of house and garden were not easy things to face, but we were supported in the hope that the change would change his [Newbolt's] *bien-être*.

The happiest days of Newbolt's life were those spent at Netherhampton, and after he left Wiltshire at the age of seventy-two his already impaired health rapidly declined. His work was by then so much out of favour that it was often derided, and he was very much aware of his reputation as an Imperialist and the extent to which his poetry had become outmoded. He acknowledged this when he wrote the following bitter comment in June 1929, in a letter written in response to a request that he provide a short biography of Richard II for a National Gallery picture postcard:

> Imperial Newbolt aged and gone to ghost
> May fill a card to stuff the penny post.

Newbolt's failing health was almost inevitably aggravated by this awareness as he grew older of the dramatic decline in popularity of his work. In October 1937 he suffered a stroke which half-paralysed him and by the time of his death on 19 April 1938, four years after leaving Netherhampton, he had become a mere shadow of his former self. Photographs reveal Newbolt in his prime as a suave, elegant and neatly dressed, tall and very upright man. Age wrought severe ravages upon him and during his terminal illness he confided to his friend Edith Olivier (who recorded that his illness had reduced Newbolt to 'a tiny, old man . . . very pale and thin, and with his neck permanently bent') that he longed for death.

Lady Margaret recorded that her husband: 'never lost his memory or his characteristically incisive way of expressing himself when spoken to, but he became more silent and withdrawn into himself'. After his death she found that he had written on a piece of paper the Latin Grace of his old college, Corpus Christi, Oxford, to read every night. He was cremated and on 10 June his ashes were buried under the yew tree at the east end of the churchyard on the tiny island in the lake at Orchardleigh, near the east end of the church in which he had married Margaret Duckworth. His son Francis read aloud the funeral scene from Newbolt's *The Old Country*. A

tiny flat inscribed stone marks his grave with a similar one for his wife.

Sir Henry Newbolt's life is well-documented in an extensive correspondence which prompted him to suggest: 'By the mass of my correspondence you'd think I'd lived nine lives'. This correspondence formed the basis of Volume One of his memoirs which he published in 1932 as *My World in My Time*. He died before the second volume was written, although it had been announced as *Yesterday*. It was finally published as *The Life and Letters of Sir Henry Newbolt* in 1942, edited by his wife Lady Margaret who, after outliving her husband for many years, died in 1960 aged ninety-three and was buried beside her husband.

Time has dealt harshly with Newbolt's reputation as a poet. Modern literary encyclopaedias are almost dismissive of him. *The Concise Oxford Dictionary of English Literature* (1974) in a four-line entry describes him curtly as the 'poet, author of many patriotic songs', and *The Oxford Companion to English Literature* (2000) grants him only ten lines and notes that he is 're-membered principally for his rousing patriotic nautical ballads'.

When visiting Edith Olivier at Wilton in 1932 Sir John Betjeman begged to see Newbolt in order that he might (according to Edith Olivier): 'savour the out-of-date flavour of a literary man of the past'. But it was Betjeman who was more generous than the literary dictionaries when he wrote in his introduction to a 1940 edition of Newbolt's poems :

> Newbolt's poetry is easy to understand, rhythmical, and full of memorable lines. Because of these qualities and because his earlier poetry is distinctly martial where it is not nostalgic, modern literary people have been inclined to dismiss him as a minor Kipling. Though this has not weakened Newbolt's popular hold, it has been the cause of neglect of his highly original qualities as a poet. There is really no parallel with Kipling, for Kipling was a great prose writer but not a great poet, and he was never a critic. Newbolt is a better poet than Kipling, and was a severe critic of his own work and an understanding one of that of others.

16 Cecil Beaton in South Wiltshire

including Edith Olivier and Rex Whistler

When parking my car at Monk's Down on the Ox Drove Ridgeway a little east of Win Green for a favourite walk in Cranborne Chase I invariably look down the private drive which plunges down the almost precipitous hill to Ashcombe House secluded in its dense wooded coombe. On these occasions I think of the times between 1930 and 1945 when Cecil Beaton entertained in this remote Wiltshire valley his many society and artistic friends, including the poet Siegfried Sassoon and the future poet laureate Sir John Betjeman, the artists Rex Whistler and Salvador Dali, Greta Garbo the actress, and Miss Edith Olivier, who found Ashcombe for him when he was looking for a house in south Wiltshire.

Ashcombe from Monk's Down

After Cecil Beaton's fifteen-year lease expired in 1945 he never entirely recovered from having to leave his beloved Ashcombe, and as he grew older he often returned to view from afar the house where he had been so happy but from which he was now excluded. At the age of sixty-five he wrote sadly:

> Often I find when motoring around Broad Chalke that I go back to the haunts that I love. Although I dare not go down the hill to visit Ashcombe for fear of being shot at or insulted by Mr Borley's son, I find myself drawn to the place like a magnet, & as I stand up outside the gate looking down into the tree covered valley towards the hidden house, I wonder, if the miracle should happen, & I was given the chance to return, whether or not it would be the wise thing to try & recapture the happiness that I had known in my youth. Perhaps, fortunately, I have not had to face the decision. The desire to return to the past is strong in most of us. It is with me . . . Perhaps it is as well that I am too busy with the future to escape too often in the past . . .

In addition to describing the life and Wiltshire associations of the photographer and designer Cecil Beaton, this chapter is devoted to his friend Edith Olivier, who introduced Beaton to Wiltshire and found for him his successive homes in the south of the county at Ashcombe and Broad Chalke. Wilton also features in this chapter because at her home, The Daye House in Wilton Park, Miss Olivier during the first half of the 20th century assembled a wide circle of artistic friends, in conscious or unconscious imitation of the 'academy' of writers and artists which Mary Countess of Pembroke had gathered at Wilton House in the late–16th century, as described in Chapter 5.

Of all the subjects of this book Edith Olivier is with the possible exception of Robin Tanner (the subject of Chapter 17) the most essentially Wiltshire person. Many of its other subjects were born elsewhere and are merely associated with Wiltshire. Other native born subjects left Wiltshire to pursue national careers, but Miss Olivier was born and lived almost her life at Wilton of which she became the first lady mayor. She wrote with immense pride and enthusiasm about her home county, and referred to the 'county spirit' at the end of the prologue to her Wiltshire county book, which was posthumously published in 1951:

> Wiltshire does possess such a spiritual unity; though Salisbury Plain, its unique physical feature, has never been a bond of union. Quite the reverse. Till the days of motors the Plain was an almost impassable division between North and South Wilts. Yet there has ever been an individual spirit knitting the county together as securely as if it were surrounded by a great wall of China.

By contrast with Edith Olivier, Cecil Beaton came late to Wiltshire, although he grew to love the county where he made his later homes, living first at Ashcombe House under Win Green and then at Reddish House in Broad Chalke. It was as a direct result of his friendship with Miss Olivier that Cecil Beaton acquired both his Wiltshire homes and a large circle of friends associated with Wiltshire.

Cecil Beaton's early career

Having been born in London Cecil Beaton (1904–80) went to Harrow school and then to Cambridge. Then, in a long and varied career extending over more than fifty years, he first achieved celebrity as a royal and society photographer and then as a stage and film designer. His success as a portrait photographer was due to his ability to capture the spirit of every age, and he produced portrait studies of over thirty members of the royal House of Windsor, from the children of George V and Queen Mary to those of Queen Elizabeth and the Duke of Edinburgh. In addition to being a royal photographer Beaton photographed many social celebrities and film stars, and after being declared unfit for military service during the Second World War he became an official war photographer.

His debut as a stage designer occurred in 1934 with his designs for C. B. Cochran's review

Beaton lived at both Ashcombe and Broad Chalke

Streamline, and he then designed scenery and costumes for many stage productions. Beaton also wrote and illustrated a number of books, and in 1959 won his first Oscar as the designer for the film *Gigi* which was followed by a second Oscar for the film version of *My Fair Lady*. After entering the film world he proposed marriage to the Swedish film star Greta Garbo (1905–90), but his proposals were rejected and he died a bachelor in 1980 having framed and kept a rose which Garbo had picked for him on one of her two visits to his home at Broad Chalke.

Miss Edith Olivier

Cecil Beaton's friend Edith Olivier (1873–1948) was the daughter of Canon Dacres Olivier, the rector of Wilton. The Oliviers were well-connected and Edith revelled in her illustrious friends and relations. She was brought up in Wilton and, being a lifelong friend of the Pembrokes, had the freedom of Wilton Park. Miss Olivier pronounced her surname in the English way as the girl's name Olivia, although other members of the family including the actor Laurence Olivier, known to Edith by the familiar name of 'Lally', used the French pronunciation. Laurence was the son of Edith's first cousin.

Edith was also related through her mother Emma Selina Eden to prime minister Sir Anthony

Edith Olivier photographed by Cecil Beaton

Eden (1897–1977), the first Earl of Avon who, after serving in the 1930s as foreign secretary, in 1940 became Churchill's secretary of state for war in which capacity he founded the Home Guard. He then became foreign secretary again in Churchill's 1951 government, and when he succeeded Churchill as prime minister in 1955 his health was already in decline. He retired suddenly at the age of sixty in 1957, was created Earl in 1961, and lived out his last years in retirement at Alvediston in south Wiltshire. He died in 1977 and was buried in the stone tomb with large lettering on the south side of Alvediston churchyard. Sir Anthony was the brother of Edith Olivier's second cousin Sir Timothy Eden, who became her particular friend when she was suffering from bad health towards the end of her life.

Edith's stern and autocratic father had been a keen sportsman who loved hunting, shooting and tennis, although he gave up sport when he felt that it was intruding upon his spiritual activities. He was by no means poor, having inherited property from an uncle who had bought the entire Blea Valley in the Lake District in order to preserve it in memory of Wordsworth, but when he died his fortune was thinly spread over a large family of eleven children, seven sons and four daughters. Edith and her sister Mildred were left very little money, but her many friends did much to alleviate Edith's comparative poverty. Lord Pembroke provided her with The Daye House in

Wilton Park for a minimal rent, Siegfried Sassoon made her an allowance of two hundred pounds a year, and Stephen Tennant of Wilsford in 1928 gave her as a present an Austin Seven car. This provided her with the mobility that enabled her to pursue her many interests.

Edith Olivier was born and lived her early life at Wilton Rectory, which stood beside the romantic Italian Romanesque church built at the centre of Wilton in the 1860s by Lord Herbert of Lea and his Russian mother Lady Pembroke. While growing up at Wilton Edith secretly longed to be an actress but such a career was forbidden to her by her strict clergyman father. She became an ardent theatregoer and her brother Alfred, to their father's disgust, become an actor.

After being taught by a governess called Helen Rootham, Edith won a Bishop Wordsworth's scholarship which enabled her to go to St Hugh's College at Oxford. Here she attracted the attention of the Rev. Charles Dodgson (Lewis Carroll: 1832–98) and was invited to dine with him tête-à-tête on condition that: 'if you don't come alone you shan't come at all'. This was strictly against college rules which were relaxed in her case. As she suffered from bronchial asthma her doctor stipulated that she must avoid Oxford in the winter. Consequently her terms were not concurrent and she returned home to Wilton rectory without taking a degree.

In his old age Edith's widowed father demanded that one of his two daughters must remain single and continue to care for him. On the only occasion that Edith took a young man home for the weekend her father made him so uncomfortable that she had to break off the relationship. Edith and her younger sister Mildred then entered into a pact never to marry and as a result became extremely close.

When Canon Olivier retired the Oliviers moved to Salisbury to 20 The Close, a Georgian house dating from about 1725 of brick with a hipped roof. It stands in the North Walk at the north-east corner of the Cathedral Close adjoining the house formerly occupied by Canon Bowles when he was a canon of Salisbury (see Chapter 12). They continued to live in this house until immediately after the Great War.

Although they had been left some shares by their father Edith and Mildred were not well-off as neither ever worked or had an income. Their mother had died in 1908 and at the death of their father in 1919 they had to move out of The Close. Edith, who was then forty-seven, and Mildred then rented for a time Fitz House at the pretty village of Teffont Magna about seven miles west of Wilton, a beautiful 17th-century stone-built house with mullioned windows. In *Without Knowing Mr Walkley* Edith Olivier described how:

> Fitz House had lately been bought by our friend Lord Bledisloe and now he offered to let it to us . . . Fitz House stands back from the village street, behind a stone wall, which was then lower than it is today . . . The house makes almost three sides of a square: the main building, a fifteenth century farmhouse, faces the road; a seventeenth century wing joins at right angles on one side, facing the long stone barn on the other.

At Fitz House Edith and Mildred lived for two years enjoying their small garden, summer evening picnics beside Great Ridge Wood, and a house frequently full of nephews and nieces, but in their hearts they longed for Wilton. When their friend Lord Pembroke heard of this he offered them for a nominal rent The Daye House in Wilton Park, so-called because it had once been the dairy to Wilton House. They jumped at the opportunity and both lived at The Daye House for the rest of their lives.

When in late 1924 Mildred died after a long illness Edith seriously contemplated becoming a nun but was rejected by the mother superior as being unsuitable. She returned to live at The

Daye House and later became the first lady Mayor of Wilton, an appointment of which she was immensely proud.

Edith's interests in the supernatural and local history

Edith Olivier was a believer in the supernatural. She knew Miss Moberly, a cousin of her mother's and a daughter of Bishop Moberly of Salisbury, and the head of St Hugh's College which Edith Olivier attended at Oxford. Edith was enthralled when Miss Moberly told her how she and Miss Jourdian believed that they were transposed back in time to the 18th century at the Petit Trianon, the experience that Miss Moberly wrote up as *An Adventure*. She also told Edith of the local legend that when a Bishop of Salisbury died two large white birds were seen. Edith also claimed that in October 1916 when driving through Avebury she saw a phantom fair taking place in the stone circle, and only discovered some years later that fairs had been held at Avebury but had been abolished in 1850. She also recorded seeing off the coast of Cornwall a vision of King Arthur's legendary Lyonesse, and after the death of her friend the artist Rex Whistler (1905–44) towards the end of the Second World War she wrote in her diary of seeing a vision of him:

> He came in, only one eye and one cheek could be seen for bandages tho' these were not injured. His arm tied up and his leg. He looked well. I said my darling Rex. He looked at me with great love – and did not speak. We kissed and stood embraced. I knew

20 The Close, Salisbury, once the home of Edith Olivier

Fitz House at Teffont Magna, for two years the home of Edith and Mildred Olivier, and later of Siegfried Sassoon

we had thought him dead and I thought this had been a mistake. It was a very still quiet dream. No words spoken except my greeting – but we felt great love. I woke happy and then cried.

Another of Edith Olivier's interests was in local history. In July 1932 she organised the lavish Wilton Pageant at which she played Queen Elizabeth and in 1941 she planned and organised a concert in honour of a Mr Henry Good at The Hut. This had been a primitive inn on the Ox Drove ridgeway two miles south of Broad Chalke and has now been rebuilt as Hut Farm. The deer stealers in Cranborne Chase were not all poor men and William Chafin, the historian of The Chase, tells us that Mr Good was a 17th-century

Henry Good and his accomplices

member of a family that had long been established at Broad Chalke. He was a skilled musician with a fondness – in addition to venison! – for the poetry of Milton and of Samuel Butler's *Hudibras*, the most popular poem of its time. Under the guise of holding musical concerts at The Hut he would snare deer and then read *Hudibras* until nightfall, when he would organise a party to help bring home the catch and enjoy the venison.

The Daye House
The Daye House is a two-storeyed building situated immediately behind the east wall of Wilton Park. It was built in the 1850s as the dairy house to Wilton House and Edith revived its old name of The Daye House. The house is in an Italianate-Romanesque style with low-pitched roofs, bracketed eaves, many round-headed and a

The Daye House in April 1942, an untitled oil painting by Rex Whistler, with his car parked in the drive

single bulls-eye window, and several chimney stacks. To the original house Edith added a single-storey timber extension which she called the 'Long Room', and in the attic she created a tiny chapel. Gradually Edith and her friends developed the long room so that it became the heart of her home and of her life. Outside it was smothered with roses and climbers and Rex Whistler embellished its interior. It was floored with square panels of ash, and bookcases lined its walls. Edith described it as: 'now a very pleasant room in which to sit, either alone or with a few friends'.

Rex Whistler painted The Daye House with Edith standing on the lawn holding a walking stick, his sports car on the drive, and showing the house embowered with trees and with shrubs scrambling up its walls. He also painted a picture of the interior of the long room with Edith lounging on a chaise-longue, David Cecil sitting at her feet at the end of the chaise-longue, Lady Ottoline Morrell leaning forward from an armchair in her customary wide-brimmed hat, and himself behind her with cigarette in hand leaning against the fireplace. This picture was one of Rex Whistler's favourite works and he told Edith prophetically: 'If I die first, please bring it with you when you come'.

Edith Olivier's artistic circle at Wilton
Although late in life she took up writing Edith Olivier is of limited importance as a writer in her own right. Her appearance in this book is entirely due to the fact that at The Daye House she gathered around her a band of young writers, artists and musicians, some of whom attained great

eminence. She sublimated her own career as a writer to theirs and entertained and encouraged artists, writers, musicians and painters in whom she recognised much more talent than she possessed. Her many artistic friends included the writers Siegfried Sassoon and the Sitwells, the composers Constant Lambert and William Walton, the artists Rex and Laurence Whistler, and the artist, photographer, writer and designer Cecil Beaton – the principal subject of this chapter. As they shared very similar tastes she was particularly friendly with the eccentric Edith Sitwell, whose verse had in 1923 been set as *Façade* by William Walton; he had escaped to Oxford from his upbringing in Oldham and became a protégé of the Sitwells. After establishing a brilliant reputation in his early life Walton was eclipsed after the Second World War by the brilliance of the younger Benjamin Britten. In 1932 Walton started to compose his first symphony at The Daye House, where he was often depressed by a conviction that his music was much inferior to the music that he heard on Edith's radio.

Edith's many friends recognised that she was a remarkable woman who encouraged the latent ability that existed in others, a fact that she recognised when she once referred to herself as 'the Queen of Coddlers' for her pampering of her young friends. Recalling these days at Edith's home at Wilton Cecil Beaton wrote:

> Of all the neighbours on whom I grew to rely more and more, Edith Olivier was perhaps always the most cherished. So many of the young writers, painters and poets came to her with problems about their work and their lives and they knew that after she had listened intently to their outpourings, her advice would be unprejudiced, wise and Christian.

Miss Olivier's published journals for the period 1924 to 1948 provide frank and interesting insights into her group and her visitors at Wilton, an example being her reference in July 1932 to John Betjeman who the following year married her friend Penelope Chetwode:

> John Betjeman arrived for the weekend. He is . . . cleaner than I expected. Knows a lot about architecture, loves Georgian churches . . . John is a Quaker,

having become one two years ago. This is surprising as his temperament has not the clear simplicity of Quakers, but a most mocking, doubling-back-upon-itself kind of humour, writing parodies on hymns and begging to see Harry Newbolt [Edith's neighbour at nearby Netherhampton] so that he can savour the out-of-date flavour of a literary man of the past . . . I like him better than I expected.

Edith and Rex Whistler

Shortly after the death of her sister in late 1924 Edith Olivier met the nineteen-year-old artist Rex Whistler (1905–44) on a visit to San Remo. He provided a welcome distraction from her bereavement and from 1925 became a frequent visitor to The Daye House. Whistler was a brilliant Slade-trained artist who prior to the Second World War achieved a considerable reputation as a mural painter, book illustrator and stage designer, who with his baroque inclinations (dem-

Rex Whistler

onstrated in his design of the headstone to Pamela, Lady Glenconner, in Wilsford churchyard) stood outside the mainstream of the modern movement in art. His brother Laurence recorded Rex's 'chronic untidiness' and his lik-

The Walton Canonry in Salisbury Close, which Rex Whistler hoped to make his home

ing for 'rich and unusual colour effects' in his dress. His choice of *The Laughter and the Urn* as the title for his biography of Rex suggests that he was very good company. He loved Wiltshire and shortly before the Second World War purchased the Walton Canonry in Salisbury Close, the house at which John Constable had stayed and painted. He intended to make this fine house his permanent home but with the outbreak of war the military authorities requisitioned it. At camp at Codford in the Wylye Valley Rex Whistler in 1942 painted murals entitled 'Surrounded by the Boys'. These were removed to London after the war when Codford Camp was cleared. From

Lady Glenconner's tombstone in Wilsford churchyard, designed by Rex Whistler

Codford Rex Whistler wrote to Edith Olivier: 'I don't remember ever having been so astonished at the beauty of Wiltshire, the ideal longed for country one only sees clearly in dreams.' He then took part as a tank commander in the Normandy invasion and was killed near Caen towards the end of the war.

Although she confided to her diary in 1927: 'He looks on me most simply as a Mother', Edith grew to love Rex Whistler but there was a great disparity of thirty-two years in their ages. Their friendship continued until his death, and when in 1935 Rex was was attracted to the beautiful Caroline Paget, the daughter of the owner of Plas Newydd in Anglesey, Edith was perhaps a little jealous when she confided to her diary that she 'minded terribly' for Rex. In fact after his death Edith finally recognised that her feelings for him were deeper than those of a woman for a surrogate son.

One of Edith's great pleasures was sightseeing, to which she devoted Chapter 19 of *Without Knowing Mr Walkley* (1939), describing enjoyable visits made in the company of Rex Whistler:

> Rex Whistler is the perfect travelling companion. He follows no prearranged plan: he is ready to respond to any unexpected invitation. When one drives out in the morning with a certain destination in mind, Rex soon wearies of the important road which leads to it and is attracted by some side road which appears to meander nowhere in particular. He turns into this. From it there diverges another byway far smaller than the first. Then yet another. Rex finds each one quite irresistible and we soon become lost in a tangle of little old roads, each narrower and more forgotten than the last . . .

They often drove together round the byways of Wiltshire visiting out-of-the-way places, one of their favourites being a tiny chapel in its derelict graveyard:

> Another evening Rex and I arrived at a little chapel buried in a wood on the borders of Hampshire . . . and felt our way along a very narrow footpath. It led to a deserted churchyard where, thrown wildly across the graves and shattering the tombstones, there lay

an enormous uprooted yew tree, its roots and its torn branches tragic in the twilight. Behind it was a little fourteenth-century chapel.

This was the tiny de Borbach Chantry, now a mortuary chapel hidden away at the north edge of West Dean on the Hampshire border, but once part of the old church of St Mary. It is sometimes called the Evelyn Chapel because it contains a number of fine monuments to this family who were related to John Evelyn the diarist, as well as others to the Pierreponts who were descended from them. During the 1750s Gilbert White (1720–93) of Selborne in Hampshire was for a time curate of West Dean, to which he would ride the thirty miles across the downs from his home at Selborne. His church would have been the old St Mary's church of which the surviving de Borbach Chantry is a fragment.

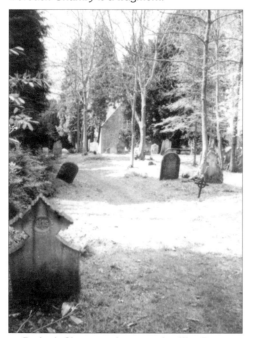

Borbach Chantry and graveyard at West Dean, visited by Edith Olivier and Rex Whistler

After 1927 Rex Whistler began to bring along to The Daye House his fifteen-year-old brother Laurence, who described another visit made by Rex and Edith in his biography of his brother Rex *The Laughter and the Urn*. He tells how one summer afternoon in 1932 they: 'set off exploring up the Avon Valley and finally arrived at Alton Barnes, under its White Horse on the Marlborough Downs'. They discovered the Saxon church and its adjoining farmhouse,

The Georgian house beside the church at Alton Barnes which Rex Whistler greatly admired

which they greatly admired, and Laurence describes how Rex expressed a hope of living there and:

> vividly pictured his days there, perhaps with some unknown companion, some not impossible "she", there came as always the reflection, "not this". His paintings would never hang in those faintly-discerned, low rooms, his clock in the hall would never chime the peaceful afternoon away as he drew, no bust of his would ever turn its back to the garden on that very windowsill. Perhaps one day, but not yet, and doubtless never here.

They then climbed on to the hills and on 'a flat grassy shoulder' under the high point of Adam's Grave enjoyed a picnic tea while they looked across Pewsey Vale below:

> Here fancy of the not-so-feasible-kind took over. Rex said he would like a Kingdom of just that size, and planned his Summer Palace just where we were sitting, and a Versailles down in the Vale. Possible and impossible were always interchangeable.

As a result of visiting Edith at The Daye House Rex Whistler met and liked her neighbours the Newbolts at Netherhampton House (see Chapter 15), a house which so chimed with his baroque taste that he considered it the best house he had ever seen.

Edith Olivier as a writer

It was at the instigation of her friend Sir Henry Newbolt that Edith became a writer. With his encouragement she published a number of novels and the autobiographical *Without Knowing Mr Walkley* (1939), a book about her life and her neighbours at Wilton. Mr A. B. Walkley had been a drama critic on *The Times* and a friend and fellow collegian of Newbolt who often mentions him. Two years after the publication of this book Batsfords asked Edith to write a book on country life and she produced *Country Moods and Tenses* (1941), describing the backgrounds and the psychology of country people and drawing attention to the vulnerability of traditional country life.

In 1935 Edith had at the suggestion of John Betjeman assisted Robert Byron (1905–41) by compiling a gazetteer for his *Shell Guide to Wiltshire*. Byron was a Wiltshire-born travel-writer and aesthete from the Byron family of Savernake Lodge who were remotely connected with Lord Byron. He wrote on eastern cultures and architecture and his best-known work is *The Road to Oxiana* (1937), in which he described a journey from Venice to Afghanistan and India exploring the origins of Islamic culture and architecture. He was considered by Bruce Chatwin to be in 'the rank of Ruskin', but was drowned at sea in the Second World War when his ship was torpedoed. Robert Byron is commemorated by a tablet in Cadley church in Savernake, which is now secularised as a dwelling.

Having also written a number of novels, some illustrated by Rex Whistler, towards the end of her life Edith was invited by Brian Vesey-Fitzgerald to write the Wiltshire volume of a series of county books which he was editing for Robert Hale. Edith was delighted and felt: 'if I could do it well, [it] would be the achievement of my life, something I would love to leave behind' (Diary, 8 December 1943). It was intended that the book should be finished by autumn 1945 and published in spring 1946, but the manuscript was not completed until 4 October 1947, probably due to Edith's poor health. It was not published until 1951 after her death. Edith, being seventy-two in 1945 and in failing health, found writing this book an arduous task. She died in 1948 and her Wiltshire book was published with a foreword by her niece Rosemary Olivier, which stressed that her aunt had neither seen the proofs nor selected the photographs. Over fifty years after it was written this book remains a useful source of information and, although unreliable in some of its detail, it exudes its author's intense love of Wiltshire.

Edith Olivier's neighbours

Edith Olivier's neighbours at Wilton included, in addition to Sir Henry Newbolt at Netherhampton, Arthur (A. G.) Street (1892–1966), who farmed Ditchampton Farm at the north end of Wilton and was married to Edith's dressmaker; she was also a sister of the Olivier's former maid Cissy Foyle. When the expansion of Wilton northwards began to impinge upon Ditchampton Farm Arthur Street moved one and a half miles north to Mill Farm at the south end of South Newton.

The Ox Drove above Ashcombe, which is to the right

During the great depression in agriculture of the 1930s when Arthur Street needed to augment his depleted income Edith encouraged him to embark on his successful writing career. In *Wessex Wins* (1941) Arthur wrote his impression of Edith's arrival in 1931 to 'advise him about his writing and to get his vote'. He tells how she 'swooped into the room as only Edith can swoop', and advised him not to pursue his intention to write a novel but to write instead about something that he knew well. He continues:

> I promised for three reasons. The first was because my work for the *Salisbury Times* had taught me that my farming stuff was saleable. The second was because it was obvious that Edith Olivier had nothing to gain by such advice, and must be offering it solely because she thought I could write a book. The third was because in that particular mood Edith Olivier was an irresistible force against which I dared not attempt to play the role of immovable object.
>
> Having obtained my promise my literary fairy godmother was eager to be off, presumably to speed and advise some of her many other godchildren . . . her final remark, "Well that's splendid, Arthur. And remember, whatever you do, dont try to be clever." Whereupon she floated airily from the room. Anyone who knows Edith Olivier at all will agree with my choice of phrase to describe her passage.

Arthur Street at Ditchampton followed Edith's advice and wrote a number of novels and books of essays, generally on farming topics. The best-known is probably *Farmer's Glory* (1932), but one for which I have a particular liking is *The Gentleman of the Party* (1936), in which he describes traditional farming in the Nadder Valley west of Wilton from about 1872 and the impact of the Great War on farming in the valley.

Arthur Street's only daughter Pamela Street became a writer and wrote many novels and *The Illustrated Portrait of Wiltshire* (1971). She was for a time the personal assistant of the historian Sir Arthur Bryant who lived in the house called Wincombe Park situated one mile north-east of Shaftesbury and about five miles north-west of Beaton's Ashcombe, an area which he described as: 'that little corner of earth where Wiltshire joins Dorset and the infant Nadder rises'. He had known

Wincombe from childhood when his uncle owned it. In 1956 he acquired the house with forty acres and kept it for seven years as a retreat from London while writing the *Alanbrooke Diaries* and *The Age of Chivalry*, but in 1963 he reluctantly sold Wincombe and in 1973 also gave up his London home and moved into The Close at Salisbury.

Cecil Beaton at Ashcombe

The house at Ashcombe, beautifully situated in its remote wooded coombe under Win Green Hill, was Cecil Beaton's home for the fifteen years from 1930 to 1945. Its situation was described by Pevsner as: 'a wonderfully secluded place, down from the downs in a sheltered hollow'. The original house on the site was a much larger one built by the Barber family, and early maps show the house surrounded by substantial landscaped grounds and occupied by the Hon. James Everett Arundell Esq. An 18th-century painting confirms the elaborate nature of its grounds, which included avenues and garden buildings set among a profusion of trees. Soon after he acquired a lease on Ashcombe Cecil Beaton heard of the existence of this painting and, determined to have it, went to see the owner of the picture, Sir Gerald Grove of Shaftesbury, who sold it to him for fifty pounds.

Ashcombe House showing Rex Whistler's doorcase and the urns that Cecil Beaton added to the parapets

The Arundells had substantially altered Ashcombe but in about 1815 the estate was bought by Thomas Grove of nearby Ferne, the brother of the poet Shelley's Harriet Grove (see Chapter 15, page 221) for £8,700. In the mid–19th century his grandson Sir Walter Grove pulled down Ashcombe House to provide building materials for the principal Grove family house at Ferne a little north of Win Green. A small part of the old house was retained and forms the core of the present house, which was in 1870 sold to the 13th Duke of Hamilton. After the First World War he sold it to Mr R. W. Borley, who lived in Shaftesbury and there became the owner of the *Grosvenor Arms*.

In her 1927 diary Edith recorded that despite being then twenty-three Cecil owned only a simple camera that had been given to him as a child and used his sister's bedroom as a studio. At first she had considerable reservations about him because he came from what she regarded as an ordinary family. In 1928 she described him as: 'rather a venomous child . . . but very amusing', but two years later she had rather changed her opinion, and wrote: 'Cecil is indeed a marvel to spring out of his very commonplace family'.

Having achieved wide recognition and become prosperous, in the late 1920s Cecil Beaton decided that he needed a house as a retreat from his hectic life in high society as a royal photographer and designer. From visiting Edith Olivier he by then knew something of south Wiltshire, and one day in April 1930 at The Daye House Edith, after expounding at length on the county's attractions, convinced Cecil that he should live in south Wiltshire. She recalled that the sculptor Stephen Tomlin who then worked from a studio in Swallowcliffe had told her how he had chanced upon a splendid isolated but semi-derelict house called Ashcombe when walking in the south Wiltshire downs. They went to see the house which they found with some difficulty. Beaton's immediate reaction was, in his own words, 'love at first sight'. He described how: 'None of us uttered a word as we came under the vaulted ceiling and stood before a small, compact house of lilac covered brick. We inhaled sensuously the strange, haunting – and rather haunted – atmosphere of the place', and he later wrote: 'None of the rooms possessed the disadvantage of being cottagey, and each window seemed to have a more dazzling view than the last'. The owner Mr Borley at first refused to sell on the grounds that sale of the house would ruin the estate, but was persuaded into a seven year lease which was later extended to fifteen years at a cost of £50 a year, with an understanding that improvements would be made.

Advised by the Austrian architect Michael Rosenauer, Cecil Beaton set in hand extensive modifications to adapt Ashcombe to his needs as a home suitable for entertaining his wide circle of artistic friends. His father saw warning signs and cautioned him not to spend too much on a leased house, but Cecil was so besotted by Ashcombe that he ignored the fact that he did not own it. He later recalled that: 'When the lease of Ashcombe was handed over to me I felt it was mine for life'. He was then only twenty-six and in spite of his fathers warnings he lavished vast expense on rebuilding and embellishing Ashcombe, all of his extravagances being observed with interest by the owner Mr Borley, who was well aware that he could repossess the house after fifteen years.

Beaton elongated the windows, linked the front and rear of the house by a corridor, added a new baroque door case designed by Rex Whistler, and placed urns on the brick parapet at the corners of the house. Statues were added to the garden, the orangery was converted into a studio, and the interiors were decorated in an extravagant style. Few of these alterations by Beaton now survive, but an ancient tramcar dating from his time at Ashcombe survives (2001) in a very derelict condition in the grounds south of the house.

Cecil Beaton's love for Ashcombe seems to have completely clouded his judgement, and for the next few years he continued to incur vast expense on improving the house in collaboration with Rex Whistler, who shared his extravagant tastes. Cecil, Edith and Rex spent as much time as they could spare at Ashcombe while the house was being renovated, with Rex advising on and designing some of its features and the contractor's lorries conveying all necessary building materials down the almost precipitous drive from Monk's Down.

Similar expense was incurred on the garden. Beaton's diaries and his book describing his stay at Ashcombe reveal that his flamboyant tastes caused him to commit fundamental gardening errors. He attempted at great cost to furnish his garden with exotic plants which took his fancy but either failed to flourish or died in the inhospitable shallow chalk downland soil. By late 1930 Edith was entering in her diary anxious comments on the amount that Cecil Beaton was expending on Ashcombe. On the 21 October she wrote: 'Cecil is spending far more than he knows or intends', and 'the road is really impassible – all cars have to be pushed up the first bit'. Four days later she wrote: 'All the rooms half built, some are window-less and doorless and none painted. The outside all heaps of bricks.' The work however proceeded at some speed and on 9 November 1930 the house was in a fit state to allow Cecil to hold his first luncheon party at his new home.

He lavishly entertained his friends at Ashcombe where they loved to dress up in ex-otic clothes. Rex Whistler recorded that Beaton would remain 'out of ordinary clothes [that is in fancy dress] for a week or ten days at a time'. Innumerable week-end parties were held and the house soon acquired a possibly undeserved un-enviable reputation in the locality. Among his other activities Beaton and his friends in July 1935 shot in the coombe at Ashcombe a pri-vately-made film of David Garnett's *The Sailors Return* (1925), which is set in Dorset and relates the conflicts between a sailor and his black Afri-can wife. The film was directed by Beaton's film-director friend John Sutro and starred Cecil as the sailor, John Betjeman as the parson, and Caroline Paget, the eldest daughter of the 6th Marquess of Anglesey (who owned Plas Newydd in Anglesey), as the wife Tulip. Edith played a small part as a village woman. The many visitors to Ashcombe at this time also included the flamboy-ant artists Augustus John and Salvador Dali.

As servants Beaton at first employed the fam-ily of Betteridge, the small-statured but fiery tempered gamekeeper who lived in the cottage in the coombe. After the Betteridges were dis-missed Cecil Beaton was looked after by Mr Dove as his gardener, Mrs Dove, and their son, who all lived at Tollard Royal. Beaton wrote very warmly about old Mr Dove after he died peace-fully in one of the Ashcombe greenhouses.

At the start of the Second World War, al-though he was only thirty-five, Cecil Beaton was regarded as being entirely unsuited for military service, and therefore worked for the Ministry of Information. A radio location station and a searchlight battery with their attendant barrack huts were built in Ashcombe and attracted a single German bomb which demolished the gamekeeper's cottage (which was soon rebuilt), and blasted Beaton's house.

After having unwisely spent a fortune on a house that he had acquired on a comparatively short lease, in about 1943 Cecil Beaton was dev-astated to be given early notice by Mr Borley's son, who had inherited Ashcombe, that his lease would not be renewed when it expired in Sep-tember 1945. Mr Borley is said to have objected to the extravagant behaviour of Cecil Beaton and his friends because they disturbed the pheasants. Despite Cecil Beaton's desperate pleas for an extension Mr Borley remained adamant, and on 31 August 1945 Edith Olivier recorded her last visit to Ashcombe: 'My last visit there, and poor Cecil was much upset. He feels going so much. We talked of our first sight of the place and of all the fun we have had there since. He is going to write a book giving a history of the 15 years he has had it.' The book appeared in 1949 as *Ashcombe: the Story of a Fifteen-Year Lease*, dedicated: 'To the memory of EDITH OLIVIER who brought me to Wiltshire'.

After moving into Ashcombe in 1946 Mr Borley continued to live there until his death in 1993, repelling intruders by setting his dogs upon them and even threatening to shoot them. He refused very generous offers for Ashcombe from Americam millionaires and gradually the house became derelict. After he was buried in the grounds its new owners restored Ashcombe to some of its former glory.

Although from above Ashcombe appears to be impenetrably wooded and the drive approach from Monk's Down is strictly private, public rights-of-way exist through the coombe. One runs east down the steep hill from Win Green and then south down Ashcombe Bottom, and another is signposted south from a point between Monk's Down and Win Green through the woods, and then also follows Ashcombe Bottom to Tollard Royal.

Reddish House at Broad Chalke

After his lease on Ashcombe was not renewed Cecil Beaton had to find a new home, and the house which he ultimately chose was Reddish House in the village of Broad Chalke in the Ebble Valley. This too was found for him by Edith Olivier. Reddish House stands on the south side of the road through Broad Chalke some distance west of the church and on the opposite side of the road from The Old Rectory. This is a former nunnery with a mill-race outside built in 1487, which was the home of the writer Maurice Hewlett (1861–1923). He included many literary figures among his visitors to Broad Chalke, one of these being the American Imagist poet Ezra Pound (1885–1972), who was indicted by the Americans for treason after the Second World War for making broadcasts on behalf of the Italians, but was judged to be insane.

Reddish is a very fine house of brick with stone dressings, one of those buildings which gains immensely from being slightly mannerist. Its description by Pevsner reads:

> Very lively early C18 brick front of four bays, not at all correct or polite. Two-bay centre with a pediment on giant pilasters. In the pediment a horizontally placed oval window with a wreath as a surround and a mask at the top. Doorway with a segmental pediment on brackets. The bust on top may be a recent addition.

Before Beaton acquired Reddish House it was associated with a painter of some importance. Cecil Beaton purchased Reddish from Dr Julius Wood, the Broad Chalke GP whose son Christopher ('Kit') Wood (1901–30) was a promising artist who had died young. He was known to Rex Whistler, who met him at a Cochran review for which Rex had designed the curtains, and he may also have been known to Cecil Beaton. Wood attained a condiderable artistic reputation in France and after going abroad in 1928 spent some time in England. Early in that year he was painting at Broad Chalke and three of his oil paintings, 'Cottage at Broad Chalke', 'Anemones in a Window, Broad Chalke', and 'The Red Cottage, Broad Chalke', are of local subjects. By 1928 he had become friendly with the painter Ben Nicholson (1894–1982), and in that year he stayed with Nicholson at his parents' house, the White House at Sutton Veny near

Warminster. Christopher Wood then returned to France from where his letters home reveal tensions between his English middle-class origins and the bohemian society that he had joined in Paris. He painted furiously, achieved some success, and became an accepted member of the

Christopher ('Kit') Wood

second phase of the Modernist movement. His show unfortunately coincided with the Wall Street Crash and he spent his last two years at the village of Treboul in Brittany, working day and night painting Breton scenes from postcards. His precarious health was further undermined by his use of opium and in 1930, at the age of only twenty-nine, he again visited England. He had formed a liaison with Meraud Guinness, who had joined him in Paris in 1928 and they wished to marry, but when her family opposed the proposal they had separated, and Meraud that same year (1928) married Alvaro 'Chile' Guevarra. Losing Meraud seems to have preyed upon Christopher Wood's mind. On 21 August 1930 he met his mother and his sister at the former County Hotel beside the River Avon in Salisbury, and after leaving them bought a ticket to Waterloo. On Salisbury station he fell under a train, apparently convinced that he was being pursued. He was buried in Broad Chalke churchyard a few yards south of the porch under a flat slab on which Eric Gill's exquisite lettering is now almost illegible.

Beaton, who was a keen practising gardener, consoled himself for his loss of Ashcombe by creating around Reddish a fine garden out of former pasture fields. The undulating ground at the rear of the house to its south was grassed and sub-divided by rollicking topiary yew hedges, and to the north of the house on the opposite side of the road he created a fine water-garden running down to the River Ebble.

After Greta Garbo had visited Reddish House on two occasions and had twice rejected his offers of marriage, Beaton lived a rather hand-to-mouth existence taking on commissions for portrait photography or designing stage or film design sets only when he needed money to embellish his house or garden. A film survives entitled by Beaton *Summer in Arcadia*, out of deference to Sir Philip Sidney, who in Elizabethan times was inspired by this part of Wiltshire to write his *Arcadia*. It shows him tending his garden and greenhouse, trug and pruners in hand and dressed in a straw hat, pink open-necked shirt with cravat, and light flared trousers. His garden at Reddish House survives, although adapted by its subsequent owners to suit their requirements.

The deaths of Edith Olivier and Cecil Beaton

After Rex Whistler's death in 1944 Edith Olivier became a close friend of Sir Anthony Eden's brother Sir Timothy Eden. She suffered from high blood pressure and severe fibrositis. Having made very little money from her writing she was never well-off and often closed down The Daye House and stayed with friends in order to

minimise her living expenses. As her sight became bad Edith at the age of seventy-five jokingly confided to her diary on 29 December 1947:

> I decided I want a man to live with me in winter when I may not drive in the dark. So I must have a driving lover, or a loving driver. Can't afford a chauffeur.

By January 1948 she was 'in the red' at the bank and on 16 April she had a minor stroke. Another stroke rendered her speechless, and she died on 10 May. After a funeral service at Wilton parish church where the mosaic behind the altar commemorates the fact that her father served Wilton as its rector for over fifty years, she was buried beside her sister Mildred in the churchyard on the south side of the church, her grave being marked with a simple wooden cross similar to her sister's, on which is carved:

R. I. P.
EDITH MAUD OLIVIER 1872–1948
BE GLAD WITH ME ALL YE
THAT LOVE ME

Sir Cecil Beaton continued to live in his Wiltshire Arcady at Broad Chalke and when he died in 1980, thirty-two years after Edith Olivier and ten years before Greta Garbo, he was buried in Broad Chalke churchyard with a simple slate headstone under a cherry tree at the west side of the graveyard, not far from the grave of his fellow artist Christopher Wood.

Olivier crosses (Edith left and Mildred centre) in Wilton churchyard

Cecil Beaton's grave at Broad Chalke

17 'A Vision of Wiltshire'

Robin Tanner at Old Chapel Field, including Francis Kilvert

In the early autumn 1930 a local man who was an admirer of William Morris supervised the cutting of the first turf for the house that he was having built at Kington Langley, north of Chippenham, as a home for himself and his prospective wife. The house, which had been designed as their wedding present in the Arts and Crafts style by his future wife's uncle Vivian Goold, was situated at Old Chapel Field on the inside of the sharp bend in the road at the west end of Kington Langley.

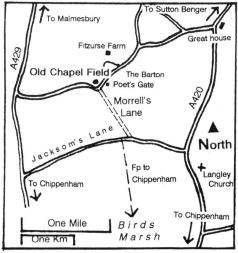

Kington Langley showing the location of Old Chapel Field

The house in Old Chapel Field was built for Robin Tanner (1904–88) and his future wife Heather (1903–93), whose maiden name was Spackman. From it for more than fifty years from 1931 to his death in 1988 Robin Tanner worked as much as the necessity to earn a living allowed on his drawings and etchings, always encouraged by his writer wife with whom he collaborated on a number of books on the countryside.

The heading of this chapter is 'borrowed' from the title of a film about their work in which Robin and Heather Tanner, with some apprehension, featured towards the end of their lives.

Of all the subjects of this book Robin Tanner is with the possible exception of Edith Olivier (Chapter 16) the most positively Wiltshire orientated, for even Richard Jefferies (Chapter 13) eventually moved away from Wiltshire. Tanner is probably the least known of my subjects but he interests me as I hope that he will interest my readers. For him Wiltshire and especially northwest Wiltshire around Castle Combe and Kington Langley held all that he ever sought in life. When he was away from home he became homesick and pined for this, his home district of Wiltshire, and throughout his long life he was exiled from Wiltshire for only two periods, first for his art training and an initial short spell of teaching in London, and later in life when serving elsewhere as a schools inspector.

Many of my other subjects were born privileged, some to royal, noble or rich families, and others into the landowning classes. Robin Tanner had no such advantages, and he is included because from humble origins he achieved by his own determination and abilities a considerable reputation in two fields of activity. When towards the end of his life in a lecture at Devizes Museum he referred to his artistic talent as 'a very minor one' Robin Tanner was being unduly modest, for he was both an artist-etcher who exhibited at the Royal Academy and a brilliant teacher of art who believed that an inherent ability at art was latent in every child. This belief enabled him to bring out unexpected artistic ability in many of his pupils, and his success as a teacher was so great that he ended his educational career as a schools inspector. After retiring he devoted the rest of his long life to his art.

Robin Tanner was a dedicated exponent of the pastoral tradition in art who throughout his life remained unaffected by modernisn. He was a follower of Samuel Palmer, the landscape painter and etcher who in about 1850 realised the potential of etching as a rewarding art form and had produced limited signed editions from his plates. Only too aware of the vast amount of time he expended on his etchings Robin Tanner refused to destroy his plates after limited editions had been taken from them and they have been preserved in the Ashmolean Museum at Oxford to allow later editions to be drawn from them. In Robin Tanner's case this appears to have increased the value of his early editions.

The appearance and characters of Robin and Heather

Robin Tanner was a short, stocky, bespectacled, and rather portly man. On one occasion when he replied to a request for his name that it was 'Tanner' his reply prompted the response: 'Yes, you look like one' ('tanner' being a slang name for the small coin valued at sixpence in the predecimal currency), and another friend likened his face to a Cox's orange pippin. When photographed, even at his etching bench or pottering in his garden, he seems to have always been very formal and wore a suit and tie, although it is significant that one of the first things that he noted after he retired in 1965 was: 'I wore old clothes'. His empathy with the natural world is demonstrated by the story which he told of how, when he was etching: 'Our bold pet robin would come in through the big open studio window . . . he would perch on the wheel of the press, then face me, and sing a sweet sub-song in minor mode, and then blow away like an autumn leaf into the hazel copse'. He loved music and sometimes worked listening to the musical setting by Gerald Finzi, who had lived at Beech Knoll at Aldbourne, of the words of the 17th-century mystic Thomas Traherne: 'Everything was at rest, free and immortal'.

Robin and Heather Tanner at Old Chapel Field

Heather Tanner was a tiny, slight, bird-like woman. The Tanners always worked together, so closely that Robin entitled his autobiography *Double Harness*. Both were ardent socialists, practising Quakers, pacifists, and devotees of the Arts and Crafts movement in the tradition of William Morris, who had died in 1896 a few years before they were born. They supported Greenpeace and the Campaign for Nuclear Disarmament, and Heather took part in the protests at Greenham Common when she was over eighty. They abhorred fox-hunting and whenever possible unstopped earths after the hunt had blocked them, and Robin in his diary described the hunt people as: 'oafish men and their hard-faced women, dressed up for murder, tearing heedlessly over any man's property in their blood lust'.

Kington Langley and its Old Chapel

Kington Langley is a long linear village standing at the top of Fitzurse Hill about two miles north of Chippenham, along the road which runs roughly west to east between the A429 Chippenham to Malmesbury road and the A420 road between Chippenham and Sutton Benger.

The village, part of which stands around a wide green, is generally charming but architecturally rather undistinguished, except for the magnificent 17th-century Greathouse which stands at its east end. About its many unpretentious stone cottages Robin Tanner wrote:

> These stone houses with thatched or stone-tiled roofs and mullioned windows were a Wiltshire version of Cotswold : something less perfect perhaps : Cotswold with a rough, earthy difference. Indeed the whole countryside was like that. Here, close to the Gloucestershire border, was a splendid building stone, but in deep rich dairy country that was West of England rather than West Midland.

In the 17th century John Aubrey recorded that at Kington Langley there was formerly: 'A Chapell dedicated to St Peter but now converted to a dwelling house', and mentioned that: 'the Revell is still kept the Sunday following St Peters day, it is one of the Eminentest Feastes in these partes'.

At the bend of the road at the west end of Kington Langley is Old Chapel Field, of which Robin Tanner wrote:

> The village where my mother was born, and where my happiest days as a teenage boy were spent, had belonged to a dissolute hunting squire whose un-tamed horses roamed the common and whose word was law . . . Here, but a few yards from my mother's and grandmother's home and the ancient moated home of my grandfather, in this silent and secluded place, we [Robin and Heather] decided we would live. For me it would be a return to the place where I belonged, and from here Heather could see the stretch of downland where her forbears once farmed. I had already spent my savings, so she paid the hun-dred-and-fifty pounds for what the sale catalogue called Old Chapel Field with her own money.

Many years before most of Kington Langley had been owned for generations by the Coleman family, who probably built Greathouse at the east end of the village. The name Old Chapel Field arose from the fact that soon after he married at the age of fifty-seven in 1778 a Walter Coleman in 1780 resolved to build a mausoleum chapel for the family. He bought Old Chapel Field, then called Batten Patch, and planned and started to

build his chapel, but died in May 1782 before the chapel was finished. He was nevertheless buried at Old Chapel Field and for a time work on his chapel was continued by James Barrett, a ma-son and one of the trustees. He too then died, work stopped, and the chapel was probably never completed. The fact that it has gone with-out trace suggests that it was probably plundered for its materials, and the only memory of the building is the name of Old Chapel Field.

Robin Tanner's description of his house at Old Chapel Field in Chapter 5 of *Double Harness* implies that it stood in isolation some way from the road. The Tanner house was in fact built on the top of the ridge within about twenty yards of the road, which was then merely a byway called Plough Lane. It stands a little north of the point half a mile east of the Plough Inn near the point where the road executes a sharp bend around Old Chapel Field near the north end of Morrell's Lane.

Old Chapel field is a short distance from Fitzurse Farm. This incorporates the remains of a manor house which was in John Aubrey's time an ancient building with a great hall, and a moat of which few traces remain. It was owned by the fam-ily of Reginald Fitzurse, who in 1170 led the four knights who murdered Thomas Becket at Canter-bury. An early representation of the murder in the British Museum shows Reginald Fitzurse leading the four knights and striking the first blow with his sword. Robin's mother's father lived at Fitzurse Farm and she was brought up in a cottage with a walled garden at The Barton on the south side of the road through the village, where Robin as child sometimes stayed with his grandmother.

Although no chapel is shown on Old Chapel Field on the first edition Ordnance Survey of about 1820, during the Second World War Robin Tanner discovered that the diarist Francis Kilvert's great-grandfather Walter Coleman had in 1778 built a private burial chapel and had been bur-ied in 'his own Chapple' at Kington Langley. In his *Beauties of Wiltshire* (1801) John Britton had written that:

> Another chapel was built here [Kington Langley] by the late William Coleman, esq., beneath which he was interred, but his remains have been since re-moved to the parish church of Kington,

although Robin Tanner found his information when examining the papers of Walter Coleman.

The Tanner house was furnished with Arts and Crafts furniture and its wild garden was densely stocked with plants, many of them obtained by Robin in payment for the drawings which he prepared for the plant catalogue of Scott's Nurseries at Merriott in Somerset.

The Tanner house is now (2001) buff-washed and it is no longer isolated, having been joined by other houses which have been built since the Tanners built their house here in isolation in 1931.

The backgrounds of Robin and Heather Tanner

Robin Tanner was born at Bristol on Easter Sunday 1904 into a humble working family which resided at Kington Langley. He was the third of six children, four boys and two girls. His father Sidney Tanner (1876–1960) was a craftsman in wood and his mother, whose maiden name was Emily Collins Baker (1876–1938), had been a housemaid. Robin later described her as 'a great Saskia of a woman', a reference to Rembrandt's substantial wife Saskia van Ulenbergh who was often drawn and etched by her husband.

The Tanners had been long established at Kington Langley. In his diary entry for 4 February 1873 the diarist Francis Kilvert (see later, pages 254-7) recorded being told: 'the story of the terrible faction fight [early in the 19th century] between the men at Chippenham and the men of the two Langleys'. Bad blood had arisen as a result of the behaviour of the Chippenham men at the annual Kington Langley festival or 'revel', which was an ancient event held annually at Kington Langley soon after the feast of St Peter. One September Saturday the Langley men to the number of thirty to forty marched into Chippenham to challenge the Chippenham men. A fierce affray followed in which about thirty Chippenham residents were injured and two were killed. Ten men of Kington Langley were indited for murder and six for riot, and among the latter was a William Tanner, presumably an ancestor of Robin Tanner. There then seems to have been a conspiracy of silence as no one was convicted owing to lack of evidence.

At an early age Robin Tanner was sent by his mother to a Primitive Methodist Sunday School. Since the family was poor their immediate inclination was to make anything that they wanted. From his earliest years Robin drew, principally natural subjects; he also developed a feeling for letter shapes and for books, and when still very young he combined these interests by creating his own illustrated books. When he disclosed his wish to become an artist his father, already concerned about Robin's left-handedness, despaired of his son ever being able to earn a living.

At the age of three Robin was in 1907 sent to school. There he was introduced to brushwork and by his own account: 'In 1909 I was declared clever'. It was at this time that he first met and was impressed by a schools inspector and when asked by him what he intended to do prophetically replied: 'What you do'. He was already demonstrating his artistic ability and was complimented by the inspector for his 'capital' picture. When he was six Robin was belatedly christened, this having been until then overlooked.

As he grew up Robin Tanner discovered that in common with many studious boys he disliked games. He also recalled an incident which occurred when he was ink monitor for his class. Every day he was required to mix the ink from powder and water but, disliking its anaemic grey quality, he decided on his own initiative to make it a good dense black by doubling the amount of powder. This led him into trouble on two counts. The authorities objected because it was wasteful and the thick mix disastrously clogged the children's pens!

Early in the Great War Robin at the age of eleven entered by scholarship the secondary school at Chippenham, where he encountered both a bullying headmaster ('In six years he never said one friendly word to me') and a saintly lady art teacher ('a meek and sensitive woman dedicated to her work'), who encouraged him in his artistic aspirations until she left to become a nun. Encouraged by this teacher he began to visit local churches, inspired by the drawings of the celebrated etcher F. L. (Frederick) Griggs in his copy of *Highways and Byways in Buckinghamshire*. At this time Robin also developed an admiration for

William Morris and all that the Arts and Crafts movement represented. His reading at this time included the west country writers Thomas Hardy, Richard Jefferies, and W. H. Hudson.

At his Chippenham school Robin met Heather Spackman who, although a little older than Robin, was to become his lifelong companion. She was daughter of Herbert Spackman (1864–1949) and Daisy, née Goold (1865–1945), of Corsham. Her father was described by Robin Tanner as: 'the most truly happy and contented man I have ever known'. The Spackmans had for generations farmed around Bromham, Cherhill, Calne, Calstone and Compton Bassett, and in Clyffe Pypard church four miles south of Wootton Bassett there is a very imposing 18th-century memorial to a member of the Spackman local building family who was a carpenter (see Chapter 18, page 265).

In 1838 Heather's grandfather Henry Spackman was articled to a grocer at Corsham, where he became a partner and ultimately took on the business which his son Herbert inherited. Henry Spackman was a close friend of Sir Isaac Pitman (1813–97), the inventor of shorthand, who was born at Trowbridge, and from the age of twelve until he was in his eighties kept a diary in Pitman's shorthand, part of which was edited and published by his daughter Heather as *A Corsham Boyhood, 1877–1891*. For this publication Robin Tanner provided a decorative title-page, chapter headings, and two illustrations.

In 1921 Heather went away to King's College, London, where she read Anglo-Saxon and obtained a first. She then became an examiner in English, and later taught at the Bath College of Art when it occupied part of Corsham Court.

Upon leaving school Robin Tanner took up a local appointment as a pupil-teacher. On Mondays the pupil-teachers met at the Tabernacle in Trowbridge which had, as the Tabernacle Mens Institute, during the Great War only five years before been frequented by the poet Edward Thomas, whose widow Helen was soon to become Robin Tanner's friend in London. The Tabernacle, described by Pevsner as 'A surprisingly earnest and imposing church', was built in 1882 adjoining the garden of George Crabbe's rectory

The Tabernacle at Trowbridge

in Church Street (see Chapter 12). At Trowbridge the pupil-teachers were taught by an inspirational teacher called Agnes Grist, regarded by Robin Tanner as the best teacher he ever knew. He was then accepted into Goldsmith's College at the University of London, but in London he was terribly homesick and recorded that: 'North-West Wiltshire was never from my thoughts or yearnings'. In London Robin learned to love music and developed a particular liking for the 20th-century English composers Delius, Vaughan Williams and Butterworth. In a letter written much later (in April 1975) he listed his preferred writers as being: 'Bloomfield and Clare and that Wiltshireman Stephen Duck, and Hudson and Hardy and Edward Thomas, and dear Wm. Barnes, and even our odd friend Jefferies. And I revere the Georgics.' During his second year at Goldsmith's Robin's abilities as an etcher developed, as did his admiration for the artist-etcher F. L. Griggs, although his proposal to produce a series of etchings of Wiltshire craftsmen was derided by his tutor.

In the 1920s and 1930s slump years Robin Tanner worked as a teacher. He first took a job at a school at Greenwich while still attending evening classes, and at this time became 'Etcher by night, teacher by day'. His etching entitled 'Alington in Wiltshire' was seen by a dealer who asked Robin to supply him with forty prints for one pound each. With the proceeds Robin Tanner bought a small etching press. When teaching at Greenwich he would come home at week-ends and return to work laden with berries, nuts, and flowers for the children. One small pupil was so impressed with such bounty that she enquired: 'Is God up in Wiltshire?'. After in 1926 haunting the Samuel Palmer exhibition at the Victoria and Albert Museum Robin resigned from his teaching post at Greenwich.

At Old Chapel Field

Throughout his time in London Robin continued to see Heather who also drew. In fact according to Robin her drawings were more accurate than his own, although by this time he had become a first-rate etcher. Heather was now working on the Welsh coast, but during her summer holiday of 1928 they met every day to draw and talk. They decided to marry, and Heather's architect uncle Vivian Goold offered to design for them a new house as a wedding present. They found the perfect site at Old Chapel Field.

Robin continued to etch and took great pains over an etching of a bird's eye view including elements of Castle Combe by moonlight, which he called 'Christmas' (1928). He memorably recalled that the preliminary sketches were made at Castle Combe by moonlight in the small hours within sound of people snoring with their windows open. From his plate Robin drew fifty impressions and exhibited one at the Royal Academy. He recorded how while seeing it hung he met the etcher whom he idolised:

> I sent a print to the Royal Academy, and on varnishing day I took a richer, more subtle impression with me, hoping it might be possible to change it. A spare, serious, gentle man, with the straight and kindly glance of a sensitive doctor, came up to me, smiled, and asked what I was carrying under my arm. When I showed it to him and he compared it with the one on the wall he at once made the change, and I blessed him. I did not know until someone called him by name that I had come face to face with the hero of my teens, F. L. Griggs. The modest bearing of this great etcher and his winning voice and smile completely held me. He liked my work. This was wonderful to me. He asked what other designs I had in mind, and I told him about an even more ambi-

'Christmas' (1928), an etching exhibited at the Royal Academy, based on sketches made at Castle Combe by moonlight

tious plate, Harvest Festival, and the small one called Wiltshire Woodman: and he showed the sort of enquiring and total interest one would give to a friend but hardly to a young stranger. I went home elevated and strengthened, and still more determined to follow my own way.

The small etching entitled 'Wiltshire Woodman' was composed from a number of sketches made at Thickwood, west of Colerne Park and a mile south-west of Slaughterford.

In 1929 Robin took a temporary local teaching post at the Ivy School at Chippenham and, finding both teaching and living once more in his beloved home district congenial, he decided that teaching should become his occupation and etching his hobby. He accepted a permanent post at Chippenham teaching general subjects including physical training and art.

The scheme for the Tanner house in Old Chapel Field progressed. In July 1930 the drawings were completed and work on site was started in the autumn, closely observed several times a week by Robin. After taking their marriage vows privately Heather and Robin were officially mar-

'Wiltshire Woodman' (1928) based on sketches made
at Thickwood near Colerne Park

ried at Corsham parish church in 1931. They then
moved into their new house from where Robin
walked daily to Chippenham down Morrell's
Lane, the broad green lane that runs south-east
from the bend in the road outside Old Chapel
Field, crosses Jacksom's Lane at Morrell Cottages,
and runs on down the east side of Bird's Marsh
and across the open fields east of Greenways to
Chippenham School south of the railway.

The Tanner house at Old Chapel Field, Kington
Langley

Robin Tanner's love of the route by which he
walked to school is evident in his description of
Morrell's Lane in Double Harness as:

the broad green glade that runs steeply from the corner of Old Chapel Field into the valley, gradually
narrowing with undergrowth and then becoming wide
again where it ends at a pair of stone cottages. A gate
spanned it here with a squeeze-belly stile, and an ash
tree on either side. Then I crossed Jacksons Lane . . .

Robin's proof-reading of Double Harness was
not infallible and he allowed the typesetter to
substitute the more probable 'Jacksons' Lane for
the correct 'Jacksoms' Lane. He continues:

Then came a wood called Bird's Marsh, and the
strong smell of its damp acid soil and foxes. Here in
autumn there were frightening fungi under the oaks
and beeches. In winter it was never lifeless, and in
spring it was a glory of anemones, moschatel, wood
sorrel, ferns, and bluebells. All through the summer
it was submerged in heavy green, looming and dark
and wet even in the driest weather. Meeting the star-
tling light as I left it and came out on the hillside under
the great chestnuts was always a shock.

Robin Tanner at work

The new house included an etching room in
which Robin spent many hours over many years
recording the beauty of a rustic England that was
rapidly vanishing. He published his etchings and
drawings in a number of books including Wiltshire
Village (1939), Woodland Plants (1981) on which
he collaborated with Heather who wrote the text,
A Country Alphabet (1984), A Country Book of
Days (1986), and his autobiography entitled

Double Harness (1987). He described his 'etched world' as 'an ideal world – a world of pastoral beauty that could be ours did we but desire it passionately enough'. The Tanners were well aware that by concentrating on recording traditional things it would be said that they were merely nostalgically recreating the past. Heather therefore justified their preference for old things by writing in her Foreword to *Wiltshire Village*: 'To call back yesterday would be foolish even were it possible; but in order that what was noble in the yesterday that still lingers might not pass unhonoured and unlamented this book has been made'.

Apart from line-drawing and etching Robin Tanner occasionally painted watercolours, and in 1933 produced his first large painting of the Coffin Way, the wide lane that descends the north side of Fitzurse Hill towards Kington St Michael, which he sold for five pounds to the Bury Municipal Art Gallery.

Robin Tanner's friendship with Helen Thomas

When working in London Robin and his friend Cyril Rice, another Wiltshireman from Chippenham who married Robin's sister Grace and also became an art teacher at Chippenham, became close friends of Helen Thomas, the widow of the poet Edward Thomas who had been killed in the Great War (see Chapter 14). In 1928 Robin visited Steep, near Petersfield in Hampshire, accompanied by Helen Thomas who showed him many of the places associated with her husband and his poetry. In her memoirs of her mother (*Time and Again*: 1978) Myfanwy Thomas wrote:

> Her books brought Helen a great many letters from people unknown to her . . . Two young men, art students in London, became Helen's friends through her books. She went to stay at the home of one of them, Robin Tanner, at Chippenham in Wiltshire. It was a lively household full of young people, presided over by the warm-hearted and hospitable 'Mother Tanner' . . . The other young man, Cyril Rice, Robin's friend at the Art School, was engaged to Robin's sister Grace. These carefree times with the eager and unaffected Tanner family made Helen long once again to live in the country, and they found her an

eighteenth-century stone-built and stone-tiled farmhouse [Starveall Farm which Helen Thomas called 'Starwell'] between Biddestone and Chippenham. The friendly farmer Harold Tucker and his wife Adeline agreed to let half of the house to Helen.

With Edward Thomas's widow Helen living at Starveall Farm not far from Kington Langley the friendship between the Tanners and Helen was renewed and Helen gave Robin the manuscript of *The Woodland Life*, her husband's first published book, which he had written as a boy in 1897. Helen and her daughter Myfanwy now became regular visitors to the Tanners at Old Chapel Field, and there were many other visitors including the writer Henry Williamson.

Francis Kilvert

During the Second World War the Tanners found great comfort in those troubled times by reading the diary of the Reverend Francis Kilvert (1840–79), the young clergyman whose pastoral duties were divided between the countrysides of Wiltshire and Wales. He was associated with the Kington Langley area of Wiltshire and in 1937

Francis Kilvert

twenty-two notebooks containing his diaries were discovered by William Plomer. They caused a sensation when they were published in three volumes in 1938, 1939, and 1940 for their unsurpassed portrayal of country life in mid-Victorian England, which immediately established them as minor classics. A. L. Rowse thought that they were 'the quintessence of England' and 'among the best half-dozen or dozen [diaries] ever written in England', and John Betjeman considered Kilvert's diary to be: 'The best picture of quiet vicarage life in Victorian England that has yet been given us'. Robin Tanner noted that:

Kilvert was born at Hardenhuish, little more than a mile off : his mother and her ancestors had lived in our village ; and much of the diary was written at his fathers parsonage at Langley Burrell, a few meadows away on the opposite side of the valley.

The Kilverts had moved to Bath from Shropshire in the 18th century and Francis Kilvert was born at Hardenhuish (pronounced Harnish) rectory near Chippenham, the second child of the rector Robert Kilvert and his wife Thermutis, a daughter of Walter Coleman of Kington Langley and Thermutis Ashe of Langley Burrell. In his diary entry for 11 March 1876 Kilvert refers to his birthplace as 'Harden Ewyas' when he writes of:

. . . the old sweet home where I was born. Harden Ewyas, sweet Harden Ewyas . . . my sweet birthplace and the dear house of my childhood . . . The house remains the white house on the hill where I was born, there is the ivied Church across the lane [now a road] to which I was first carried to be baptised. . .

Kilvert is associated with two Wiltshire churches, Hardenhuish and Langley Burrell.

Hardenhuish Church

Hardenhuish, where his father was rector, is situated at the north edge of Chippenham. Its church is a fine classical Georgian one built in 1779 and designed by John Wood the Younger of Bath. In its churchyard is the grave of David Ricardo (1772–1823), the political economist and writer who after being educated in Holland made a fortune on the London stock exchange, became a radical MP, and died at his seat at Gatcombe Park in Gloucestershire.

The other Wiltshire church associated with Kilvert is Langley Burrell, which stands in the grounds of the manor house north-west of Langley Burrell village towards Kington Langley. This church, at which he became curate, is a fine church with a Norman north arcade and a (probably) 14th century tower. It survives surrounded by trees just as Kilvert must have known it. Pevsner describes it as: 'a delightful church, not neglected, but also not over-restored'. When I was last there in October 2001 it was locked because it had been robbed of some of its furniture.

Francis Kilvert went to Wadham College, Oxford, entered the church and was from 1863-4 curate of Langley Burrell, where his father had become rector. He then spent some time at Clyro in Wales, but from 1872-6 was back as curate of Langley Burrell, until in 1877 he became vicar of Bredwardine in Herefordshire. He married in August 1879, died of peritonitis the following month whilst still in his thirties, and was buried at Bredwardine.

Kilvert was a contemporary of Thomas Hardy and was born in 1840 only eight years after the death of the Rev. George Crabbe (see Chapter 12). His duties often took him, as had Crabbe's, into the humble and sometimes squalid cottages of his parishioners, and he assumed in prose some of Crabbe's mantle as a realistic depicter of the rural poor whose poverty he diligently recorded in his diary.

Throughout his life and for sixty years after his death Kilvert remained entirely unknown. In deep isolation in remotest Wales and rural north Wiltshire he lived a full and apparently happy life and wrote up his diary in a beautiful limpid prose that created a sensation when it was published long after his death. It is this fact that makes Kilvert so fascinating, for we are curious about his elusiveness, his reason for writing his diary, and the fact that he remained unrecognised for so long after his death. On the subject of his diary-writing

Kilvert pondered on 3 November 1874 after walking in Lord Lansdowne's park at Bowood:

> Why do I keep this voluminous journal? I can hardly tell. Partly because life appears to me such a curious and wonderful thing that it almost seems a pity that even such a humble and uneventful life as mine should pass altogether away without some such record as this, and partly too because I think the record may amuse and interest some who come after me.

Francis Kilvert was a keen walker and once described his 'peculiar liking for a deserted road'. On 31 August 1874 he described wandering in the Kington Langley area:

> I love to wander on these soft gentle mournful autumn days, alone among the quiet peaceful solitary meadows, tracing out the ancient footpaths and mossy overgrown stiles between farm and hamlet, village and town, musing of the many feet that have trodden these ancient and now well nigh deserted and almost forgotten ways and walking in the footsteps of the generations that have gone before and passed away.

He could evoke a landscape in fine prose, as in this May 1874 description of Seagry Mill situated on the Avon a few miles south-east of Malmesbury:

> This afternoon I drove with my Father to Seagry through the snowy May bushes and golden brown oaks and lovely hedgerows of Sutton Lane. Charles Awdry went with us to the river and Seagry Mill, and we lay back on the river bank talking while my Father fished. It was a glorious afternoon, unclouded, and the meadows shone dazzling like a golden sea in the glory of the sheets of buttercups. The deep, dark river, still and glassy, seemed to be asleep and motionless except when a leaf or blossom floated slowly by. The cattle by the mill plashed and trampled among the rushes and river flags and water lilies in the shallow places, and the miller Godwin came down with a bucket to draw water from the pool.

In several diary entries Kilvert reveals his sense of humour. On 7 December 1873 he recorded how a housebound elderly lady when asked how she passed her time replied: 'Aw ther, I do rock and sway myself about', and on 4 March 1875 he wrote: 'Old William also told the story of how old Squire Sadler Gale of Bulwich House [now Bolehyde Manor] at Allington made himself wings and flew off the garden wall. "Watch I vlee!" he cried to the people. Then he dashed down into the horsepond.' He sometimes revealed an almost Aubreyesque credulity, as when he wrote on 22 July 1871 of 'the woman frog' and related that: 'Her head and face, her eyes and mouth are those of a frog, and she has a frog's legs and feet. She cannot walk, but hops.' He then explained that she: 'wears long dresses to cover and conceal her feet', and attributed her strange condition to the fact that when her mother was pregnant she turned away a beggar woman and her children saying: 'Get away with your young frogs, and so she was cursed and her daughter was a frog!'

Kilvert's intimate knowledge of the Tanner countryside around Kington Langley is confirmed by his diary entry for 19 June 1876. Having visited Chippenham in the morning, that afternoon he:

> . . . went down out of the heat and glare of the summer day into the cool green shades of the Happy Valley [the valley immediately south of Kington Langley]. Thence I went up the opposite slope of the green hill through the beautiful meadows to Langley Fitzurse [the old name for Kington Langley]. As I mounted the slope there were lovely glimpses of the far blue hills and chalk downs seen through the tops of the luxuriant elms of the Happy Valley, which lay beneath me, a sea of bright green foliage.

Kilvert's mother was Thermutis (born 1808), the daughter of Walter Coleman of Kington Langley, of the family who had owned Old Chapel Field. The brother of Kilvert's sweetheart Ettie Meredith Brown lived in the double-roofed stone house on the Ridge near Old Chapel Field and Kilvert often visited this house. Ettie's father the Reverend Meredith Brown (died 1895) owned Nonsuch House, a little east of Tom Moore's cottage at Westbrook near Bromham. Kilvert also often visited Nonsuch but he never married Ettie as there was a problem over his position as a curate lacking a living of his own. Three years after being 'warned-off' in April 1876 by a letter from Ettie's mother, Kilvert married in August

1879 Miss Elizabeth Rowland (1846–1911), a lady he had met in Paris. They honeymooned in Scotland but the following month Kilvert died from peritonitis aged only thirty-nine. His grave at Bredwardine bore the epitaph which was prophetic in view of the posthumous publication of his diaries: 'He being dead, yet speaketh'.

Three years before his death Kilvert wrote in 1876:

> I went on past the head of the steep green lane [Morrell's Lane] in the site of the Old Chapel and burying place where my great- grandfather was laid to rest . . . I lingered some time leaning over my favourite gate, the Poet's Gate, and looking at the lovely view . . . At length twilight began to fall on the wide and lovely landscape. I turned away with a sigh and a heart full of sad sweet tender memories and passed over the village green among the pleasant friendly greetings of the kindly village people. I always seem to feel at home among these people in the village [Kington Langley] of my forefathers.

From this description we know that this gate, a field gate situated on the south side of the road opposite Old Chapel Field and about twenty yards east of the north end of Morrell's Lane, was known as the Poet's Gate before Kilvert was here, an intriguing fact that invites speculation about the identity of the poet it commemorated. Robin Tanner loved elegant old timber gates with their wooden staples and catches and in the late 1940s the Tanners bought the field of the Poet's Gate in order to ensure that it remained as Kilvert knew it. They erected the new Poet's Gate with a beautifully lettered inscription indicating that the meadow to its south was dedicated to Francis Kilvert because he had loved the view from this gate. In *Double Harness* Robin Tanner relates how he:

> . . . sought out lingering examples of country craftsmanship to record before they perished. I had no desire however to represent the accidental, photographic, surface appearance of things, but rather to probe beyond the material likeness to their inner life. The meadow stile at Kilverts 'Poet's Gate', a stone's throw away from my workroom [at Old Chapel Field], and the unchanged pastoral landscape fading away to the Marlborough Downs, filled me with

The Poet's Gate opposite Old Chapel Field

a longing to make an etching that would portray not just that particular stile but would speak for all the 'squeeze-belly' stiles that had ever been made by Wiltshire carpenters and joiners. The gate itself had been made from a measured drawing of an older one, by Alan Duckett, a distinguished woodworker employed by our local firm of builders, and Walter Cowen, a Yorkshire friend, had made the incised inscription on it to Francis Kilvert's memory.

Robin Tanner as teacher and school inspector

Largely as a result of his ability to illustrate his teaching Robin had now become an inspiring teacher who also gave evening classes in Swindon for the Workers Educational Association. He also began lectures to other teachers which took him all over Wiltshire. His pupils at Chippenham School were now busy painting murals under his direction on the inside of the walls of their school. His qualities now became widely recognised and in 1935 he joined the schools inspectorate, just as he had suggested he would like to do when as an infant he met the schools inspector at Kington Langley.

This work took him away from Wiltshire to Leeds, where Robin and Heather consoled themselves for being exiled from Wiltshire by collaborating in their spare time on *Wiltshire Village*, Heather writing the text and Robin providing the illustrations based on the drawings he had been making for many years of the farms and cottages, stiles, barns and wagons of North-West Wiltshire. In 1937 he was delighted to be transferred from Leeds to Gloucestershire, as this appointment allowed the Tanners to resume living at Old Chapel Field. Robin then bought a car to facilitate travelling and as part of the purchase was taught to drive.

Despite their long and happy marriage Robin and Heather had no children, although shortly before the Second World War broke out they corresponded with a young German Jewish boy called Dietrich Hanff and they applied for permission for him to come to England as a farm trainee. This was after some difficulties granted; he was found work on a local farm, he was adopted by Robin and Helen and he stayed with them for the rest of his life. In *Double Harness* Robin Tanner left a moving word picture of young Dietrich standing at a window in the house at Old Chapel Field listening to records of his beloved Bach and Beethoven while struggling to learn the complexities of the English language. Early in the Second World War Dietrich was declared exempt from internment, but the decision was suddenly rescinded. He was interned as an alien on the Isle of Man and not allowed to correspond with the Tanners, but in 1942 he was released and allowed to return to Wiltshire where he ultimately became a teacher and died fifty years later in 1992, outliving Robin but predeceasing Heather.

In September 1956 Robin was transferred to Oxfordshire where he spent his last eight years in his employment as a schools inspector. There he spent the happiest days of his working life, for in Oxfordshire he felt that he worked more effectively as a result of being at the centre of Oxfordshire educational activities. In 1965 he retired from regular employment and was enabled to devote his last twenty-three years re-learning etching, writing, and with Heather pursuing their pacifist and anti-nuclear activities. One of the first etchings that he produced in retirement was 'Easter', which he dedicated to F. L. Griggs.

The Tanners in later life

At Old Chapel Field Robin was opposed to having the telephone because they went to bed at ten o'clock and he feared that their rest would be disturbed by late callers, although he relented in 1969 when it became possible to have the cable run underground.

Robin Tanner was a fine calligrapher who believed that, if a letter was worth writing, it should be beautifully written, including the address on the envelope. He took infinite pains over his letters and often embellished them with illustrations, making each letter a minor work of art. Consequently a great many of his letters have survived, for their recipients understandably felt that they must not destroy such exquisite creations. The survival of so many letters and their publication by a former colleague in a book entitled *From Old Chapel Field* are a great help in recreating the life and career of this distinguished but little-known Wiltshire artist.

During the 1950s Robin illustrated Geoffrey Grigson's King Penguin Book *Flowers of the Meadow*, and this probably led to the commission to ilustrate Merriott's plant catalogue. *Woodland Plants* with text by Heather Tanner, and Gray's *Elegy* with illustrations by Robin Tanner were published in 1981. The former had been first contemplated in 1940, and Robin must have been relieved to see it published at last.

In 1987 the Tanners overcame their dislike of publicity and with some reservations featured in a BBC Television documentary film about their lives and work entitled *A Vision of Wiltshire*. Robin's letters reveal that in spite of their apprehension, when they saw it they were very pleased with the sensitive approach and quality of the film. Towards the end of their lives Robin and Heather Tanner also helped set up the Crafts and Study Centre at the Holburne Museum, which was opened in June 1977 at the end of Great Pulteney Street in Bath.

Among the things that Robin and Heather most deplored were the accelerating modern decline in country life, the appointment of Margaret Thatcher as Minister of Education, and the spread of supermarkets. They enthusiastically supported the peace and anti-nuclear movements and denoted to them all that they could spare from their earnings.

After his retirement Robin Tanner resumed etching, which he diligently practised for the rest of his life. He now took photographs to assist him in the preparation of his etchings and in this he was assisted by Dietrich, who had become a proficient photographer. His late publications were *A Country Alphabet* and *A Country Book of*

Days, the former an alphabet of capital letters embellished with decorative representations of country objects. In early December 1984 the entire edition of two hundred copies was brought to Old Chapel Field to be autographed. Robin was delighted with the quality of the book, which was published by The Old Stile Press, and throughout the summer of 1984 he worked at the twenty-six illustrations for *A Country Book of Days*.

Less than two years before he died Robin Tanner gave a short talk on 5 July 1986 at the opening of the Summer Exhibition of his work at Devizes Museum, in which he disclosed a good deal about his life and his philosophy of art and teaching. He spoke of his: 'two long, happy lives – in education and in art', how: 'the one has never stifled the other', and said:

> Nor have I a high opinion of my work: if I have a talent it is a very minor one. I regard what I have produced as the natural overflow of my deep love of Wiltshire countryside, where most of my life has been spent . . .

He quoted Thomas Traherne ('Everything is at rest, free and immortal') and William Blake's reference to 'the real and eternal world', and explained why he had remained an etcher rather than becoming a painter, saying:

> a painting can be owned by only one person, whereas – with care – a large number of perfect impressions can be printed from a steel-faced etching plate.

He also pointed out that:

> Within its chosen limits an etching can say all. Men like Dürer, Goya, Meryon, and our own Palmer and Griggs and many more have worked wonders on copper.

Towards the end of his address Robin Tanner said:

> Nor can I claim great success as an etcher. The pursuit of excellence involves a long struggle. I am goaded on to produce a superb etching. The vision I have is glorious, but I'm afraid the reality is always a partial failure. Yet something urges me to continue the pursuit. Etching designs seek me out and crave to be born: there are seventeen in the queue! I am in the midst of three exacting plates at the moment.

He was then eighty-two.

An evaluation of Robin Tanner's work

Robin Tanner's finest etchings are arguably his more restrained work, the flower drawings, his Samuel Palmer-like etchings such as 'Wiltshire Woodman', and many of his simpler landscapes, including 'Christmas' and 'June', with its typical stone-slabbed North Wiltshire stile. His flower and plant drawings are beautifully restrained, but the opulent romanticism of a few of his etchings, including the illustrations for Gray's *Elegy* are sometimes a little overpowering.

'June', etched to celebrate the end of the Second World War.

It is in the nature of an etcher to be meticulous, and Robin Tanner was particularly disciplined. His drawings and etchings are usually formally confined within rigid rectangular margins and he almost invariably etched right up to these margins so that the entire area of the plate was generally filled. This practice sometimes gives his work a certain rigidity and lack of vitality compared with that of his mentor F. L. Griggs who, although he often drew frames around his drawings and etchings, did not necessarily etch right up the frame, and sometimes left large areas of his drawings and etchings as a bold blank white to great effect. If Robin Tanner had a weakness it was this reluctance to leave any part of a plate unetched, and it is this characteristic that gives some of his etchings such an opulent character. But this is perhaps to carp, for he was undoubtedly a magnificent etcher. It is also often difficult to decide whether his work is the ultimate in craftsmanship or pure art, but the point at which craftsmanship becomes art is always debatable and raises a perennial question.

Although there may be some truth in the old saying 'travel broadens the mind' Robin Tanner provides a reassuring example of a man who throughout his long life remained entirely content with his native locality. Although he travelled over most of Wiltshire, and sometimes further afield, his artistic and literary activities were generally confined to the countryside of north-west Wiltshire around Kington Langley, the beautiful rural world of the inhabited working countryside of his childhood that he recorded in his work.

He particularly loved the By Brook, Castle Combe, Slaughterford and Biddestone, and its Broadmead Brook tributary with its stone clapper bridge near Nettleton, which he depicted in his 1972 etching 'The Clapper Bridge'. The following year he produced the etching 'Full Moon' based upon Woodford Brake on the Broadmead Brook between Nettleton and Castle Combe. The 'Old Thorn' illustrated the wooden stile in Kington Langley where his parents met.

By concentrating his activities in this restricted area he put into practice the beliefs expressed by Richard Jefferies and Thomas Hardy, that it is better to know a small area of countryside intimately than to know a large area superficially. In *Double Harness* he wrote:

> All that I wanted to say on copper – indeed, all that I still want to say – is contained in a few square miles of N.W. Wiltshire – a land of Cotswold stone, but a countryside that is Cotswold with a Wiltshire difference: warmer and more lush than Gloucestershire: pastoral dairy country with small meadows and high hedges. And there is an ancient church every three miles or so in any direction.

With 'The Cheese Room', which depicted the cheese room of a farm at East Coulston three miles east of Bratton in west Wiltshire, Robin Tanner for once departed from depicting his immediate home area. In 1979 he rediscovered the old stone drinking trough beside the road which descends to Castle Combe which he had first seen seventy years before, and in 1980 he produced an etching 'The Drinking Trough', with an added inscription which read 'DRINK THY FILL'.

Having concentrated on his drawing and etching I must not overlook the considerable talent that Robin Tanner demonstrated as a writer. An anonymous *Country Life* reviewer of *Double Harness* offered rare praise when he wrote: 'With its poetic turns of phrase and close observations of nature, this book is a worthy successor to the writings of Edward Thomas and Richard Jefferies'.

Since he had earned a regular income and a retirement pension from his years of teaching and as a schools inspector Robin Tanner always enjoyed the freedom of being essentially an amateur artist. He knew neither great success nor failure and he enjoyed the satisfaction of practising his art free from the frustrations which professional artists frequently suffer, from having to compromise their art in order to live. Craftsmen who live uncomplicated lives are frequently happier than artists and more serene, as a result of the immense satisfaction that they derive from their work. Robin Tanner, who was always a great admirer of rural craftmanship, appears to have been a meticulous craftsman as much as an artist. He died in May 1988, aged eighty-four.

Heather lived for a further five years and Dietrich predeceased her. When he died she commented to her friends: 'What a blessing that Dietie has not been left alone', and the following year she too died aged ninety in June 1993. The Tanners both appear to have been secretive about their funeral arrangements and none of the many obituary notices that I have read indicate their place of interment. As they were conservationists it seems likely that they may have been cremated and their ashes scattered, perhaps in the garden at their beloved Old Chapel Field, or alternatively beside the Broadmead Brook between Nettleton Shrub and Castle Combe which Robin so much loved and where I always remember him.

When reflecting on his life at the end of his autobiography Robin Tanner wrote of his 'two long lives– in education and in art'. He concluded that he had succeeded in integrating these two consuming interests of his life and had been blessed with a particularly happy marriage. On the debit side, he felt that he was leaving a world that he believed to be declining into chaotic disorder.

Subsequent events have done little to prove him wrong.

18 Pevsner at Little Town
including Geoffrey Grigson and John Betjeman

How many people going for a walk or a drive have asked: 'Have you remembered the Pevsner?' Sir Nikolaus Pevsner's county volumes of *The Buildings of England* are essential works of reference which provide an immense stimulus and aid to the enjoyment of visits to cities, towns, villages, or to almost any individual historic building in England. They have been described as being 'though occasionally indigestible, indispensable', and are found on the shelves of most serious local historians. The progressive publication of these forty-two volumes commenced just after the end of the Second World War and soon made their author famous.

The Little Town of the heading to this chapter is a place-name which may not be known even to some who are reasonably familiar with Wiltshire. Lying a few hundred yards north-east of Broad Town in the north of Wiltshire and a little over three miles south-east of Wootton Bassett, it consists of

Little Town with, left to right, Little Town Farm, the White Horse, and Pevsner's cottage in the trees

an isolated farm and cottage standing beneath a White Horse, which is cut into the secondary and lower escarpment of the Marlborough Downs. Several deserted settlements formerly existed along the spring line under this western escarpment, and Little Town has the feel of being an old settlement, which is confirmed by its appearance as *Lytelton* in a deed of 1247.

When in the 1930s the Nazis gained power in Germany Nikolaus Pevsner, a German professor of art, fled to England because having Jewish blood he feared for the future of himself and his family in Nazi Germany. Germany's loss was Englands gain, for Professor Pevsner became a leading scholar and writer on English art and architecture, and the instigator and author of the authoritative *Buildings of England* series of county books. These list, briefly describe, and sometimes criticize, all the buildings that he considered to be worthy of notice in England.

Pevsner's early life

Pevsner (1902–83) was born at Leipzig, the younger son of Jewish parents, and was christened Nikolaus Berhard Leon Pevsner. He was educated at St Thomas's School at Leipzig and the universities of Leipzig, Munich, Berlin, and Frankfurt. His elder brother died young in 1919. In 1923 Pevsner married Karola ('Lola') Kurlbaum whom he described as 'the most important influence on his life' and they had two sons and a daughter. In 1924 Pevsner joined the staff of the Dresden Gallery and became its assistant keeper. He held this appointment until 1929 when he became lecturer in the history of art and architecture at Göttingen University. In 1930 he visited England for the first time and as a result of this visit developed a particular interest in the differences between English and Continental architecture. Pevsner then lectured in Germany on English architecture but, despite having become a Lutheran at the age of nineteen, as he was born a Jew he was in 1933 barred from teaching by the Nazis. Fearful for his future and possibly for his life he emigrated with his family to England, where he published the influential *Pioneers of Modern*

*Geoffrey Grigson (far left), Sir Nikolaus
Pevsner (left), and Sir John Betjeman
(above)*

Design, from William Morris to Walter Gropius
(1936). He then obtained a one-year research
fellowship at Birmingham University. There he met
Sir Gordon Russell and, by becoming his adviser
on modern furniture, Pevsner influenced the bet-
ter-designed furniture of the 1930s. Pevsner's fur
trader father Hugo Pevsner died in 1940, and his
mother committed suicide in 1942 to avoid being
sent to a concentration camp.

While establishing a new career in an alien
country Professor Pevsner was very poor. For
example when he visited the excavations then
being conducted by the Finnish professor Tancred
Borenius at the former royal palace of Clarendon
in south-east Wiltshire, it is said that he had to
borrow the taxi fare back to Salisbury station.
Clarendon Palace had been long neglected, allowed to fall into dereliction, and had become
overgrown by trees. Many years later Pevsner was
to make a strong plea for its preservation in his
Wiltshire volume of *The Buildings of England*,
when he wrote: 'One crag of walling stands up.
Surely, out of respect for English history if for no
other reason, these remains ought to be as clearly
visible as those of Old Sarum.'

When war broke out with Germany in 1939
Pevsner was initially interned in the Isle of Man as
an enemy alien but by the influence of his friends
he was released. He was then employed on clearing bomb damage in London, and it is perhaps
ironic that Pevsner should have been engaged
upon clearing away the rubble of buildings which,
had they survived the attentions of his country-
men, he would have later recorded in *The
Buildings of England*. At this time he wrote the

authoritative *An Outline of European Architecture*,
an account of the history of European architecture from the 6th century which was published
in 1943 and dedicated 'To My Three Children'.

The Buildings of England

Pevsner's ambitious aim in writing *The Buildings
of England* was to visit and describe in a comprehensive series of county volumes every
significant building in England. He was destined
to realise most of this ambition, but as he became
older recognised that despite his dedication and
industry he would be unlikely to complete this
task, so arranged for some of the counties to be
covered by others. Today fifty years after its com-
mencement the series covers Scotland, Wales
and Ireland as well as England.

The fieldwork for *The Buildings of England*
was done between 1951 and 1974 as a summer
holiday occupation fitted between Pevsner's educational and writing commitments. The only
criterion for inclusion was the aesthetic value of
the buildings, Pevsner's remit being strictly to ignore buildings which had historic, literary or
musical associations but no architectural merit.
He was of the decided opinion that buildings
should be of their time and his books were sometimes critical, his particular dislike being 20th
century architects who had chosen to ignore the
modern architectural movement and had in his
estimation decadently designed pastiche buildings in outmoded styles of the past. When he
came upon an example of this practice he would
either discreetly dismiss and exclude the building as being not worthy of notice or, when his

feelings were particularly strong, he would include the building and castigate it, sometimes in very strong terms. Dan Cruikshank in the *Daily Telegraph* for 1 March 1997 criticised this attitude when, having generously assessed *The Buildings of England* volumes as being 'breathtaking in the scope and depth of their learning and in the information that they contain about historic buildings', he then deplored the fact that: 'paradoxically they display a contempt for any contemporary architect rash enough to contemplate working in a style inspired directly and honestly by historic precedent'.

Pevsner could be extremely critical, as for example when he dismissed the Victorian church at Oare near Pewsey in his Wiltshire volume with a withering entry: 'HOLY TRINITY. By Teulon. 1857-8. It may well be considered the ugliest church in Wiltshire'.

Pevsner may be criticised for his tendency to emulate the Victorian topographical writers by demonstrating an ecclesiastical bias. He sometimes devoted excessive space to churches to the detriment of secular buildings, a practice that probably arose from his evident preference for the gothic over the classical style of architecture. As their title implies *The Buildings of England* volumes were primarily concerned with architecture, although they also included some archaeological field monuments for which he relied upon the advice of specialists whom he acknowledged.

In *The Leaves of Southwell*, written immediately after the war in 1945, Pevsner expressed the view that:

> . . . works changes in style and outlook, and the man of genius is not he who tries to shake off its bonds, but he whom it is given to express it in the most powerful form.

Pevsner's method was to cover each county in about a month of concentrated activity undertaken during the summer holidays when he had less teaching commitments and could make best use of his students. The work was intensive, taking place on seven days a week and extending from dawn to dusk. Pevsner then sat up most of the night writing up his notes while the visits were fresh in his memory. He once 'did nineteen par-

ishes in a single day' and he was not always scrupulous. One of his students recalled driving at walking pace round the drive of a country house without stopping, while Pevsner dictated a brief description of the house watched by its astonished owners who were taking drinks on the front lawn attended by their butler!

The series was almost universally well received, a review in *The Architect's Journal* being typical of its reception:

> Inventories these books are, and wonderfully detailed ones . . . But they are much more than that. On every page one is continually made aware – sometimes by a single sentence or comment, sometimes by as little as a single word, sometimes even by what isn't said – of learning, intelligence and taste at work, placing, testing, and assessing. So far as architecture is concerned, this series will relegate most other guides to the status of picture books.

Pevsner's associations with Wiltshire

In visiting, assessing and describing all the historic buildings of architectural merit for his Wiltshire volume Pevsner must have visited every part of the county since, as he pointed out in his introduction to *The Buildings of England: Wiltshire* (1963): 'I have myself seen everything that I describe'. He in fact already knew Wiltshire, from a particular association with the county which dated from about 1946, when at the age of about forty-four he obtained his country cottage at Little Town beside Broad Town in a remote part of Wiltshire. For the rest of his life he used this cottage, wedged into the escarpment beside Little Town farmhouse, as his country retreat.

Grigson/ Pevsner cottage under the cliff at Little Town

Post-War

From 1942 to 1945 Pevsner as its stand-in editor effectively ensured the survival of the influential *The Architectural Review* during the absence on military service of its regular editor. In 1946 he became a naturalized Briton, and in addition to working on the editorial board of *The Architectural Review* and as art editor of Penguin Books, he was from 1949 until 1955 Slade Professor of Fine Art at Cambridge. In 1950 he became a founder member of the William Morris Society and in 1963 chairman of the Victorian Society, which he had also helped to found. In 1955 he gave the BBC Reith Lectures on 'The Englishness of English Art', which were later published in an expanded and annotated version by The Architectural Press under that title in 1956, and reprinted by Penguin Books in 1964. From 1942 until his retirement in 1969 he also lectured at Birkbeck College in the University of London.

Pevsner's admiration for the gothic style was demonstrated when immediately after the war he published *The Leaves of Southwell* (1945), a book in which he lovingly described the exquisite early gothic foliage carving at Southwell Minster in Nottinghamshire. He then made two proposals to Sir Allen Lane who had founded Penguin Books in 1935. Both were accepted. His idea for a series of county books on English architecture was commenced in 1951 as *The Buildings of England*, and his *Pelican History of Art* was launched in 1953.

To enable him conveniently to achieve the immense amount of travelling demanded for the site visits for *The Buildings of England* Sir Allen Lane provided Pevsner with an old 1933 Wolsey Hornet car, although he never learned to drive. He relied upon his wife Lola to drive him around the countryside, often with young students or historians crammed into the back seats of the car, with a pile of reference books to assist with the work. These students often recall him as being something of a slave-driver. His method was to search out the buildings of interest by taking in sequence one kilometre squares of the Ordnance Survey map. When the work was falling behind schedule he would sometimes lose patience and summarily dismiss an unlikely-looking square

without properly investigating it. This practice probably explains his occasional lapses in missing remote buildings, an example being the exquisite ruined gothic Chapel of St Martin situated in a farmyard on the ramparts of Chisbury hillfort in north-east Wiltshire. This chapel, which is now looked after by English Heritage, is freely accessible to the public and is well worth visiting.

Pevsner's friend Geoffrey Grigson

Pevsner came to Wiltshire as a result of his friendship with Geoffrey Grigson (1905–85), a Cornish born writer and poet who had been successively schoolmaster, journalist, publisher, and a radio producer for the BBC. In the 1930s Grigson was editor of the influential *New Verse*, he became self-employed as a critic and also wrote much poetry and many books. In 1957 he expressed in *The Wiltshire Book* feelings for Wiltshire which are shared by many lovers of the county: 'So Wiltshire has a delightful emptiness, a landscape windy and suggestive, stimulating and soothing . . . Not too far from London, not too close, Wiltshire is in the blessed situation of persisting as a backwater, fed by the past.'

Geoffrey Grigson was the youngest of seven brothers, five of whom were killed in the two World Wars. He gained a reputation as a writer and journalist and as a very severe and uncompromising critic. In addition to criticism Grigson wrote a great deal on the countryside in general and on Wiltshire in particular. Among his Wiltshire writings his many articles in *Country Life* and his little book of photographs with short texts entitled *The Wiltshire Book* (1957) are of especial interest. His more general reference books including *The Shell Country Book* (1962) and *The Country Alphabet* (1996) reveal his very profound knowledge of rural England. He also wrote poetry, books, essays, articles and reviews on many subjects including art and literary criticism. *The Englishman's Flora* (1958) and the *Dictionary of English Plant Names* (1974) demonstrate his expert knowledge of botany and the associations of wild plants.

Geoffrey Grigson's third wife was the famous cookery writer Jane Grigson who died in 1990, and his daughter Sophie Grigson now (2000) presents cookery programmes on television.

In about 1936 Grigson on a walking tour in north Wiltshire with Norman Cameron discovered the attractive though semi-derelict cottage under the escarpment at Little Town. He bought the cottage for forty pounds, renovated and lived in it for some years. When in 1946 he moved into Broad Town Farmhouse (the house with the

Broad Town Farm, Grigson's home for the latter part of his life

pillared porch at the road junction in Broad Town) in which he lived until the end of his life, he offered his vacated cottage at Little Town to Pevsner, who was his neighbour in London. Pevsner took it on as his country retreat and his Wiltshire volume of *The Buildings of England* (1963) was dedicated 'To Nicholas and Paul, this volume on the county of the cottage'.

In *The Crest on the Silver* (1950) Grigson described this cottage as 'a minute three-roomed house in ruins under an inland cliff in Wiltshire'. The house is said to have at one time had an outside toilet which Grigson sited in consultation with the sculptor Henry Moore to take advantage of the fine view across the wide Malmesbury Plain from the garden, a view which Grigson likened to the background to Rubens painting of the Chateau de Steen in the National Gallery.

Grigson eloquently described this remote part of Wiltshire in which his cottage and farmhouse were situated as:

Rather desolate fields without or with only a few paths or tracks stretched away from the farmhouse I bought in Wiltshire [Broad Town Farmhouse] at the end of the war. Curlew flighted from an escarpment to these damp fields, the damp meadows of long coarse grass, saying *curlu*, *curlu*, as if it were Yorkshire and not Wiltshire.

The poet Edward Thomas (the subject of Chapter 14) knew these fields when as a boy staying with his grandmother at Swindon towards the end of the 19th century he would often walk across them to visit an old lawyer friend, Willie Gough of Wootton Bassett. When many years later Willie Gough met Grigson they talked at length about Edward Thomas, and Willie invited Grigson to visit him and see the letters that Thomas had written to him many years before. Grigson never took up the offer and when Willie Gough died in the 1940s his papers were burnt on a bonfire in his garden and the Edward Thomas documents were lost.

Grigson also recorded that the farmer who had rented his farmhouse at the crossroads in Broad Town before him had known Edward Thomas and had taught him to make hay ropes. This house has on its stone chimney the inscription 'R S 1 6 6 8', and after examining his deeds Grigson found that these initials were those of a local builder called Richard Spackman. When he extended his house he was astonished to find that the builder who undertook the work was another Richard Spackman. This family must have been in building in this district for many generations because a very large and elaborate marble monument to a prosperous local carpenter called Thomas Spackman, who died in 1786, stands in Clyffe Pypard church. This monument, which is signed by the well-known sculptor John Deval the Younger (who succeeded his father as Master Mason to the Royal Palaces), is illustrated by Rupert Gunnis in his definitive *Dictionary of British Sculptors, 1660–1851* (1951), where it is described as an 'exciting and arresting work'. It stands about eighteen feet high and is surmounted by a life-size full length figure of Thomas Spackman standing on an inscribed pedestal incorporating a basket of carpenters tools. In the 1963 Wiltshire volume of his *Buildings of England* Pevsner, then presumably unaware that he would ultimately lie in Clyffe Pypard churchyard, devoted a long description to this memorial and describes Thomas Spackman as standing: 'on a pink marble base, dressed in ideal clothes with a long flowing mantle and holding an eloquent pose'. Helen Spackman who married Robin Tanner, the subject of Chapter 17) came from this family.

The Devals, father and son, were master masons and sculptors who deserve more recognition than they have received. The Spackman monument was the most important monument sculpted by John Deval the Younger (1728–94), the son of another John Deval (1701–74). The older Deval was chief mason to the royal palaces and worked in Wiltshire for the Hoares of Stourhead and the Lords Radnor of Longford; he also built the famous Palladian bridge at Wilton for the Earl of Pembroke. The younger Deval, in addition to sculpting the Spackman monument, in 1777 built the mausoleum for the Earls of Radnor in Britford churchyard, which was altered when the church was rebuilt in 1873.

Pevsner achieves wide recognition

In 1953 Pevsner was made a CBE, and soon after commencing *The Buildings of England* he was in 1955 invited to deliver the BBC Reith Lectures. Aware that his German birth, education, and early career might provoke criticism Pevsner attempted to forestall this by suggesting in his Foreword to the resulting book that: 'the very fact of having come into a country with fresh eyes at some stage, and then of having settled down gradually to become part of it, may constitute a great advantage'. By 1956 his work was becoming widely admired and the success of *The Englishness of English Art* ensured that he became a recognised authority on English art and architecture. At his retirement in 1969 he was knighted for his services to English art and architecture, although his wife Lola who had died in 1963 sadly did not live to see this honour accorded to her husband. She was buried nearby at Clyffe Pypard, and twenty years later Pevsner was buried beside her. In his early days as a scholar and as a celebrated professor in Germany Pevsner cannot have dreamed that he and his wife would be buried in a remote English village churchyard. They lie towards the east end of Clyffe Pypard churchyard beneath a segmental-headed slate gravestone. Since this was originally

set up to commemorate Lola her name takes precedence over her husband's in the inscription.

The Pevsners' grave (right) at Clyffe Pypard

Pevsner's appearance and character

Pevsner is the one subject of this book whom I can describe from personal experience. As a young architect interested in the history of architecture I recall in the early 1960s having a long discussion with him when he came to Trowbridge to lecture. My recollection of him is as a quietly-spoken courteous man whose speech was particularly precise. In appearance he was scholarly, tall, lean, balding and bespectacled with wire-rimmed glasses. He dressed in a very restrained way, often in an unassuming raincoat, so that he was on one occasion mistaken for the gas man! This would have amused him for he had a wry sense of humour and could stand a joke at his own expense. He was a workaholic, and it is said that his preferred food was spaghetti because it could be swallowed so rapidly that it allowed him to resume his work with minimal interruption for eating. His few recreations included swimming and walking, at which he was inexhaustible. He would walk twelve miles to see a building and one of his conducted visits to a Medieval cathedral is said to have taken nine hours. Such energy and enthusiasm prompted Giles Worsley to describe Pevsner as 'a phenomenon'.

Geoffrey Grigson left us an account of an amusing incident which befell his friend at Little Town. The tall and scholarly Pevsner was ineffectually picking with a spade at the ground in his garden, vaguely attempting to dig a cess-pit. A local resident for a time watched his pathetic efforts over the hedge in utter disbelief until, unable to stand it any longer, he pushed through the hedge saying: 'Let I do it Doctor Pevsner, Let I do it!' – and soon completed the job!

The great strength of Pevsner as a critic of art and architecture was his immense breadth of knowledge. One commentator referred to his 'omnivorous appetite and discriminating taste that gained him the admiration of scholars throughout the world'. The quality of his writing in English, which was an alien language to him, was excellent, and he demonstrated deep learning, generally sound judgement, and occasionally a mischievous sense of humour, as for example when in conversation he would for a joke disconcertingly depart from his very correct English with a very slight foreign accent into broad cockney or ultra-superior 'toffee-nosed' English. He even dedicated one of his *Buildings of England* volumes to 'the inventor of the iced lolly'!

Pevsner versus Betjeman

With his Germanic method and thoroughness Pevsner was at odds with the perhaps over-enthusiastic and occasionally uncritical approach to architecture of his near contemporary Sir John Betjeman (1906–84), who regarded buildings through the romantic eyes of a poet, in marked contrast to Pevsner who viewed buildings with the analytical and critical eyes of a German scholar. This prompted one architectural critic (Roderick Gradidge in *The Field*) to suggest that Pevsner had forced architectural criticism into 'a Prussian corset', to which a Pevsner enthusiast responded by suggesting that Betjeman had adorned architectural criticism with 'seaside bloomers'. Pevsner has often been criticised for viewing and recording buildings and places in his cold and analytical way, seldom acknowledging that they were inhabited by real people. His books have been

derogated because they are structured, read like catalogues, and generally fail to arouse the enthusiasm with which Betjeman sometimes fires his readers, but *The Buildings of England* volumes should be recognised as critical gazetteers, a fact which was acknowledged by their author when he used the word 'gazetteer' in his Forewords to the series.

The two men did not necessarily disagree in their judgements, merely in the way that they were presented. For example at Mildenhall, a short distance east of Marlborough, the early church with Saxon windows in its tower was in 1816 fitted out with polished oak fittings, including a reredos, canopied pulpits, high box pews, a west gallery, and even small benches for the children. The whole ensemble, which is unique in Wiltshire, elicited from Betjeman the comment that going into this church was like entering a Jane Austen novel, while Pevsner merely described it as: 'a perfect example of the small village church of many periods' with: 'charmingly Gothick fitments'. The verdicts were similar, but Betjeman's reaction was more literary and personal than that of the more restrained Pevsner.

Pevsner and Betjeman both cared profoundly about architecture despite their very contrasted characters. Betjeman had a jolly and impish sense of humour that often caused him to see the funny side of serious matters, as he demonstrated in his broadcasts on television – a medium in which he excelled. This characteristic could create the impression that he was superficial, which was very far from the case. Pevsner was less relaxed and more serious, although he had a wry sense of humour and told against himself the story of how he was mistaken for the gas meter reader.

John Betjeman was in fact an emotional, eccentric and insecure character who had been bullied at school. He found himself at odds with his father after he decided to be a poet, and refused to become the fourth generation Betjeman to enter the family business of inventors and high-class cabinet-makers. He suffered from agoraphobia, was unnerved by long walks in the open air, and sometimes wore a mackintosh with a straw boater and carried his belongings in a carrier bag. He liked buildings probably more than he liked people, and his teddy-bear Archibald apparantly more than either. He had Archibald from the age of two and always refused to be parted from him because he considered that he had 'never let him down'. As a young man Betjeman was susceptible to young ladies and proposed to several. Having in 1928 left Oxford without a degree he was at Longford Castle near Salisbury introduced by the Countess of Radnor to Penelope Chetwode, a field marshal's daughter whom he married in July 1933. That his marriage was troubled was partly due to the fact that his wife was an ardent horsewoman and John was terrified by horses, so that when Penelope finally contrived to get him on a pony he clung on desperately crying: 'You are trying to kill me'. Penelope also converted to catholicism, whereas John is generally assumed to be Anglican, although according to Edith Olivier in 1932 he was a Quaker. Consequently for thirty-three years of his marriage Betjeman had a relationship with Lady Elizabeth Cavendish, a daughter of the Duke of Devonshire and a lady-in-waiting to the queen.

As he was educated at Marlborough College and lived for part of his adult life at Uffington in an adjoining county, John Betjeman was often in Wiltshire indulging his 'topographical predelictions' for visiting churches, and examples of the Victorian and Edwardian architecture which were his particular interest. He was generally unhappy at Marlborough College although he nostalgically recalled his days there in his long autobiographical poem *Summoned by Bells*, which contains evocative descriptions of Wiltshire places including Manton Lane and Hackpen Hill. Elsewhere Betjeman wrote about many obscure Wiltshire places, including the railway halt (he loved steam railways) at Dilton Marsh near Westbury, and he wrote a poem about the incongruity of that essential Irishman Tom Moore being buried in Bromham churchyard (quoted above, page 178). He was a friend of Sir Cecil Beaton at Ashcombe and of Edith Olivier at Wilton (see Chapter 16).

After the Betjemans made their home for a time in a rented farmhouse at Uffington Betjeman became particularly fond of Highworth, a small town in the north of Wiltshire about six miles west of Uffington, about which he wrote enthusiastically in 1950:

> When I am abroad and want to recall a typically English town, I think of Highworth. Countless unknown lanes lead up the hill to it. It is the sort of town you read about in novels . . . We walked down one of those narrow lanes, between garden walls, that lead under archways in the High Street . . . Sun and stone and old brick and garden flowers and church bells. That was Sunday evening in Highworth. That was England.

In 1950 Betjeman also contributed an essay headed 'Architecture' to *Studies in the History of Swindon* published by Swindon Borough Council. His essay begins: 'To write a short architectural study of Swindon is easier than to write a long one' because: 'There is very little architecture in Swindon and a great deal of building'. He admires the 1729 Georgian house in Cricklade Street as: 'one of the most distinguished town houses in Wiltshire'. Pevsner later described this house as: 'the best house in Swindon by far'. Betjeman also liked the surviving relics of the Wilts and Berks Canal and the Great Western Railway housing around Cambria Place in New Swindon, both of which were so dear to Edward Thomas (Chapter 14).

In the 1930s Betjeman was employed in the publicity department of Shell-British Petroleum where, with Rex Whistler and Edward Ardizzone, he was one of the publicity manager's group of 'Young Gentlemen'. During the Second World War he served as an attaché to the Bristish ambassador in Dublin, and is said to have been marked down by the IRA for assassination; but he was reprieved because a senior IRA officer considered that it would be a shame to deprive the world of his poetry.

Although he became poet laureate in 1972 and the most popular English poet of the 20th century Betjeman's slight eccentricity, which he amply demonstrated in the popular media of film and television, and his enthusiasm for architecture, have tended to obscure his literary talents which attracted a wide and admiring public at the time when in literary circles he was regarded as a lightweight.

After initially disagreeing as a result of their contrasted attitudes to architecture Betjeman and

Pevsner finally quarrelled and carried on a protracted feud. It is said to have begun in 1941 when the influential *Architectural Review* carried Pevsner's obituary notice of the architect C. F. A. Voysey in preference to Betjeman's. This prompted Betjeman at least to pretend to hate Pevsner, to write a particularly critical review of his Durham volume, and from that time refer to him petulantly as variously the 'Herr Doktor Professor', 'Granny', and as 'a new refugee scholar' in his letters. In deliberately contrasted photographs reproduced in Timothy Mowl's *Stylistic Cold Wars: Betjeman versus Pevsner* (2000) the ascetic severely thin and scholarly Pevsner peers with a serious expression through steel-rimmed spectacles over two piles of his complete county volumes, while the jolly portly Betjeman reclines in a deck chair sporting a straw hat at a rakish angle and roaring with laughter, with a characteristically disordered pile of documents on his lap. Existing feelings between the two men were exacerbated when *The Buildings of England* volumes achieved immense popularity and began to supersede the Betjeman-edited *Shell Guides* which had been begun in the 1930s. It is pleasing to record that in their old age when both men suffered from Parkinson's disease they corresponded and seem to have been at least half-reconciled.

Pevsner and Betjeman in fact had much in common, which may have accounted for some of the antipathy that arose between them. They were both of Continental origin, the Betjemans having originated in Holland, where their name had been Betjemann. Both wrote architectural guide-books to Britain, and they also shared a particular interest in churches which led them both to tend to underestimate secular buildings, especially country houses. Pevsner and Betjeman were both generally referred to by their surnames, were knighted in the same year (1969), and both lived for at least part of their lives in the Wessex downlands. Betjeman died in 1984, a year after Pevsner, and was buried in a Cornish churchyard that is even more remote than Clyffe Pypard, where Pevsner lies. Even their segmental-headed headstones are similar.

After Betjeman's death his daughter Candida Lycett Green lived for a time at Huish Farm, opposite Huish Church in the Vale of Pewsey.

John Piper

A great friend of John Betjeman was the romantic painter, photograper and writer John Piper (1903–92) a man who had many Wiltshire associations. Piper was for a time joint editor with Betjeman of the *Shell County Guides* and became sole editor when Betjeman resigned. Piper collaborated on writing the revised edition of *The Shell Guide to Wiltshire* (1968) which he illustrated with his own photographs. He was also a friend throughout the Second World War of Geoffrey Grigson, although they too quarrelled in 1950.

When he was young Piper was, like Robin Tanner (Chapter 17), greatly influenced by the topographical illustrations in the *Highways and Byways* series of county guides, particularly those by F. L. Griggs. He left the Royal College of Art in 1928 and for most of his working life after 1935 lived in a Buckinghamshire farmhouse. In 1930 he wrote a particularly critical review of Cecil Beaton's *Book of Beauty* and the two men did not speak until shortly before Beaton's death. From 1936 John Piper worked for *The Architectural Review*.

As a boy Piper developed an interest in archaeology, became a member of the Wiltshire Archaeological & Natural History Society, and at the age of almost eighty in 1981 designed a stained glass window for the gallery in Devizes Museum. This consists of a composition depicting several Wiltshire archaeological field monuments, including round barrows, the Devil's Den at Clatford, some Avebury monoliths, and Cherhill hillfort and White Horse. He also produced fine paintings of such diverse Wiltshire scenes as the interior of Mildenhall church, Salisbury Plain, Chisbury chapel, Devizes market place, the Stourhead landscape, Inglesham church, and the Fonthill gateway, many of which are beautifully reproduced in *Piper's Places: John Piper in England and Wales* (1983) by Ingrams and Piper.

Pevsner's achievement, later life, and death

Pevsner entered upon the English architectural scene at a time when architectural history was almost invariably written by art historians. He directed his discerning and unprejudiced Conti-

*Memorial plaques to Lola and Nikolaus Pevsner on
the gates to Clyffe Pypard church*

nental eye at English architecture, researched and
catalogued county by county most of the buildings of historic interest in England, and listed them
with generally brief descriptions in *The Buildings
of England*. He was by no means infallible. The
sheer scale of his undertaking and his occasional
impatience meant that some errors, generally errors of omission rather than of fact, were inevitable,
a failing which he recognised by appealing to readers to draw his attention to errors and omissions.

Pevsner's books have continued to be invaluable and have been revised and updated by a
team operating from the Penguin offices directed
by Bridget Cherry, the series editor who became
Pevsner's research assistant in 1968. In 1997 BBC
Television broadcast a series of five programmes
in which five different presenters – Lucinda
Lambton, Patrick Wright, Germaine Greer, Janet
Street Porter, and Michael Bracewell – each chose
a favourite county in which they visited some of
the buildings which Pevsner had recorded in his
Buildings of England volumes. The programmes
must have been successful because a follow-up
series was broadcast in late 1998, and in 2001
Penguin Books celebrated the fiftieth anniversary
of the publication of the first volume of *The Buildings of England* by publishing *The Buildings of
England: a Celebration*.

Pevsner's last years were marred by
Parkinson's disease. He remained in his London
home, 2 Wildwood Terrace in Hampstead,

where he had lived since 1941, and there he
died in 1983.

Having been inspired into verse by the incongruity of the burial of the essentially Irish poet
Thomas Moore in a remote Wiltshire churchyard
(see Chapter 12, page 178), John Betjeman
would have been interested in the improbable
burial of the German Professor Pevsner in another Wiltshire graveyard. Pevsner was brought
to Wiltshire to be buried beside his wife at Clyffe
Pypard, where they are commemorated by their
initials 'L P' and 'N P' on plates fixed to the commemorative gates at the west end of the
churchyard. It is curiously appropriate that the
extrovert poet-laureate Sir John Betjeman should
be given the honour of a memorial in
Westminster Abbey, and that the more reticent
Sir Nikolaus Pevsner is commemorated by a
simple plaque on his London house and by these
unobtrusive and to most people anonymous
plaques on the gates to the churchyard of the
remote village of Clyffe Pypard.

The first editions of *The Buildings of England*
have been in existence for so long that they have
generally been revised and re-issued by later
writers, and it is these indispensable volumes
(which were once described as being 'something
of a monument in their own right), rather than
plaques on houses and in churchyards, that are
the true memorials to the industry and scholarship of Sir Nikolaus Pevsner.

*Little Town Farmhouse from the escarpment,
showing the view from Pevsner's cottage*

Index

This index is restricted to persons and places. Subjects are excluded, and only Wiltshire places are included. Page references to illustrations are printed in italics. Bracketed references in bold type after many places [for example (**B4**)] enable that place to be located on the map on page vi.